THE TWILIGHT STRUGGLE

THE TWILIGHT STRUGGLE

What the Cold War Teaches Us
about Great-Power Rivalry Today

HAL BRANDS

Yale

UNIVERSITY PRESS

New Haven and London

Published with assistance from the income of the Frederick John
Kingsbury Memorial Fund and with assistance from the foundation
established in memory of Philip Hamilton McMillan of the
Class of 1894, Yale College.

Yale University Press books may be purchased in quantity
for educational, business, or promotional use. For information,
please e-mail sales.press@yale.edu (U.S. office) or sales@yaleup.co.uk
(U.K. office).

Set in Janson type by IDS Infotech Ltd., Chandigarh, India.
Printed in the United States of America.

Library of Congress Control Number: 2021935428
ISBN 978-0-300-25078-7 (hardcover : alk. paper)

A catalogue record for this book is available from the British Library.

This paper meets the requirements of ANSI/NISO Z39.48-1992
(Permanence of Paper).

10 9 8 7 6 5 4 3 2 1

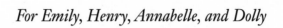

For Emily, Henry, Annabelle, and Dolly

Contents

Acknowledgments

I AM DEEPLY GRATEFUL to the Smith Richardson Foundation for helping me conceive and generously supporting this book; Johns Hopkins University and the American Enterprise Institute for giving me intellectual homes while writing it; and Yale University Press for publishing it. I also thank James Baker, Seth Center, Jaya Chatterjee, Tarun Chhabra, Robert Doar, Eric Edelman, Frank Gavin, Chris Griffin, Toby Harshaw, Seth Jones, Robert Kagan, Tom Mahnken, John Maurer, Andrew May, Mira Rapp-Hooper, Rafe Sagalyn, Mary Sarotte, Kori Schake, David Shipley, James Wilson, and Toshi Yoshihara. Finally, I owe a great debt to those scholars whose work I learned from while writing this book—and a heartfelt apology to those whose work space constraints precluded me from citing.

INTRODUCTION

Twilight Struggles,
Then and Now

GREAT-POWER COMPETITION—PROLONGED, dangerous, even deadly geopolitical rivalry—is more normal than we think. From antiquity to the present, nations have vied for influence and advantage. Athens and Sparta clashed for dominance of the Greek world. The United Kingdom played its "great game" against Russia during the nineteenth century. America and the Soviet Union locked horns during the Cold War.[1]

These contests have often been smoldering long-term rivalries punctuated by war or the threat of war. They have typically blended geopolitical and ideological conflict, involving the balance of ideas as much as the balance of power. And these struggles are so intense because the consequences are so profound. From the Peloponnesian War to the Cold War, great-power rivalry has shaped world order.

Today, America is facing new twilight struggles—high-stakes, long-term competitions against China and Russia. So far, these competitions are occurring in the no-man's-land between peace and war, although the danger of military conflict is growing. They represent fierce geopolitical struggles over power and influence, but also deeply ideological conflicts between authoritarianism and democracy. These competitions will determine whether the twenty-first century extends the relatively peaceful, prosperous world to which Americans have become accustomed or thrusts us back to a darker past. They will influence the fate of freedom in countries around the globe.

Many books have been written about how America should wage great-power competition in the coming decades. This one is different. Here, I seek insight about the future by examining the past. Protracted rivalry against powerful authoritarian countries feels unfamiliar to Americans after the generation of great-power peace that followed the Cold War. But long-term competition seems new only because it is very old. Rediscovering the lost art of long-term competition requires only that we reacquaint ourselves with history.

During the Cold War, competition was a way of life. For 45 years, U.S. officials grappled with a dangerous adversary in the ambiguous space between peace and war. They devised generational strategies while responding to crises and surprises. They racked up impressive achievements and committed grievous errors. Ultimately, they defeated a powerful adversary peacefully, decisively, and without disfiguring their own nation beyond recognition.

History never repeats itself precisely. America's current struggles are not exact replicas of the Cold War. It is a serious mistake, moreover, to think that America's Cold War strategy was wholly successful. The road to victory was littered with failures and higher-than-expected costs.

But examined properly, the Cold War offers insights about long-term rivalry and about America's strengths and weaknesses in such a contest. In 1947, Secretary of State George Marshall said that no man "can think with full wisdom and with deep convictions" about the Cold War "who has not at least reviewed in his mind the period of the Peloponnesian War and the fall of Athens."[2] The United States needs this same historical sensibility today. To prepare for new twilight struggles, we must reexamine how America waged an earlier twilight struggle. Winning the contest for the world's future will require learning from our past.

That this contest is under way is undeniable, even if some American officials were, not so long ago, trying to deny it.[3] The U.S.-led international system is threatened by authoritarian powers seeking to redraw the world's geopolitical map and make the twenty-first century an age of autocratic ascendancy. "The central challenge to U.S. prosperity and security," the 2018 *National Defense Strategy* states, "is the *reemergence of long-term, strategic competition* by . . . revisionist powers."[4]

It wasn't supposed to be this way. The Cold War ended with the geopolitical triumph of the West and the ideological triumph of democracy. After the Cold War, U.S. strategy sought to make these victories permanent. Multiple presidents promoted democracy and free markets overseas. They expanded America's global presence to prevent resurgent instability. Most important, they worked to discourage potential rivals from upsetting the post–Cold War order through a mixture of military deterrence and economic integration. In short, Washington aimed to relegate great-power rivalry to history by keeping prospective challengers in check until they were pacified by globalization and liberalization.

This strategy deserves more credit than it often gets. By remaining deeply engaged after the Cold War, instead of retreating across the oceans as it had done after World War I, America provided insurance against a rapid reversion to vicious global anarchy. U.S. promotion of democracy and globalization made the world richer and more humane. If the decades since 1945 have been a time of unprecedented peace and prosperity, it is principally because America worked to make it so after World War II and then persisted after the Cold War. Alas, the idea that great-power rivalry itself could be vanquished went wanting, for three reasons.

The first was a failure of integration. U.S. officials hoped that China and Russia would become responsible stakeholders in an American-led world. But authoritarian leaders had other ideas. Unwilling to sign their political death warrants, they fortified their systems against liberalization (China) or rolled back reforms that had occurred in the 1990s (Russia). Once prospects for democratization faded, authoritarian regimes committed to suppressing liberalism at home were sure to feel threatened in a world where a democratic superpower reigned supreme.

In fact, Russian and Chinese leaders saw U.S. policy not as a source of stability but as a threat to their security and power. Washington was not wrong to expand the North Atlantic Treaty Organization (NATO) into Eastern Europe, give Taiwan shelter against Chinese coercion, and prevent Moscow and Beijing from dominating their surroundings as great powers have long done. But Russia and China resented a hegemonic America imposing its will in their backyards and thwarting their geopolitical designs.

That resentment might not have mattered absent a second factor: the shifting balance of power. So long as America's might was unrivaled, even dissatisfied countries were loath to incur Washington's wrath. Yet U.S. supremacy became more contested, partially owing to the prosperity the American-led system fostered. Russia's constant-dollar gross domestic product (GDP) doubled between 1998 and 2014, and military spending quadrupled. Between 1990 and 2016, Chinese GDP increased twelvefold, and military spending, tenfold. As Russia escaped its post-communist paralysis, as China rose meteorically, countries that disliked the status quo now had the wherewithal to challenge it.[5]

This shift was exacerbated by a third factor: distraction, disinvestment, and disengagement by the United States. After the attacks of September 11, 2001, America spent a decade focused on the Middle East rather than rising geopolitical rivals. For another half-decade after that, Washington slashed its military capabilities in response to budgetary pressures and political dysfunction. And following the 2008 financial crisis, American presidents showed growing ambivalence about global leadership, first subtly under Barack Obama and then flagrantly under Donald Trump. The barriers to great-power rivalry were weakening as the stimulus to rivalry was growing stronger. The resulting challenges have become sharp indeed.

The Chinese challenge is the graver of the two because Chinese power and potential are so great. Although U.S. officials long hoped that Washington could avoid competing with China, the Communist government has been pursuing its "Chinese Dream" at America's expense.

This means, first and foremost, displacing the United States as the premier power in the Asia-Pacific—leaving Asia to the Asians, as Chinese leader Xi Jinping has said.[6] Over a quarter-century, China has conducted a determined military buildup so it can overawe its neighbors and prevent America from defending them. China has also blended coercion and seduction to undermine U.S. alliances and increase its own influence; it has used creeping expansion to control large swaths of the Western Pacific. Like virtually all rising powers, China seeks primacy in its geopolitical backyard. Pushing America out is the prerequisite to pulling that region into China's grasp.

Yet regional primacy is less a destination than a springboard. China's Belt and Road Initiative is a multi-continent project to organize Eurasia into a geoeconomic space oriented toward Beijing. China's military influence is following its economic and political influence. Meanwhile, China is striving to dominate key areas of high-tech innovation. And having once shunned international institutions, China is now building its own while working aggressively to capture others. To see Beijing's assertiveness amid the COVID pandemic—the bullying of international critics, the coercion of neighbors from India to Vietnam, the destruction of Hong Kong's autonomy, the threats against Taiwan—was to glimpse how China will behave as its influence grows. In "continually broadening our comprehensive national power," Xi has argued, Beijing is "laying the foundation for a future where we will win the initiative and have the dominant position."[7]

China envisions a far less democratic world as well. As Beijing builds a hypermodern police state at home, it works assiduously to strengthen autocracy and weaken democracy abroad. China has exported the tools and techniques of repression to countless autocrats. It has used corruption and economic pressure to distort decision-making and suppress free speech in democratic countries. It has promoted autocrat-friendly global norms on human rights and internet management while advertising authoritarian capitalism as superior to liberal democracy. The more prevalent illiberal forms of government are, Chinese leaders calculate, the more secure autocracy in China will be.[8]

The sources of Chinese conduct are complex. Chinese leaders see weakening America's influence as the best guarantee of their own security and survival. Yet China is also spurred onward by vaulting ambition and a sense of historical destiny. This is a country, after all, that traditionally viewed its domain as "all under heaven."[9] Chinese behavior is driven by ideology and geopolitics, insecurity and aggrandizement—the same potent cocktail that has energized rising powers throughout history.

That cocktail is energizing Vladimir Putin's Russia, too. Moscow's long-term prospects are dimmer than Beijing's, so its challenge has been more aggressive. Like China, Moscow desires dominance of its "near abroad." Under Putin's leadership, Russia has dismembered former Soviet republics that were leaning toward the West while using intimidation and subversion to undermine NATO and the European Union—efforts backed by an impressive military modernization campaign.[10]

Military power is not Moscow's only weapon. The Kremlin uses economic leverage to pull countries in Eastern Europe and Central Asia close. Nor are Moscow's geopolitical horizons confined to its near abroad. Putin reestablished Russia as a player in the Middle East and Africa through arms sales, proxy wars, and even direct intervention. Moscow has used military, intelligence, and other resources to shape events and protect friendly rulers as far away as Latin America. Russia cannot create a Moscow-centric global order, but it can act as a foil to American influence and drag the world back to a more predatory, disordered condition.

Indeed, the weaponization of disarray is central to Russian statecraft. Putin has unleashed political meddling, cyberattacks, and "influence operations" meant to weaken and divide countries opposing him. In 2013, General Valery Gerasimov, Russia's chief of general staff, described "new generation warfare" as the fusion of informational, intelligence, and other tools to paralyze an enemy by infiltrating and disrupting its political system. Russia's sophisticated attack on the U.S. presidential campaign in 2016 was the most spectacular example of this strategy. And like Beijing, Moscow supports friendly autocrats while inveighing against the alleged failures of liberal democracy.[11]

In Putin's eyes, it is not Moscow but Washington that is the dangerous revisionist power. Yet if Russian policies seek to halt the encroachment of democratic norms and U.S. influence, they are hard to distinguish from offensive efforts to restore Russia as a global power. What Russia wants, remarked Foreign Minister Sergei Lavrov, is a transition to a "post-West" world.[12]

To be clear, neither China nor Russia is determined simply to blow up the existing order, as Napoleon or Hitler did. Yet both are seeking a dramatically altered international environment, one in which spheres of economic and geopolitical influence have returned, American power is constrained, and authoritarianism advances as democracy retreats. They can succeed only if the U.S.-led order is rolled back and weakened. Because Russia and China share this objective, they have forged an uneasy but productive strategic partnership—an authoritarian International for the twenty-first century.

So far, competitions with China and Russia have remained cold rather than hot. Yet China and Russia could become more confrontational if they conclude that a war against the United States or its allies would be successful, and both countries are working very hard to tip key regional military balances in their favor. The likelihood of a Sino-American war over Taiwan has risen dramatically in recent years and will likely keep rising in years to come. In the meantime, Washington will face all the dangers of great-power rivalry: high-stakes diplomatic crises, proxy conflicts and covert skullduggery, arms races and the shadow of war.

America could avoid these burdens by opting out of competition. It could hope that its authoritarian challengers, which face serious internal problems, burn themselves out. Yet doing so would only increase the danger. Russia may be in long-term decline, but it has compensated with creative tactics and risk-taking. China, even if its power eventually falters, could still be the most formidable opponent the United States has ever faced. The price of retreat would be the steady erosion of the world America has built. The price of preserving that world is competing effectively.

What is long-term competition? The idea that studying geopolitical struggle in one era can help us navigate rivalry in another implies that long-term competition has core features that endure across history even as the specifics of two contests may differ dramatically.[13] In essence, long-term competition is an *ongoing, open-ended contest for influence between great powers.* Beyond this, the concept has several persistent traits.

First, long-term competition happens at a geopolitical twilight, between the sunshine of peace and the darkness of war. Geopolitical rivalry is not peace. The threat of violence is omnipresent, and some competitions do culminate in war. In long-term rivalry, the U.S. diplomat George Kennan noted, "There is no real security and there is no alternative to living dangerously."[14] Yet competition is not all-out military conflict. It may blend rivalry and cooperation. Before World War I, for example, the United Kingdom and Germany were commercial partners and strategic foes. Competition may also feature wars that are deliberately kept limited. Indeed, the fact that long-term rivalry is long-term—that it is not brought swiftly, violently to a conclusion—presumably indicates that the protagonists share an interest in preventing matters from spiraling out of control.

Second, long-term competition is interactive: it requires outplaying an antagonist that is trying to outplay you. This means that a central challenge is getting inside the opponent's head by studying how he thinks. It also means that the best competitors will find ways of shaping a dynamic interaction to their benefit by exploiting an opponent's weaknesses, steering the competition into areas of particular advantage, or even molding the larger international environment to limit the adversary's options. Long-term competition doesn't happen in a vacuum. Affecting the wider world can be a profoundly powerful way of constraining a dangerous rival.

Third, long-term competition occurs in a world of finite resources. No one has the advantage in every dimension of rivalry; countries must tolerate weakness somewhere if they are to enjoy strength anywhere. The essence of long-term competition, then, is strategic choice. Countries must choose where to focus and where to economize; they must deftly apply limited means while forcing a competitor to squander its own. Above all, long-term competition rewards countries that pit their strengths against a competitor's vulnerabilities and translate moments of opportunity into lasting advantage.

Fourth, long-term competition is comprehensive. The military balance invariably casts its shadow over any competition, but power is multidimensional, so struggles over power are multidimensional, too. Rivalries involve economic statecraft, intelligence, and diplomacy; they play out in the realm of culture, values, and ideas. Long-term competition thus requires integrating multiple forms of influence into a coherent whole.

All this takes time, which leads to a fifth point: Long-term competition is often unsatisfying and indecisive by nature. It plays out over years, decades, generations. It rewards the incremental strengthening of position rather than the quest for quick, decisive triumph. As a result, long-term competition demands seemingly contradictory qualities: the ability to deploy power effectively while husbanding it for the long haul, the ability to advance consistently while retaining flexibility along the way. Commitment is imperative, but there are no prizes for what Lord Salisbury called "sticking to the carcass of dead policy."[15] And since long-term competition takes time, it makes time a weapon. Smart strategists seek an edge by exploiting windows of opportunity and manipulating the pace of the rivalry.

Sixth, long-term competition is a test of systems as much as statecraft. It is a measure of whose political, social, and economic model can best generate and employ power. There are no purely domestic issues. Matters that affect the performance of a country's institutions, economy, and society may determine its geopolitical fate. The best strategies strengthen a nation's system by spurring it to undertake needed reforms; the cardinal sin is to pursue policies—foreign or domestic—that undermine a nation's vitality. And because long-term competition is a contest of systems, shrewd players will ruthlessly exploit a rival's internal weaknesses.

Long-term competition might thus be considered the graduate level of strategy. It involves mastering a dynamic interaction while synchronizing initiatives across time, space, and the various dimensions of national power. It requires creating asymmetric advantages and imposing disproportionate costs, rather than simply overwhelming an adversary everywhere. It involves straddling the line between tranquility and violence and, not least, fortifying a state's domestic system while defending it from the strains that foreign dangers invariably impose.

Finally, the pressures to succeed in long-term competition are enormous given the costs of failure. Winners of great-power rivalries receive vast influence and the opportunity to shape the world. Losers can fall into decline, even disaster. All of which means that the United States will need every bit of intellectual preparation it can get for the tests it now confronts.

If Americans aren't well versed in long-term competition today, it is because they haven't had to face it recently. It has been 30 years since America was last engaged in great-power rivalry. Few living policymakers have deep experience with that challenge. America, as a result, has precious little muscle memory in dealing with powerful, persistent foes.

That wasn't always the case. In the decades after World War II, America conducted what President John F. Kennedy called a "long twilight struggle" against the Soviet Union.[16] The superpowers competed fiercely for geopolitical influence. They fought, as President George H. W. Bush said, over the "soul of mankind"—over what set of political values would emerge supreme.[17] As the Cold War shaped the postwar world, it put long-term competition at the heart of U.S. statecraft.

For two generations, American officials devoted vast resources and intellectual energy to competing with the Kremlin militarily, economically, diplomatically, and ideologically. They designed generational strategies while coping with unending strategic shocks. They developed defensive policies to check Soviet thrusts and offensive policies to exploit Soviet weaknesses; they used American power assertively but also sought to prevent competition from escalating into disastrous conflict. The demands of competition even reshaped American government and society.

Through all this, the United States suffered mistakes and setbacks. Prominent Americans on the left and the right wondered whether the effort was worth making. Yet the Cold War was, fundamentally, a period when long-term competition was intimately familiar to U.S. officials, and when America eventually accomplished nearly everything it wanted to. So Cold War history has much to teach us about how America wages great-power rivalry and how to get long-term competition right.

To be clear, the Cold War is not a perfect analogue for today's rivalries. Neither China nor Russia is driven by an ideology as messianic as Soviet communism. Putin's Russia is a shadow of the Soviet Union, and China lacks the global military punch Moscow once possessed, even though it is a stronger economic competitor than the Kremlin ever was. There is far greater economic and technological interdependence, and a far more complex relationship, between America and China than ever existed between the Cold War superpowers. Moreover, the strategic context is different. Now, Russia and China are confronting a well-established, if beleaguered, international order. After World War II, the Soviet danger was so immense because there was no order; chaos convulsed much of the globe. We can't rerun the Cold War playbook in a very different world.[18]

History, in fact, can never fully solve our strategic problems. Events are like snowflakes: no two are exactly alike. Luck, circumstance, and human choice ensure that there are no iron laws of history. Yet policymakers still study the past for guidance in confronting the future because the past is the only place we *can* look to understand things that haven't happened yet, and history can give us a deeper reservoir of insight than we might otherwise possess. "Fools learn by experience," German chancellor Otto von Bismarck once said. "Wise men learn by other people's experience."[19] Indeed, there are several reasons why wise strategists should revisit America's Cold War.

First, although the Cold War isn't a precise match for today's competitions, it isn't such a bad one, either. The Cold War was a global duel over power and world order, just the sort of contest that is now under way. The Cold War was about ideology and geopolitics; so are America's new twilight struggles. The Cold War was a contest of systems and a test of strategy; here, too, history rhymes. The Cold War tested America's ability to develop long-range strategies and build international coalitions. It required mobilizing the U.S. government and society for rivalry while intensely studying an opaque adversary. It entailed finding areas of cooperation amid hostility, and figuring out how, and whether, to split rivals and attack their political systems. It forced hard choices about how to employ U.S. power across multiple theaters; it required tradeoffs between America's strategic interests and its cherished values. All these tasks will be essential in the coming years. It would be strategically lazy to mindlessly apply Cold War solutions to post–Cold War problems. But it would be intellectually wasteful to ignore the insights the Cold War offers.

Second, the Cold War is a vast repository of knowledge about long-term competition. It was unique in many respects; no prior rivalry played out in the nuclear shadow. But the Cold War was also one of many great-power rivalries dating back millennia. If Carl von Clausewitz could write the defining treatise on war by studying the Napoleonic conflicts, if Thucydides could learn basic truths about geopolitics from the Peloponnesian War, then surely a struggle as epic as the Cold War can teach us something fundamental about long-term competition.

Third, the Cold War can teach us about how America does great-power rivalry. The Cold War is the only time America has waged a twilight struggle, across continents and decades, against an authoritarian foe. It is the only time America's strengths and weaknesses in such a struggle have been on display. Put simply, the Cold War is the only history of sustained competition that America has. To prevent policymakers from using that history badly, scholars must help them use it well.

Offering that help is the goal of this book. It tells the story of U.S. strategy in the Cold War, an analysis that should stand on its own as history while also informing our thinking about America's new twilight struggle. The book unfolds not chronologically but thematically, with each of ten historical chapters covering a Cold War–era strategic challenge that has obvious relevance for waging global competition today.[20] The final chapter brings us back to the present, offering the Cold War's lessons for American leaders in the twenty-first century.

Alas, no amount of history can provide precise answers to hard policy problems. History can, however, give us greater intellectual depth ahead of the coming trials. Relearning the history of America's Cold War can rebuild muscle memory that has atrophied in recent decades. It can provide vicarious experience so that strategic dilemmas appear less foreign when encountered in real life.[21] Long-term competition seems less novel once we remember how normal it once was. Embracing the past is indispensable to thriving in our competitive future.

CHAPTER ONE

Forging a Strategy

"NO ONE STARTS A war—or rather, no one in his senses ought to do so—without first being clear in his mind what he intends to achieve by that war and how he intends to conduct it."[1] This Clausewitzian dictum applies equally to long-term rivalry. The first imperative of competition is to determine what sort of contest one faces and how one will win it. Having that theory of victory is critical. It ensures, as General Omar Bradley said, that a country's actions are "guided by the stars" and "not by the lights of a passing ship."[2]

The theory of victory that America chose in the Cold War—containment—has attained near-mythical status. Since the Soviet collapse, containment has been revered for its clarity and effectiveness. Its originators in the Truman administration have been lauded for plotting a 45-year roadmap to victory. The era of containment's founding, wrote former Council on Foreign Relations president Leslie Gelb, was a "golden age of U.S. foreign policy."[3]

Containment has achieved fame for good reason. It persisted for two generations. It delivered the greatest peaceful victory in the history of great-power rivalry. Yet the retrospective veneration of containment makes one wonder how much the U.S. foreign policy community remembers about the Cold War.

Containment was not an immaculate, detailed blueprint set down by George Kennan. It was pieced together, incrementally and often chaotically, and almost immediately took on characteristics that Kennan found appalling.

The strategy triggered fierce political fights almost from the outset; it faced withering critiques from left and right, hawks and doves, for decades thereafter. And not surprisingly, because containment had plenty of drawbacks—its plodding pace, its dangers and costs, its moral compromises—and often looked to be failing until it triumphed. The idea that the Cold War was a golden age would have been news to those who experienced it. Containment looks so pristine, so impressive, only in hindsight.

This doesn't make containment's origin story irrelevant to our problems. Exploring how containment took shape, and how the Truman administration crafted a political consensus to support it, is critical to understanding how long-term strategy really works. The legend of containment may be alluring. But the true, messy history is more rewarding, for it reminds us just how arduous and contested the strategy-making process is. It shows that containment's most frustrating qualities were also its greatest virtues. And it reveals what made a strategy that was so thoroughly imperfect so successful in the end.

Strategy looks forward to a better future but is often inspired by a traumatic past. Such was the case with containment. That strategy was Washington's answer to the situation after 1945, when the United States faced a totalitarian foe in a shattered world. Yet containment rested atop an intellectual architecture constructed during World War II.

If that conflict ended in a decisive victory for America, its strategic legacy was lasting vigilance born of insecurity. The war demonstrated that America was not immune from instability and aggression overseas. It illustrated the tight interconnections between economic prosperity and geopolitical security, since the collapse of the former had preceded the breakdown of the latter. Above all, it revealed how cataclysmically the global order could buckle when assaulted by aggressive regimes. America was "the most powerful nation in the world," wrote Secretary of War Robert Patterson in 1945. "But our present triumph may hold the seeds of our future destruction," he argued, if Americans did not heed these lessons.[4]

The upshot was a strategic revolution. Prior to 1941, most Americans assumed that the country could protect its vital interests by dominating the Western Hemisphere and limiting its commitments in Eurasia. By 1945, however, most elites accepted Franklin Roosevelt's view that America could never survive "as a happy and fertile oasis of liberty surrounded by a cruel desert of dictatorship."[5] The United States could protect its interests only by dramatically expanding its definition of those interests; it must assure its own security by creating a world that was secure from depression, coercion, and war.

Creating this world would require heroic exertions. Washington must anchor an open international economy that would prevent another slide into misery and radicalism. It must lead international institutions that would promote diplomatic cooperation. It must confront aggressors early and stand up for values—self-determination, freedom from coercion— that had been trampled before World War II. Not least, it must prevent any hostile power from controlling Eurasia and amassing the resources to threaten America itself. "The strategic defenses of the United States are not at the three-mile limit in American waters," journalist Walter Lippmann wrote, "but extend across both oceans and to all the transoceanic lands from which an attack by sea or by air can be launched."[6]

Cold War strategy thus began to form before most Americans had ever contemplated the possibility of a Cold War. Coming out of one epic global trauma, U.S. officials already knew what sort of world they wanted and what catastrophe—a return to violent anarchy—they must avoid.

They did not necessarily realize that the Soviet Union would need containing. It was obvious that World War II had catapulted the USSR into a position of tremendous influence by destroying the natural barriers to Soviet power. That the Kremlin ran a tyranny just as murderous as the Nazi regime, with an ideology just as hostile, was also ominous. "A future war with Soviet Russia is as certain as anything in the world can be certain," wrote Undersecretary of State Joseph Grew.[7] But this remained a minority opinion at war's end. Americans made the transition from hot war to cold war reluctantly.

Throughout World War II, President Franklin D. Roosevelt had labored to moderate Moscow's behavior and alleviate its insecurity. At the Yalta conference in 1945, FDR tacitly blessed Soviet domination of Eastern Europe in hopes that Moscow would rule with a light hand. Until his death, he argued that cooperation with Joseph Stalin was the key to ending "the system of unilateral action, the exclusive alliances, the spheres of influence, the balances of power, and all the other expedients that have been tried for centuries . . . and have always failed."[8] After the war ended, the alliance deteriorated swiftly; the glue of a common enemy no longer held it together. Yet President Harry S. Truman, too,

held out hope for a diplomatic understanding with Stalin. The Soviet ty-
rant, he judged, "was a fine man who wanted to do the right thing."⁹

U.S. policy changed in 1946 for two reasons. The first was growing
alarm at Soviet behavior. By this point, Moscow was making a farce of
self-determination in Eastern Europe. Stalin demanded territorial concessions from Turkey and sought geopolitical gains around the Mediterranean rim. The Kremlin hesitated to withdraw troops from Iran and
Manchuria. And in February 1946, Stalin gave a major speech in which
he blamed capitalism for World War II and asserted that it would inevi-
tably precipitate World War III.¹⁰ Stalin, it appeared, was rejecting
America's vision of a cooperative world, and his ambitions would be limited only by U.S. resistance. "Unless Russia is faced with an iron fist and
strong language another war is in the making," Truman wrote.¹¹

The second reason was unrelenting global chaos. Throughout Europe,
political radicalism simmered and famine threatened. Instability and radicalism roiled critical countries from the Atlantic to the Pacific. A crippled, bankrupt Britain could no longer exercise global leadership. "There is a situation
in the world," Assistant Secretary of State Dean Acheson explained, "which
threatens the very foundations, the whole fabric of world organization."¹²
The world was falling apart again, with Stalin poised to scoop up the pieces.

To be clear, the Cold War was not entirely Moscow's fault. The Soviets undoubtedly felt threatened by America's power and ambitions, and
the inherent ideological clash made matters worse. But U.S. leaders were
not wrong in concluding that Stalin viewed the capitalist world with fundamental hostility (even as he also hoped for U.S. economic assistance),
and that the Soviet Union was determined to increase its power at the
West's expense. Even if the West "were suddenly to give in and grant all
Russian demands," former foreign minister Maxim Litvinov acknowledged, it would simply invite the "next series of demands."¹³

The climate of growing alarm in Washington led to an unmistakable
stiffening of U.S. policy. Truman demanded that Soviet troops withdraw
from Iran and used the Sixth Fleet to face down Stalin's bid for the Dar-
danelles; U.S. troops lingered in southern Korea to prevent a takeover by
the Communist-led North; the administration aided China's Chiang Kai-
shek in his civil war against Mao Zedong's Communists. All the while,
however, the American military was shrinking from 12 million personnel
in 1945 to under 2 million in 1947. "We were spread from hell to break-
fast," said one U.S. official, "all over the world."¹⁴ The president also
waited until March 1947 to issue a public declaration of Cold War, in a

major speech to Congress in which he sought emergency aid for Greece and Turkey and argued that America must "support free peoples" against the march of tyranny.[15]

It took time, then, to accept that creating a healthy world would require waging a geopolitical struggle with the Soviet Union. Yet that reluctance was arguably a strategic blessing. As the diplomat Charles Bohlen later wrote, Americans had to feel that their government had tried to "work out a better world" before they would accept the imperatives of survival in a tragic one.[16] That America had not rushed into the Cold War made the country more effective in conducting it.

The onset of competition with Moscow did not, however, answer the question of how to wage it. There was nothing like an American strategy in 1946–1947. From Europe to Korea, the Truman administration was piling up commitments as its resources dwindled. Internally, the administration was beset by rivalry and disorganization. While U.S. views of Moscow were hardening, there remained confusion regarding how, precisely, to define the threat and America's objectives. It fell to Kennan, the State Department's leading Sovietologist, to provide clarity.

Kennan's writings—notably his Long Telegram from the U.S. embassy in Moscow in February 1946 and his "X Article" in *Foreign Affairs* in July 1947—were as much about eliminating bad options as illuminating better ones. Kennan doused hopes for a diplomatic settlement. The Soviet Union harbored a pervasive, unconquerable suspicion: "Nothing short of complete disarmament, delivery of our air and naval forces to Russia and resigning of powers of government to American Communists" could convince Stalin of America's goodwill, and even then he would "smell a trap."[17] More fundamentally, Soviet aims made long-term coexistence impossible. Moscow believed it was essential "that the internal harmony of our society be disrupted, our traditional way of life be destroyed, the international authority of our state be broken, if Soviet power is to be secure."[18]

This hostility flowed from a toxic combination of history and ideology. Russia's experience of living on a vast, vulnerable plain created unshakable insecurity that led to compulsive expansion: The only defense was a good offense. Soviet ideology added the belief that capitalism must be destroyed for communism to triumph. Russian leaders, Kennan wrote, would "seek security only in patient but deadly struggle for the total destruction of rival power."[19]

Yet if accommodating the Soviet Union was unwise, taking up arms was unnecessary. Soviet leaders understood how badly World War II had devastated their country. They respected America's military and economic might. And because Soviet ideology held that capitalism was doomed, Moscow could be patient in seeking its demise. The Soviet Union was a fundamentally different adversary from the one America had just defeated. It could be deterred, whereas Hitler could not. The Kremlin might be "impervious to logic of reason" but was "highly sensitive to logic of force."[20]

This diagnosis produced three key insights that formed the core of America's Cold War strategy. First, peace did not require appeasement, and victory did not require war. This was not as obvious then as it would seem in hindsight. Stalin himself had publicly declared that the third world war could only be postponed, not avoided. Eminent statesmen such as Winston Churchill argued that America should smash the Soviet Union while it had the chance.[21] Yet if Kennan was right, outright conflict was not necessary. Instead, Soviet expansion could "be contained by the adroit and vigilant application of counterforce at a series of constantly shifting geographical and political points."[22]

Second, containment need not bring perpetual stalemate. The Soviet Union was externally formidable but suffered from severe internal weaknesses: the irrationality of the command economy, the fatigue and resentment of the population, the vicious yet sclerotic political system. The Kremlin's chief strength was its confidence that it would eventually overpower a dying capitalist world. But if America could disprove this thesis, it could shatter the Kremlin's ideological certitude; if it blocked Soviet expansion, it could force Moscow to face its internal infirmities. America could "increase enormously the strains under which Soviet policy must operate" and "promote tendencies which must eventually find their outlet in either the breakup or the gradual mellowing of Soviet power."[23] Containment could bring about regime change; a conservative policy could achieve transformative ends.

Third, the best way to contain Soviet power was to rebuild a healthy Western community. "World communism is like [a] malignant parasite which feeds only on diseased tissue," Kennan wrote. Combating the underlying disease would foreclose opportunities for mischief. It would demonstrate that the noncommunist world could attain a prosperity and vigor that the Soviet empire could never emulate. Containment, then, was a team sport. What Washington did with its friends was more important than what it did to its enemy.[24]

Admittedly, Kennan's writings offered few concrete policy proposals. Their value lay in explaining how the United States might succeed and what it might eventually win. Turning this theory of victory into an actual strategy would preoccupy U.S. officials through the late 1940s and after.

It is tempting to look back on the legendary initiatives of the Truman years—the Truman Doctrine, the Marshall Plan, the North Atlantic Treaty, the Korean War—as logical steps in a visionary plan. But this is not how long-term strategies emerge. Containment was an ever-shifting mass of policies; it evolved in dramatic and unexpected ways. The golden age of American strategy was "one of great obscurity to those who lived through it," Acheson recalled.[25]

That obscurity wasn't for lack of deliberate thought. "This is only the beginning," Truman remarked after his speech on Greece and Turkey; there were crises everywhere.[26] To get ahead, the administration engaged in a frenzy of planning. The new secretary of state, George Marshall, tapped Kennan to run a Policy Planning Staff tasked with developing long-range strategy. The Joint Chiefs of Staff studied which countries Washington should prioritize.[27] In July, the National Security Act created the Central Intelligence Agency and the National Security Council and brought the military services under a secretary of defense, James Forrestal. The United States, Forrestal believed, must "advance on a solid front and not on a jagged and spasmodic line."[28]

This planning process produced an elegant strategy of containment. That strategy rested on the idea that containing the Soviet Union meant preventing it from dominating Eurasia—but that doing so meant being highly selective in applying American power. Washington should focus on key centers of industrial activity, namely Western Europe and Japan, that could shift the global balance if they fell under Soviet control. America would fortify these areas by using its unmatched strengths—economic muscle, capital, technology—to restore their economies, revive their self-confidence, and fortify them against subversion and pressure. "Any world balance of power means first and foremost a balance on the Eurasian land mass," noted Kennan. "That balance is unthinkable as long as Germany and Japan remain power vacuums."[29]

At the heart of this strategy were concepts of comparative advantage and calculated risk. Rather than matching Moscow tank for tank, soldier for soldier, Washington would employ tools it possessed in abundance to re-create natural barriers to Soviet power. Because U.S. officials, buoyed by CIA estimates, believed that the Soviets would not initiate war so long as America possessed superior overall power, Washington could risk antagonizing an enemy that commanded dominant land power at key points across Eurasia. "As long as we can outproduce the world, can control the sea and can strike inland with the atomic bomb, we can assume certain risks otherwise unacceptable," Forrestal wrote.[30]

This strategy underpinned two landmark initiatives of 1947–1948: the Marshall Plan and the "reverse course" in Japan. The former was an unprecedented $13 billion aid package meant to jump-start European economies and stymie radical forces. The latter was a shift from a punitive to a restorative occupation, meant to stabilize Japan as an anticommunist bastion. Notably, this strategy also informed what America did not do in 1947–1948: undertake a major military buildup, rescue Chiang Kai-shek from defeat in China's civil war, or commit to defending unstable regimes on a conflict-plagued Asian mainland. America must identify "what parts of the Pacific and Far Eastern world are absolutely vital to our security," Kennan noted, and relinquish the rest.[31]

U.S. policy still had an improvisational character. The Marshall "Plan" was announced before U.S. officials had any real idea of how it would work. The CIA threw together covert campaigns to stop Communists from surging to power in Italy and France. The crush of problems was such that "the only way we could ever hope to solve them would be if we could persuade the world to stand still for six months," Kennan lamented.[32] In these circumstances, it was doubly impressive that Truman's policies were so effective.

Indeed, this early period of containment represents what we commonly think a long-term competitive strategy should be. U.S. officials differentiated between greater and lesser threats; they accepted peripheral setbacks to achieve victories in places that mattered more. "That means peace in the world," Truman remarked, "if we can get recovery in Europe."[33] U.S. strategists understood the importance of time: They calculated that Washington had a window of opportunity to address the political and economic instability that was making Europe and Japan vulnerable. Not least, the Truman administration emphasized asymmetry and leverage, by deploying America's unrivaled economic power to build positions of enduring geopolitical strength. This was competitive strategy par excellence—and it didn't even survive the 1940s.

Almost as quickly as containment emerged, it started morphing into something different. In 1947, there was no thought of creating a permanent military alliance with Western Europe. That alliance became reality in 1949. Truman had abandoned Chiang's government in China on the grounds that mainland Asia was a strategic backwater. By mid-1949, however, now-Secretary Acheson termed it a "fundamental decision of American policy" not to "permit further extension of Communist domination on the Continent of Asia."[34] Also in 1949, U.S. forces pulled out of South Korea to conserve scarce resources. By the next summer, Washington was desperately fighting to defend that country. And whereas Truman had rejected rearmament in the late 1940s, in 1950 he approved a tripling of the defense budget.

The new attitude infused a top-secret document drafted under the aegis of the National Security Council, NSC-68. The Cold War was a conflict between freedom and slavery, NSC-68 stated. "The assault on free institutions is world-wide now" as the Soviets surged and America's position slipped. Washington must prevent further setbacks wherever they might occur; it must develop the comprehensive military strength to keep a ruthless enemy in check. "Without superior aggregate military strength, in being and readily mobilizable, a policy of 'containment' ... is no more than a policy of bluff."[35] Containment had now gone global; it had become less discriminate and more militarized. The reasons why U.S. policymakers moved from one version of containment to another demonstrate just how hard it is for long-term strategy to remain static.

The most obvious reason is that the world didn't stand still between 1948 and 1950. The Cold War intensified dramatically; the danger was palpable. The year 1948 saw a Communist coup in Czechoslovakia and the onset of the Berlin blockade. The following year brought the Communist victory in China, prompting fears of a rout across Asia, and the first Soviet nuclear test. In June 1950, North Korea invaded South Korea, triggering U.S. intervention; in November, China entered the conflict, smashing American forces and stoking fears of World War III. "We are faced with the most terrible situation since Pearl Harbor," Truman said.[36] This epochal succession of shocks laid bare several key issues that reshaped U.S. strategy.

The first factor was that U.S. commitments had a tendency to snowball in an interconnected world. The initial strategy of containment was *too* elegant. It held that America could revitalize Europe and Japan without getting deeply involved elsewhere, that it could emphasize economic recovery while avoiding military entanglements. Yet the postwar world was stubbornly indivisible. "The Marshall Plan for Europe," Forrestal explained, "could not succeed without access to the Middle East oil."[37] Similarly, Japan was the priority in Asia, but Japan needed resources and markets on an increasingly vulnerable mainland. The world seemed psychologically indivisible, too. Although South Korea itself mattered little, abandoning that country to flagrant Communist aggression could demoralize allies elsewhere. "You may be sure that all Europeans to say nothing of the Asiatics are watching to see what the United States will do," one U.S. diplomat wrote.[38]

It proved equally difficult to segregate economic and military issues. For the Marshall Plan to succeed, Western European governments had to eject obstructive Communist ministers, but that step provoked strikes and riots. The Marshall Plan also required countries that had just been terrorized by Germany to cooperate in its reconstruction. Yet the prospect of reviving an old enemy while antagonizing a new one was alarming, and only an explicit U.S. security commitment—embodied in the North Atlantic Treaty—could provide the necessary reassurance. Western Europe needed "economic revival," conceded State Department official Philip Jessup, but also "the feeling of security and hope without which a man can't put his heart into his work."[39]

A second factor was that America could not implement containment in a vacuum. Strategy always involves intense action-reaction dynamics. If Soviet expansionism had initially elicited containment, containment then elicited alarming Soviet responses. The Marshall Plan provoked Stalin to cement his control of Eastern Europe by approving the Czech coup, which terrified Western European governments and catalyzed planning for the transatlantic alliance.[40] The U.S. effort to rehabilitate the German economy caused Stalin to retaliate with the Berlin blockade, which prompted the Berlin airlift and the conclusion of the North Atlantic Treaty. The Europeans were " 'completely out of their skin, and sitting on their nerves,' and hope must be recreated in them very soon," Marshall said.[41]

North Korea's invasion of South Korea created even greater blowback. That event was triggered not by American assertiveness but by American retrenchment. The pullback of U.S. troops in 1949, and Acheson's subsequent declaration that South Korea lay outside Washington's defense perimeter, helped tempt an opportunistic Stalin to approve the attack. Yet by

convincing Truman that America's enemies would "now use armed invasion and war" to achieve their aims, the assault had transformative global
effects.[42] It led to U.S. intervention in Korea, the dispatch of additional
troops to Europe, the transformation of the North Atlantic Treaty into a
real, integrated alliance (the North Atlantic Treaty *Organization*), and a
vast military buildup. The enemy gets a vote in strategy, as in war. By revealing deep vulnerabilities in the U.S. position, Stalin provoked a stronger, more global version of containment.

This phenomenon related to a final issue, which was that weaknesses
tolerable in 1947–1948 became less tolerable with time. Kennan may have
been correct in insisting, as he did throughout the late 1940s, that the Soviets would not invade Western Europe.[43] But a military imbalance could still
undermine the political will of U.S. allies. And amid escalating tensions,
how could anyone be sure the Kremlin would show restraint? "We are
playing with fire," worried Marshall in 1948, "while we have nothing with
which to put it out."[44] Once the Soviets acquired their own atomic device
and North Korea invaded South Korea, discounting the possibility of war
seemed downright reckless. The military buildup associated with NSC-68
was dramatic, Acheson acknowledged, but "the only thing that was more
dangerous than undertaking this program was not undertaking it."[45]

Kennan could never accept this transformation of containment. His
strategy had escaped him. He had the feeling of having "inadvertently
loosened a large boulder from the top of a cliff and now helplessly
witness[ing] its path of destruction in the valley below."[46] Yet it is not clear
that U.S. policymakers reasonably could, or should, have ignored the surging dangers that made the limited-liability approach untenable. Kennan
was dismayed that containment took on attributes he never intended. But
it was just that malleability that kept his strategy relevant under Truman
and all the Cold War presidents who followed.

Strategy, however, is political as well as geopolitical, and containment
could not have endured without a solid domestic foundation. The typical
interpretation is that Truman oversold containment by whipping up an
overwrought Cold War fervor.[47] More accurately, the Truman administration legitimized containment with a concerted, and basically honest,
education campaign.

That campaign was necessary because Americans were not naturally
predisposed toward confrontation with Moscow. On V-J Day in 1945, 54

percent of Americans trusted and wanted to work with the Kremlin. In 1947, 82 percent opposed undertaking major initiatives without approval of the United Nations. Many Americans suspected that containment was really a policy of protecting British imperial interests; many liberals initially favored accommodating Stalin. And even as views of Moscow hardened, the reality of competition did not translate into support for the investments needed to win it. Opposition to foreign aid was fierce just as Europe careened toward disaster.[48] Getting America "into European politics," Truman remarked, "means the greatest selling job ever facing a president."[49] His sales pitch fused geopolitics, ideology, and political leadership.

The geopolitical argument was that inaction would jeopardize everything America had won in World War II. The loss of Greece and Turkey, warned Truman in 1947, could lead to Soviet domination of the Mediterranean rim, imperiling critical countries throughout the Middle East, North Africa, and Europe.[50] A year later, Marshall told Congress that failure to aid Europe would invite "economic distress so intense, social discontents so violent, political confusion so widespread," that the continent might collapse and reemerge "in the image of the tyranny that we fought to destroy in Germany."[51] The United States had just sacrificed 400,000 lives to prevent aggressive dictatorships from dominating the globe. If America hesitated now, it would again risk being reduced to an isolated democracy in a hostile world.

Avoiding this nightmare required unprecedented peacetime expenditures. But the administration framed these commitments as insurance against the harsher sacrifices that would be required if Washington let the world go to pieces. "We must be prepared to pay the price of peace," Truman explained, "or assuredly we shall pay the price of war."[52] Even as the administration brought America into NATO and the Korean War, even as the defense budget ballooned, this preventive logic remained the same. The Cold War would be hard for Americans; declining to wage it would eventually inflict hardships far more severe.

Yet the Cold War was not simply about geopolitical interests. It was also about the larger principles—self-determination, democracy, human rights—that America had shed so much blood to defend. Allowing the world "to work out a way of life free from coercion," Truman explained, was a "fundamental issue in the war with Germany and Japan." At a time when "nearly every nation must choose between alternative ways of life," Americans must once again recognize that totalitarian aggression represented a threat to their values as well as to international peace.[53] The

United States was competing for something greater than power, Truman repeatedly argued. It was struggling to defend "the things we believe in most deeply," to "get the right sort of peace in the world."[54]

Kennan himself was uncomfortable with this universalistic language; critics charged that the Truman Doctrine elided the authoritarian tendencies of America's friends.[55] But Truman acknowledged that the Greek and Turkish governments were flawed, and he relied on soaring rhetoric for good reasons.

Framing the Cold War as a struggle for American values was critical to refuting the charge that Washington was practicing cynical Old World diplomacy or rescuing the British empire. The idea of "pulling British chestnuts out of the fire," one official noted, had caused a "very adverse reaction" from congressional leaders.[56] Truman's approach allowed the administration to break with one hallowed tradition, abstention from European politics, by inaugurating another tradition of supporting free peoples against totalitarianism. Additionally, his rhetoric transcended partisan divisions by invoking the ideals around which Americans had rallied in World War II. "The missionary strain in the character of Americans," noted a British diplomat, "leads many of them to feel that they have now received a call to extend to other countries the blessings with which the Almighty has endowed their own."[57]

Truman always erred on the side of stark language; he insisted that his speeches be "free of hesitation or double talk." But this doesn't mean U.S. officials used deception to "scare hell" out of the American people.[58] Rather, Truman and his aides remembered how slowly America had responded to gathering threats in the 1930s. They understood that only clear, piercing messages could move the domestic audience. "Qualification must give way to simplicity of statement, nicety and nuance to bluntness, almost brutality, in carrying home a point," Acheson wrote. So they sought to educate Americans, frankly and compellingly, about what was at issue.[59] "If we can sell every useless article known to man in large quantities," said the adviser Robert Lovett, "we should be able to sell our very fine story in larger quantities."[60]

Selling U.S. policy also required careful guidance by American elites. It was critical, noted one interagency paper, "to bring about an understanding by the American people of the world strategic situation."[61] Through the end of his presidency, Truman spoke forcefully about the stakes of competition with Moscow. The administration enlisted prominent citizens, both Democratic and Republican, to press the case for initiatives such as the Marshall Plan.[62] Most consequentially, the administration built bipartisan support for its policies (for a time) by courting Arthur Vandenberg, the Republican chair and later ranking member of the Senate Foreign Relations Committee. Truman and his aides incorporated Vandenberg's ideas into the North Atlantic Treaty and other ventures. They entrusted him with shepherding critical bills through the Senate. This process, and the flattery it involved, grated on Kennan. "I could not accept the assumption that Senators were all such idiots that they deserved admiring applause every time they could be persuaded by the State Department to do something sensible," he groused. The indignities were rewarded, for Vandenberg kept the Republican Party's isolationist wing at bay.[63]

With Vandenberg's help, Truman won congressional support for the crucial initiatives of the period. But many of the key debates were nearer-run things than the final vote tallies indicated. It took nearly a year for Congress to approve the Marshall Plan. As one senator scoffed, "This is not our first attempt to fill up a leaking barrel by pouring more water into it."[64] The North Atlantic Treaty attracted scorn from Senator Robert Taft and other Republican isolationists. And all the administration's efforts might have failed absent a final factor: timely Soviet assistance.

The Marshall Plan appropriation was proceeding lethargically until the Czech Communists carried off their coup. The Berlin blockade ensured Senate support for the North Atlantic Treaty. The invasion of South Korea enabled a heretofore-impossible level of defense spending. For decades to come, Soviet aggressiveness would be the worst geopolitical fear and best political ally of America's Cold Warriors. The Soviet Union, National Security Adviser Brent Scowcroft later noted, "had periodically rescued us from ourselves by some singular act of brutality to remind us what they were really like and that we couldn't let our guard down."[65] Whenever Americans tired of containment, Moscow would eventually deliver the provocation needed to reinvigorate a Cold War consensus.

Were there drawbacks to this consensus? Absolutely. Truman's grand rhetoric hardly made U.S. officials mindless ideologues. But it did make it harder to explain why the loss of China, the world's most populous country, was not a strategic disaster, and to resist pressure to push deep into North Korea in late 1950 despite the risk of Chinese intervention. The administration's own language also made it difficult, following Chinese intervention, to argue that the Korean conflict must be kept limited so Washington could remain focused on Europe. "Are we to take the position that human freedom is less worth supporting in Asia than it is in Europe?" Republican senator William Knowland asked.[66] Even more troubling was that sweeping, values-laden public statements fed a charged Cold War climate that could be exploited by demagogues like Senator Joseph McCarthy. The Truman administration's fusing of geopolitics and ideology was necessary to create a Cold War consensus. But a consensus strong enough to enable constructive policy was also strong enough to support more destructive impulses.

None of this meant that containment was immune from criticism. If the standard lore is that politics stopped at the water's edge, the reality is that the period of peak bipartisanship lasted about two years. From 1949 on, brutal political fights—over the loss of China, the alleged presence of Communists within government, the conduct of the Korean War—were the warp and woof of Cold War politics. "Remember that the words Truman and Democrat mean diplomatic failure, military failure, death and tragedy," Republican Thomas Dewey thundered during the Korean War.[67]

In fact, containment took fire from all sides. Progressives like Henry Wallace deemed it a reckless crusade: "The tougher we get the tougher the Russians will get."[68] Lippmann, the liberal icon, labeled containment a "strategic monstrosity" that would force unending interventions on behalf of "satellites, puppets, clients, agents about who we know very little."[69] On the right, old isolationists such as Herbert Hoover and Joseph Kennedy called for Washington to abandon its allies and withdraw to the Western Hemisphere. The goal, Kennedy said, must be to "conserve American lives for American ends, not waste them in the freezing hills of Korea or on the battle-scarred plains of Western Germany."[70] Other conservatives derided containment for being too weak and called for Truman to attack Communist China or roll back Soviet power at its source. Even friendly observers were skeptical. "If one is honest," said Robert Oppenheimer in 1950, "the most probable view of the future is that of war, exploding atomic bombs, death, and the end of most freedom."[71]

The Truman administration beat back these assaults by pointing out that geopolitical retreat might be suicide on the installment plan, whereas dramatically escalating the Cold War risked inciting the conflagration that containment was meant to avoid. But within the administration, there were nagging doubts. "Our resources are not inexhaustible," said Truman as the Korean War dragged on. "We can't go on like this."[72] Not surprisingly, in 1952 President Dwight Eisenhower and Secretary of State John Foster Dulles inaugurated one of the stand-out political traditions of the Cold War by condemning the strategy—the "negative, futile, and immoral" policy of containment—that they ended up pursuing.[73] What is now the most revered strategy in American history was, at the time, more frequently a magnet for opprobrium than an object of praise.

And not without reason. Containment was plodding and indecisive; it entailed bearing overseas burdens that Americans would have rejected out of hand not long before. Over time, containment would require running tremendous risks and navigating perilous crises; it would demand construction of a peacetime "national security state" without precedent in the country's history. Cold War logic would draw America into disastrous interventions and require ethical compromises aplenty. Those who worried that containment would tax America financially, militarily, and morally were not entirely wrong.

Yet for all the rhetorical arrows aimed at containment, the basic strategy proved more prescient and resilient than the critiques. Presidents who took office pledging to overhaul containment generally opted to embrace it; the Cold War eventually concluded roughly as containment's founders had envisioned. "When history says that my term of office saw the beginning of the Cold War," Truman said in 1953, "it will also say that in those 8 years we have set the course that can win it."[74] So what permitted containment to survive and thrive over time?

First, containment was firm in the strategic direction it provided, but flexible in the adaptation it allowed. Kennan's insights provided conceptual guardrails to prevent U.S. statecraft from running off the road. But the very vagueness of those ideas ensured room for maneuver en route to the final destination. Indeed, containment would eventually accommodate multiple variations on the underlying strategy (sometimes within a single administration), as well as vibrant debates over specific initiatives. For this reason, the strategy was well suited to a world that itself changed enormously as the U.S.-Soviet competition wore on.

Second, containment suited America's political system. Containment drew on Americans' hopes and fears, their tangible interests and their loftiest ideals, to rally a broad coalition. It was simple and clear enough to be operationalized by the bureaucracy: containment did not require a single, Bismarckian genius. Most important, because containment combined straightforward logic with significant flexibility, it could persist across multiple presidencies while allowing the adjustments that are unavoidable in democratic politics. If statesmanship, as one Truman-era official wrote, "is a working alliance between leadership on the one hand

and the bureaucracy and the people on the other," containment proved congenial to preserving that alliance over time.[75]

Third, containment combined incremental methods with transformative aspirations. A key difficulty of containment was that it was never easy to tell, at any given moment, how close America was to its ultimate objective—the breakup or mellowing of Soviet power. Yet the intermediate goal—checking Soviet expansion—provided a useful target for America's day-to-day exertions. Containment, then, focused the nation's energies in the short-term while helping it advance toward a more distant horizon. In doing so, it allowed America to pursue radical goals while still exercising tremendous strategic patience.

Fourth, containment prospered because it used U.S. strengths to attack the weaknesses of the adversary's system and strategy. As Kennan understood, Stalin needed external victories to mask Soviet debilities. Soviet officials believed they could attain those victories because the capitalist world couldn't hold together. Cooperation between America and the United Kingdom would never last, the Soviet ambassador to Washington assured Stalin in 1946.[76] Containment's virtue was that it eventually brought the infirmities of the Soviet system into the open by denying the Kremlin the geopolitical gains that it desired.. By prioritizing the construction of a vibrant free world, moreover, containment defeated Soviet strategy by showing that time was not on the Kremlin's side. This approach took decades to bear fruit, but the results were eventually devastating to Soviet policy and the Soviet Union itself.

Finally, containment was not a brilliant strategy, but it was the best of bad alternatives. No reasonable person would have thought that prosecuting a dangerous standoff with the Soviet Union was an attractive approach. It was only in comparison to other plausible possibilities—diplomatic appeasement or a catastrophic showdown—that containment's merits became clear. The theologian G. K. Chesterton once observed that since Christianity was attacked from so many angles, on so many contradictory grounds, perhaps that religion was actually right and true.[77] In the same way, if containment was assailed by some for being too weak and by others for being too provocative, then perhaps it had the balance about right. Middle-ground approaches like containment are inherently unsatisfying. But in a long struggle, a strategy that gradually advances while avoiding disasters on both sides is probably good enough.

CHAPTER TWO

Creating Situations of Strength

THE UNITED STATES PASSED the first test of long-term competition: forging a lasting strategy. Yet the virtues of containment became evident only with time, as U.S. officials did the hard work of translating that strategy into initiatives to check Soviet power. No aspect of that endeavor was more important than America's multidecade effort to build the "free world."

When we think of competition, we usually think of policies meant to harm or constrain a rival. But competition is not simply a bilateral affair; it occurs in a larger global environment. The smartest players use what political scientists call "milieu strategies"—strategies that shape the world in ways that frustrate an opponent's plans and expose its weaknesses.[1]

During the Cold War, America pursued history's most successful milieu strategy. It wrenched the noncommunist world out of its long, self-destructive spiral and set it on the path to unmatched prosperity, freedom, and internal peace. In doing so, Washington closed off Moscow's best bet for victory and put the Soviet Union at a lasting disadvantage. In effect, America outplayed the Soviet Union by remaking the world around it—by turning a weak and divided community into a vibrant coalition whose achievements Moscow could not equal. Dean Acheson liked to talk about constructing "situations of strength."[2] This was the ultimate situation of strength: a free-world community that could resist Soviet pressure while exerting a great deal of its own.

The United States scored this competitive coup *against* the Soviet world by transcending the rhythms of competition *within* the Western world. America's ambition to transform global politics—to remove the causes of aggression, misery, and extremism—had first been articulated by President Woodrow Wilson. During the Cold War, Washington used its power to create a Wilsonian order within the West. This revolutionary "inside game" enabled a devastating "outside game." By liberating the free world from the anarchy of global politics, America and its allies seized command of a cut-throat Cold War.

Nothing about this process was straightforward. Building a strong, cohesive Western community involved ratcheting back America's wartime ambitions: the United States could not create "half a world" until it gave up on transforming the whole world. Pursuing that objective required more than a change in U.S. strategy; it required fundamental shifts in how America calculated national advantage. No single policy or initiative ushered in a new future for the noncommunist world; the promotion of security, prosperity, and democracy was an indivisible package. Even then, the free world was shakier than we remember; its collapse often seemed imminent. Holding the free world together did not require Washington to defer to its allies on all matters, but it did demand an enlightened approach to the task.

Leading the free world, Acheson explained, "requires that we take no narrow view of our interests." America must "conceive them in a broad and understanding way so that they include the interests of those joined with us in the defense of freedom. . . . We cannot dictate, we cannot be irresponsible, if we are to fulfill the mission of leadership among free peoples. The pattern of leadership," he concluded, "is a pattern of responsibility."[3] Only by accepting that responsibility could Washington change the trajectory of the noncommunist world and create an enduring advantage in the Cold War.

If building the free world was a monumental undertaking, it marked a retreat from America's objective during World War II. At that time, few officials were fixated on building up a noncommunist bloc against the Kremlin. The aim was to create "one world"—a single, integrated system that would deliver prosperity and cooperation. "Let us not fail to grasp this supreme chance to establish a world-wide rule of reason," Truman declared in 1945—"to create an enduring peace under the guidance of God."[4]

This idea captivated the American imagination because it was a remnant of an earlier faith. During World War I, Wilson had argued that preventing the next great conflagration required transforming international affairs. America must stymie the forces of instability and aggression by leading a liberal trading system, promoting democracy and self-determination, and erecting an international organization that would provide collective security. "There must be, not a balance of power, but a community of power," he declared, "not organized rivalries, but an organized common peace."[5] Yet Wilson's concept of a new global order had foundered on European enmities and American retrenchment, and the dream of one world was again frustrated after World War II.

Part of the problem was the sheer magnitude of wartime destruction. "More people face starvation and even actual death for want of food today than in any war year and perhaps more than in all the war years combined," Truman reported in 1946. Survival, not global transformation, was the immediate challenge.[6] Part of the problem was that Stalin had little interest in joining a unified world. Moscow rejected membership in the institutions—the World Bank and the International Monetary Fund—meant to govern a collaborative global economy. It sought security not through cooperation but by pulling down, in Churchill's words, "an iron curtain" across Europe.[7]

Charles Bohlen captured the resulting strategic shift in 1947: "There are, in short, two worlds instead of one." The United States must not chase the illusion of global integration. The non-Soviet world must instead "draw closer together politically, economically, financially, and in the last analysis, militarily" to "survive in the face of the centralized and ruthless direction of the Soviet world."[8] In Acheson's phrasing, America's charge was now to build "half a world, a free half . . . without blowing the whole to pieces."[9]

Making even half a world would be an exercise of epic proportions. The world was just a decade removed from a global depression that had revealed the most self-destructive tendencies of capitalism. Twice in a generation, the capitalist powers had torn each other to pieces. As Dwight Eisenhower remarked, "It seems almost as if the nations of the West have been, for decades, blindly enacting parts in a drama that could have been written by Lenin."[10] Creating a free world strong enough to confront present dangers meant breaking the tragic cycles of the past.

———

The key was to make a healthy free-world economy. During World War II, U.S. officials had identified economic dysfunction as the root of all evils. Beggar-thy-neighbor policies had worsened the depression, incubated radicalism, and exacerbated rivalry. A functioning world could be built only on a foundation of economic cooperation. "Peace, freedom, and world trade" were inseparable, Truman declared; "the grave lessons of the past have proved it."[11]

This was the rationale for the Bretton Woods system of international trade and finance. Bretton Woods did not go as far as dedicated free-traders had hoped, but it established the principle of using multilateral negotiations to reduce tariffs and trade quotas. It also created a system of fixed but adjustable exchange rates meant to prevent wild currency swings. The system would provide the stability permitting collective prosperity while also giving governments the flexibility to pursue social-welfare and full-employment programs at home. The whole endeavor was anchored by Washington, which led the push for freer trade and pegged the dollar to gold at $35 per ounce.[12]

Yet Bretton Woods was nearly stillborn. Most European countries were in such desperate economic straits—and so short of the dollars needed for trade—that they could hardly think of joining a more open system. Economic misery was threatening to destroy European civilization. "Millions of people in the cities are slowly starving," Undersecretary of State William Clayton reported in May 1947. "Economic, social and political disintegration" were imminent.[13] Clayton's warning helped catalyze the Marshall Plan. That program, combined with U.S. assistance to Japan, amounted to nearly 5 percent of U.S. gross national product in 1948. It also signaled the shift from a one-world to a two-worlds economic policy.[14]

The United States invited the Soviets to partake in Marshall Plan assistance, but only on the expectation that Moscow could not accept without losing control of its satellites. The plan focused instead on stabilizing the free world politically by countering the economic exhaustion that was ripening Western Europe for communism.[15] It was also a last-ditch effort to save the idea of a free-world economy by preventing Western European governments from reverting to protectionism in a desperate bid for survival. If help did not come quickly, the British government warned, it might have to "abandon the whole concept of multilateral trading" and "eke out a painful existence" by other means.[16]

The resulting program was highly intrusive. U.S. experts were deeply involved in formulating European economic policy. The State Department demanded that European governments throw out Communist ministers. "We are in it up to our necks," said Senator Henry Cabot Lodge Jr., "and almost everybody except a few political leaders will be damned glad to see us interfere."[17] Yet Washington could also be remarkably undoctrinaire in its interventions. The Marshall Plan permitted the nationalization of key industries, which was often enacted by social democratic governments that embraced central planning. "Be liberals or *dirigistes*," Clayton told French officials. "Return to capitalism or head toward socialism." So long as plans were economically sound and totalitarian influences excluded, "we shall help your country, for its prosperity is necessary to peace."[18] The Marshall Plan fused hegemony and deference, with the latter making the former tolerable.

The Marshall Plan thus refined Bretton Woods for a divided world, and it enshrined a set of principles for U.S. economic statecraft. European recovery must be attained cooperatively; America would not underwrite rivalrous practices that had earlier led to disaster. The United States would also provide the hegemonic leadership and coordination that had gone wanting during the depression. Not least, America would take on tremendous, unequal burdens to revive the free world. "Between a war that is over and a peace that is not yet secure," Truman explained, "the destitute and oppressed of the earth look chiefly to us."[19]

These ideas set the pattern for the postwar era. The United States performed the managerial tasks necessary for an open economy to function: serving as lender of last resort, driving multiple rounds of trade negotiations, stabilizing and lubricating the monetary system. Washington supported European economic integration because subsuming West Germany's strength within a collective framework was the only way to enable recovery without unleashing rampant insecurity. "Americans were the best Europeans," West German chancellor Konrad Adenauer remarked.[20]

Crucially, America also made asymmetric concessions to strengthen weaker parties against Soviet pressure. U.S. aid and technology flowed into countries around the world, some of which had recently been America's enemies. Japan, for one, received $2.4 billion in assistance between 1945 and 1953. The United States cut tariffs further and faster than its trading partners, with its average tariff on dutiable imports falling from 33 percent in 1944 to 13 percent in 1950.[21] The goal of all this was not to hoard but to decrease the advantages America possessed after World War II. Making the international economy hum, Acheson explained, required reducing "a disparity between production in the United States and production in the rest of the world that is staggering in its proportions."[22]

"There is no charity involved in this," Acheson continued. "It is simply common sense and good business."[23] Indeed, Washington would not have assumed such outsized responsibilities had it not expected to benefit—even if it did not always seem that America was getting a good bargain.

America backed European integration even though doing so meant creating a powerful economic competitor that discriminated against U.S. exports. It stuck with Bretton Woods for a quarter-century even though that system hurt American exports by keeping the dollar overvalued. The United States exposed its industries to foreign competition in return for later and lesser concessions from allies. Partially as a result, America's share of global manufacturing and GDP steadily declined after World War II—and U.S. officials counted this a victory. "We have borne the burden because we think it is in the interest of free world security," one Kennedy-era official would observe; "we know that our security is intimately tied up with that of other major nations in the free world."[24]

This vision of U.S. national interest, then, was extremely broad and extremely patient. It was rarely based on near-term calculations of material gain because such transactional arithmetic rarely added up. "The weighing of costs and benefits cannot be in purely economic terms," said U.S. official Richard Bissell in 1948, for doing so meant ignoring the "magnitude of the political stakes for which we are playing."[25] U.S. policy was rooted in a gauzier, longer-term notion: that carrying onerous responsibilities was essential to making a world safe from Soviet predations—and from its own worst impulses.

A similar logic underpinned America's security commitments. A lasting military presence in Europe—much less a globe-spanning alliance system —was the last thing U.S. planners had intended during World War II. FDR had categorically rejected the idea that U.S. troops would indefinitely pacify the Old World.[26]

The creation of NATO in 1949 thus resulted from European insistence rather than U.S. initiative. "Any defense arrangements which did not include the United States were without practical value," said Belgian prime minister Paul-Henry Spaak.[27] And at first, America was a diffident protector. The Pentagon initially dispatched no additional troops to Europe. Congress insisted on writing the North Atlantic Treaty to give America as much leeway as possible in determining how and even whether to respond to aggression. Senator Vandenberg warned that "if this North Atlantic Pact is going to take on the overriding character of a permanent military alliance . . . there just ain't going to be any North Atlantic Pact."[28]

Here Vandenberg was wrong. By the early 1950s, NATO had an integrated command structure and plans to defend Western Europe at the Rhine. Additional deployments of U.S. and European troops were giving NATO real punching power, and the alliance was moving, slowly and painfully, toward rearming West Germany. Meanwhile, the U.S. alliance network was going global through pacts involving Japan, Australia, New Zealand, the Philippines, and other countries. By 1953, over 900,000 U.S. service members were stationed in Europe and East Asia.[29] America's task, said Acheson, was "to organize the free world so that the peace could be made secure."[30] Far from remaining a diffident protector, the United States now labored to develop the doctrines and capabilities needed to protect its allies, for it repeatedly found itself embroiled in hair-raising crises that tested its commitment and credibility.

These security arrangements were so important because they served a dual purpose: they protected the free world both from its enemies and from itself. NATO and other U.S. alliances drew red lines against Soviet aggression and gave vulnerable countries the fortitude to resist intimidation. Yet they also suppressed the arms races and security competitions that had previously ripped apart Western Europe and the Asia-Pacific. American alliances removed any chance that Germany or Japan could again become the scourges of international security by hugging those countries so tightly that they became strategic adjuncts of the United States. Those alliances reassured former victims that America would shield them from former victimizers. The beauty of NATO, British foreign secretary Ernest Bevin realized, was that it would make the "age-long trouble between Germany and France . . . disappear."[31]

The alliances also served a third purpose: increasing the predictability of the United States. It may have been, as Kennan argued, that America's geopolitical interests required it to defend Western Europe, treaty or no treaty.[32] Yet formal alliances and troop deployments provided reassurance that American prestige and troops would be involved in any crisis from the beginning—that "if trouble did come," as Bevin said, the Europeans would not "be left waiting as in 1940 in a state of uncertainty."[33]

It is easy to forget how revolutionary this approach was. America's ambition was not simply to contain Soviet power or ease fears of a resurgent Germany. It was to radically reshape the geopolitics of the world's crucial regions. America's security commitments would make possible unprecedented cooperation between former rivals, allowing Japan and Germany to be revived as engines of regional prosperity rather than perpetually subdued as menaces to stability. America's military commitments would thereby secure the Wilsonian dream of a "community of power" in half the world even as the West pursued a balance of power vis-à-vis the other half.

If the benefits of this approach seem obvious in hindsight, though, the burdens weighed heavily in real time. America was now required to defend countries on the other side of the world. It shouldered a disproportionate share of the free-world military mission, while other countries invested in generous welfare states. Unsurprisingly, American policymakers periodically sought relief from the strain. Dwight Eisenhower hoped that Western Europe would become "a third great power bloc" so America could "sit back and relax somewhat"; as president, he searched, unsuccessfully, for ways of pulling back U.S. troops.[34] The role of securing the free world always came somewhat unnaturally.

The United States stuck with the role because it saw little alternative. Only America, with its unmatched power, could provide security in conflict-plagued regions. Only America could strengthen free nations while tamping down the tensions between them. Were there better ways, Acheson asked, "to stop Soviet expansion without a catastrophic war," better ways to protect the free world by solving the problems "which were holding it back, dividing it, weakening it?" Were there better ways to create a fundamentally "new world environment?"[35] The answer was no. Altering the fate of the Western world required altering America's own conception of responsibility and self-interest.

Yet transforming the economic and security climate of the Western bloc might not have sufficed unless the political culture was also transformed. The crackup of the capitalist world before World War II had followed the rise of totalitarian ideologies: aggression at home promoted aggression abroad. America now sought to reverse that equation—to hold the free world together by ensuring the primacy of democratic politics at its core.

The eventual success of this endeavor can lead us to forget how daunting it appeared. Democracy's future was in doubt after World War II, given its failure to resolve the economic and geopolitical crises that had caused that conflict. Into the late 1940s, fragile European democracies were menaced by the Communist left and the authoritarian right.

Nor was Washington irrevocably committed to democratizing former enemies. The U.S. occupations of Germany and Japan initially focused on disarmament and deindustrialization. America, Kennan confessed, was "not sure the Germans can ever be democratized within our time."[36]

Despite these doubts, the spread of democracy became the third pillar—alongside the provision of security and prosperity—of America's free-world project. There was a competitive logic here: ensuring liberty within the Western world would create a sharp contrast with the dreary authoritarianism across the Iron Curtain. "Freedom," said one British diplomat, "was essential to us but a corrosive poison to the countries of the East."[37] Yet the promotion of freedom was a competitive advantage over the East bloc in part because it was the surest safeguard of tranquility within the West. Long before political scientists articulated the "democratic peace" theory, U.S. officials concluded that democracies were the best international citizens—that their domestic habits of compromise had a pacifying influence on their external behavior. "The record is . . . one of economic oppression and exploitation at home, aggression and spoliation abroad," wrote General Douglas MacArthur, America's proconsul in Japan. Changing politics was vital to changing geopolitics.[38]

With this in mind, the United States promoted rehabilitation through reform. In western Germany, U.S. occupation authorities purged Nazi officials and supporters, enshrined democratic electoral processes, and supported a free press and a liberal educational system. "Evil consequences to all men flow from the suppression and corruption of truth," read instructions to General Lucius Clay. "Education is a primary means of creating a democratic and peaceful Germany."[39] U.S. officials threw their support behind Adenauer and other pro-democracy elites, providing them with critical advantages. On the other side of Eurasia, Japan was simultaneously becoming, in MacArthur's phrasing, "the world's great laboratory for an experiment" in democratization. U.S. authorities shattered the old regime by dissolving the Japanese military and purging 200,000 elites. U.S. advisers rewrote the Japanese constitution, empowered a democratic legislature, and undertook land and labor reforms.[40] The bargain that Washington offered Tokyo and Bonn was the same: vanquished enemies could become valued friends by embracing democratic rule.

Critically, the pursuit of liberal reform involved linking Japan and Germany to an open international economy and a free-world security system. If zero-sum economic competition had strengthened authoritarian elements in the 1930s, giving these countries access to markets and raw materials would reinforce democracy. Similarly, Japan and Germany no longer needed to pursue security through aggressive expansion, which made possible the defeat of militarism at home.[41]

The United States was simultaneously strengthening democracy elsewhere. The Marshall Plan was not simply an economic recovery program; it was also an effort to defend weak democracies against encroaching totalitarianism. America's "deepest concern," said Truman, was to protect nations that "constitute a bulwark for the principles of freedom, justice and the dignity of the individual."[42] American officials maneuvered, sometimes covertly, to head off Communist coups or electoral triumphs for fear that once radical elements took power, they would never relinquish it. The CIA and the State Department schemed to ensure the victory of the Christian Democrats in Italian elections in 1948 through covert financial support and implicit threats to withhold Marshall Plan assistance if the Communists triumphed. "Every action of the U.S. will have a direct bearing on the outcome," wrote Ambassador James Dunn.[43]

Washington also created incentives for democratization by giving preferential treatment to the truly free members of the free world. Fascist Spain, for example, was excluded from NATO until it democratized. Most broadly, the United States promoted democracy by tamping down the trade and security conflicts that had previously played into the hands of aspiring authoritarians, restraining a deeply antidemocratic Soviet Union, and bringing the world's leading democracies into a formidable strategic community. America had "welded alliances that include the greater part of the free world," Truman remarked, and joined with "other free countries" to create "a healthy world trade."[44]

Americans were not purists, of course, and the United States would not have fared well if they were. Authoritarian Portugal was part of NATO from the beginning; the United States often found that friendships with dictators, particularly in the developing world, suited its near-term objectives just fine. There was, moreover, something unsavory about seeking to save democracy through covert skullduggery. But on the whole, America created an environment in which democratic practices could flourish. By the late Cold War, Washington was becoming ever more assertive in pushing those practices outward, from the core of the free world to the periphery.[45]

Those efforts to make the noncommunist world more democratic also made it more cohesive. They helped the free world sort out disagreements —and there were many—through the bargaining and compromise that characterized democratic politics. So long as America was dealing with an "organization of freedom-loving nations," State Department official Jack Hickerson predicted in 1948, it could be "confident that we could settle any differences with them."[46] Just as important, U.S. policy gave that community an identity rooted in fundamental values as well as shared interests. "Our ties with the great industrial democracies," Secretary of State Henry Kissinger would aver, "are ... not alliances of convenience but a union of principle in defense of values and a way of life."[47]

The creation of the free world, then, was a project every bit as ambitious as containment of the Soviet Union, even if the former was, in many ways, a means to the latter. The United States set out to build a community in which steadfast cooperation prevailed, seemingly timeless rivalries were suspended, and democratic values displaced dangerous ideologies. The three key elements of this endeavor were all mutually reinforcing. Economic openness facilitated democracy and peace. The American security blanket sheltered democratic nations and created a positive-sum economic calculus. Democratic values encouraged the cooperation that made shared prosperity and security possible. "Peace, freedom, and world trade" were indeed a single package.[48] America's free-world mission could succeed only as an integrated whole.

In retrospect, that mission did succeed brilliantly. The free world achieved historic, unprecedented gains and eventually left the Communist world in its wake. Japan's portion of world GDP quadrupled between 1950 and 1970, while GDP in Western Europe increased by an average of 5.5 percent annually.[49] The number of democracies rose from around a dozen during World War II to 39 by 1974, to 76 by 1990, to 120 by the year 2000.[50] The prospect of wars between major capitalist powers became nearly unthinkable; the leading democracies created a strategic community Moscow could neither intimidate nor outperform. Yet treating the history of the free world as a just-so story is dangerous because doing so can make us forget how crisis-ridden the postwar period was.

The Bretton Woods era is often remembered as a time of growth and cooperation. In reality, it was also a time of friction and turmoil. Bretton Woods rested on a contradiction. It required the United States to fix the dollar to gold but also to run a payments deficit to enable global growth and liquidity. The inevitable result was to undermine the real value of the dollar and the stability of the system. By the 1960s, international monetary crises were commonplace. American officials were terrified that the allies might exchange their greenbacks against the limited U.S. supply of gold, while the allies were frustrated at being asked to hold dollars of declining value. The climax came when President Richard Nixon severed the link between the dollar and gold in 1971, setting off a decade of economic instability and trade battles. "European leaders want to 'screw' us and we want to 'screw' them in the economic area," Nixon remarked.[51] The halcyon days of capitalism often felt like a period of disarray.

The free-world security architecture wobbled as well. During NATO's first half-decade, the alliance was severely tested by debates over the Korean War and German rearmament. In 1956, it nearly ruptured when Britain and France tried to salvage their imperial role in the Middle East by attacking Gamal Nasser's Egypt, only to be pummeled economically by a furious Eisenhower. "Those who began this operation should be left ... to boil in their own oil," Ike said.[52] During the 1960s, Charles de Gaulle's France withdrew from NATO's military command and insisted that all U.S. soldiers leave the country. "Does that include the dead Americans in military cemeteries, as well?" Secretary of State Dean Rusk rejoined.[53] During the Arab-Israeli war of 1973, the European Community openly repudiated the United States. "We must break the EC," Kissinger fumed.[54] In the 1980s, many Europeans viewed President Ronald Reagan as a greater threat to peace than his Soviet counterpart, Leonid Brezhnev. The most successful alliance in history was riven by the most serious disputes.

Indeed, NATO's obituary was written repeatedly. The alliance, Acheson warned in 1952, was "marking time while ... historic decisions are being made elsewhere."[55] In 1955, Ike worried that "enthusiasm for NATO was dying out."[56] Throughout the postwar decades, U.S. and allied officials spoke about each other in the nastiest terms. Kissinger labeled the French "unadulterated bastards"; he and Nixon commiserated when a lump on West German chancellor Willy Brandt's throat proved *not* to be malignant.[57] Brandt's successor, Helmut Schmidt, considered President Jimmy Carter a diplomatic amateur; Carter once referred to a summit among democratic allies as "one of the worst days of my diplomatic life."[58]

These tensions within the Western world were not merely the result of personality conflicts. They also reflected structural splits. The interests of Washington and its allies were convergent but hardly identical. The varying geographies, histories, and economies of free-world states drove them toward divergent positions on issues from military strategy to trade negotiations. "Is the Grand Alliance going to founder over chickens?" Kennedy asked during one dispute.[59] The great ambition of America's free-world project therefore came with an inherent challenge, since the search for consensus among a large and diverse group of nations was often an exercise in frustration.

In fact, the success of the free world generated new strains. America's aspiration was not to crystallize the post-1945 balance of power forever; it was to strengthen U.S. friends so they could become more effective allies. Yet this ethos was destined to destabilize the free-world compact. Washington would surely demand that its allies do more for the collective defense as they recovered; it would become less inclined to make asymmetrical economic concessions. America could not keep paying "for the military protection of Europe" while its allies were "living off the 'fat of the land,' " Kennedy said.[60] The Europeans and the Japanese, for their part, would desire greater influence as their power and confidence rose. NATO was founded upon "the weakness of the European powers," de Gaulle lectured Kennedy in 1961. But the old arrangements were "not acceptable" anymore.[61]

These dynamics meant that neither the United States nor its partners were ever fully satisfied with their relationship. Americans started complaining about European free-riding shortly after the North Atlantic Treaty was signed, and they never stopped. The NATO countries, one U.S. secretary of defense scolded, had chosen "added annual vacation time" over "adequate military strength."[62] The allies complained that America was unhelpful with their efforts to maintain their overseas empires and insensitive to the concerns of countries that would be on the front lines of any U.S.-Soviet war. They were more correct than they knew. If Western Europe had been conquered by the Soviet Union, the United States would have nuked its own allies rather than see their industry harnessed to the Kremlin's war machine.[63]

Indeed, alliance relations could be a bare-knuckle affair. During the 1950s and 1960s, U.S. officials threatened to withdraw troops from Europe if the allies did not integrate West Germany into NATO or offset the outflow of dollars by purchasing U.S. military equipment. The American position, complained one German statesman, was that "unless we get our offsets, we will go home and sacrifice you to the Russians."[64] During the 1970s and 1980s, America used its economic and security leverage to force the allies to revalue their currencies, and it employed trade sanctions to extract concessions involving autos, agricultural products, and semiconductors. "Japan has little choice but to negotiate the best terms it can for access to U.S. and West European markets," the CIA explained. "It has nowhere else to go."[65]

The allies could be pretty cold themselves. De Gaulle menaced Washington with the prospect of a run on the dollar. He eventually quit NATO's military command on the calculation that this would not affect French security in the slightest. Threatening to withdraw the U.S. security guarantee from France "is like threatening to abandon Kentucky in the face of a land attack by Canada," National Security Council adviser Francis Bator acknowledged. "It is hard to do unless one is prepared to throw in Ohio."[66] Leaders in West Germany and Japan occasionally hinted that they might slide toward neutralism if America did not accommodate their concerns. During the 1970s and 1980s, Tokyo's commitment to the West did not prevent it from pursuing trade policies that endangered entire swaths of U.S. manufacturing. Japan, one Reagan-era official remarked, was "the rotten apple that poisons the entire world trade barrel."[67]

America's free-world project was never free of conflict; it sometimes seemed that the endeavor might come undone. Yet the free-world community persisted and outperformed all reasonable expectations. What held it together in the end?

The simplest reason the free world survived is that the Kremlin left it no choice. No matter how viciously America and its allies quarreled, the disputes were trivial compared to those between the free world and the Soviet bloc. America could not contain the Kremlin without a cohesive Western community; the allies knew that the failings of U.S. leadership were minor compared to the evils of Soviet domination. Likewise, the Kremlin threat gave the capitalist countries incentive to prevent periodic economic crises from turning into economic free-for-alls. "Fear makes easy the task of diplomats," John Foster Dulles observed, "for then the fearful draw together and seek the protection of collective strength."[68]

But coalitions have fragmented even when confronted by a looming threat: Napoleon's enemies were regularly divided before they were conquered. The United States avoided that fate during the Cold War by following six essential principles of coalition management.

The first was distinguishing between greater and lesser evils. U.S. officials were consistently frustrated by the free-riding, the diplomatic disputes, and the economic quarrels, but they kept that frustration in perspective. Bearing the onus of hegemonic leadership was the price America paid for fostering a resilient capitalist economy. Tolerating free-riding was the cost of breaking the cycle of catastrophic conflict. To be clear, the United States was rarely silent about the inequities of alliance leadership. In the end, though, it accepted slow, partial progress rather than risk blowing up the system by demanding complete satisfaction. Dulles could threaten an "agonizing reappraisal" of U.S. commitments to Europe, but he knew America would share in the agony if a rupture ever occurred.[69] This moderation made it easier for America's free-world allies to recognize that U.S. leadership was itself a lesser evil. As U.S. analysts concluded in 1969, "NATO has endured for twenty years, not because it meets all the needs of all its members, but rather because it satisfies more of them than any other arrangement conceivable under present circumstances."[70]

Second, a successful superpower could not continually coerce its allies. Kissinger's complaints notwithstanding, U.S. diplomats didn't break the EC during the 1970s because—State Department officials warned—divide-and-rule methods would make friends feel that "they had been treated much more like enemies."[71] Similarly, American negotiators generally refrained from squeezing every possible concession out of the allies because coalitions based on unsatisfying compromises were more resilient than those based on brute force. It may have been true, the CIA reported, that Japan's economic dependence on Washington conveyed "strong U.S. tactical leverage." But use of "serious threats" would backfire by making Tokyo wonder whether the alliance was a devil's bargain.[72]

Third, the United States stimulated the initiative and input of weaker members. The allies' acceptance of American leadership involved surrendering some influence, even sovereignty, to Washington. Yet even if America was always the senior partner, influence flowed both ways, which made the power imbalance more bearable. The superpower generally listened when its friends complained loudly enough, as when European fears inhibited Washington from escalating the Korean War in late 1950 or waging economic warfare more aggressively against the Soviet bloc.[73] Throughout the Cold War, America's followers could become leaders, too. The allies were the early movers on key initiatives from the formation of NATO to decisions on nuclear strategy in the late 1970s and early 1980s.

The free world also proved resilient because of a fourth virtue: America's reliance on institutions. U.S. leadership was mostly expressed through institutions—NATO, the International Monetary Fund, the World Bank—which arguably diluted the power Washington might have wielded one-on-one. Yet this was the point. The reliance on institutions took the edge off America's dominance by giving allies access to forums in which they could engage and influence the United States. It ensured routinized cooperation even when ties were frayed at the political level. And it provided forums for dealing with the most difficult issues.[74]

When the free world confronted severe economic volatility in the 1970s and early 1980s, the response was to construct new institutions—in this case, the G-5 (later G-7) summits of finance ministers and heads of state. These groupings enabled leaders to compare diagnoses and created mechanisms for multilateral responses. "We feel like members of a fraternity; we share problems and political analyses, try to understand different national perspectives, and cooperate," wrote Carter. These institutions eventually helped the allies preserve an open Western economy as technological innovation and financial globalization ushered in a new era of prosperity lasting beyond the Cold War.[75]

This feature is related to a fifth principle: an understanding that key relationships must periodically be renegotiated. America was never prepared to relinquish leadership on security issues. Yet Washington reworked the U.S.-Japan alliance in the late 1950s to defuse growing anger at the American presence; it also gave European allies a greater voice in alliance strategy by creating the Nuclear Planning Group during the 1960s.[76] Similarly, the United States applied "shock treatment" to its allies by ending the dollar-gold linkage in 1971. But U.S. policymakers treated those shocks not as the end of economic cooperation but as prelude to the negotiation of new arrangements that would keep everyone committed to the system. If the deep crises of the free world were real enough, they were also part of a messy process of adapting that project over time.

Finally, the free world held together because America put so much effort into the task. The United States could be a difficult friend, but only rarely could it be accused of taking its relationships for granted. For the most part, American officials engaged in what Secretary of State George Shultz called "gardening"—the unending cultivation of partnerships. U.S. leaders met frequently with their free-world counterparts, even when they hardly wanted to; they built trust and goodwill before a crisis to maximize support once the crisis hit. And when Washington did occasionally lapse into periods of neglect or high-handedness, those periods were invariably followed by efforts at revitalization and repair. America got so much out of its free-world project because it never stopped investing in it.

The benefits were tremendous; the investment paid outsized returns. America's free-world project did not just reverse the momentum of history within the noncommunist world. It also provided decisive competitive benefits in the Cold War.

For one thing, the success of the free world closed off the most likely path to Western defeat. In 1947, French officials had described that scenario. The capitalist world would lapse into a "profound depression," which would sever the links between the old world and the new by ending "American aid for European reconstruction." American abandonment "will mean that European economies will disintegrate," with chaos leading to takeovers by "well organized Communist Parties."[77] This scenario was by no means outlandish in the late 1940s, yet it never materialized. The free world climbed to soaring heights, ensuring that the Soviets never confronted a weak, demoralized enemy that it might have defeated without firing a shot. Instead, Moscow faced a vigorous community that was more than capable of holding its own.

Over time, the resilience of the free world tilted the global balance sharply in America's favor. Early on, Bohlen had worried that Soviet domination of Eastern Europe would give the Kremlin a notable advantage. Yet whatever benefits Moscow extracted were dwarfed by the geostrategic gains America reaped from heading the Western world. The world's most powerful nation led a coalition that vastly accentuated its own strengths by linking it to other dynamic economies, augmenting its military capabilities, and giving it access to critical territory around the Eurasian periphery. The American alliance system, stated Dulles in 1953, "has staked out the vital areas of the world."[78] Nothing was guaranteed. There were moments when it looked as though the military balance was tipping toward Moscow. But so long as the free world held together, the overall geopolitical playing field was slanted in America's favor.

Meanwhile, the free world's progress was destroying Moscow's ideological position. The Soviets were certain, Kennan assessed in 1947, "that we will not be able to muster . . . the leadership, the imagination, the political skill, the material resources, and above all the national self-discipline necessary to bring material stability, confidence, and hope for the future."[79] But if Stalin believed capitalism's failures would pave the way for communism's triumph, what would happen if the capitalist world found strength and unity instead? The answer became clear as the Cold War progressed.

In 1959, Soviet leader Nikita Khrushchev claimed that communism would "bury" capitalism. In succeeding decades, though, the free world's ascent left the Soviets irretrievably behind. By 1990, per capita income in the West was nine times that of the Soviet bloc, and the free world accounted for over 60 percent of global economic output.[80] Soviet leaders were "starting to recognize that something has gone hideously wrong," wrote one U.S. analyst. "History is no longer on Moscow's side—if ever it was."[81] This realization set off soul-searching within the Kremlin, which precipitated reforms that brought the Soviet empire crashing down. The arc of the free world did more than disprove Moscow's theory of victory. It brought excruciating pressure on the Soviet Union itself.

Over 40 years earlier, British foreign secretary Ernest Bevin had predicted that this might happen. If the free countries fell into disunity, he warned, they would be doomed "to repeat our experience with Hitler." But if they could "become really organised," they might "turn the whole world away from war" and eventually "save Russia herself."[82] Bevin was exactly right. Revolutionizing international affairs in half a world was vital to outperforming and transforming the other half. A milieu strategy could be a lethally effective weapon of competition.

CHAPTER THREE

Competing in the Nuclear Shadow

T HE ACHIEVEMENTS OF THE free world meant Moscow could not win the Cold War by awaiting capitalism's demise. Yet what if the Kremlin battered or intimidated its enemies into submission? Even U.S. officials who thought that Moscow didn't want war could not be sure war would not happen. Much less could they forget that the balance of military power would shape the balance of global influence even if conflict never occurred. Winning the Cold War would thus require winning, or at least not losing, the military competition.

We often view that competition as an "arms race"—an inexorable, mindless accumulation of weapons. There were certainly moments when policymakers felt trapped in pointless, escalating rivalry. "The United States is piling up armaments which it well knows will never provide for its ultimate safety," Eisenhower said in 1956. "We are piling up these armaments because we do not know what else to do."[1] Yet we shouldn't dismiss the arms race as an exercise in absurdity. Doing so shortchanges the complexity of the challenges involved and the sophistication of the strategy America eventually devised.

Ideally, a long-term strategy should do more than hold the line. A good strategy should reduce an opponent's freedom of action, cause its costs to rise, and eventually make it give up the game. An effective strategy, moreover, must do this without bankrupting one's country economically or politically; it should expose the weaknesses of the opponent's system without destroying one's own. Finally, a long-term strategy should pressure the adversary without causing the very conflagration a strategist hopes to avoid. This last requirement took on particular gravity in the nuclear age, when hot war could endanger civilization itself. The Cold War was not just an arms race. It was a test of American minds as well as American weapons.

By the 1980s, America had passed that test. It had developed a devastatingly effective military strategy, one that ruthlessly pitted U.S. strengths against Soviet weaknesses and threatened to put an exhausted enemy at an enduring disadvantage. America's military efforts were hardly futile: they secured the free world and helped bring the Cold War to an end.

The road to success, though, was long and winding. For decades, America struggled with the contradictions of competition in the nuclear age. Through the 1970s, the free world's military shield seemed to be cracking. It was only amid much adversity that a sharper, more punishing strategy emerged. It was only when the Kremlin reached the pinnacle of its military power that its crippling vulnerabilities were exposed. America won the military competition, but only after it was in danger of losing that competition. And navigating that contest required U.S. officials to confront an awful truth of Cold War rivalry: that strategic *advantage* and strategic *stability* did not always go hand in hand.

Few rivalries are symmetrical in nature because few rivals are evenly matched across all domains. Military competitions are defined by asymmetries— differing strategic situations, strengths, traditions—that create opportunities to exploit and vulnerabilities to mitigate. America's Cold War statecraft was shaped by five key asymmetries.

The first asymmetry was geographic. From 1945 on, Washington had superior overall military power as well as superior military potential, given its vast industrial might. Yet America was thousands of miles from the Cold War's central theaters, whereas the Soviet Union had a commanding central position in Eurasia. Especially in the early Cold War, this geographical asymmetry—combined with Moscow's dominant land power—allowed the Kremlin to muster decisive force almost anywhere along the East-West divide. America's task, then, involved using greater total power to offset local weaknesses. "The USSR has an overwhelming preponderance of immediately available power on the Eurasian continent," the CIA explained. America's deterrent was "the superior warmaking potential of the United States."[2]

The second asymmetry was diplomatic. U.S. planners always understood that Washington could not balance Soviet power without the manpower, economic resources, and strategic geography that friendly Eurasian
nations provided. The New World "must have the support of some of the
countries of the Old World," Pentagon analysts argued.[3] Yet U.S. alliances
also created formidable difficulties. Washington had to protect vulnerable
countries in the shadow of Soviet power; it had to reassure allies that it
wouldn't provoke war unwisely but would risk its own destruction to defend them if war came. "One country may support another's cause," Clausewitz wrote, "but it will never take it so seriously as it takes its own."[4] Cold
War statecraft represented a half-century effort to disprove this aphorism.

Ideology constituted a third asymmetry. During the Cold War, the
United States constructed an unprecedented peacetime military establishment. Yet Americans never lost their fear of an illiberal, overmilitarized
"garrison state." If the free world became "a huge garrison, concerned only
with defense," Truman said, it would lose the very freedoms that Cold War
strategy was meant to protect.[5] The enemy faced no such restraints. A totalitarian state could devote far higher levels of wealth and manpower to defense. In the long run, this asymmetry was a blessing for America because it
forced U.S. officials to focus on a factor—sustainability—that Soviet officials ignored. In the near term, it exacerbated fears that a decentralized democracy could not compete against a Communist leviathan.

The geographic, diplomatic, and ideological issues made a fourth
asymmetry—technology—crucial. America's military might was a product of technological prowess, which gave it global reach and striking
power. Moscow's power was a function of mass—infantry and tanks in
Europe and, later, heavy intercontinental ballistic missiles (ICBMs). This
asymmetry was never perfect. The Pentagon relied on quantitative edges
in key capabilities, while the Soviets were occasionally first to reach mile-
stones like space satellites. But generally speaking, America used superior
technology to offset Soviet numbers.

Yet the reliance on technology highlighted a fifth asymmetry: the vast
gulf in destructive power between nuclear weapons and everything that
came before. In theory, that disparity heightened the advantage of whoever
dominated the nuclear rivalry. But the same disparity raised hard questions
about whether weapons that were inherently indiscriminate—and, after
the thermonuclear revolution, civilization-shattering—could ever again
be used in combat; about whether victory in nuclear war was possible;
about whether rivals might have a higher interest in stabilizing a military

competition than winning it. "Thus far the chief purpose of our military establishment has been to win wars," strategist Bernard Brodie wrote after Hiroshima. "From now on its chief purpose must be to prevent them."[6] The central dilemma of Cold War statecraft lay in exploiting weapons so revolutionary that they might be unusable.

These asymmetries were at the top of Harry Truman's mind. During the late 1940s, Truman's aides believed that war was improbable but hardly inconceivable—and that the more successful U.S. policy was, the more dangerous the situation might become. Moscow did not want a show-down, wrote intelligence analysts, but that could change "when the Soviet Government is convinced that measures short of war will fail to secure its objectives."[7] Even if the guns stayed quiet, military hopelessness could create diplomatic paralysis. European countries might feel forced to appease Moscow; they could drift into its orbit. With enough military power, Stalin might not have to fight.

Truman's answer was to use unique assets to compensate for glaring vulnerabilities. He kept the armed forces, particularly the Army, far below the level needed to defend U.S. interests outside the Western Hemisphere. The Pentagon would instead rely on atomic bombardment to punish Soviet aggression until such time—two years—as it could mobilize to liberate Europe. In essence, Washington would play its trump card—the threat of a one-way atomic war—for all it was worth while using the country's latent power to offset its dearth of existing forces. The years when America alone had the bomb, wrote Forrestal, were "our years of opportunity."[8]

This strategy accomplished a lot with a little. The atomic monopoly provided the confidence necessary to remain in Berlin during the Soviet blockade; it lent the assurance required to undertake the Marshall Plan and create NATO. "If Western Europe is to enjoy any feeling of security," noted one NSC directive, it was because the atomic bomb counterbalanced "the ever-present threat of Soviet military power."[9] Indeed, although Stalin professed not to fear the bomb, its existence reinforced his reluctance to push America too far.[10] U.S. strategy was politically savvy, too. By keeping military spending low—$13.2 billion, or 4.8 percent of GDP in 1949—Truman avoided a domestic blowup at the start of the Cold War.[11]

Yet the nuclear shadow that American strategy exploited was shorter than it first appeared. Through the late 1940s, America lacked the number of bombs necessary to break Soviet war-making potential, as well as the intelligence—and intercontinental bombers—needed to deliver them effectively. "It would be the height of folly," warned Pentagon officials, "for us to assume that a war could be won by any single weapon."[12] The Berlin crisis, in fact, showed as much weakness as strength, since the B-29s that Truman ostentatiously brandished were not equipped to deliver nuclear weapons. Nor were America's allies thrilled about a strategy that would allow them to be conquered while Washington waged atomic warfare over their heads and even against Red Army units on their soil.[13] Then there was the matter of what would happen when the Soviets built their own device, as they did in 1949.

The Soviet nuclear test changed little militarily. Into the early 1950s, Moscow had scant ability to deliver nuclear weapons in combat. Yet the psychological effect was extraordinary. In the future, any atomic war would be a two-way contest, with Moscow striking U.S. bases in Europe and perhaps targets in America. That prospect might shatter U.S. defense strategy by deterring Washington from using nuclear weapons. And as America's relative position grew weaker, the Soviets might become bolder by waging localized conflicts or engaging in diplomatic blackmail. The Kremlin would "take greater risks than before," the CIA predicted; it could "weaken seriously the power position of the United States without resorting to direct military action."[14]

The Korean War soon confirmed that Moscow and its proxies were acting more belligerently. It also revealed how feeble U.S. conventional capabilities were. American forces could respond only because the Pentagon had poorly trained occupation troops in Japan. After Chinese forces intervened, Truman chose not to strike targets in China for fear of provoking a devastating Soviet reaction. If global war occurred, Joint Chiefs of Staff (JCS) Chairman Omar Bradley warned, "We might be in danger of losing."[15] Even in such terrible circumstances, the mere hint of using atomic weapons in Korea provoked panic among U.S. allies who feared being sucked into the resulting vortex. Nuclear threats, said Acheson, might not "worry our enemies" but would "frighten our allies to death."[16] America's posture was both too weak and too provocative.

These events caused drastic changes in U.S. strategy. Lest an asymmetric advantage become an asymmetric vulnerability, the administration sprinted to develop the hydrogen bomb, and it expanded the U.S. atomic arsenal from 299 bombs in late 1950 to 841 bombs in 1952. The military also undertook an across-the-board buildup that more than doubled the size of U.S. conventional forces; by 1952, NATO commanded 25 active divisions and over 5,000 aircraft.[17] This buildup was the precondition to a strategy based not on select advantage but on comprehensive strength. Washington must be able to repulse aggression wherever it occurred; it must be able to defend rather than liberate its allies; it must impose restraint upon an aggressive enemy. "The Soviets respected nothing but force," Truman said. "To build such force . . . is precisely what we are attempting to do now."[18]

This shift enhanced America's leverage at a critical moment. In the early 1950s, it was the Kremlin that was deterred from precipitating a crisis as Washington rearmed West Germany and strengthened NATO. Stalin, Khrushchev later scoffed, "developed fear, literally fear of the United States."[19] As U.S. military power increased, Truman and Eisenhower felt freer to expand the Korean War if the Communist powers did not accept a cease-fire, which they did after Stalin's death. "The Communist world," Acheson gloated, was being "forced to adjust its tactics" by "the growing strength of the free world."[20]

Yet the administration's strategy was vulnerable because it upset the balance between America's competing objectives. Defense spending surged to nearly 14 percent of GDP, necessitating taxes, deficits, and inflation controls. The public would not long support such measures, warned Truman's Budget Bureau, "in a situation short of all-out war."[21] The allies complained that increased military outlays were threatening economic recovery—that NSC-68 might undo the Marshall Plan—even as it remained unlikely that NATO could hold the line short of nuclear war.[22] All this raised doubts about whether the free world could ever sustain enough military power to check aggression anywhere along a global perimeter, much less force Moscow to draw in its horns.

The Truman years thus illustrated the range of military options for the United States. On one end was a minimalist strategy that embraced asymmetries rather than fighting them; on the other was a maximalist strategy that aimed to overpower the dilemmas of Cold War defense. The former provided bang for the buck but left the free world dangerously exposed; the latter provided confidence and credibility at an unbearable price. The task for Truman's successor was to forge a strategy for the long haul, one that was neither riven with vulnerabilities nor exhausting to sustain.

The Soviets were planning for "an entire historical era," Dulles remarked in 1954, "and we should do the same."[23] America, Dulles and Eisenhower believed, could not perpetually remain in a state of military hypervigilance without destroying its economy and its democracy. Waging a generational rivalry required shifting the competition back onto more advantageous ground.

The resulting strategy, termed the "New Look," had several distinguishing features: slashing the size of the armed forces, particularly the Army; relying on frontline allies for troops while making U.S. conventional forces a strategic reserve; and using nuclear striking power as the primary sanction for aggression. Caricatures notwithstanding, this strategy did not entail firing off nuclear weapons at the slightest Soviet infraction. Rather, Washington reserved the right to respond to major offenses in devastating ways. If Washington ruthlessly exploited its nuclear superiority—if it made the cost of aggression astronomical—then fear of escalation would deter the Communists from forcing the issue, even where they had a conventional edge. Washington could not check enemy thrusts "at all danger points around the Soviet orbit," Dulles explained; it must rely on the "deterrent of striking power as an effective defense."[24]

Yet the New Look was not another atomic strategy that lacked usable atomic capabilities. It required America's arsenal to be massive and primed for use. The number of U.S. warheads rose from 1,169 in 1953 to 22,229 in 1961, preserving a ten-to-one edge over Moscow.[25] The administration built a more secure, diversified "triad" featuring land-based missiles, ballistic missile submarines, and intercontinental bombers. To offset Soviet numerical superiority, the Pentagon also deployed smaller battlefield weapons around the Eurasian perimeter.[26] Most important, NATO approved a defense concept emphasizing brutal, rapid escalation. The U.S. commander of NATO possessed predelegated authority to use nuclear weapons in wartime; Ike planned to smash the Soviets immediately, even preemptively, if aggression seemed imminent. "Our only chance of victory," he said, was "to paralyze the enemy at the outset of the war."[27]

The New Look also informed what America did not do under Eisenhower: fight major conventional wars. In 1954, the administration refused to save French forces in Indochina, even though this meant losing part of Southeast Asia to communism. "No one could be more bitterly opposed to ever getting the United States involved in a hot war in that region than I am," Ike insisted.[28] Instead, the administration contested communist gains in the Third World through covert action and regional military alliances backed by U.S. striking power.

Staying out of peripheral quagmires was an achievement in its own right. The danger of economic exhaustion also receded. Military spending fell from nearly 14 percent of GDP under Truman to 9 percent under Eisenhower.[29] Yet Eisenhower ran into trouble substituting European for U.S. soldiers: only U.S. troops, he grudgingly realized, could convince allies that Washington would be in the fight from the beginning, so the legions must stay there "almost indefinitely."[30] As for how the New Look fared in deterring Moscow, the evidence was mixed.

The New Look failed to dissuade the Soviets from provoking crises and pushing for advantage. During the 1950s, Khrushchev believed he had to challenge Eisenhower precisely because the Soviet Union suffered from nuclear inferiority. Otherwise, he feared, Moscow would face unending coercion by a stronger power. Khrushchev's impetuousness was matched by his ambition: his "dearest dream" was to break the link between America and NATO. As the Soviets built a nascent intercontinental arsenal—long-range bombers and then ballistic missiles—Khrushchev hoped that even a primitive capability would yield improved geopolitical running room. "Let this device hang over capitalists like the sword of Damocles," he said. If both sides could hit each other with nuclear weapons, the leader with stronger nerves would prevail.[31]

Eisenhower thus encountered a blizzard of threats and crises. In 1956, the Kremlin threatened—superfluously but menacingly—to incinerate London and Paris unless they halted their attack on Egypt. In 1957, the launch of *Sputnik* created a widespread but mistaken perception of Soviet missile superiority. The next year, Khrushchev demanded the withdrawal of foreign forces from Berlin—a city surrounded by Soviet armies—and warned that missiles would fly if America resisted. Mao Zedong also squeezed vulnerable positions. In 1954–1955, and again in 1958, his forces shelled Nationalist-held islands in the Taiwan Strait.[32] American adversaries were testing the central proposition of Ike's statecraft: that nuclear superiority offset local disadvantages. In doing so, they unleashed all the conflicting pressures on U.S. strategy.

In Berlin and Taiwan, Eisenhower worried that retreat would dishearten allies and deplete U.S. credibility. In both cases, however, defending exposed garrisons would require rapid escalation, which would lead quickly, American planners explained, to the use of tactical nuclear weapons and then to "general nuclear war between the U.S. and the USSR."[33] The very allies Washington meant to reassure were horrified by that scenario. "For God's sake," exclaimed Adenauer. "Not for Berlin."[34]

Eisenhower himself realized there was something ridiculous about threatening global catastrophe over Western rights in Berlin or strategically useless islands off China's coast. If a full nuclear exchange happened, he warned, "it would literally be a business of digging ourselves out of ashes, starting again."[35]

In practice, then, the New Look paired restraint with resolve. Eisenhower refused to cave to Khrushchev's demands or Mao's cannons; he affirmed that America would "push its whole stack of chips into the pot" if war came. Yet an experienced statesman also walked gingerly on dangerous ground. Ike refused to call up the military reserves in the Berlin crisis—"we will not be served by ultimatum," he said, "but we will not be truculent"—and agreed to diplomatic discussions to defuse the crisis.[36] In the Taiwan Strait, the U.S. Navy evacuated Nationalist forces from the most exposed islands in 1955; in 1958, Ike quietly reopened a diplomatic channel to Beijing to lower tensions.[37] Ike wielded U.S. nuclear superiority as a club while staying calm and offering adversaries face-saving exits.

His strategy worked, for now. In each case, America's opponent backed down from fights in which it would be destroyed. So long as America's deterrent was "superior to Russia's and ... the Russians knew it was superior," said Dulles, "we could call checkmate on the Soviet Union."[38] Indeed, as Eisenhower suspected, even after *Sputnik*, Soviet intercontinental forces were incredibly vulnerable to a U.S. first strike. From a long-term perspective, however, these crises highlighted real problems.

For one thing, if U.S. strategy required nuclear superiority, the best America could expect was an unending, expensive quest to stay ahead. "Neither side can afford to lag or fail to match the other's efforts," one top-secret report concluded. "There will be no end to the moves and countermoves."[39] Such a strategy was also highly vulnerable to the appearance of shifts in the strategic balance: *Sputnik* had changed little militarily, but its psychological impact was severe. More profoundly, as Ike said in 1959, if "global conflict under modern conditions could mean the destruction of civilization," then what advantages did nuclear superiority really bring?[40]

In this situation, both sides might be deterred from going nuclear: the awesome power of the ultimate weapon might make that weapon impotent. As Khrushchev had realized, the critical variable would then be not the balance of power but the balance of resolve: who was willing to run greater risks in a crisis. Meanwhile, the allies would be terrified by fears of destruction; opportunistic opponents might engage in limited aggression or insurgency, confident that America would not escalate by unleashing

Armageddon. "Retaliatory theory collapses when you have creeping aggression," Ike had admitted in 1954.[41] An emerging stability in the nuclear competition might unleash greater instability at lower levels of conflict.

These problems loomed as Eisenhower's presidency wound down. A Communist insurgency in South Vietnam and Fidel Castro's takeover in Cuba showed that nuclear deterrence was irrelevant to pressing Third World problems. As Soviet intercontinental attack capabilities improved, NATO began to explore conventional defense options, in recognition that Washington might not fight a nuclear war if doing so would devastate America itself. The president himself was still a true believer, even as Soviet intercontinental capabilities improved. But he admitted that the SIOP—his Single Integrated Operational Plan for nuclear war, which envisioned striking 20,000 targets—"frighten[ed] the devil out of me."[42] And he often wondered whether America could escape an unending arms race either by seeking détente or by vaporizing the Soviet Union while Washington had the upper hand. "We can't go on the way we are," Eisenhower said. A strategy for the long haul was running out of road.[43]

That strategy had steered the country through a remarkably perilous time with remarkably few major losses. Yet by 1960, the same nuclear revolution that had enabled Ike's approach was undoing it. Washington was facing a vexing problem of long-term rivalry: What do you do when your best competitive advantage begins to wane and perhaps even becomes unusable?

The Democratic administrations of the 1960s, connected principally by Defense Secretary Robert McNamara, tried to solve this problem but ended up hopelessly ensnared in it. Their strategy, Flexible Response, was based on familiar critiques of the New Look: that it was useless in combating brushfire wars and insurgencies; that it weakened NATO by requiring Europeans to believe America would commit suicide on their behalf; that it left too many gaps for a creative enemy to exploit. The free world, wrote adviser Walt Rostow, must close off "all areas of vulnerability, if we wish to minimize the number and effectiveness of Communist probes."[44]

Flexible Response would do so by providing better options: options to fight limited wars on the periphery, options for conventional defense in Europe, options to use nuclear weapons short of all-out war. If Eisenhower and Dulles had used uncertainty—the threat of retaliating "by means and at places of our choosing"—to keep the Soviets off balance, Kennedy believed that only certainty—the ability to "convince all potential aggressors that any attack would be futile"—could make deterrence work.[45]

Strategy in the 1960s thus involved more conventional power and more "rational" nuclear options. Kennedy created five new Army divisions, doubled the number of ships in the Navy, expanded the Air Force, and invested in special operations forces. The Pentagon adopted a "2.5 war" strategy meant to allow nearly simultaneous operations against the Soviets in Europe, against China in Asia, and in one minor conflict. On the central front, the administration believed, a fortified conventional defense could at least "prevent any cheap and easy seizure" of key territory. It could thereby buy time—time to issue warnings or engage in thoughtful deliberation—before the leap to nuclear warfare.[46]

If America did cross the nuclear threshold, it would still have graduated options. NATO could employ battlefield nukes without using strategic weapons. At the strategic level, McNamara pushed for "sub-SIOP" options involving attacks on a fraction of the targets in Ike's plan. He also advocated a "no cities" doctrine in which the Pentagon would target any major nuclear strikes—even after a Soviet surprise attack—against the enemy's military capabilities rather than its people, in hopes of limiting the overall damage a general war would cause. Waging nuclear war "while preserving our own societies is . . . a not wholly unattainable military objective," McNamara said. For U.S. nuclear power to be credible, it had to be usable. That meant that its employment could not be inherently apocalyptic.[47]

Challenges to this strategy arose immediately. In 1961, Khrushchev renewed the Berlin crisis by demanding withdrawal of Western forces and threatening to settle things unilaterally if Kennedy refused. The next year, he touched off the most dangerous crisis of the Cold War by shipping nuclear-tipped missiles to Cuba. Khrushchev had multiple motives in these affairs: damming the gusher of refugees fleeing East Germany through Berlin, protecting a Cuban regime Kennedy had tried to overthrow, reducing the strategic imbalance by using Cuba as a base for intermediate- and medium-range missiles that could hit U.S. targets. But in both cases, he was gauging whether the theory he had tested in the 1950s—that an emerging balance of terror created opportunities for the bold—might succeed against Ike's greener successor.[48]

At first glance, these crises appeared to vindicate Flexible Response. Kennedy drew a hard line against Soviet threats in Berlin while also mobilizing reserves and increasing the strength of the Army. Whereas candidate Kennedy had cultivated the myth of the "missile gap," President

Kennedy made it known that America had a massive nuclear advantage. Washington possessed "a second strike capability which is at least as extensive as what the Soviets can deliver by striking first," Deputy Secretary of Defense Roswell Gilpatric announced.[49] The resulting standoff was incredibly tense; at one point, Kennedy asked his advisers to assess the possibility of a surprise first strike against the Soviet Union.[50] But Kennedy's posture ultimately convinced Khrushchev to solve the refugee problem not by pushing the West out of the city but by locking its Eastern residents in with the Berlin Wall.

Kennedy also achieved a good-enough outcome in Cuba. There he used graduated coercion—a naval blockade and preparations for airstrikes and an invasion, backstopped by the threat of nuclear war—to show resolve and pressure a chastened Khrushchev. "We do not want to unleash a war," Khrushchev conceded. "We only wanted to threaten them."[51] U.S. conventional superiority in the Caribbean left Moscow with no way to defend its position other than nuclear war, and U.S. nuclear superiority made that option prohibitive. "The Soviet Union was not prepared to use its nuclear power," McNamara explained. "And it had no other force it could effectively use."[52] The lesson, it seemed, was that wielding a range of credible military capabilities was essential to resolving crises on U.S. terms.

Unfortunately, the truth was not so simple. The central premise of Flexible Response was that America could use force in a calibrated manner. Behind the scenes, though, both crises left Kennedy gravely troubled that violence of any sort could spiral out of control. During the Berlin crisis, he had therefore refused to send an armed probe down the autobahn. In Cuba, he had rejected early strikes against the missile sites. And in that case, despite possessing a seven-to-one advantage in strategic weapons, he had concluded that if even one or two Soviet missiles hit American cities, the damage would be unacceptable. In the nuclear age, Kennedy remarked, any use of force was "one hell of a gamble." This was why he discreetly made concessions in both crises. In 1961, he quietly signaled that Washington would not contest the division of Berlin. "A wall is a hell of a lot better than a war," he reasoned. The next year, Kennedy publicly agreed not to invade Cuba—and privately pledged to remove U.S. missiles from Turkey—if Moscow withdrew its rockets. Khrushchev, by this point, was more impressed with U.S. superiority than Kennedy was.[53]

The Cuban Missile Crisis also underscored the horrifying prospect that nuclear war could break out by accident. There were several close calls—a U-2 spy plane that strayed into Soviet airspace, a U.S. warship that dropped depth charges near a Soviet submarine carrying nuclear-armed torpedoes—that eviscerated the confidence that superpower crises could be precisely managed.[54] Any remaining hope that America might escape epochal destruction in a nuclear war was vanishing as Soviet strategic forces grew. By late 1962, military officials warned that "we were approaching a point where both sides hold a Sword of Damocles."[55] Kennedy, like Eisenhower, deserved credit for avoiding disastrous retreats and disastrous wars. Yet U.S. strategy was starting to unravel.

For if any nuclear war would cause unacceptable destruction, and if any use of force could escalate uncontrollably, then Flexible Response was a fantasy. "The line between non-nuclear war and nuclear war is distinct and observable," McNamara admitted. But "once the momentous decision has been made to cross that line, everything becomes much more confused."[56] Indeed, how could rational American leaders ever use nuclear weapons, no matter how bad the conventional situation? They could not, McNamara later admitted. He had secretly recommended that the presidents he served not "ever initiate, under any circumstances, the use of nuclear weapons."[57] Had he said this publicly, the U.S. alliance structure might have collapsed. U.S. officials were caught between their belief that a credible collective defense required calibrated uses of force, backed up by meaningful nuclear threats, and their creeping fear that that calibration was impossible and nuclear war unimaginable.

The latter sentiment overtook the former after the missile crisis. McNamara and President Lyndon B. Johnson leveled off the U.S. nuclear buildup; the Pentagon ditched the no-cities doctrine; and the Johnson administration shifted to an "assured destruction" posture (commonly called "mutual assured destruction," MAD) rooted in the idea that the best way to prevent nuclear war was to *maximize* its horrors. This meant pursuing "counter-value" strategies—targeting the enemy's population—rather than "counter-force" strategies, which targeted its nuclear assets. In the nuclear age, the thinking went, the most stable situation was one in which neither side felt vulnerable to a disarming first strike nor thought it could escape a society-shattering second-strike from the enemy. Safety would come from accepting, not resisting, a grim "balance of terror."[58]

For this reason, McNamara and Johnson also resisted pressure to construct a large-scale antiballistic missile (ABM) shield.[59] And U.S. officials began taking steps to cap the military competition by negotiating the Limited Test Ban Treaty in 1963 and later seeking talks on strategic weapons and antimissile systems. "We do not want a nuclear arms race with the Soviet Union," McNamara declared. "The action-reaction phenomenon makes it foolish and futile."[60] All these initiatives represented an intellectual breakthrough of sorts—a realization that safety might require prioritizing stability over advantage. The Soviets reciprocated, in their way, by dumping Khrushchev and following a less truculent policy after the missile crisis. Such crises subsequently became less frequent; the Cold War became less terrifying.

The problem was that this emerging logic of stability undercut the enduring logic of competition. MAD was lethal to a military strategy that required nuclear escalation to compensate for America's inability to defend far-flung allies conventionally. That inability, unhappily, remained. Concerns about the balance of payments eventually led Johnson to reduce, rather than increase, U.S. deployments in Europe.[61] There were "gaping holes in all strategic options," LBJ's advisers reported. General war was "virtually suicidal," conventional defense "seems less attainable than heretofore," and tactical nuclear war was "full of uncertainties."[62] When NATO was surprised by the Soviet invasion of Czechoslovakia in 1968, that event only underscored how overmatched the alliance was.

By this point, the shifting military balance was opening up fissures in the West. In 1966, de Gaulle withdrew from NATO's military command, years after Paris had developed its own nuclear weapons owing to doubts about U.S. strategy. Now that the superpowers "each can destroy the other," he had told Kennedy, "the U.S. will find it extremely difficult to ... use nuclear weapons."[63] Others were singing the same tune. "West Germany cannot really depend on the Americans," Vice Chancellor (soon to be Chancellor) Brandt argued.[64] By decade's end, it was hardly absurd to think the Soviets might fracture NATO even without the histrionics of the Khrushchev years.

The logic of stability posed another problem: McNamara's insistence that MAD was a "fact of life" required assuming that the Soviets thought so, too. Surely, McNamara calculated, the Kremlin realized the futility of seeking true nuclear parity or even nuclear advantage, particularly because it led a poorer country whose economy was beginning to slow.[65] Yet this assumption required overlooking the possibility that a regime obsessed with the "correlation of forces" might see value in catching up to, even passing, the United States. Sure enough, by the mid-1960s Moscow was exploiting the American slowdown to whittle away Washington's strategic advantages, even as McNamara insisted that the Soviets had "lost the quantitative [arms] race."[66] And however much Khrushchev's successors feared nuclear war, they resisted the idea that security lay in vulnerability. When McNamara urged Premier Alexei Kosygin to forgo an ABM race in 1967, Kosygin angrily replied that "defense is moral, aggression is immoral!"[67] McNamara had a strategy for dealing with the enemy he wanted, not the enemy he faced.

The weakening of America's position was exacerbated by the one case in which Flexible Response was applied most faithfully. The sad story of U.S. intervention in Vietnam is covered in the next chapter. But that conflict was part of America's broader preoccupation with alliances and credibility, and it featured a calibrated approach—first advisers, then airpower, ultimately a 500,000-strong troop presence—designed to stymie aggression without provoking unwanted escalation. The result was catastrophe: an intervention that drained America's resources, crippled its military, and created vast opportunities for Moscow. "While we have been heavily engaged in Southeast Asia," wrote Nixon's first secretary of defense, Melvin Laird, "the Soviet Union has built a military momentum relative to the U.S. in virtually all aspects of military strength."[68]

By 1969, American strategy was in disarray. Flexible Response had not overcome America's conventional inferiority in Europe, but it had carried the country into a quagmire that undermined its strength worldwide. American strategy increasingly hinged on the dubious belief that the Soviets would not push for strategic parity or superiority, even though they were now doing so. Worse, following a series of traumatic crises U.S. officials were placing greater value on strategic stability, even though America required strategic instability to make its commitments credible. Depending on how one prioritized those objectives, things were about to get either much better or much worse. The 1970s represented the high point of MAD—and the low point of America's military fortunes.

If Washington had long struggled with the dilemmas of Cold War defense, it had at least done so from a position of strength. By the 1970s, however, the margin of safety was closing. The Cuban crisis persuaded McNamara that nuclear superiority was worthless, but it convinced Soviet officials that superiority was worth a great deal. "You Americans will never be able to do this to us again," Deputy Foreign Minister Vasili Kuznetsov said.[69] Moscow thus undertook a determined buildup that would last nearly two decades.

The focus was on strategic forces. By the early 1970s, the Soviets were nearing parity in strategic delivery vehicles. The Kremlin then kept pushing. The Soviet Union followed the Americans in producing MIRVs (missiles with multiple, independently targeted warheads) and building heavier, more accurate ICBMs. Moscow also modernized its intermediate-range forces, deploying high-speed, mobile SS-20 missiles that could, as one Soviet general put it, "hold all of Europe hostage."[70]

The Soviets were simultaneously improving their conventional forces. On the Cold War's central front in Europe, the Red Army fused new capabilities—better tanks, logistics, and attack aircraft—with new concepts that emphasized using massed echelon attacks to achieve shattering breakthroughs. Mobile maneuver groups would destroy NATO's tactical nuclear weapons before the alliance could use them; Moscow's improved theater and strategic capabilities would deter Washington from escalating.[71] All the while, the Soviets made unprecedented investments in aircraft carriers, long-range airlift and airborne assault units, and other forces with global reach. "We have seen a massive power shift," Secretary of Defense Donald Rumsfeld observed in 1976. Moscow was "becoming a true superpower."[72]

America was moving in the opposite direction. Constant-dollar defense spending fell by nearly 40 percent between 1968 and 1976 because of economic troubles and post-Vietnam cutbacks. The number of aviation squadrons fell by 46 percent, the number of ships by 47 percent, and the number of combat divisions by 16 percent between 1964 and 1974.[73] "We have been methodically and continually reducing our military forces," JCS Chairman Thomas Moorer remarked, while "the Soviets have been building up all across the board."[74]

The military balance was changing fundamentally. Through the 1970s, most U.S. officials believed America had a narrow advantage. But the gap had shrunk dramatically, and key trends looked unfavorable. Some analysts feared that America was entering a "window of vulnerability"— that Moscow could use its heavy ICBMs to execute a disarming first strike. Even more sanguine observers worried that America risked finding itself outgunned in a crisis. "The main purpose of our forces is diplomatic wallop," Nixon said, but that wallop was dwindling.[75]

The shifting balance certainly made Soviet influence harder to contain in the Third World. During the 1970s, Moscow deployed forces to Egypt in the "war of attrition" with Israel, threatened to intervene in the Arab-Israeli war of 1973, intervened decisively—by delivering Cuban troops and Soviet arms—in conflicts in Africa, and invaded Afghanistan in 1979. "Never before in its entire history," crowed Leonid Brezhnev, "has our country enjoyed such authority and influence in the world."[76]

Soviet military power was increasing the strain on NATO, too. The problem, Nixon understood, was not the threat of invasion but "a more subtle mix of military, psychological and political pressures" meant to bend Europe to Moscow's will.[77] During the 1970s, the Kremlin buildup was bringing Moscow closer to this goal. Brandt's *Ostpolitik*—outreach to the East, combined with subtle distancing from Washington—was partly rooted in doubts about the U.S. commitment. Kissinger feared that Europe might slide toward "Finlandization," as the allies refused to risk Moscow's wrath.[78] The SS-20 deployment made this fear very real. By underscoring the nuclear imbalance within Europe, it threatened to produce a divided, demoralized free world. For most of the 1970s, America seemed to have only incomplete answers to the Soviet military challenge.

This was certainly true of superpower arms control. In one sense, the agreements of the 1970s—the Strategic Arms Limitation Treaty (SALT), which imposed numerical limits on SLBMs (submarine-launched ballistic missiles) and ICBMs; the ABM Treaty, which restricted missile defenses; the signed but never ratified SALT II—were possible only in an age of parity. Moscow had, unsurprisingly, declined to limit the arms race until it had caught up; it now capped its quantitative buildup in exchange for recognition as America's strategic equal. Moreover, the pairing of SALT and the ABM Treaty seemed to show a mutual acceptance of mutual vulnerability, a recognition that striving for narrow advantage was pointless in an era of nuclear plenty. Arms control, Nixon said, was the keystone of an emerging "structure of peace."[79]

But Nixon didn't really believe this, and for good reason. Sure, Brezhnev desired greater stability in superpower relations—who wanted nuclear war? But he defined stability as a Soviet superiority that would allow Moscow to protect its interests and assert its prerogatives.[80] Indeed, even as the Kremlin signed SALT and the ABM Treaty, it was feverishly building ICBMs suited to a first-strike strategy. Nixon, for his part, privately scorned the "pathetic idealism" of the arms controllers; he understood that strategic stability was the enemy of competitive advantage.[81] "We may have reached a balance of terror," he remarked. "Our bargaining position has shifted."[82] Nixon and Kissinger thus saw arms control primarily as a competitive tool for containing the Soviet buildup while America was weak after Vietnam, and they continually sought to locate new sources of strategic leverage.[83]

This crafty policy produced uneven results. The accords of the 1970s did yield a strategic breather for an exhausted superpower. "Neither in

what we say nor what we do, would we want to force the pace of armaments," Kissinger warned.[84] What SALT could not do was prevent the
Soviets from aggressively enhancing the quality of their strategic forces
or deploying lethal theater forces such as the SS-20. In theory, Washington could match and exceed Soviet qualitative improvements, and eventually it would. For now, though, the Soviets had the jump, while the
Pentagon was constrained by the post-Vietnam backlash.

Amid the ups and downs of arms control, U.S. leaders tried other
ways of escaping the straitjacket imposed by MAD. Nixon rejected the
idea that nuclear weapons should not be used for coercion. He sought,
rather, to squeeze additional juice out of America's forces by manipulating
the balance of resolve. If, as Khrushchev had recognized, MAD would
deter both sides from waging nuclear war, then the side willing to come
nearer the brink would prevail in crises. Nixon thus emulated Khrushchev's nuclear saber-rattling with his "madman strategy." His administration conducted a "secret" nuclear alert in 1969—meant to be visible to
Soviet intelligence—to prod Moscow to put pressure on the North Vietnamese. The administration conducted another strategic nuclear alert in
October 1973 after the Soviets threatened to intervene against Israel.[85]
The strategy, Kissinger explained, was "to maneuver very dangerously, so
that the other side doesn't think it is riskless to challenge."[86]

The October 1973 alert succeeded in exposing a Soviet bluff. "We
should not take the road of sending our troops," said Foreign Minister
Andrei Gromyko. "That would mean confrontation with the United
States." Yet the 1969 alert failed, and as the balance shifted, the risks that
Moscow might eventually call an American bluff—with catastrophic implications for U.S. credibility—became unacceptable. "This is the last
time we will ever be able to get away with this," Kissinger conceded in
1973.[87]

The search for limited nuclear options yielded equally mixed results. If
massive retaliation was now suicidal—"SIOP is a horror strategy," Kissinger complained—and non-use of nuclear weapons threatened to destroy
U.S. alliances, the only solution was to make nuclear war more thinkable
by making it less destructive.[88] Presidents Nixon and Gerald R. Ford
pushed the Pentagon to devise plans for selective strikes against Soviet military assets and targets in the Warsaw Pact countries, as well as for strikes
simply for signaling purposes, as a way of halting Soviet aggression by
showing that the war was getting out of hand. "Now we have parity,"
Nixon said, "so now we need an option other than all or nothing."[89]

Over the long term, the search for limited options promoted fresh thinking about how to employ nuclear weapons in conditions of near parity. But for now, discriminate options required a degree of precision and real-time situational awareness that U.S. forces lacked.[90] Those options also required testing a supremely dicey proposition: that nuclear war would not escalate uncontrollably. "Conducting a limited strategic strike against Soviet territory would entail incalculable risks," wrote Kissinger's advisers, even if it seemed "to offer the last chance of bringing the Soviet Union's leaders to their senses."[91]

Through the 1970s, U.S. officials were whipsawed by the reality of parity and the requirements of global strategy. The result, frequently, was conceptual ambiguity or confusion. In one notorious episode, Kissinger defended the Ford administration's arms control agenda by publicly deriding the value of strategic superiority. "What is the significance of it, politically, militarily, operationally at these levels of numbers?" he asked. "What do you do with it?" In private, he was working to prevent America from falling into a position of inferiority that he realized could be quite dangerous.[92]

Carter's struggles were greater because his aversion to nuclear weapons was more visceral. "We have to do everything possible to stop this mad race," Carter believed.[93] Upon taking office, Carter canceled or delayed key strategic programs. He also considered a no-first-use declaration despite its obvious incompatibility with U.S. plans to defend NATO.[94] The president ultimately achieved the most complex arms control pact yet—SALT II—but failed to get it ratified, largely because of a growing perception that America was falling dangerously behind. "The future will be terrifying if the Allies do not and we do not carry out our defense programs," Secretary of Defense Harold Brown said.[95] America looked to be losing the military competition. In fact, it was gradually devising a strategy that would win that contest decisively.

The coming change of fortunes owed as much to Soviet missteps as to American ingenuity. Moscow had made large military strides during the 1970s, but only by overburdening a fragile economy. Because the U.S. economy was three to six times bigger than the Soviet economy, and because Soviet industry was so inefficient, Moscow could become a global rival to Washington only by spending prodigiously—upward of 25 percent of its gross national product (GNP) on defense.[96]

The Soviets could do this for a while because there were few political or ideological constraints on what Soviet leader Mikhail Gorbachev
called "the insatiable Moloch of the military-industrial complex."[97] Yet
over the long term, this freedom encouraged self-defeating behavior:
military spending that badly strained a wheezing economy. The Soviet
buildup thus had paradoxical effects. It provided unprecedented global
influence, but it meant that Moscow, not Washington, was most vulnerable to further intensification of the rivalry. "We were at the peak of our
power in 1979," one Soviet official recalled, but "it was the period when
the country's back began breaking."[98] By pushing so hard for military advantage, the Soviets had put America in a position to exploit its own superior economic strength.

It didn't help that Soviet enemies were multiplying. The Sino-Soviet
split announced itself to the world in 1969 with a fierce border conflict.
Thereafter, the Kremlin had to assume that any general war would be a
two-front conflict against NATO and China.[99] Conversely, the U.S. opening to China allowed the Pentagon to downshift to a more realistic 1.5 war
strategy, while the end of the Vietnam War permitted the armed services
to refocus on high-end competition instead of brushfire conflicts.

Elsewhere, too, the story of the 1970s was more complex than it
seemed. Arms control treaties didn't immediately halt the ebbing of America's military edge. But by capping the quantitative arms race, they ensured
that qualitative factors mattered more. That shift would eventually favor
the United States because it played to America's strengths in computers,
sensors, and other information-age technologies. These technologies were
now enabling revolutionary improvements in the lethality of modern
arms—but only for countries with flexible economies and open information
ecosystems. As Laird predicted, America could "keep ahead" because "we
have the technological capability that far outstrips the Soviet Union."[100]

As the structural conditions of the competition were shifting, so was
America's intellectual approach. If the adverse shifts of the decade put
great strains on U.S. strategy, they also triggered great innovation. Andrew Marshall, the defense intellectual and Pentagon official, put it suc-
cinctly in 1972: "The United States will have to outthink the Soviets since
it is doubtful that it will continue to outspend them substantially." In an
era of rough parity, America had to drive the military rivalry through
targeted investments that would play to U.S. strengths and negate major
Soviet programs. The objective, Marshall wrote, was "to induce Soviet
costs to rise" and erode Moscow's competitive position; the method was

"seeking … areas of U.S. comparative advantage, and … steering the strategic arms competition into these areas." Washington should focus less on stability and more on exploiting favorable instabilities.[101]

Doing so required seeing the world through the enemy's eyes. Here, too, the United States was making gains by drawing on new intelligence and old history. The Soviets were scarred by the memory of Nazi air attacks in 1941. By fielding even a small number of penetrating bombers, Marshall wrote, Washington could cause Moscow to devote disproportionate resources to air defense.[102] Similarly, Pentagon and CIA analysts learned that the Kremlin was constructing—at a cost of 1–2 percent of its GDP—underground bunkers to protect its leaders during war. It followed that targeting those bunkers was a resource-efficient way of threatening what Soviet leaders valued most, their own survival.[103]

Additionally, the Pentagon was using small wars to prepare for big ones. In long-term rivalries, proxy wars and limited conflicts serve as laboratories. The Vietnam War pitted American fliers against Soviet-made jets and tactics, exposing glaring deficiencies in U.S. air-to-air combat. The October War highlighted the devastation that advanced air defenses, antitank munitions, and precision-guided munitions (PGMs) could wreak. "The tactical possibilities" of PGMs "are far reaching," noted a Defense Department memo. "Perhaps we can now guarantee to stop the tank, making it obsolete."[104] The small conflicts promoted intense intellectual ferment, focusing U.S. strategists on new technologies, competencies, and operational challenges. During the 1960s, Washington had hit an intellectual impasse. During the 1970s, America was beginning an intellectual—and strategic—renaissance.

Viewed against this backdrop, U.S. defense choices during the 1970s look more purposeful. Even amid prolonged austerity, successive administrations invested in a new generation of strategic assets: Minuteman III and MX ICBMs, Trident ballistic missile submarines and Trident D5 SLBMs, air- and ground-launched cruise missiles, improved nuclear warheads. By Soviet estimates, the resulting accuracy improvements would produce a threefold gain in destructiveness and a vastly improved ability to destroy Moscow's land-based nuclear forces.[105] *"With M-X deployed,"* U.S. officials projected, "the Soviets could expect to lose *nearly 90 percent* of their *total* strategic warheads from a US first strike in the mid-1980s."[106] Even in a situation of numerical parity, the *Soviets* might soon face a window of vulnerability.

Strategy was following technology. Largely on Brown's initiative, the Carter administration approved and selectively leaked a new targeting policy, PD-59, focused on destroying Soviet leadership bunkers, military forces, industrial targets, and other assets that would be required to recover after war. PD-59 went in concert with improvements in command, control, and communications meant to allow the U.S. leadership to survive and, if necessary, wage an extended nuclear war. Washington, Brown reassured the allies, had "no illusion that a large-scale nuclear war" could be a "sensible, deliberate instrument" of policy.[107] But the ability to fight a protracted war—and kill Soviet leaders in the process—would reinforce deterrence by ensuring that the Kremlin could not profit from any nuclear exchange.[108]

A similar transformation was under way in general-purpose forces. "Technology can be a force multiplier," Brown believed. It could "offset numerical advantages of an adversary."[109] As part of this "offset strategy," the Defense Department began developing technologies that would revolutionize the East-West military balance. Stealth fighters and bombers would render Soviet air defenses irrelevant; precision-guided munitions would wreck tank columns; improved sensors and strike capabilities would extend the battlefield deep into the Soviet rear. Technological breakthroughs were systematically eating away at Moscow's greatest advantage: its superiority on the central front. Those advances were also making it possible to develop vastly enhanced military power without distorting America's economy—or harnessing its manpower—in the politically toxic manner of Korea and Vietnam. "For the first time in our conventional rivalry," Marshall commented, Washington was "really moving toward gaining the upper hand."[110]

Many of these capabilities were nascent in the late 1970s, and there still was not enough defense money to go around. But Soviet behavior was solving that problem, too. In 1979, NATO approved plans to deploy Pershing II intermediate-range ballistic missiles (IRBMs) and Tomahawk cruise missiles to Western Europe. Like MX, the Pershing II was a Soviet nightmare, a mobile, fast-flying missile that could strike targets deep within the Soviet bloc in less than 10 minutes. Meanwhile, the number of Americans who wanted higher defense spending rose from 17 percent to 56 percent between 1974 and 1980. "The continuous Soviet military buildup," noted Brown, "has finally sunk into American consciousness as an important fact."[111] As the 1970s ended, the Soviets were in a position of deep vulnerability, and America was preparing to race forward again—this time, with a sharper strategy that the pressure of adversity had helped to forge.

Ronald Reagan was uniquely suited to lead this offensive because of his unorthodox views on the central dilemma of the military competition. Reagan had always hated MAD, which he likened to "two westerners standing in a saloon aiming their guns at each other's head—permanently."[112] He believed that strategic superiority mattered enormously and that Moscow wanted it to "intimidate, 'Finlandize,' and ultimately neutralize Western Europe."[113]

To be sure, Reagan was not an uncompromising hawk. He hoped that the superpowers could eventually find a new type of strategic stability based on dramatic reductions in, and perhaps even elimination of, nuclear weapons. Yet doing so first required reestablishing more pronounced advantages. Moscow "is up to its maximum ability in developing arms," he said in 1980. "They know that if we turned our full industrial might into an arms race, they cannot keep pace with us."[114] By accelerating the competition, America could confront Moscow with painful choices—and perhaps even exhaust the Soviet system itself.

The first element of Reagan's offensive was simple: turning on a gusher of defense spending. Pentagon outlays more than doubled in nominal dollars between 1980 and 1987.[115] Secretary of Defense Caspar Weinberger poured resources into key nuclear and conventional capabilities, and Reagan pushed ahead with the plan to station intermediate-range missiles in Western Europe. "The Soviets have a great fear of the Pershing," Weinberger said. It was a system that played on Moscow's historical fear of surprise attack.[116]

The Pershing deployment touched on a second element of Reagan's strategy: investing in capabilities that would create painful Soviet dilemmas. PGMs and improvements in intelligence, surveillance, and reconnaissance threatened to make the battlefield larger and more lethal for Soviet forces. Terrain-hugging cruise missiles and stealth aircraft would challenge generational Soviet investments in air defense. Improved ICBMs would endanger Soviet command-and-control facilities and land-based missiles, assets on which Moscow had spent enormous sums. The U.S. buildup, noted one Pentagon document, should "impose disproportionate costs, open up new areas of major military competition and obsolesce previous Soviet investment."[117]

Third, Reagan employed new capabilities in aggressive ways. The Army's AirLand Battle and NATO's Follow-on Forces Attack would utilize the emerging reconnaissance-strike complex to smash Soviet forces before they hit the front lines. At the same time, armored units would launch a "counter-blitz" to disorient and roll back the attackers. The Navy's Maritime Strategy would employ America's naval striking power to attack exposed Soviet lines of communication and territories.[118] In the nuclear realm, the administration—building on PD-59—planned to use penetrating bombers and highly accurate missiles to cripple Soviet nuclear forces and the "military and political power structure."[119] As during the 1970s, forward-leaning strategies rested upon a more thorough knowledge of the enemy. By the 1980s, pilfered Warsaw Pact plans had yielded new insight into the Soviet vision for war in Europe and focused U.S. planners on breaking up enemy mass before it slammed into NATO's defenses.[120]

A fourth initiative was to open up new areas of competition. During the 1970s, Nixon had little choice but to press pause on an ABM contest. Yet such a contest was in America's long-term interest because it emphasized technologies in which Washington excelled. During the 1980s, Reagan proposed a Strategic Defense Initiative (SDI) that would render nuclear missiles "impotent and obsolete."[121] That project reflected Reagan's deep discomfort with MAD. It also threatened the major Soviet strategic accomplishment of the Cold War—the construction of the world's largest ICBM force—and might eventually force Moscow to choose between strategic inferiority and unaffordable military rivalry. If the Soviets "want an arms race," Reagan said, they would have to "break their backs to keep up."[122]

Reagan announced SDI on national television to maximize the psychological impact of a program that was many years from fruition. This was a fifth aspect of the offensive: influencing Soviet calculations by selectively revealing U.S. advantages. From 1980 on, the Pentagon dribbled out information about the revolutionary potential of Stealth aircraft. U.S. submarine commanders, armed with vastly improved intelligence, simulated sinking Soviet ballistic missile submarines under polar ice caps to show that they could destroy Moscow's most "invulnerable" assets. NATO began showcasing new capabilities in exercises that included up to 120,000 personnel. Shortly thereafter, Soviet military observers warned that "new technology was threatening tanks with obsolescence."[123] In peacetime competition, the perception of the future military balance was as important as the military balance itself.

Many of these initiatives represented a rebellion against MAD and strategic stability. Strategic defenses meant to render Soviet missiles irrelevant, the development of advanced counterforce capabilities, the explicit targeting of Soviet nuclear forces and even Moscow's political leadership—all were intended to build powerful U.S. leverage, and all subverted mutual vulnerability. "They have been building a 20-minute launch-on-warning capability," Director of Central Intelligence William Casey explained, "but the Pershing only provides 8 minutes."[124] As a result, Reagan's policies often invited criticism from Europeans who demonstrated against NATO's efforts to defend itself and from others who saw MAD as the only path to safety in the nuclear age.

That criticism informed a final element of Reagan's strategy: pursuing the most aggressive arms control agenda to date. "Let us agree to do more than simply begin where ... previous efforts left off," Reagan said. His administration called for deep cuts in strategic forces and elimination of intermediate-range nuclear forces in Europe.[125] There was little expectation that Moscow would accept these proposals, which required throwing away prized capabilities, anytime soon. But they might lay the groundwork for successful negotiations after America had built a position of strength.

The Reagan offensive thus exploited tools and ideas that had been emerging since the early 1970s. It abruptly shifted the military competition against a vulnerable opponent. It unmistakably prioritized military advantage, although Reagan hoped that doing so might permit improved stability later. This surprisingly sophisticated strategy succeeded because it put Moscow under pressure on multiple fronts while throwing its longer-term competitiveness into doubt.

Everywhere Soviet officials looked—the theater nuclear balance, the strategic arms race, the conventional military competition—the situation was becoming more menacing. Pershing II missiles and new ICBMs were creating terrifying vulnerabilities; revolutionary advances in situational awareness and striking power were transforming the balance on the central front. "Currently there is no direction of military efforts, and no type of armaments, where U.S. and NATO do not strive for superiority," Soviet defense minister Dmitri Ustinov said.[126] Most ominously, SDI showed that the very nature of the strategic competition was changing, in ways that potentially imperiled a Soviet ICBM force that represented—as Kremlin adviser Andrei Grachev later said—"the essence of Soviet power in the international arena."[127]

SDI was years, if not decades, away from deployment, and many key weapons systems were still in their infancy. Yet the U.S. offensive shifted the psychological balance immediately by showing that Washington was now driving the pace and by threatening to leave the Soviets at a lasting disadvantage. "We will never be able to catch up with you in modern arms until we have an economic revolution," admitted the chief of the Soviet General Staff, Nikolai Ogarkov. "And the question is whether we can have an economic revolution without a political revolution."[128] The problem was not simply that the Soviet Union was falling behind. It was that a closed totalitarian system had no way of catching up.

By the mid-1980s, America was decisively winning the military competition. If war broke out, Moscow would now find itself at a severe disadvantage, which meant that, even short of war, Washington would have a crucial coercive edge. America's new capabilities, said Foreign Minister Andrei Gromyko, would "be used to bring pressure on the Soviet Union" and "to blackmail the USSR."[129] Before long, a new generation of Kremlin officials would cite America's growing military lead—and the burdens it imposed on the Soviet system—as reason to de-escalate the Cold War. "If we won't budge from the positions we've held for a long time, we will lose in the end," conceded Gorbachev. "We will be drawn into an arms race that we cannot manage."[130]

Yet Gorbachev's epiphany was still in the future, and in the near term, the price of America's emerging advantage was renewed instability. The Soviets did not take the U.S. rejection of MAD quietly. During the early 1980s, Moscow was so alarmed by Reagan's offensive—in the military arena and others—that the threat of confrontation rose significantly. "The Reagan administration has inaugurated open preparations for war," Ogarkov warned. "In several fields, the battle is already going on."[131] As we will see, the build-down that America's build-up enabled would come only after a final Cold War crisis.

The Cold War is sometimes remembered as a period of stability, when the iron logic of nuclear deterrence kept the peace.[132] It didn't feel that way at the time. The Cold War featured intense, dramatic swings in the military balance. Deterrence was not self-regulating: it required a continual evolution of plans and capabilities, all organized around the grim premise that preserving peace required credibly threatening to kill untold millions in war. The "balance of terror" was not inherently robust but inherently delicate, strategist Albert Wohlstetter wrote. Deterrence would be "the product of sustained intelligent effort, attainable only by continuing hard choice."[133] This made the Cold War military competition incredibly dynamic: it featured moves and countermoves that played out over decades.

Some analysts believe that this competition was an exercise in irrelevance—that in the nuclear age, the military balance mattered only in the minds of policymakers.[134] Yet the military balance mattered in reality precisely because it mattered in the minds of policymakers. In tense crises, perceptions of strength or weakness loomed large for Cold War leaders. Even when war seemed distant, the military equation affected the cohesion of America's alliances and the dynamics of superpower statecraft. In any long-term rivalry, the military balance shapes risk-taking, decision-making, and the ebb and flow of influence.

Washington did not always perform brilliantly in that rivalry. The Cold War subjected U.S. strategy to competing pressures: stability versus advantage, economy versus security, strength versus sustainability. American policymakers sometimes seemed lost in the conundrums of the nuclear age. Looking back, we can see that America was fortunate to have faced an enemy that, though opportunistic and occasionally aggressive, was generally cautious about risking major war.

In the end, a winning approach took more than three decades to assemble. That approach fused revolutionary technological advances to innovative strategic ideas; it punished specific Soviet weaknesses while intensifying the overall military competition beyond anything the opponent could stand. In that way, America's strategy wrung maximum benefit out of enduring competitive asymmetries while using new concepts and capabilities to offset longstanding weaknesses. Over the course of the Cold War, Washington was just effective—and lucky—enough to hold the free world's defenses together. Then it used a moment of opportunity to seize control of the contest.

That breakthrough, in turn, was only possible because the outlook had recently appeared so dim. In retrospect, the trauma of the 1970s forced U.S. strategists to think creatively about how to reclaim the advantage within a tighter competition and how to exploit an adversary's fears. In the same vein, nuclear parity had ironic effects. It threatened to undermine America's global strategy, but it also triggered a qualitative, information-age race in which the Soviets were at a hopeless disadvantage. Not least, the 1970s saw the Soviets make the grave error of trying to compete globally with a superior power—a mistake that soon proved fatal. By the 1980s, America could use insights and innovations developed at a time of relative weakness to make the most of its competitive strengths. The sharpest strategic thinking often occurs during the hard times and can set up a devastating counteroffensive once conditions improve.

Yet the military rivalry also compelled American officials to face a final reality: that the requirements of managing competition and the requirements of winning are not always the same. The nuclear age created an overarching imperative to avoid global war and foster stability—thus the logic of MAD. But the asymmetries of the Cold War required America to seek strategic instability so that it could coerce its enemy and reassure its allies. This was why U.S. officials tried to escape the implications of MAD long after McNamara had insisted it was pointless to do so. This was why leaders like Nixon who pursued arms control in public often spoke the rougher language of unilateral advantage in private. And this was why America eventually won the military contest with a strategy that built leverage by de-emphasizing near-term stability. In the nuclear age, there were no panaceas. Not even a brilliant strategy could deliver maximum safety *and* maximum advantage.

CHAPTER FOUR

Contesting the Periphery

THE HOTTEST BATTLES OF the Cold War happened in the most out-of-the-way places. Western Europe and Japan were the blue-ribbon prizes, but most movement happened in the Third World, that collection of Latin American, African, and Asian countries linked by underdevelopment and the experience of colonialism. The geopolitical fault lines here were less entrenched than in the "First World," and the internal instability was more severe. From Vietnam to Afghanistan, Guatemala to Angola, great-power policies and local politics collided, often explosively.

The Third World was also where America faced its most vexing competitive difficulties. Here, the world often seemed to be slipping away as decolonization created space for radical ideologies and Soviet influence. America seemed perpetually on the defensive, paying rising costs to stave off disaster. And here America suffered its most damaging reverses, while relying on expedients that contradicted its values. U.S. policy in the Third World has come in for withering criticism from historians; it is an aspect of the Cold War almost no one wants to relive.[1]

It won't be relived, in any exact fashion, in today's rivalries because the underlying turmoil is not nearly as pronounced. The collapse of the European empires redrew the world's political map, birthing nearly 100 countries in a quarter-century. The political, economic, and ideological changes that developing nations experienced were epochal. Whatever happens between America, China, and Russia in the future won't look precisely like what happened in the Cold War. Yet we shouldn't assume that the struggle for the Third World has nothing to teach us. After all, Washington and its authoritarian rivals are already jockeying for influence in these regions. More important, America's Cold War experience remains revealing because of the multilayered competitive dynamics it entailed.

That experience is a case study in how a country can, despite misgivings, be drawn into competition on unfavorable ground. It illustrates the difficulties of closing off near-term vulnerabilities without increasing long-term troubles. It underscores the challenges of aligning policy with morality—and the dangers of not doing so. The contest for the Third World reveals, moreover, how the same vigilance and ambition that permitted tremendous achievements in some circumstances led to trouble in others. Finally, it points to the overriding importance, in long-term competition, of pacing oneself—and of learning and recovering from mistakes. By the 1980s, America was dominating the struggle for the Third World. But reaching that point took some fortuitous global changes, and it required that America fundamentally rebuild a strategy that had led to disaster and exhaustion not long before.

Some principles of strategy seem obvious. Don't compete on the enemy's favored terrain. Don't relinquish the initiative. Don't get on the wrong side of the cost curve. By this logic, Washington should have avoided the Third World altogether.

To be sure, America's superior overall power always gave it a boost in the developing regions. Washington also enjoyed some ideological sympathy there, thanks to its political traditions and support for self-determination during World War II: Ho Chi Minh quoted Thomas Jefferson in his declaration of Vietnamese independence.[2] But by and large, the Third World was a harsh competitive landscape.

America suffered, diplomatically and ideologically, from its ever-closer association with Europe's fading imperial powers. A witch's brew of underdevelopment, surging nationalism, and political instability seemed more likely to benefit Moscow than Washington. In the Middle East, Acheson remarked, "we had a situation which might have been devised by Karl Marx himself."[3] Amid the profound change that decolonization was bringing, the sowing of disorder would be cheap and easy; the defense of a fragile global perimeter, difficult and expensive. "The Russians can defeat us," Lippmann warned, "by disorganizing states that are

already disorganized, by disuniting peoples that are torn with civil strife
and by inciting their discontent which is already very great."[4]

In the late 1940s, most U.S. officials agreed. Kennan thought it
"probably unavoidable" that many underdeveloped countries would fall
"under the influence of Moscow"; Truman largely avoided major commitments in the Third World.[5] This relaxed attitude didn't last, however,
and U.S. officials were soon fighting furiously to protect endangered positions in nations from Southeast Asia to Latin America. By 1961, Kennedy would anoint "the whole southern half of the globe" as "the great
battleground for the defense and expansion of freedom today."[6] America
had been drawn, irreversibly, onto shaky competitive ground.

The simplest reason for this was the impossibility of sealing off entire
regions from bipolar rivalry. Third World countries lacked industrial
might, but they had resources and markets the First World required.
There was, additionally, the danger—unquantifiable but unshakeable—
that U.S. setbacks in one area might demoralize allies and embolden rivals
in another. If the lesson of the 1930s had been that aggression begat aggression, the implication for Cold War policymakers was that Communist
gains anywhere could set the dominoes toppling. It is easy, but wrong, to
mock such concerns now. In 1949–1950, Mao's victory in China precipitated a mini-domino effect, encouraging North Korea's invasion of South
Korea and an intensification of Ho's Communist rebellion in Indochina.[7]

Sealing off entire regions ideologically proved difficult as well. The
Cold War was not a bloodless chess match. It was a competition for the future of humanity, an impassioned struggle between radically different
models of politics, economy, and society. If the world was, as LBJ declared,
"a vast battleground between two systems of thought and two philosophies
of society," then the choices of emerging nations—just now working out
their destinies—might determine the outcome.[8] Here, ideological imperatives collided with domestic politics. The freedom-versus-tyranny themes
that U.S. policymakers sounded in the late 1940s helped generate the
Cold War consensus. They also made it harder to maintain the nuanced
geographical distinctions that Kennan had originally sought to draw.

Additionally, because rivalry is interactive, the enemy got a say in
where the Cold War unfolded. The West's grave vulnerabilities in the
Third World gave Moscow strong incentives to probe there. The weakness
of the developing regions looked all the more inviting because America
was creating situations of strength in Europe. Stalin, at first uninterested in
the Third World, began pushing for advantage after the Chinese revolu-

tion. Khrushchev pushed even harder, declaring that decolonization would "bring imperialism to its knees."[9]

During the 1950s, Moscow used economic assistance, military sales, and other tools to woo governments or just bleed Washington. "They will give you more aid as soon as we give you aid," Khrushchev told India's foreign minister.[10] That competitive dynamic gave Third World leaders an opportunity to manipulate America by threatening to defect to the Soviet camp or warning that their governments might otherwise collapse. By decade's end, the competition was ratcheting up quickly, with Khrushchev pledging to promote the "national liberation" movements and Communist insurgencies sweeping across the global south.[11]

Finally, America was pulled into the Third World by its own irrepressible faith in itself. As difficult as the situation seemed, U.S. officials could never fully shake a quintessentially American optimism about the country's ability to use its power for constructive ends. America's success in rebuilding Europe fostered a remarkable confidence that it could transform other continents, too. The Marshall Plan, stated former diplomat Joseph Jones, showed "not the limits but the infinite possibilities of influencing ... other countries by statesmanship in Washington."[12] The strength of this attitude waxed and waned over time, but the basic idea was ingrained in the nation's psyche.

Competition in the Third World was thus unavoidable and deeply problematic. For America quickly found itself stretched along a precarious frontier where the balance of possibilities favored an opportunistic opponent. This was Washington's central dilemma in the Third World, one it would take decades to escape.

One approach to that dilemma would have been to flip America's competitive dilemma on its head. If profound change was upending a Western-oriented status quo, then perhaps the United States—itself the product of an anticolonial revolution—should align with the forces of upheaval. By supporting decolonization, Washington could make itself an ally of self-determination. By tolerating nonalignment—the idea that emerging states would balance between East and West—it could help emerging countries avoid Communist domination even as they escaped European control. "If we put ourselves sympathetically on the side of ... nationalism," said Acheson, "we have put ourselves on the side of the thing, which more than anything else can oppose communism."[13]

Truman and Ike both tried to make the strategy work. Truman proposed a program of economic and technological aid to the underdeveloped world, warning that the alternative was losing entire regions to communism.[14] Much to the annoyance of British officials, Truman and Eisenhower initially urged moderation in dealing with radical nationalists, such as Egypt's Nasser or Iran's Mohammad Mossadegh, who challenged London's quasi-imperial prerogatives. Not least, U.S. officials pushed their European allies, sometimes firmly, to quit colonial locales from Indonesia to Algeria. "The spirit of nationalism was the most powerful force in the world today," Ike averred, and a natural ally in the long struggle against Soviet hegemony.[15]

Yet playing the long game is difficult when near-term pressures are intense. For every Indonesia, where ending colonialism dampened the appeal of communism, there were two Malayas, where well-organized Communists were positioned to grab power after a colonial exit. Similarly, pushing too hard for self-determination in the Third World could break the First World: forcing France out of Indochina might fracture NATO. Funding for development was, simultaneously, whittled down by Republican opposition and the enormity of U.S. commitments in Europe. Furthermore, if nonalignment and nationalism seemed incompatible with Soviet imperialism in the long run, they might in the short run open the door to political chaos or anti-Western sentiments that Moscow or Beijing could exploit. Washington got a taste of this in 1955. When nonaligned states gathered at Bandung, China's Zhou Enlai stole the show with his bid (unsuccessful but unnerving) to swing that movement toward the Sino-Soviet bloc. Bandung "might establish firmly in Asia a tendency to follow an anti-Western and 'anti-white' course," Dulles said.[16]

If Bandung worried Eisenhower and Dulles, Nasser flummoxed them. Nasser was no communist, but he was a wildly ambitious Arab nationalist who pitted the superpowers against each other. In 1955, he secured a U.S. pledge to fund construction of his Aswan High Dam while also recognizing Mao's China and buying East-bloc arms. The ensuing fury with Nasser's "blackmail" led Eisenhower to cancel funding for the dam; Dulles hoped the project would turn into a costly, Soviet-backed fiasco.[17] But that decision merely gave Nasser a pretext to nationalize the Suez Canal, which led the British and French, in cahoots with Israel, to attack Egypt. Ike was horrified. "How could we possibly support Britain and France," he asked, "if in doing so we lose the whole Arab world?"[18] Eisenhower responded to the attack by striking his own blow for Arab nationalism, applying ruinous financial and diplomatic pressures that made Paris and London back off.

Ike's stand buoyed America's reputation with the Arabs. But not for long, because it also destroyed British and French influence in the Middle East, creating a vacuum that Moscow might fill. Eisenhower declared in response that America would do whatever was necessary, including military intervention, to stave off Communist advances, and Dulles constructed a coalition of conservative, pro-Western regimes. Predictably, this "Eisenhower Doctrine" convinced many Arabs that Washington was trying to contain Nasser and the nationalism he represented, a suspicion confirmed in 1958, when Eisenhower panicked and sent in the Marines during a political crisis in Lebanon. That intervention, Ike acknowledged, "would involve great problems," but it would be worse "to do nothing and permit Lebanon to fall."[19] All this pushed Nasser closer to the Soviet bloc; an administration that had tried to make a virtue of nationalism became its target instead.

The story was similar in South Asia. Ike worked hard to maintain respectful relations with Jawaharlal Nehru's India. U.S. aid and technology made vital contributions during the postwar decades toward helping India feed itself.[20] Yet Washington never got much diplomatic credit because fears of Soviet encroachment simultaneously led Eisenhower to seal an alliance with Pakistan. That alliance yielded benefits—namely, the ability to operate U-2 spy planes from Pakistani bases. But it also got Washington crosswise with India, the larger of the two South Asian powers and a leader of the nonaligned movement. More broadly, Ike's tendency to throw up Third World alliances, such as SEATO and CENTO, as checks on Communist expansion made America seem to be replacing colonial rule with quasi-imperial structures of its own. The "tendency to rush out and seek allies was not very sensible," Eisenhower admitted, even if there were few good alternatives.[21]

This sense of being trapped between the reality of accelerating change and the continuing imperative of anticommunism was most pronounced in Southeast Asia. By the early 1950s, U.S. support for the French war in Indochina was destroying Washington's reputation as an ally of self-determination. "We are more and more becoming colonialists in the minds of people," a young John Kennedy wrote.[22] But pulling support would lead to a Communist takeover. America had little choice, State Department officials lamented, but to "continue to pour treasure (and perhaps eventually lives) into a hopeless cause."[23] When the French

position collapsed anyway in 1954, Ike wisely avoided military intervention. Yet by decade's end, the same dilemma had ensnared him: his administration provided $1.5 billion in U.S. aid to a corrupt South
Vietnamese government under Ngo Dinh Diem.[24]

Throughout the Third World, processes of change were exploding in
radical directions, and an initially progressive American policy was becoming more reactionary. When Eisenhower concluded that Mossadegh—
whom Washington had earlier protected—was softening up Iran for a
political collapse in 1953, he approved a CIA-backed coup against him.
When Ike judged, the next year, that Jacobo Árbenz was empowering Guatemala's Communists, the CIA repeated the performance. Covert action
and paramilitary operations became tools of choice against unfriendly governments; anticommunist authoritarians became partners of first resort.
Ike's CIA tried to foster a separatist revolt in Indonesia as Sukarno became
more radical, and it plotted to kill Congolese leader Patrice Lumumba
amid postindependence chaos.[25] The president, one CIA official recalled,
saw Lumumba as "a thorough scoundrel" and wanted him "got rid of."[26]
Ike's spies didn't end up killing Lumumba, but his other enemies did.

In fairness, all of these initiatives reflected genuine fears of Soviet
breakthroughs. All represented cost-conscious approaches to containing
instability. Some even produced low-price successes: the coup against
Mossadegh secured a friendly Iran for another quarter-century. Operations in Indonesia and other countries failed, however, sometimes em-
barrassingly. They also created an unmistakable impression that
Washington had lost faith in self-determination. "The U.S. can win
wars," UN ambassador Henry Cabot Lodge remarked, "but the question
is can we win revolutions."[27]

The question was equally whether America could defend its interests
without resorting to indefensible tactics. The moral rationale for covert
intervention was that nothing could be worse than communist tyranny.
"We are facing an implacable enemy whose avowed objective is world
domination," a secret CIA report had concluded. "There are no rules in
such a game."[28] The problem was that the chosen methods blurred the
moral clarity of America's struggle and, if exposed, risked enraging the
populations whose support Washington wanted to win.

Blowback was already materializing. The coup against Árbenz incited
anti-Americanism across Latin America and convinced radicals that violent revolution was the only path to change. Two such radicals, Ernesto
"Che" Guevara and Fidel Castro, subsequently carried out such a revolu-

tion in Cuba and edged closer to the Kremlin. That move triggered another covert U.S. undertaking, the Bay of Pigs invasion, which backfired catastrophically, precipitating the Cuban Missile Crisis and a Cuban campaign to spread revolution throughout the hemisphere. Washington "will not be able to hurt us," Castro said, "if all of Latin America is in flames."[29] The United States now found itself in exactly the quandary it had sought to avoid: defending, through questionable methods, a deteriorating perimeter at a time of intensifying upheaval. In a protracted rivalry, aligning with strong historical currents makes sense. But when doing so exposes glaring vulnerabilities, the sound move may prove devilishly difficult to execute.

The Democratic policymakers of the 1960s recognized this dilemma and believed it could be overcome. Eisenhower's preoccupation with stability had bought time, they argued, but at a cost of alienating the United States from the political revolutions sweeping the globe. Escaping this trap would require using America's unmatched power to transform the competitive landscape.

The intellectual impetus for this policy was modernization theory, which featured a radical optimism about America's ability to drive constructive change. Modernization theory held that there was a single, universal path to capitalist prosperity and democratic stability. America's task was to thrust Third World countries down this path. Washington would provide capital, technology, and expertise; it would help reformist elites confront tenant farming and other quasi-feudal institutions that slowed growth and turbocharged extremism. "There is no longer any question that radical change will occur in the world, but only a question of what direction it will take," the CIA predicted.[30] If America had held back history in the 1950s, it would now accelerate history and control its course. By promoting rapid, even revolutionary change, modernization theory would also reconnect U.S. policy with America's self-image as a moral force for global liberation. "To those people in the huts and villages of half the globe struggling to break the bonds of mass misery," Kennedy declared, "we pledge our best efforts to help them help themselves, for whatever period is required."[31]

During the 1960s, modernization theory influenced the creation of institutions such as the Peace Corps and the U.S. Agency for International Development; it informed initiatives in Southeast Asia and Iran.

But the acid test came in Latin America. That region was aflame with
radicalism and Cuban-supported insurgencies; the CIA warned that "revolution or attempts at revolution are definite possibilities in twelve of the
twenty-three countries to our south."[32] To meet that danger, Kennedy
unveiled the Alliance for Progress. Over ten years, Washington would
provide $20 billion in loans, grants, and investment. Latin American gov-
ernments would generate $80 billion in public and private funds while in-
stituting land reforms, progressive tax systems, and other sociopolitical
changes. "Those who make peaceful revolution impossible will make violent revolution inevitable," Kennedy declared. Democratic progress and
sustainable prosperity were the best insurance against Soviet influence.[33]

Still, Kennedy and Johnson did not slight the sharper tools of U.S.
power. "Vitamin tablets," said Dean Rusk, "will not save a man set upon
by hoodlums in an alley."[34] It was essential to suppress violent radicalism
until social and economic reforms could work. The United States thus
invested in counterinsurgency programs and police training. Both Kennedy and Johnson also committed to using U.S. power decisively to prevent additional Communist takeovers. "How many troops could we get
into the Dominican Republic in a 12-24-36-48 hour period?" Kennedy
asked. "How many into Honduras? How many into Venezuela?"[35]

Given how disastrously things might have gone in Latin America,
the results weren't bad. In a few countries, such as Venezuela, economic
assistance and political support helped consolidate relatively stable democracies. Land redistribution and other reforms, even incomplete ones,
drained support from guerrilla movements in Peru, Bolivia, and Colom-
bia. Counterinsurgency programs battered guerrilla groups that were
weakened by factional splits and self-defeating behavior; Guevara himself was captured and killed by a U.S.-trained unit in Bolivia in 1967. By
1968, the CIA could report that "the establishments which now control
the larger Latin American countries are far stronger than any proponents
of revolutionary violence."[36]

Yet the goal of U.S. policy was not simply to halt revolution. It was
to remake the region so that Washington would not have to rely on repressive militaries and other blunt instruments. "What we are asking is
that the philosophy of Jefferson and the social reforms of FDR be tele-
scoped into a few years in Latin America," wrote Undersecretary of State
Chester Bowles.[37] That ambition went unrequited.

The obstacles to rapid development proved more formidable than
anticipated owing to glaring infrastructure gaps and low commodity

prices. At the same time, even a superpower lacked the skilled adminis-
trators and local experts required to be effective across a diverse region.
"The Alianza has the same trouble as the Washington Nats," assessed
one official. "They don't have the ballplayers."[38] And all too often, powerful Latin Americans hoarded their privileges by thwarting reform and
repressing dissent. The Alliance for Progress had channeled the Marshall
Plan ethos of working through committed local partners. Yet Latin
America, unlike Europe, proved remarkably resistant to U.S. power because Washington was seeking changes that were frequently anathema
to the elites who were meant to enact them. "Then we helped to rebuild
a shattered economy whose human and social foundation remained,"
Kennedy said. "Today we are trying to create a basic new foundation, capable of reshaping the centuries-old societies and economies of half a
hemisphere."[39]

In fact, the Alliance offered a rude lesson in unintended consequences.
Throughout the region, it increased instability, in part by intensifying the
revolution of rising expectations at work—expectations most countries
could not meet. Yet since the mere possibility of reform terrified conservatives, polarization was the result. "The hazards of governing may be increasing rather than lessening in Latin America," the CIA reported in 1964.[40]

The perverse upshot was to leave America more dependent on covert action, counterinsurgency, and military intervention. Although the
Alliance was meant to strengthen democracy, Washington ended up supporting military coups from El Salvador to Brazil. The CIA meddled in
elections from Chile to Costa Rica. In Guatemala, U.S. advisers helped
the security services wage counterinsurgency using modern surveillance
technology as well as torture and other timeless brutalities. U.S. forces
even intervened directly in Panama and the Dominican Republic in
1964–1965. "We either got the power or we haven't," said Johnson, "and
if we got it, I'm gonna use it, period."[41]

Johnson certainly had the power to stamp out a Cuban-backed insurgency or topple an unreliable government. In many cases, however,
the effect was to tie America to unjust and unsustainable domestic arrangements. Counterinsurgency was "running wild," State Department
officials wrote. In Guatemala, the government was using U.S. support
not just against Marxist insurgents but "against an alarmingly broad
range of Guatemalans."[42] If Kennedy and LBJ had sought to create the
image of a kinder, gentler America, they failed: U.S. intervention in the
Dominican Republic elicited jeers throughout the region and beyond. By

decade's end, Latin America was no closer to lasting stability. Yet America's Third World strategy was nearing a moral reckoning.

Senator Frank Church had already warned that America was supporting "so many tottering governments afflicted by decadence and despotism and frequently despised by their own people." The United States, American diplomats acknowledged, was backing tactics that "resembled those of the guerillas themselves: kidnappings, torture, and summary executions."[43] Unfortunately, Latin America wasn't the only place this was happening. In 1965, the CIA helped the Indonesian military save that country from Sukarno and a possible Communist takeover—at the mind-numbing cost of perhaps 500,000 civilian deaths.

The Alliance for Progress aimed to use America's advantages—its resources, its idealism—to defeat Third World radicalism. Yet it exacerbated internal volatility and left U.S. policymakers clinging to stability wherever they could find it. The Alliance, Richard Nixon remarked in 1969, had exposed "the illusion that we alone could remake continents."[44] In doing so, it revealed a lesson that America's war in Vietnam was teaching even more painfully: that doubling down on lofty ambitions in unfavorable terrain can lead to disaster.

U.S. officials had long feared losing the Cold War in the Third World. That almost happened, but not in the way they expected. The Vietnam War overshadowed everything else America did in the 1960s. It was meant to demonstrate Washington's will and ability to compete in the developed regions. Instead, it produced a geopolitical nightmare that cost 58,000 American lives and showed just how uncompetitive U.S. strategy had become.[45]

How did Washington become so disastrously committed in a small, out-of-the-way country? Because Vietnam brought together the insecurities and ambitions that drew America into the global south. Vietnam itself was never the issue. America's intervention reflected larger concerns about political score-settling, falling dominoes, and weakness on the periphery undermining strength at the core. "If we are driven from the field in Viet-Nam," LBJ warned, "then no nation can ever again have the same confidence in American promise, or in American protection."[46] Yet the U.S. war in Vietnam also reflected vaulting optimism in the efficacy of American power. In private, U.S. leaders expressed severe misgivings: "It's the damn worse mess that I ever saw," Senator Richard Russell told LBJ.[47]

But in public, they averred that the world's foremost superpower could defeat the Communist insurgency and transform the entire region. "The task," Johnson maintained, "is nothing less than to enrich the hopes and the existence of more than a hundred million people."[48]

The Vietnam War was also a product of American strategy in the 1960s. The emphasis Kennedy and Johnson placed on avoiding reverses anywhere increased the perceived value of commitments everywhere. Their faith in the calibrated use of American power made waging large-scale limited war—accompanied by ambitious political and economic programs—more palatable. The plan was for U.S. economic and technical aid to spur growth and win the loyalties of the South Vietnamese population; escalating pressure would squeeze the enemy without provoking Chinese or Soviet intervention. Most important, the willingness to accept higher costs in search of lower risks made it conceivable to fight a brushfire conflict that ultimately required more than 500,000 troops and bore no promise of quick success. "Let no one doubt for a moment," said LBJ, "that we have the resources and we have the will to follow this course for as long as it may take."[49] A victory in Vietnam, U.S. officials believed, would resonate globally. It would, wrote National Security Adviser McGeorge Bundy, "set a higher price for the future upon all adventures of guerilla warfare."[50]

That's not what happened. Admittedly, U.S. resistance in Vietnam probably limited Communist gains in Southeast Asia by preserving the lead domino until the others were no longer so wobbly.[51] Yet any benefits came at an astronomical price, and Washington eventually failed even to sustain an independent South Vietnam. That sorry outcome was rooted in a threefold failure: a failure to reform, a failure to coerce, and a failure to stop.

Washington's prospects for success depended on getting the Saigon government to earn the people's support. Yet the challenges were daunting because the same characteristics that made South Vietnam vulnerable to subversion—its artificial nature; its immature political institutions; its religious and socioeconomic cleavages—made good governance elusive. More challenging still, Eisenhower and Kennedy found that no amount of cajoling, and no amount of aid, could convince an autocratic Diem to embrace reforms that might jeopardize his hold on power. "We have still to find the technique," Walt Rostow wrote, "for bringing our great bargaining power to bear on leaders of client states to do things they ought to do but don't want to do."[52] The despair produced by Diem's polarizing rule caused Kennedy to back a bloody coup in 1963, which triggered political chaos ended only by the ascent of another corrupt regime. In this climate, U.S.-backed projects misfired or backfired. If anything, the influx of U.S. money and personnel destabilized the society it was meant to protect, fanning corruption and making Saigon look like a puppet of another colonial power.

America was also discovering, in Vietnam, that an asymmetry of power did not trump an asymmetry of motivation. U.S. strategy aimed to attrite the Viet Cong in the South and coerce the Communist leadership in the North, thereby finding the enemy's breaking point. The Pentagon applied firepower, mobility, and technology in devastating fashion, killing 179,000 enemy troops between 1965 and 1967 and dropping 643,000 tons of bombs on North Vietnam between 1965 and 1968. But that strategy produced mostly frustration, for several reasons: because the Soviets and the Chinese generously supported North Vietnam, because the strategy was ill suited to the guerrilla war America faced rather than the conventional war the Army had trained for, and because the enemy was willing to pay a nearly unlimited price. "The North will not count the cost," North Vietnamese general secretary Le Duan remarked.[53] This tenacity let Hanoi outlast America's will to fight a costly war for nebulous ends, and then launch a major attack, the Tet Offensive, that broke Washington's flagging commitment to a faraway struggle.

The obvious question is why Johnson had not stopped before reaching this point. That failure stemmed from bureaucratic issues, such as the military's reliance on misleading metrics—the infamous "body counts"—that gave an illusion of progress. It stemmed from disbelief that a Third World enemy could withstand American punishment forever. Above all, it showed that fear of losing in Vietnam—and the determination to overwhelm the challenge there—had produced a complete breakdown of Washington's cost-benefit calculus. "It would be worth any amount to win," Rusk said in 1964.[54] The comment exposes how much the United States had departed from its initial view of the Third World and hints at the problems that had accrued to America's strategy.

For starters, America had totally lost the initiative. That Washington had risked and lost so much in a war that its top leaders knew might be unwinnable revealed that America's rivals were dictating where and how the Third World struggle played out. Within Vietnam, the practical effect of calibrating U.S. pressure to enemy provocations was that those enemies determined the rhythm of the fight. The Nixon administration learned this lesson and engaged in escalations—bombing Hanoi, mining

Haiphong harbor, attacking sanctuaries in Laos and Cambodia—in hopes of gaining diplomatic leverage. But by this point, political support for the war was collapsing, and so was America's influence. "To be in a hurry when your opponent is not puts one in a very weak negotiating position," remarked one U.S. official.[55]

A second reason for America's failure was that it had put itself on the wrong side of a steepening cost curve. By the late 1960s, the demands of the air war and the massive U.S. presence in South Vietnam meant that America was paying $9.60 for every $1.00 of damage done to North Vietnam. This strategic profligacy might have been acceptable for a short time against a weak enemy. But it gave the Kremlin a golden opportunity to bleed *its* enemy, the United States, particularly through deliveries of anti-aircraft weaponry that took a horrific toll on American aircraft. By one estimate, from 1966 to 1971 Washington spent over $100 billion fighting the war; the Soviets spent only $5 billion shoring up North Vietnam and punishing the United States.[56] America found itself hemorrhaging lives and money in a conflict its principal adversary paid a pittance to protract.

Third, Vietnam confirmed that overreach anywhere could cause problems everywhere. The war in Southeast Asia delayed the Soviet split with China by ensuring that Sino-American differences remained prominent through the 1960s. It weakened America's ability to defend NATO and other allies. It produced a global wave of anti-Americanism. "The picture of the world's greatest superpower killing or seriously injuring 1000 non-combatants a week, while trying to pound a tiny, backward nation into submission on an issue whose merits are hotly disputed, is not a pretty one," McNamara conceded. Not least, the war consumed American energy that might have been better directed elsewhere. "While the United States is tied down in Viet Nam," Nixon noted, "the Soviets are loose in the World."[57]

Finally, America's Third World strategy had become a source of profound division at home. The war, Senator Mike Mansfield warned LBJ in 1965, was stirring "deep concern and a great deal of confusion which could explode at any time."[58] Sure enough, U.S. action in Vietnam triggered a powerful antiwar movement. But the conflict also became, in Kissinger's terms, "a national nightmare that stimulated an attack on our entire postwar foreign policy."[59] By the late 1960s, the war had fused with racial tensions and urban unrest to create severe domestic instability; it had badly undermined the country's faith in its own morality and effectiveness on the global stage.

Two decades earlier, Lippmann had warned that the Third World could become a competitive trap for America. Vietnam was where this prediction was, most tragically, born out. The conflict showed that the result of failing to pace oneself strategically—of failing to temper ambition and vigilance with prudence—was not just defeat but exhaustion and disillusion. So Vietnam raised another question that all competitors must confront: How do you recover from a calamitous mistake?

It wouldn't happen quickly. The 1970s were, in many ways, worse than the 1960s. That decade marked the high tide of Third World radicalism. Decolonization reached its climax. Frustration with slow development led Third World countries to excoriate the capitalist order. Middle Eastern countries—including two close U.S. allies, Saudi Arabia and Iran—demonstrated their economic liberation by engineering major oil price hikes that threw the West into turmoil. "We are now living in a never-never land," Kissinger said, "in which tiny, poor and weak nations can hold up for ransom some of the industrialized world."[60]

The Soviet Union, meanwhile, was shifting into overdrive. Soviet officials interpreted the collapse of South Vietnam in 1975 as evidence that America was losing its ability to suppress Third World revolutions. They saw the collapse of the Portuguese empire in Africa as evidence that new horizons were opening up for national liberation. The expansion of Soviet power-projection capabilities was simultaneously giving the Kremlin an unprecedented ability to intervene overseas.[61] The Soviets increased their military, intelligence, and advisory presence from Peru to Vietnam, and their arms deliveries to the Third World rose from $9.2 billion between 1966 and 1975 to $35.4 billion between 1978 and 1982. "The world was turning in our direction," one KGB officer recalled. Moscow was surging in the global south.[62]

New partnerships, meanwhile, were amplifying Soviet power. The willingness of Castro's Cuba to fight in Africa gave the Kremlin a committed proxy force. The Soviets and the Cubans were also exploiting the dynamism of Black liberation movements in southern Africa. The resulting alliance showed promise in 1975–1976, when a Soviet airlift of Cuban troops helped a Marxist faction defeat two U.S.- and South African-backed groups in Angola's civil war. In 1977–1978, Moscow airlifted Cuban troops, along with Soviet equipment and advisers, to help Marxist

Ethiopia defeat neighboring Somalia. "In Africa," Castro exulted, "we can inflict a severe defeat on the entire reactionary imperialist policy."[63]

As the Soviets advanced, America was paralyzed. During the 1970s, the experience of one quagmire left Congress determined to avoid another. "The perception quickly grew," longtime CIA official Robert Gates recalled, "that it would be a cold day in hell before the United States again involved itself militarily in a Third World struggle."[64] Disgust over American support for authoritarians led to legislative restrictions on foreign aid; revelations of CIA-backed coups and assassination schemes dating back to the 1950s led lawmakers to rein in that organization. This new atmosphere crystallized in 1975–1976, when Congress terminated Kissinger's covert bid to help anticommunist factions in Angola just as Castro and Brezhnev were making their move. "We are living in a nihilistic nightmare," Kissinger griped.[65] Overreach in the 1960s produced underreach in the 1970s.

The worst came in 1979. That year, the Carter administration watched impotently as revolutions in Iran and Nicaragua replaced pro-American dictators with anti-American radicals. The former revolution shattered the balance of power in the Persian Gulf; the latter presaged a decade of bloody conflict in Central America. In the Caribbean, another Marxist revolution empowered a pro-Soviet regime in Grenada. And in December, 80,000 Soviet troops invaded Afghanistan, raising fears of a Kremlin push into the Gulf. "Afghanistan is the seventh state since 1975 in which communist parties have come to power with Soviet tanks and guns, with Soviet military power and assistance," National Security Adviser Zbigniew Brzezinski wrote. If America did not stop the onslaught, its strategic position might crumble.[66] It was a fair warning. But by the time Brzezinski issued it, the United States was piecing together the more effective strategy it had been seeking for decades.

The new strategy was not the product of a single epiphany or planning exercise. It emerged gradually, amid scattered successes and many failures, during the 1970s; it would not fully cohere until the 1980s. A winning Third World strategy required learning and experimentation. It had four components.

Limiting America's strategic liability was the first. This did not mean reducing the geographic scope of U.S. involvement: Interventions in Angola and Afghanistan during the 1970s and 1980s showed that U.S. policy remained truly global. Yet it did mean decreasing the costs of those interventions in order to increase the durability of U.S. strategy. Nixon put it most directly: "We need a new policy to prevent more V. Nams."[67]

The resulting "Nixon Doctrine" held that Washington would defend its Asian allies from nuclear or conventional aggression, but those allies must primarily defend themselves against insurgency and internal threats.[68] More broadly, the administration quietly supported "regional sheriffs" that could maintain security in key areas. In South America, Nixon courted a Brazilian junta that aggressively combated leftist movements from Uruguay to Chile to Bolivia. "I wish he was running the entire continent," Nixon said of Brazilian ruler Emílio Médici.[69] In the Persian Gulf, Nixon deputized the Shah of Iran. "The Shah is a tough, mean guy," Kissinger said. "But he is our real friend."[70]

The Nixon and Ford administrations were still willing to act forcefully in the Third World. If Washington seemed impotent, Kissinger feared, there might follow a "complete collapse of the world's psychological balance of power."[71] As we have seen, Nixon threatened to use force in several Third World crises. Nixon and Ford also employed economic pressure and covert action to undermine pro-Soviet regimes, such as the Allende government in Chile.[72] Yet the guiding principle remained that America must rely primarily on quiet or indirect measures because it could not risk another consuming quagmire. "America cannot—and will not—conceive *all* the plans, design *all* the programs, execute *all* the decisions and undertake *all* the defense of the free nations of the world," the administration explained.[73]

The Nixon administration also contributed a second component of a rejuvenated strategy: retaking the initiative by creating dilemmas for the enemy rather than merely responding to its thrusts. An opportunity came in the Middle East, where the Six-Day War of 1967 had left Israel and its Arab neighbors locked in a tense standoff.

Here Kissinger aimed to split Moscow from its most important Arab client, Egypt. The gambit first involved obstructing any Arab-Israeli diplomatic settlement, to show that the Kremlin—for all the arms it provided—could not deliver the political breakthroughs Egypt required to recover its lost lands. That ploy succeeded too well, inducing Egypt's Anwar Sadat, in coordination with Syria, to launch a surprise attack. Yet the administration quickly recovered, using the October 1973 war to build diplomatic leverage. Nixon authorized a major airlift to resupply Israel, demonstrating that the Arabs could not triumph militarily. At the same time, the war—which was bloody and traumatic for Israel—showed that the Jewish state was utterly reliant on U.S. backing. "The best outcome," Kissinger explained, "would be an Israeli victory but it would come at a high price." The Israelis would then conclude that they could "ensure their security only through negotiations, not through military power," and the Arabs would realize "the only way to peace was through us."[74]

The U.S. maneuver was impressive, if cold-blooded. It led to intensive back-and-forth negotiations that separated Israeli and Arab forces, booted the Soviets to the sidelines, and opened the way for an eventual Egypt-Israeli peace deal. The chain of events was an early sign that Moscow had developed its own Third World vulnerabilities and that agile U.S. policy could make the Kremlin play defense for a change.

Unfortunately, by the mid-1970s Kissinger himself was playing defense. The reliance on regional sheriffs purchased some stability but hardly solved America's larger strategic problem—that its policies too often seemed reactionary in a revolutionary era. Relying on the Shah's Iran, for example, tied America to a regime that was living on borrowed time. Meanwhile, Kissinger's statecraft put Washington on the wrong side of another revolution, because it involved condoning, even supporting, appalling violations of human rights.

Chile was one of the foremost examples. The Nixon administration destabilized a popularly elected government under Salvador Allende, then encouraged the succeeding junta to crack down brutally. "However unpleasant they act," said Kissinger, "the government is better for us than Allende was."[75] Kissinger also protected Argentine leaders as they conducted a "dirty war" (1976–1983) that eventually claimed nearly 30,000 lives; Ford supported Indonesia's invasion of East Timor in 1975 to crush—at a long-term cost of 200,000 deaths—an independence movement with suspected communist ties.[76] Whatever the strategic merits of these tactics, they rubbed salt in the moral wounds left by Vietnam. So they produced a backlash at home, contributing to the legislative restrictions—on arms sales, covert action, military assistance—that Kissinger deplored.[77] A third contribution to Third World strategy—realigning American policy with American ideals—would have to come from the next president, Jimmy Carter.

Carter put human rights and democratic values at the forefront of U.S. policy. From Southeast Asia to Latin America, his administration prioritized several key categories of rights—"integrity of the person," "basic economic and social rights," and "civil and political liberties"—through the use of tools ranging from foreign aid to quiet diplomacy.[78] America, Carter declared, faced "a new world that calls for a new American foreign policy.[79]

Several motives were at work. Carter saw human rights policy as a way of expiating America's Cold War sins—of rejecting "that inordinate fear of communism which once led us to embrace any dictator who joined us in that fear."[80] A competitive logic also came into play. By the mid-1970s, the world was undergoing a human rights revolution. The rise of advanced communications technologies and a global network of humanitarian organizations was focusing attention on the plight of those abused by repressive regimes. At the same time, the world was on the verge of a decades-long democratic ascendancy, thanks to factors ranging from postwar economic growth to the outward radiation of liberal norms from the center of the free world.[81] "The world's population," Brzezinski observed, "is experiencing a political awakening on a scale without precedent in its history." Perhaps history was actually turning in America's direction.[82]

Promoting human rights and democracy was thus smart strategy. It would align Washington with the global desire for freedom. It would create a marked ideological contrast with the Soviet model, which preached national liberation while empowering a new class of authoritarians. It would thereby allow America to retake the ideological offensive by showing that its values, not Moscow's, represented the wave of the future. "The moral heart of our international appeal," Brzezinski wrote, was "as a country which stands for self-determination and free choice."[83]

This visionary policy proved endlessly vexing to execute. The administration was perpetually divided on how strongly to pressure authoritarian allies like South Africa and Guatemala. Charges of hypocrisy were inevitable, for Carter censured some regimes—particularly in Latin America—while excusing the abuses of others, such as China and Saudi Arabia. And whatever the long-run value of the human rights policy, in the near term it alienated important anticommunist allies just as America's grip was slipping. "Our influence has diminished," wrote JCS Chairman George Brown. "Our policies have left bad feeling in their wake."[84]

Even worse, Carter's policies stoked the revolutions in Iran and Nicaragua that made 1979 such a blighted year. In both cases, Carter saw political reform as the solution to popular unrest. In both cases, he pressured anticommunist rulers to refrain from all-out crackdowns and move toward liberalization. Unfortunately, by this point the Shah and the Somoza dynasty had so alienated their populations that modest reforms could not restore their legitimacy. Those reforms, could, however, undermine the governments—and energize their most radical challengers—by making the authoritarian rulers seem weak and forsaken by Washington.[85] "Moderation and democracy" were Carter's goals, neoconservative intellectual Jeane Kirkpatrick mocked. "Khomeini and the Ortega brothers" were the results.[86] Reform without realism could lead to catastrophe.

Yet if criticism was merited, the critics were missing something. Carter's policies reidentified the United States with universal aspirations for human dignity and combated a dangerous Cold War amorality. "The administration's stand on human rights," the CIA reported, was "heartening to many of those who feel oppressed by tyrannies of either the right or left."[87] In Ecuador, Bolivia, and the Dominican Republic, Carter used diplomatic leverage to safeguard fragile democratic governments or transitions.[88] When strong democratic forces were pushing for change, the application of U.S. power—at the right moment, in the right way—could make the difference. Most important, Washington had begun to reclaim the ideological high ground. "The growth in democracy ... should be cause for American confidence," Vice President Walter Mondale wrote. America should "help our friends ... along that road."[89]

By this point, a final aspect of U.S. strategy—punishing Soviet overextension—was taking shape. This development confirmed what the human rights and democratic revolutions had hinted: that the competitive landscape was shifting in America's favor. Decolonization was virtually complete; the wave of postcolonial radicalism was now ebbing. "Moscow's misfortune," one U.S. analyst wrote, "is that it has acquired the technological prowess for strutting on the imperialist stage just at the time the curtain is coming down."[90] Soviet ideology was also losing its allure. Socialism had now been tried in Third World countries and had produced, in Ghana, Tanzania, and Cuba, breathtaking economic disasters. Conversely, Asian countries that had embraced capitalism—Taiwan, South Korea, Singapore—were taking off.

Meanwhile, Moscow had blundered into America's earlier predicament: defending a fragile, repressive status quo. The problems began in the boom years, when U.S. failure in Vietnam and Soviet success in Angola had created a sense of boundless opportunity. "As soon as a leader in Mozambique, Angola, Ethiopia, or Somalia mentioned the word 'socialism,' " adviser Anatoly Gribkov recalled, "our leaders immediately ... decided that this particular country would become socialist."[91] Yet this attitude encouraged the Soviets to assume burdens throughout the Third

World. The burdens proved heavy indeed, because Soviet advances left the Kremlin supporting insolvent, illegitimate Marxist regimes that would soon become targets of anticommunist insurgencies. "Like an overanxious chess player," the CIA reported, "Moscow ... has exposed lines of attack to its adversary, placed advanced pawns in jeopardy and acquired positions that it must defend at high cost."[92]

The invasion of Afghanistan showed how deadly these excesses could be. Far from a strategic win, that invasion was a strategic blunder. It was triggered by the follies of the Communist regime in Afghanistan, which was destroying itself through factional infighting and efforts to communize a Muslim society. When Soviet forces intervened, they were stalemated in a nightmarish insurgency. The asymmetry of motivation they faced there was just as severe as the asymmetry America had confronted in Vietnam. "The Soviet soldier whose father fought heroically at Stalingrad does not have a cause in Afghanistan," wrote one U.S. intelligence analyst, "but his opponent is fighting a holy war."[93]

In 1979–1980, the Carter administration began exploiting this asymmetry by offering modest support for anticommunist rebels in Afghanistan and elsewhere. "Through political pressure and covert action," Brzezinski wrote, Washington must "make life as difficult as possible for the Soviets."[94] The United States would now harness the forces of national liberation; it would use committed insurgents to impose staggering costs on the enemy. The Reagan administration would soon weave these various initiatives into a comprehensive strategy.

That strategy had defensive and offensive components. When Reagan took office, he and CIA director William Casey worried that U.S. allies were near collapse from Latin America to southern Africa. Avoiding another setback was critical, and the administration first focused on preventing a Cuban-backed insurgency from toppling the government of El Salvador. "We must not let Central America become another Cuba on the mainland," Reagan said.[95] Extending an initiative begun in Carter's final days, Reagan rushed military aid to defeat a rebel "final offensive." His administration subsequently poured billions of dollars in economic and security assistance into El Salvador while pushing the notoriously repressive government to reform in hopes of weakening the insurgency ideologically. "A victory there could set an example," Reagan believed. Success in El Salvador could turn the tide.[96]

Turning the tide also meant attacking Soviet outposts. America would "do to the Soviets what they have been doing to us," NSC aide Richard Pipes said. "At a very low cost . . . we can make it very hard for them."[97] Afghanistan was the fulcrum of this emerging Reagan Doctrine, because it was where Moscow's forces were most exposed. Casey's CIA worked with Saudi Arabia, Pakistan, and other partners to support the Afghan mujahedin. U.S. assistance—including lethal Stinger missiles—would amount to $650 million annually in the late 1980s.[98] The administration also provided guns, money, and other support to anticommunist insurgents in Nicaragua, Angola, and Cambodia. The precise aim—whether defeating or simply attriting enemy forces—varied by case. What was unambiguous was the goal of relentlessly punishing an overextended rival.

The policy was aggressively interventionist. Yet the president mostly resisted calls to commit U.S. forces in the Third World. "The press would like to accuse us of getting into another Vietnam," Reagan cautioned.[99] The exceptions came in Lebanon, where Reagan deployed U.S. troops on a peacekeeping mission but withdrew them after matters turned bloody, and in Grenada, where the administration intervened to rescue U.S. citizens and depose an increasingly radical, but utterly overmatched, regime. "Now it is their dominoes that are toppling," one aide subsequently wrote.[100] That bravado concealed a belief that competing effectively in the Third World still required limiting America's exposure.

What tied these offensive and defensive programs together was the final element of Reagan's strategy: seizing command of the ideological competition. The Third World debt crisis that erupted in 1981–1982 was a near catastrophe for the global economy. It was also a golden strategic opportunity. Over nearly a decade, Washington tied the provision of new lending and, eventually, debt relief to the enactment of pro-market reforms. The debt "can and should be used as leverage," U.S. officials wrote.[101] Reagan also recommitted the United States—even more ambitiously than Carter had—to encouraging democratic practices around the world.

It wasn't this way at first. Reagan was initially so focused on strengthening America's strategic position that he took a dim view of human rights and reform. "There will be no more Irans," presidential emissary Vernon Walters declared. America would "stay by the side of our allies."[102] Sure enough, Reagan first worked on repairing relations with alienated authoritarians. When he visited Guatemala, he claimed that its murderous dictator—then presiding over a counterinsurgency that claimed perhaps

100,000 lives—was getting a "bum rap."[103] The policy was short-lived but damaging. Government-backed death squads ran rampant in Central America; human rights violations increased as America's concern decreased.[104]

As early as 1982, however, the push for democracy was gathering strength. This was partly for political reasons. As Kissinger had learned, there was no winning domestic support for U.S. policy in El Salvador and other hot spots absent a meaningful focus on human rights and democratic values. "We will never maintain wide public support for our foreign policy unless we can relate it to American ideals and to the defense of freedom," State Department officials wrote.[105] As Reagan's presidency progressed, he also accepted the multilayered logic of promoting democracy: that democratic legitimacy was the best guarantee of stability in friendly countries; that demands for democratic reform could be used as a hammer against Soviet client states; and that supporting American values was the best way to take the ideological fight to the enemy. "The U.S. must make clear to the world that democracy, not Communism, is mankind's future," one NSC report asserted.[106]

The question was more how than whether. Learning from Carter's experience, the administration refused to push friendly authoritarians to step down if there was no moderate alternative prepared to step up. Reagan, moreover, was perfectly willing to work with repressive security services to hold the radicals at bay until liberalization with stability could be achieved. When facing "the Communist dictatorship seeking to expand," he explained, Washington could not forsake "the imperfect democracy seeking to improve."[107] Crucially, the administration also saw itself as engaged in political reform, not social engineering. Reagan generally promoted democratic openings in countries where the momentum was already running in that direction, rather than remaking entrenched socioeconomic structures from the ground up.

Yet these concessions to pragmatism were part of a very aggressive approach. During the 1980s, Reagan's representatives (and Congress) pressured El Salvador to respect human rights and liberalize politically; they put the restoration of democratic values at the core of the campaign against Sandinista Nicaragua; they pushed authoritarian governments to step aside in countries as varied as South Korea, the Philippines, and Chile. In support of such initiatives the United States created the National Endowment for Democracy. Its charge was to fund the longer-term development of political parties, trade unions, and other building blocks of democracy. "If the Endowment is successful," its officials wrote, "it could help resolve one of the most difficult dilemmas facing the United States in the world—the absence of democratic alternatives to authoritarianism."[108]

Reagan, then, brought together the post-Vietnam innovations in American strategy. His administration aimed to recover the initiative and make Moscow pay for its excesses. It assertively promoted economic reform and democratic values. It turned up the pressure while avoiding draining military embroilments. This multipronged strategy had coalesced over many years. It was meant not just to hold the line but to win the fight for the Third World.

By no means did this strategy solve all the problems—strategic, moral, or political—that had plagued U.S. policy. The Reagan Doctrine involved siding with ruthless characters such as Islamic radicals in Afghanistan. "There are degrees of evil," Kirkpatrick (now Reagan's ambassador to the United Nations) explained: Washington had to back bad people to defeat worse ones.[109] U.S. policy in Central America bled the people as well as the government of Nicaragua, where the death toll during the 1980s was higher, in proportional terms, than American fatalities in the Civil War, the world wars, and the Korean and Vietnam wars combined.[110] It also carried the Reagan administration into felonious misconduct when U.S. officials circumvented a congressional ban on aid to the *contras*. Not least, the president himself was continually conflicted about how hard to push old anticommunist friends like Ferdinand Marcos, which occasionally gave a lurching quality to U.S. diplomacy. No American strategy could transcend the difficulties of operating in a fraught, unstable environment. What was possible was to make the most of the global opportunities that had emerged.

The U.S. debt strategy gradually nudged dozens of countries down the path of economic reform, not by imposing that reform but by strengthening pro-market technocrats and politicians. "The debtor nations themselves," said Treasury Secretary James Baker, "are increasingly adopting market- and growth-oriented reforms."[111] American pressure on authoritarians and American solidarity with democratic reformers advanced political openings in perhaps a dozen countries in Latin America, southern Africa, and the Asia-Pacific. America was working toward what one official called "the mirror image of the Brezhnev Doctrine"—a policy that "insures the irreversibility of democratic gains."[112] That local actors usually did most of the heavy lifting was precisely the point.

Washington could now support strong historical forces sweeping the Third World.

The strategic effects of the Reagan Doctrine were particularly pronounced. In Nicaragua, the U.S.-backed *contras* could not overthrow the Sandinistas, but they did severely strain the regime. "It apparently doesn't take much to disrupt the feeble economy and infrastructure of Nicaragua," wrote one NSC aide.[113] In Afghanistan, U.S. aid intensified the resistance and enabled the mujahedin to inflict rising and ultimately unbearable damage. Across the board, U.S. covert programs imposed heavy costs while shattering the Kremlin's sense that history was on its side. As early as 1982, Nikolai Ogarkov lamented that "there are trouble spots on every continent."[114] Gorbachev later labeled Afghanistan, where Moscow lost 15,000 lives, a "bleeding wound" for Soviet power.[115]

By the late 1980s, America had flipped the script in the Third World. Moscow, not Washington, was struggling to hold the line; America, not the Soviet Union, was dominating the cost-exchange ratio. To be sure, the Soviets weren't giving in. De-escalating the struggle for the Third World would require de-escalating the larger Cold War. Yet America had positioned itself superbly for the endgame. It was all a testament to how significantly the conditions in the Third World had changed—and to how well Washington had rebuilt its strategy after struggling terribly not so long before.

The Third World was the site of America's worst failings—moral and strategic—in the Cold War. It was also where America scored some of its most gratifying competitive successes. The very fact that the dilemmas were so painful in the Third World made it all the more noteworthy that Washington eventually fashioned a winning approach.

One insight from this experience is that competition can take a country to places it did not originally intend to visit. Few U.S. policymakers would have predicted, in 1947, that Washington would find itself obsessing over Angola or Afghanistan. Few would have welcomed a costly, open-ended struggle on a field so obviously tilted in Moscow's favor. Yet the pressures—strategic, ideological, psychological—of an intensifying superpower competition quickly gave America's Cold War a truly global character. That expansion caused the United States, not to mention the Third World, plenty of trouble. The momentum of great-power competition can make it hard for even the smartest policymakers to resist the most problematic commitments.

In such adverse circumstances, reconciling short-term and long-term imperatives becomes tricky. In an extended rivalry, any competent strategist should harness the power of nationalism and ride the major currents of the time. But when facing immense upheaval, surviving in the short term may require some desperate expedients. Why could America not "get some of the people in these down-trodden countries to like us instead of hating us?" Ike asked in March 1953—not long before backing coups in Iran and Guatemala.[116] Different administrations addressed this dilemma in different ways, but only in the late 1970s—when postcolonial radicalism burned itself out and Moscow made itself a target of Third World nationalism—did the basic dilemma ease. Until then, the American record underscored the difficulty of taking the long view when pressures are unrelenting and dangers are imminent.

America's travails point to another theme: that the same qualities that make a country effective in one place can be a source of grief in another. In general, the intense vigilance and ambition that drove America's Cold War strategy were a blessing. How else would Washington have tried something so audacious as altering the arc of history in the free world? Yet when taken to extremes, in the more challenging setting of the Third World, vigilance and ambition produced high-cost failures; they promoted an overinvestment in the periphery that undermined America's competitiveness around the globe. Winning requires tempering tendencies toward excess. That means balancing the dynamism and energy that good policy requires with the prudence that is essential to avoiding overreach and the ills that follow.

The idea of balance also pertains to the relationship between strategy and morality. International politics is an unforgiving game; a willingness to practice the dark arts can be indispensable. But a long-term strategy must be sustainable morally as well as geopolitically, and moral sustainability requires that the gap between the nation's policies and its values not become too wide for too long. This is what U.S. policymakers discovered in the 1960s and 1970s; it was this gap that Carter and Reagan sought, in varying and imperfect ways, to close. Aligning American strategy with American principles, however roughly, is not just a moral issue. It is a requirement for staying engaged and effective in the world.

The United States did ultimately succeed in the struggle for the Third World. By the 1980s, the developing regions were turning in Washington's direction, while U.S. policymakers had learned from failure and repositioned the country for success. There was nothing magical about this process, which took years and many missteps. But it was effective because American officials consciously corrected deep problems that the Vietnam War had revealed. What emerged was a fundamentally rebuilt strategy that was aggressive without being hyperactive, that made the most of ideological currents that were now flowing America's way, and that imposed asymmetrical costs on an overtaxed Soviet Union. If U.S. strategy had hit its nadir in the late 1960s and 1970s, a decade later it hit its stride. In long-term competition, mistakes are inevitable. It is the recovery that makes the difference.

CHAPTER FIVE

Taking the Fight to the Enemy

"IT HAS OFTEN BEEN alleged," said George Kennan in 1948, "that our policy ... was a purely negative policy, which precluded any forward action. ... That is entirely untrue."[1] Containment was primarily a defensive strategy, but it had an offensive component, meant to weaken the Soviet Union, fragment its alliances, and hasten the end of the Cold War. America's policy, explained Kennan, involved "holding our own world together" and "increasing the disruptive strains in the Soviet world."[2] It entailed not just contesting Kremlin positions on the global periphery but also attacking the core of the Soviet bloc.

Discussions of Cold War political warfare often call to mind Dulles and the thundering rhetoric of "liberation." Yet political warfare—efforts, short of war, to divide a rival's coalition, destabilize its political system, and drain its energies—was the norm, not the exception. Over the decades, U.S. political warfare took many forms, sometimes openly confrontational, sometimes subtly subversive. But America was almost always undermining the enemy in one way or another.

This shouldn't be surprising. Political warfare is as old as competition itself. During the Peloponnesian War, Athens and Sparta sought to widen each other's internal divisions. During the Cold War, it would have been odd had America *not* waged political warfare against the Kremlin, since the nuclear revolution made it so essential to win without violence. "There is but one sure way to avoid total war—and that is to win the cold war," Eisenhower said.[3]

That effort raised some hard questions. Was political warfare about over-throwing the enemy or just throwing the enemy off balance? Did carrots or sticks work better in dividing the opposing camp? Was it better to wage po-litical warfare aggressively and unilaterally or moderately and with allies? How far should Washington go in provoking a nuclear-armed adversary? How long should it take political warfare to work? The same questions, of course, could be asked about almost any modern political warfare campaign.

In the end, U.S. political warfare achieved a lot. Washington ex-ploited, over time, the divisions between Moscow and its allies and fanned subversive flames within the Soviet bloc. By the 1980s, U.S. pol-icy was punishing an empire that was suffering from pervasive internal rot. If long-term competition involves targeting the asymmetric vulnera-bilities of rivals, Cold War political warfare delivered results by targeting the entrenched pathologies of repulsive regimes. The U.S. record wasn't bad, all things considered. But it was freighted with failures, frustrations, and unresolved dilemmas.

If anyone embodied those dilemmas, it was Kennan, who would later dis-own political warfare despite fathering it. In 1948, as the director of the Policy Planning Staff (PPS), he advocated "inauguration of organized po-litical warfare" against Moscow. "Political warfare," he wrote, "is the logi-cal application of Clausewitz's doctrine in time of peace. In broadest definition, political warfare is the employment of all the means at a na-tion's command, short of war, to achieve its national objectives. Such oper-ations are both overt and covert. They range from such overt actions as political alliances, economic measures . . . , and 'white' propaganda to such covert operations as clandestine support of 'friendly' foreign elements, 'black' psychological warfare and even encouragement of underground re-sistance in hostile states."[4] The Cold War, Kennan believed, was not a tra-ditional military conflict. Rather, it was an epic struggle that would feature all "measures short of war."[5]

Political warfare could be defensive in nature: It might involve sup-porting friendly governments under pressure, as Washington did by co-vertly aiding noncommunist forces in France and Italy. Yet there was also a more aggressive side, where actions could be taken to create breaks and exploit tensions within the enemy camp. The Soviets were masters of subversion, after all. To refrain from fighting back would have meant unilateral disarmament against a treacherous foe.

Restraint would also have meant passing up a major strategic opportunity. In the late 1940s, Soviet power in Eastern Europe was not yet secure. Political and even paramilitary resistance lingered in some countries. U.S. officials also believed that the Soviet regime was brittle, because its citizens were disillusioned with a system that had produced such misery and repression. Perhaps the iron strength of Soviet rule represented its greatest weakness, in the sense that the Kremlin's domineering tendencies would alienate the subjects it controlled. "The Soviet position," CIA analysts concluded, was "vulnerable to psychological warfare aimed at exploiting . . . deep-rooted resentments."[6]

These strategic calculations dovetailed with political and moral concerns. As the Cold War began, U.S. policymakers had little desire to be seen as simply accepting Soviet domination of Eastern Europe. There was also genuine moral revulsion at the tyranny Moscow imposed during the late 1940s, as well as guilt that Washington had tacitly blessed the current division of Europe at the end of World War II. America could not "stand idly by . . . while individual rights and free institutions . . . are destroyed and people reduced to enslaved condition," diplomat Foy Kohler argued.[7] Both motives would become more pronounced in the 1950s, when the Eisenhower campaign used the appeal of "liberation" to court voters of Eastern European descent and condemned containment for leaving "countless human beings to a despotism and godless terrorism."[8]

But even before that, Truman used political warfare as part of a low-cost offense to bolster a desperate defense. NSC-20/4, approved in 1948, called for placing "maximum strain on the Soviet structure of power and . . . the relationships between Moscow and the satellite countries."[9] After the Korean War began, the administration intensified these activities to exert comprehensive pressure on the enemy. The United States, NSC-68 declared, must take "dynamic steps to reduce the power and influence of the Kremlin inside the Soviet Union and other areas under its control."[10]

There were limits. It would be "very dangerous" to seek the outright overthrow of the Soviet government, Kennan acknowledged. Moscow might even "resort to violence" rather than lose Eastern Europe.[11] Partially as a result, there were ambiguities about just how aggressively to wage political warfare and to what end. Different policymakers and policy papers proposed different objectives, from simply taxing Moscow's resources to actively rolling back Communist rule. The distance between these objectives would loom large in assessing how effective America's campaign had been.

That campaign was ambitious and wide-ranging. It included hard, coercive measures as well as softer subversion. At the aggressive end were efforts to foment violent resistance. After World War II, anticommunist partisans still operated from the Balkans to the Baltic. Over the next half-decade, the U.S. and British governments parachuted anticommunist émigrés into Eastern Europe to join the resistance or incite violence themselves. These operations focused on states, such as Albania, that were geographically accessible and not occupied by Soviet troops, but they targeted nearly every Eastern bloc country and even Ukraine.[12] Unrest in Eastern Europe, the CIA reported, represented "the first major battle to be won or lost in the 'Cold War.' "[13]

Washington simultaneously promoted schisms between Eastern European regimes and Moscow. Those relationships, Kennan believed, were unstable because Soviet imperialism required perpetually subordinating Eastern European nationalism. Through clever diplomacy, America might "foster a heretical drifting away process" and encourage even Communists to assert greater independence.[14] Here Marshall Plan aid—which Kennan insisted on offering to the Soviet bloc—had a nefarious intent. If the Soviets let the satellites participate, those countries would have to open themselves to Western influence. If Moscow refused, it would destroy its moral standing among Eastern Europeans by revealing itself to be callously insensitive to their needs. Over time, moreover, the success of the Marshall Plan would reveal the failure of communism in the Soviet bloc. As Western Europe flourished, Kennan wrote, "the communist regime in eastern Europe . . . would never be able to stand the comparison."[15]

By offering aid to Moscow, the Marshall Plan required taking political risks at home. So did another form of political warfare: backing independent-minded Eastern European regimes. In 1948, the Tito-Stalin split exposed the first rupture in the Communist world. Truman deplored Tito's brutality—"I am told that Tito murdered more than four hundred thousand of the opposition"—but valued his apostasy.[16] Consequently, just as Truman was building a Cold War consensus by stressing the stark divide between democracy and authoritarianism, his administration provided economic aid—$336 million between 1950 and 1953— and military assistance to Tito's regime. Washington even made known that it would oppose a Soviet military assault on Yugoslavia. By sustaining Tito's defiance, America might encourage others to emulate his example. "The possibility of defection from Moscow, which has heretofore been unthinkable for foreign communist leaders, will from now on be present . . . in the mind of every one of them," Kennan wrote.[17]

The prospects for dramatic change in the bloc were still limited by the shadow of the Red Army. So Washington used economic coercion to gradually intensify the strains. U.S. exports to the bloc essentially ceased between 1947 and 1950, and American officials pressured Western Europe to follow suit.[18] A Western embargo would deny Moscow goods needed to improve its military power. It would also force the satellite states to seek key commodities from the Soviet Union—commodities Moscow could not provide. That failure, U.S. diplomats wrote, would show the Eastern Europeans "that the Soviets are unable, or unwilling, to contribute to their economic well-being."[19]

Then there was the psychological offensive featuring Radio Free Europe (RFE) and Radio Liberty (RL). Frank Wisner, a key player in U.S. political warfare, wrote that the "Cold War radios" were meant "to prevent, or at least to hinder," the subjugation of captive peoples.[20] Broadcasts emphasized Soviet economic exploitation and political domination; they called particular bloc officials to account for their abuses. In one episode, RFE sought to inflame Polish nationalism by utilizing a high-ranking defector, Józef Światło, to reveal "secret police torture, rigged elections, and, especially, the mechanisms through which Soviet officials controlled Polish life." In other psychological operations, balloons dropped anticommunist literature, such as *Animal Farm*. Such methods would not "quickly bring the walls of the dictatorships tumbling down like those of Jericho," a CIA official wrote. But they might demoralize the ruling regimes while emboldening the people the regimes repressed.[21]

All these efforts required building a sprawling bureaucracy. The CIA rapidly enlarged its covert apparatus; the military, State Department, Economic Cooperation Administration, and Commerce Department developed their own capabilities. To provide greater coherence, Truman created the Office of Policy Coordination (OPC), charged with guiding and executing "any covert activities related to: propaganda; economic warfare; preventive direct action, including sabotage, anti-sabotage, demolition, and evacuation measures; subversion against hostile states ... and support of indigenous anti-Communist elements in threatened countries of the world."[22] Wisner aggressively built OPC, which grew in personnel, from 302 to 2,812, and funding, from $4.7 million to $82 million, between 1949 and 1952.[23] America now had a globally capable political warfare apparatus.

The earliest days of containment also represented the high tide of rollback. The Truman administration was seeking to provoke eruptions in the Soviet camp while keeping dissent simmering. That policy reflected a fierce urgency to avoid losing the Cold War as well as a hope that America might quickly win it. "Soviet ideas and practices run counter to the best and potentially the strongest instincts of men," NSC-68 stated. If pressured, the Soviet system "might prove to be fatally weak."[24]

It didn't work out that way, at first. If the goal of U.S. policy was to bring the empire crashing down, the results were disappointing. U.S.- and British-backed paramilitary operations flopped, done in by the ruthlessness of Communist authorities, the dearth of reliable assets behind the Iron Curtain, and Soviet spies within the Western intelligence community.[25] Nor did Titoism catch fire. Stalin's ferocious purges of suspected Titoist elements prevented further defections. The lesson was simple but important: not even aggressive action could break Soviet control of Eastern Europe so long as Moscow had the ability—and will—to brutally stamp out perceived threats.

Meanwhile, political warfare was straining America's alliances. U.S. economic pressure caused discord with the Western Europeans, who had far more extensive trade relationships with Eastern Europe than Washington did and needed all the export markets their fragile economies could get. Truman considered using sanctions to compel the allies to cut ties with the Soviet camp. But he concluded that America "must enlist the cooperation and support of other nations" and accepted a compromise that limited strategic exports to the bloc.[26] Just as this controversy faded, British officials grew alarmed that U.S. covert operations in Eastern Europe might cause a disastrous military escalation amid the high global tensions caused by the Korean War. It was necessary to "deflect the Americans from unwise and dangerous courses," the British Foreign Office commented. Even U.S. officials were having second thoughts. Covert operations were "inadequate and ineffective against the Soviet political system," wrote Wisner's deputy.[27] Political warfare could not slay the totalitarian dragon.

Bureaucratic mayhem added to the frustration. By rapidly expanding its writ, OPC became a rival to the CIA's covert operations directorate. The infighting soon became unmanageable. In response, Truman merged OPC with CIA clandestine services and created the Psychological Strategy Board as "the nerve-center for strategic psychological operations."[28] Yet departments and agencies still worked at cross-purposes. Once, the CIA even sought to overthrow Tito while the rest of Washington was trying to sustain him.[29] Political warfare was a new discipline for America, and it showed.

As a result, historians have used phrases like "tragic comedy of errors" to describe this period.[30] But that judgment is too harsh, because it sets the bar for success too high. If we measure U.S. policy not by its near-term failure to roll back the Iron Curtain but by its success in exploiting scarce opportunities and exacerbating long-term frictions, the record looks more creditable.

Although the Marshall Plan represented an unconventional form of political warfare, it succeeded brilliantly. The Soviets considered participating, but then declined—forcing the satellites to follow—after realizing the economic openness required. That turnabout deprived Eastern Europe of desperately needed reconstruction money while underscoring the cynical nature of Soviet hegemony. "I went to Moscow as a Foreign Minister of an independent sovereign state; I returned as a lackey of the Soviet Government," said Czech foreign minister Jan Masaryk.[31] The Russians were "smoked out in their relations with satellite countries," Kennan gloated. "Maximum strain placed on those relations."[32]

Similarly, even if efforts to spread Titoism failed, preserving Titoism where it existed was a triumph. To be sure, Tito's survival despite assassination attempts and military intimidation was mostly due to his own cunning. Yet U.S. assistance offset Yugoslavia's isolation. Tito had become "confident of Western determination to maintain him as a continuous irritant to the Kremlin," the CIA reported.[33] U.S. diplomatic support may also have discouraged Stalin from using the more drastic measures he periodically considered.[34] Truman helped Tito prove that Communists everywhere need not obey Moscow, a performance Mao would later emulate.

U.S. psychological operations also had an impact. Evidence from defectors soon confirmed that there was a thirst for outside information. RFE broadcasts, aimed at Eastern Europe, were "widely heard, particularly in . . . Czechoslovakia, Hungary, and Poland"; RL broadcasts, aimed at the Soviet Union, had an audience in military and other key groups.[35] In some cases, specific psychological initiatives shook bloc regimes. The Światło revelations, for example, forced resignations by members of the Polish secret police. More broadly, the radios and the balloon-delivered leaflets deprived totalitarian regimes of their information monopoly and gave their abuses a wider airing. Czech officials angrily protested the practice of denouncing particular officials as "this scandalous method, which incites to murder"; the Soviets started jamming the broadcasts, at considerable expense.[36] Given how little the CIA spent on these activities within Eastern Europe and the Soviet Union—$11 million in 1953—it seems fair to conclude, as in one assessment, that broadcasting was "one of our best available weapons in the cold war."[37]

Even failures had ironic effects. Stalin and his lieutenants took paramilitary operations in Eastern Europe seriously, in part because the CIA spread disinformation making the resistance look more formidable than it was. In response, Stalin cracked down on dissidents of all types, undertaking crippling purges of Eastern European regimes.[38] By doing so, Stalin crushed any perceived disloyalty, but he also crushed the prospect of ruling Eastern Europe through anything but fear. This dynamic would make the region a fount of continual insecurity for Moscow. Eliciting harsher repression could, paradoxically, be a form of success.

At relatively modest cost, then, U.S. policy weaponized the failings of bloc regimes, intensified strains between Moscow and the satellites, and encouraged the latent dissidence that would periodically flare into something greater. Given that the West would win the Cold War because the Soviets never extinguished this dissidence, America's achievement was no mean feat.

Yet the Truman years also raised nagging questions. Was America committed to rolling back Soviet power or just harassing Moscow? How far should Washington go in stimulating revolts that might end in tragedy? How could America destabilize the enemy while stabilizing the Cold War? The emphasis on political warfare was "cruel and misleading," Charles Bohlen argued, because it implied there was "a cheap and easy way of dealing with the menace of the Soviet bloc." America must decide, he wrote at another point, whether to seek "the overthrow of the Kremlin regime" or "even a temporary *modus vivendi*."[39] Truman never resolved these issues. They hit Eisenhower head-on.

The Eisenhower era should have been springtime for subversion. During the 1952 campaign, Republicans had (misleadingly) condemned Truman's "defensive policy of 'containment' " and (vaguely) promised to liberate Eastern Europe. Under the New Look, Dulles and Eisenhower were looking for more initiative at less cost, and they believed, as Dulles said, that the empire could be "burst asunder from inner strains."[40] When Stalin's death rocked the Kremlin in March 1953, the time seemed right for an all-out attack.

Yet that offensive never materialized. Prospects for covert action were limited by all the problems inherited from Truman, including the difficulty of infiltration and the paucity of reliable assets and intelligence. The bigger challenge involved the changing nature of the Cold War. As the Soviet nuclear arsenal grew, Ike wondered "how much we should poke at the animal through the bars of the cage."[41] Britain's Winston Churchill and other allies—who would bear the brunt of any conflict—favored a turn to diplomacy and détente. The tradeoff between political warfare and alliance solidarity reasserted itself. Policies meant to "split the Soviet bloc," said Dulles, might "cause the disintegration of the free world."[42]

A surprisingly moderate policy resulted. Following Stalin's death, Ike launched a peace offensive, meant to reassure the allies and claim the moral high ground, rather than a political warfare blitz. Caution also prevailed after East Germany erupted spontaneously in mid-1953. The Psychological Strategy Board called for action: "Popular resentment in all the European Satellites is near the boiling point."[43] Eisenhower worried, however, that arming the rebels might be "just inviting a slaughter of these people."[44] U.S. radio broadcasts did fuel the protests by denying the Soviets an information blackout. "You could start the ball rolling," one official recalled, simply by spreading news of the resistance. Yet Washington did not interfere when Moscow violently suppressed the unrest.[45]

This restraint caused acute frustration within an administration that had boldly promised liberation. But Ike realized there were limits to how far America could go in testing a nuclear-armed enemy. NSC-162/2, Eisenhower's guiding strategy document, stated that "the detachment of any major European satellites from the Soviet bloc does not now appear feasible except by Soviet acquiescence or war."[46] America had to find a middle ground, creating problems for Moscow without provoking doomed revolts or deadly conflict. The guidance the CIA received, Wisner wrote, was to "keep the pot simmering—but to avoid boiling it over."[47]

Accordingly, Ike increased funding for RFE and RL, and when Khrushchev caused an earthquake in the Communist world by denouncing Stalin in a private speech in 1956, the CIA intensified the aftershocks by seeing that its text was well distributed within the bloc.[48] Overall, however, the administration gradually deemphasized paramilitary operations while shifting toward increased diplomatic engagement. In 1955, the Western powers met Soviet leaders at Geneva, in a meeting that led to the diplomatic neutralization of Austria and made it harder to ostracize the Kremlin. CIA director Allen Dulles remarked: "The very acceptance of the conference was a step toward recognition of the Soviet Union's equality."[49]

To be sure, Ike was not abandoning political warfare. Rather, he was refining it in response to changing Cold War realities. The neutralization of Austria was rollback-lite because it secured the withdrawal of Soviet forces from a small part of the bloc. Along the same lines, Eisenhower sent humanitarian assistance after natural disasters in several bloc countries to remind the populations of the inadequacy of their own governments.[50] As the Cold War became normalized, America would subtly impose accumulating costs on the enemy. "We must know in our hearts that Communism contains the seeds of its own destruction," John Foster Dulles explained. "External pressures hasten the destructive process."[51]

This was a responsible strategy for a long rivalry. The problem was that it created a yawning gap between the administration's early rhetoric and its later policies. Even insiders were confused. When Ike informed UN ambassador Henry Cabot Lodge that Washington was "against violent rebellion," he was "amazed" to find that Lodge "was in ignorance of this fact."[52] The disjunction left Ike facing a dilemma: U.S. policy depended on encouraging instability, but America would not intervene should resistance ignite.

The administration understood this dilemma. Some officials argued, cynically, that violent repression in Eastern Europe was a good thing because it imposed high moral and ideological costs on Moscow. "You can't make an omelet," said Allen Dulles, "without breaking eggs."[53] Others argued that encouraging hopeless dreams of liberation was morally indefensible. "Heads would roll" if America were to "fan the flames of discontent," adviser C. D. Jackson pointed out at one meeting. "The heads would be those of our friends," Eisenhower responded.[54] For years, the administration chose not to choose, avoiding calls for violence while stoking discontent.[55] The upheavals of 1956 made the issue impossible to finesse.

The epicenters were Poland and Hungary; the trigger was Khrushchev's de-Stalinization speech. That speech, which Dulles termed "the most damning indictment of despotism ever made by a despot," unleashed pent-up anger across the bloc.[56] In Poland, it caused a shake-up within the regime and the rise of "reform communism." In Hungary, the fall of 1956 saw a popular uprising against the regime, then Hungary's attempted exit from the Warsaw Pact, then Soviet intervention that brought the country to heel.

Because massive bloodshed was averted in Poland, Ike could respond with a moderate policy. His administration supported the emergence of Władysław Gomułka's modestly reformist regime, and Dulles publicly renounced any intention to wrest Poland from the Warsaw Pact.[57] In Hungary, the tragic outcome made the contradictions of U.S. strategy impossible to evade.

Moscow responded with force in Hungary because Communist rule and Soviet dominance were seriously endangered. And despite anguished pleas from Wisner, Eisenhower declined to intervene militarily, send CIA-trained paramilitaries into combat, or arm the rebels. The cruel truth was that Washington was not willing to pursue rollback to the point of a showdown with the Soviets. "In view of the serious deterioration of their position in the satellites," Eisenhower asked, "might not they be tempted to resort to very extreme measures and even to precipitate global war?"[58] The administration kept a propaganda spotlight on the crisis to maximize the reputational damage Moscow suffered. Footage of Soviet tanks killing Hungarians, Ike said, should "immediately be disseminated through our Embassies all over the world."[59] Yet the president otherwise stood aside as the Soviets made the streets of Budapest run red with blood.

This outcome was even more wrenching because America had fostered the upheaval in Hungary, first by disseminating Khrushchev's de-Stalinization speech and then by rebroadcasting rebel appeals to revolt. Due more to lax supervision than to deliberate policy, RFE made other incendiary broadcasts of its own. Those broadcasts "implied that foreign aid would be forthcoming"; they recommended sabotaging railroads and telephone lines.[60] All this made the situation more difficult for Moscow. It also produced deep feelings of betrayal among the rebels. "Where the hell's your help, West?" one asked. "Are we supposed to beat the Russians all by ourselves?"[61] Indeed, the perception that America had stirred up and then abandoned a captive people had lasting repercussions. CIA-trained émigré forces were disbanded and talk of liberation faded. The era of sharp political warfare aimed at subverting Soviet dominance in Eastern Europe was, for the moment, over.

On the plus side, the events of that era had confirmed America's ability to exacerbate tensions within the Eastern bloc and thus confront the Soviets with a costly choice between intervening and losing control. Yet those events also showed the limits and moral costs of destabilizing the enemy, as well as the tensions between prosecuting and stabilizing the Cold War. After Hungary, the difficulties loomed larger and U.S. officials were losing faith in the idea of shortening the Cold War by attacking the Soviet empire at its core. So the focus of political warfare now shifted elsewhere.

Elsewhere was the Sino-Soviet relationship. That alliance was a singularly imposing geopolitical fact—and a singularly attractive target for political warfare. The Sino-Soviet axis united the world's leading Communist regime with the world's most populous country; it created a Red bloc spanning Eurasia. If Washington could split Moscow and Beijing, however, it would create a balance of power within the Communist world, which would weaken the Kremlin's ability to cause trouble beyond its borders. It would also demonstrate that communism was so repulsive that not even communists could stand each other. The effort to divide China and the Soviet Union would take a quarter-century, requiring remarkable patience and exquisite opportunism. It ultimately showed that pushing opponents together may be prelude to pulling them apart.

The effort began even before Mao took power in 1949. When the Chinese civil war ended, U.S. officials doubted that Moscow and Beijing would easily get along. China was not some vassal state occupied by Soviet troops. It had a proud civilization and was led by a man with sterling revolutionary credentials. The Chinese would surely bridle at the obeisance Stalin demanded; the divisive power of nationalism would surely overcome the ideological glue of communism. The trick was to hasten the division by ditching Chiang Kai-shek, now seeking refuge in Taiwan, and by pursuing a sophisticated policy toward Mao. The idea was for the United States to resist Chinese aggression while offering trade and other benefits should Mao remain outside Stalin's orbit. America didn't mind "if the devil himself runs China," Acheson said, so long as "he is an independent devil."[62]

This "wedge strategy," unfortunately, rested on two false premises. First, Mao was no Tito, at least at first. He saw Stalin's support as a badge of ideological authenticity and wanted Soviet backing against the hostility he expected (wrongly, but not unreasonably) from the world's leading capitalist power. Second, Truman never crafted a nuanced policy. Mostly for political reasons, the administration couldn't break free of Chiang. Mostly for ideological reasons, Truman and Acheson couldn't fully suppress their hatred for Mao's vicious regime. By 1950, the rise of McCarthyism made even talk of Sino-American détente toxic. The result was a mess—tentative outreach to Beijing, continued support for Chiang, abortive efforts to incite anticommunist resistance within China—that helped solidify the emerging Sino-Soviet alliance.[63] By February 1950, Mao had a defense pact with Stalin. By November, America and China were at war.

Yet this deepening confrontation gave birth to a new scheme for splitting the Communist giants. Part of the plan was to wait. Dulles believed that Mao—"an outstanding Communist leader in his own right"—

would not forever play second fiddle to the second-raters who succeeded Stalin. America could hasten the divorce by—paradoxically—forcing those countries into a closer embrace. "The best hope for intensifying the strain ... would be to keep the Chinese under maximum pressure," Dulles explained. That "would compel them to make more demands on the USSR which the latter would be unable to meet."[64]

Eisenhower followed this policy faithfully. His administration slapped Beijing with trade restrictions more stringent than those placed on Moscow. The CIA ran covert operations in China and Chinese-controlled Tibet. More forcefully still, Ike threatened nuclear war if Mao pushed too hard in the Taiwan Strait. All of these policies had multiple aims, but all were geared toward making Beijing more dependent on Moscow and thereby making Moscow resent Beijing. "I have a feeling that the Chinese Communists are acting on their own on this and that is considerably disturbing to the Russians," Ike said during the 1954–1955 crisis.[65]

Even so, progress was slow in coming. America might have to "play this thing for 25 years," Dulles said. "Could we afford to wait that long for a split?"[66] It was a reasonable question, given the costs. The pressure strategy required opposing Japan and NATO allies who wanted increased trade with China. It forced Washington to endure dangerous confrontations. The entire strategy, moreover, rested on a thesis that was counterintuitive and, for the moment, unprovable. Although Mao and Khrushchev might fall out, Dulles admitted, there was "no early prospect of a division there which would be helpful to the West."[67]

Yet Ike's strategy was politically astute: He sought to split hostile regimes in a way that could never be described as soft on communism. And his policy was based on a sound reading of how America could leverage its strengths. Washington could never match Soviet aid—economic support, a defense pact, assistance in building an atomic bomb. A "competition with Russia as to who would treat China best," said Dulles, would "put China in the best of both worlds."[68] What America could do was expose deep-seated tensions by pushing China to demand more than Moscow could give.

Ike was right about the Taiwan crises: Khrushchev was alarmed by Mao's recklessness, while Mao was outraged by Khrushchev's late and reluctant support. Likewise, the U.S. embargo influenced China's rising requests for assistance, which troubled Kremlin officials, given the enormity of Beijing's needs. Yet when Khrushchev offered more aid in return for closer integration, Mao accused the Soviets of trying to control China.[69]

Years earlier, U.S. analysts had predicted that Chinese independence would eventually lead Moscow to seek "greater disciplinary control over the Chinese Communists," which would leave the alliance "critically endangered."[70] Exactly this was happening by the late 1950s.

To be sure, the Sino-Soviet split mostly flowed from factors beyond U.S. control. Mao saw de-Stalinization and Khrushchev's periodic bids for détente as evidence that Moscow was going soft. The fundamentals of geopolitics and ideology also worked against the alliance. How could two huge, ambitious neighbors, who were part of a movement that could have only one leader, forever coexist? This, however, was just the point. U.S. leaders understood that tectonic forces would eventually drive Moscow and Beijing apart, and used their influence to magnify those forces. That they did so by indirection made the achievement all the more impressive.

Yet fully exploiting the split would require replacing the Sino-Soviet alliance with a Sino-American entente, which would take another decade. In America, the scars of McCarthyism remained raw through the 1960s. In China, the Cultural Revolution produced both external aggression and diplomatic paralysis. Moreover, if Sino-Soviet relations were collapsing, Sino-American relations were venomous. Beijing was waging an anti-imperialist crusade in Asia and beyond; America was fighting a war in Vietnam to contain Chinese expansion. Kennedy considered Mao's China the epitome of a rogue state and worried that its acquisition of nuclear weapons "would so upset the world political scene it would be intolerable."[71]

By the late 1960s, however, the stars were aligning. The madness of the Cultural Revolution was easing, and America elected a president whose former militancy gave him great political flexibility. Only the "original anti-Communist" could make peace with the "original Communist," Nixon quipped.[72] Meanwhile, the fact that America had effectively lost in Vietnam made U.S. policy less threatening to China, while Soviet behavior was becoming more menacing. By early 1969, skirmishes along the Ussuri River had brought Moscow and Beijing to the brink of war. "The Soviet revisionists" now posed "a more serious threat to our security than the U.S. imperialists," Mao's advisers wrote.[73] In August, a Soviet diplomat secretly inquired "what the U.S. would do if the Soviet Union attacked and destroyed China's nuclear installations."[74]

The Nixon administration replied by discouraging a Soviet strike, thereby supporting the more radical of its enemies against the less radical one.[75] Nixon then initiated a secret opening to Beijing, meant, among other things, to complete the work of fragmenting the Communist world by making America the arbiter of its conflicts. Washington, said Nixon, should "tilt towards the weaker" enemy to balance the stronger.[76]

The logic of rapprochement was easy, but transcending a generation of estrangement was hard. Nixon and Kissinger had to overcome entrenched opposition from State Department officials—which they did by cutting them out of the process. They had to contend with the political scorn that an opening to Beijing would invite from conservatives. Given the paucity of existing channels to Beijing, the administration also had to seek dialogue via a motley crew of third parties: France, Romania, and especially Pakistan.[77]

This issue of go-betweens touched on a larger challenge: the troubling moral choices involved in courting China. Reestablishing relations with Mao meant betraying Chiang, one of America's most vulnerable allies. "It's a tragedy that it has to happen to Chiang at the end of his life but we have to be cold about it," Kissinger said.[78] It also meant condoning appalling behavior by intermediaries. This, Nixon did in 1971, by backing Yahya Khan's Pakistani government as it pursued quasi-genocidal policies against its Bengali population and launched a disastrous war against India. "One doesn't burn down a bridge which has proved useful," Nixon said.[79] Dividing the Communist world required cutting deals with the devil.

With two devils, really, because Khan's sins were nothing compared to Mao's. The Chinese leader was a mass murderer whose body count surpassed Stalin's; he was a committed Communist who opposed nearly everything America stood for. The Chinese were "hard realists who calculate they need us," wrote Kissinger, but also "tough ideologues who totally disagree with us on where the world is going."[80] The China gambit required holding hands with evil to avoid the greater evil of Soviet ascendancy. It was impossible to wage political warfare while remaining morally pure.

The Nixon administration had to confront these issues just to get to the summit with China, in the form of dramatic trips by Kissinger and Nixon to China in 1971–1972. Yet this breakthrough led to another challenge: building a stable relationship with a regime that had so recently been a sworn enemy. America, Kissinger explained, had to move quickly. To deter Moscow from smashing China, it needed to "make plausible the notion that an attack directed against China could be an attack on the fundamental interests of the United States."[81] Yet that proposition seemed tenuous because U.S.-Chinese ties were minimal. So the administration focused the relationship on intangibles, namely the development of a common strategic worldview.

This is why Nixon and Kissinger shared sensitive intelligence on Soviet troop dispositions in the Far East, and why they pushed for meetings with Mao and Zhou Enlai even when those meetings seemingly produced little of substance. "The Sino-American dialogue concentrated on strategy," Kissinger wrote, because "we had nothing else to talk about in those early days."[82] The going was rocky. Mao and his aides doubted America's intentions as well as its staying power.[83] But over two or three years, the Sino-American dialogue cemented a shared commitment to opposing Soviet hegemony and a tacit agreement to sideline disputes over Taiwan and other issues. "They're our best NATO ally!" Kissinger exclaimed.[84]

The China gambit transformed the Cold War's geometry. America, the Soviet ambassador in Washington, Anatoly Dobrynin, reported, was "building a new strategic alignment of forces in international politics": Moscow now had to contain adversaries that were cooperating to contain it.[85] The opening had even greater ideological impact. The Sino-American relationship exposed Mao's successor, Deng Xiaoping, to the potential of market-oriented reform.[86] It also opened the floodgates to trade and technology that helped that reform succeed. China's turn to the market would soon underscore, to the world and the Soviets themselves, how outmoded the command economy had become. By the late 1980s, Reagan was hailing—in Moscow—China's reforms as evidence that "the power of economic freedom" was "spreading around the world."[87] America was helping one Communist power destroy the ideological appeal of another. Political warfare doesn't get any better than this.

If the Sino-American rapprochement exacted a high price in friends abandoned and moral compromises made, that price was worth paying. The long process of encouraging and then exploiting the Sino-Soviet split showed that determined, patient pressure could open the door for bold, opportunistic engagement—just as events in Europe were showing that the reverse was also true.

On the surface, America gave up subverting Moscow's European empire during the 1960s and 1970s. Washington hardly encouraged the Prague Spring in 1968; it hardly protested when Brezhnev crushed that movement and asserted Moscow's right to suppress challenges to socialism anywhere. By the mid-1970s, the United States had formally acknowledged the post–World War II division of Europe; it appeared to be affirming Yalta rather than undermining it. Yet in reality, the Soviet bloc was being softened up for a renewed onslaught—and a flawed strategy of engagement was doing the softening.

The move toward engagement was partially a concession to reality—the reality that NATO was afraid to aggressively challenge the Communist bloc and that the allies were now clamoring for an expansion of East-West trade. The move toward engagement also marked a philosophical shift. Early American political warfare had generally featured pressures meant to exacerbate weaknesses. Yet many NATO allies had long believed that poisoned carrots were more potent weapons than sharpened sticks. Communist regimes thrived in autarkic darkness, the thinking went, but could not withstand the sunlight of integration. "Economic warfare is as out of date as the Zeppelin," said the head of Britain's Board of Trade in 1962. Commerce could strengthen pro-Western tendencies and infiltrate subversive ideas.[88]

America tentatively tried subversion-cum-engagement during the 1960s, yet the Europeans were calling the pace. De Gaulle challenged the "policy of blocs" by forging stronger ties with Moscow. Bonn's *Ostpolitik* strategy reduced tensions with East Germany, the Soviets, and the bloc as a whole in hopes of increasing openness and interchange and perhaps easing the strains that made the Iron Curtain necessary.[89]

Nixon and Kissinger never liked *Ostpolitik* because they worried that Bonn might prioritize accommodation with Moscow over alliance with Washington. Yet the Nixon administration's theory of change in the Soviet bloc wasn't much different from Brandt's. Nixon and Kissinger always prioritized state-to-state relations, in part because they believed that reform in Eastern Europe would come only in a climate of superpower détente. By alleviating the fears that impelled Moscow to dominate Eastern Europe, the West could induce the Soviets to permit increased liberalization and autonomy—"Finlandization" in the East—over time. The idea, said State Department counselor Helmut Sonnenfeldt, was to make "the relationship between the Eastern Europeans and the Soviet Union an organic one," not one characterized by upheaval and repression.[90]

The administration applied the same logic to the Soviet Union itself. The immediate reason for augmenting U.S. trade ties with Moscow was to gain leverage over Soviet policy—so "we can turn it off if their political behavior becomes threatening," Kissinger said.[91] By 1973, though, there was a hidden, secondary logic for engagement: it would undermine the isolation on which hard-liners depended. "Brezhnev's gamble," wrote Kissinger, was that détente "will not undermine the very system from which Brezhnev draws his power and legitimacy. Our goal ... is to achieve precisely such effects."[92]

East-West trade skyrocketed under détente, rising sixfold between 1970 and 1979.[93] Yet the idea of using commerce for political ends immediately ran into problems. That strategy would work best if the allies coordinated their policies. Yet the quest for profit (and diplomatic rivalries between Western leaders) caused a fratricidal race to Moscow. Even within the U.S. government, careful calibration proved elusive. In 1972, the Soviets hoodwinked the Department of Agriculture, buying up the U.S. grain crop before anyone realized what was afoot.[94] And in 1974–1975, Congress scuttled a major U.S.-Soviet economic agreement by insisting that Moscow permit dramatically higher levels of Jewish emigration—a condition the Kremlin angrily rejected. "We have now lost the leverage," Kissinger sighed.[95]

The emigration imbroglio highlighted a larger debate over whether to use economic leverage to seek near-term political change. Nixon and Kissinger were adamantly opposed. "One of the riskiest things is to try to play around with the domestic structure of a revolutionary government," Kissinger said.[96] The secretary of state did work privately with Moscow to secure higher emigration levels. But there was no point in publicly demanding that a totalitarian regime change its ways: "Emigration policy is none of our business."[97]

Senator Henry Jackson disagreed. Détente, Jackson argued, mustn't lead to "capitulation on the issue of human rights." It was a mistake, he said, to give Moscow the benefits of trade without making it pay a price.[98] Kissinger's position was that soft-pedaling these issues now would promote warmer relations, which might ease Soviet repression later. But the extended time horizon, uncertain prospects, and near-term moral compromises of that approach made it hard to defend. When Ford declined to see the dissident Aleksandr Solzhenitsyn in 1975 in deference to Moscow's sensitivities, even Chief of Staff Dick Cheney objected: engagement should not "imply also our approval of their way of life."[99]

The clash of visions intensified in 1975 with the signing of the Helsinki Final Act, a set of agreements on economic, security, and political issues in Europe. The Soviets had long sought that accord as a seal of approval for their dominance in Eastern Europe. The NATO allies valued the pact as a way of reducing tensions and facilitating potentially subversive exchanges. Liberty, French president Georges Pompidou said, was like syphilis: it was a "contagious disease that spreads through constant and repeated contact." Kissinger, however, thought of Helsinki as a bargaining chip for Soviet concessions on arms control. He deprecated provisions on human rights and pushed for them only because the allies insisted.[100] What Helsinki could accomplish, in his view, was to deepen the superpower diplomacy that might create room for change. Soviet "political domination in Eastern Europe," he maintained, was "more likely to be undermined in détente than in cold war."[101]

The problem was that the Helsinki accords seemed to bless Communist authority in the here and now by accepting the postwar borders of Europe. The *Wall Street Journal* called Helsinki "a formal version of Yalta, without Yalta's redeeming features."[102] Kissinger was incredulous, pointing out the accords left the door open to peaceful change. "Sometimes I think we are in a nut house," he said.[103] The defense fell flat, with fellow Republicans, including Reagan, charging that détente was strengthening the Iron Curtain.

It was, for the moment. The Soviets and the satellites pointed to the diplomatic legitimacy they had won through the Helsinki agreements to bolster their domestic legitimacy. They used Western loans and credits to temporarily conceal the accumulating failures of their economic model.[104] Moreover, if Kissinger aimed to undermine the bloc eventually, his preoccupation with near-term stability had the demerit of implying that Eastern European demands for freedom, rather than Moscow's brutality, constituted the real threat to peace. America seemed more distant than ever from breaking down the Soviet sphere; the engagement strategy had come apart. Beneath the surface, however, that strategy was accelerating the crisis of the Soviet bloc.

The premise of political warfare had always been that the Soviet empire suffered from grave weaknesses. By the 1970s, those weaknesses were quietly multiplying. Behind a smokescreen of high oil prices, Soviet productivity was plummeting and growth was grinding to a halt.[105] Alcoholism and infant mortality rose as life expectancy declined; political dissidence flourished as ideological commitment waned. Young people had "nothing of the ideology and romanticism of the 1930s," one Soviet official lamented.[106] Ominously, a geriatric leadership showed no ability to cope with this malaise. A fatally diseased Soviet system was slowly dying, even as Soviet military power grew.

The same was happening in Eastern Europe. The East-West commerce of the 1970s had hidden fundamental problems. As bloc countries
binged on foreign loans, the region's debt ballooned from $6 billion in
1970 to $56 billion in 1980. Subservience to Moscow had long ago
robbed these regimes of their legitimacy, and dissatisfaction now intensified as citizens learned how badly West had left East behind. There was
lots of political tinder, one Soviet general warned. "All it will take to
bring down the entire house is just one spark."[107]

Soviet leaders had hoped the Helsinki agreements would serve as political flame retardant. They did not. Provisions addressing human and
political rights highlighted the systematic violation of those rights by
East-bloc governments. And because the text was published widely
within the bloc, the accords became a focal point for dissent. Helsinki
"watch groups" documented abuses; these groups, the KGB reported,
"inflict serious political damage on the Soviet state."[108] Critically, Helsinki also created a follow-on process—the Conference on Security and
Cooperation in Europe (CSCE)—that allowed continued Western scrutiny. Détente, the CIA concluded, had made it harder for the bloc to act
"in authoritarian ways abhorrent to Western sensibilities."[109]

Indeed, engagement had unleashed profoundly subversive forces. Expanded travel exposed citizens—and future elites—to just how backward
their countries had become.[110] The debt that Warsaw Pact countries
racked up was largely held by Western banks, leaving those countries in
hock to their enemies and conscious that violently repressing dissent could
cause economic strangulation. "We are integrally tied to the capitalist
economy," Soviet adviser Anatoly Chernyaev wrote.[111]

Behind the scenes, an even more critical change was happening: the Soviets were losing the will to kill in Eastern Europe. Necessity, not enlighten-
ment, was the cause: the Kremlin could no longer afford the economic and
diplomatic costs of slaying protestors and stabilizing unruly provinces. The
invasion of Afghanistan was the exception that proved the rule, for the widespread opprobrium and the Western sanctions imposed after that intervention showed that a repeat performance in Eastern Europe would be
disastrous. When Poland erupted in 1980–1981, with the rise of Solidarity—
an independent trade union that soon enlisted 10 million members—and
countrywide protests, Moscow was trapped between the dangers to Communist rule and the dangers of intervention. "If troops are introduced, that
will mean a catastrophe," one Soviet official said.[112] The bloc was seething
with dissidence as the tools of Kremlin dominance were corroding.

The twenty years after 1956 were hardly halcyon days of political warfare; engagement often appeared morally and strategically obtuse to its critics. Yet ironies abounded when it came to subverting the Soviet bloc. The soft techniques of the 1970s paved the way for the harder political warfare America would now resurrect.

That restoration occurred mostly under Reagan, but it featured tools that Carter developed. Carter was an ambivalent warrior; his desire to challenge the Soviet system competed with his desire to deepen détente. Yet his administration did reverse a long downward trend in funding for RFE and Voice of America (VOA). It began slowly rebuilding a covert action capability that had been gutted during the 1970s.[113] Most important, Carter embraced human rights. The president met with exiled Soviet dissidents, and his diplomats used the CSCE to focus international attention on continuing abuses. "Human rights," Carter informed Soviet foreign minister Andrei Gromyko, "were one of the main differences between us."[114] If nothing else, his advocacy showed how powerful a weapon human rights was, because the bloc regimes reacted hysterically to the slightest mention of the issue. Carter's human rights policy, a foreign ministry official observed, was "a well-thought-out, well-planned campaign of psychological warfare."[115] It hit totalitarian governments where their armor was weakest: their relationship with their own people.

Reagan was primed to exploit that weakness. For years, he had argued that morality was an underutilized American asset: "It's time to remind *ourselves & others* of the difference in culture, in morals and in the levels of civilization between the free world and the communist ant heap."[116] He believed that the Soviet system was inherently precarious— "a temporary aberration which will one day disappear from the earth"— and getting weaker day by day.[117] The key was to stop legitimizing the Kremlin's rule and start poking at its vulnerabilities.

The resulting political warfare offensive had short-term and longer-term objectives. At a minimum, intensified political warfare would inflict pain and impose costs. "A little less détente with the Politburo and more encouragement to the dissenters might be worth a lot of armored divisions," Reagan wrote.[118] At best, it might weaken the foundations of totalitarian rule. Washington, NSC staffer Richard Pipes argued, should "exert maximum possible internal pressure on the Soviet regime" as a way of "encouraging anti-expansionist, reformist forces inside the Communist bloc."[119] If Kissinger had sought reform through seduction, Reagan would use blunter methods to make the Kremlin face the full extent of its failings.

Poland was the focal point. "We are seeing the first, beginning cracks," Reagan said in 1981, "the beginning of the end."[120] The administration initially sought to avert a Soviet crackdown, with Reagan warning Brezhnev of "very serious" consequences if the Red Army moved in.[121] Moscow temporarily outfoxed Reagan by convincing the Polish government to declare martial law in December 1981. At this point, U.S. policy shifted to keeping Polish opposition alive. Driven by Casey, the CIA provided radios, computers, printing presses, and other technology that helped Solidarity function after it was driven underground. RFE and VOA broadcast details of the repression and relayed messages from Solidarity. "We can't let this revolution against Communism fail without our offering a hand," Reagan wrote.[122]

The Polish crisis also catalyzed a second line of action: raising the costs of repression. Reagan suspended Poland's most-favored-nation trade status and canceled an aid package to punish Warsaw and force Moscow to bear the cost of supporting Poland economically. The administration also hit Moscow directly, suspending exports of high-technology goods and oil and gas equipment. "The Soviet Union is economically on the ropes," Reagan said. "This is the time to punish them."[123]

Indeed, Reagan wanted to declare economic warfare on the Soviet bloc. Yet he rejected a proposal to declare Poland in default on its foreign loans for fear of endangering Western banks. Another effort to bleed Moscow—by preventing construction of an energy pipeline that would connect Siberia to Western Europe—also foundered.[124] Close U.S. allies were outraged when Reagan imposed sanctions on European companies involved with the project. Britain, Prime Minister Margaret Thatcher announced, had been "deeply wounded by a friend.[125] Political warfare, Reagan discovered, required being aggressive enough to hurt the enemy without unduly hurting the allies.

Still, the episode was not a complete setback. U.S. opposition delayed the pipeline by at least two years, and Secretary Shultz eventually secured NATO's agreement to limit the provision of credits and strategic goods to the Soviet bloc.[126] More quietly, Reagan's representatives discouraged private banks from lending to Warsaw. "Private sources of long-term credit to the Bloc have largely dried up," CIA analysts reported.[127] Having become hooked on international lending, the Warsaw Pact nations were about to go through a painful withdrawal.

They were also about to suffer systematic de-legitimization. Détente had demonstrated that the bloc regimes craved diplomatic legitimacy but were determined to maintain tight political controls. Reagan made sure Moscow could not have it both ways. The president publicly labeled the Soviet regime "an evil empire"; he argued that a system so morally and practically bankrupt could not endure. "The West won't contain communism, it will transcend communism," he declared. "It will dismiss it as some bizarre chapter in human history whose last pages are even now being written."[128] The purpose was to remind Soviet leaders that the world was witness to their crimes and, at the same time, make common cause with those trying to change the system from within. "The long-term weaknesses of the Soviet system," noted one strategy document, "can be encouraged in part simply by telling the truth about the USSR."[129]

The idea of strengthening reformist tendencies underpinned a final U.S. initiative: pushing Western ideas into the Soviet bloc. The budget for RFE and RL more than doubled during Reagan's presidency; the radios also received technological enhancements that allowed them to better circumvent Soviet jamming.[130] Programming focused on subjects such as the upheaval in Poland, the costs of the war in Afghanistan, and the writings of Soviet dissidents. The radios would later publicize the Chernobyl nuclear power plant disaster, which supercharged anti-Soviet sentiment in Ukraine and the Baltic. "Of America's nine Cold War presidents," RFE bureau director Arch Puddington wrote, "none was as committed to the mission of the radios as Ronald Reagan."[131]

The goals of this multifaceted assault were spelled out in classified decision directives, which made it U.S. policy to promote political liberalization within the Soviet Union and "loosen the Soviet hold" on Eastern Europe.[132] All of these elements were nested within a larger global campaign. The Reagan Doctrine targeted the Third World but also fostered a contagious sense of empowerment among those challenging Communist rule.[133] The U.S. military buildup sharpened the dilemmas that Kremlin leaders faced in keeping a moribund economic and political structure intact. Reagan's campaign marked the culmination of Cold War political warfare, and it would have dramatic effect.

Timing was crucial. One of the challenges of earlier campaigns was that the Soviet system, while profoundly flawed, was growing stronger as it recovered from World War II. The opposite was true in the 1980s. All the inbuilt pathologies were worsening; the iron will to crush dissent by force was fading. These trends left the Soviet Union susceptible to pressure.

In Eastern Europe, U.S. support preserved Solidarity as a potent political force and symbol of dissent. High-tech communications equipment and printing presses allowed Solidarity to spread its message under martial law; RFE dramatically expanded the organization's informational reach. According to one study, "The circulation of one *samizdat* rose from a maximum of eighty thousand when distributed on paper to many millions when transmitted by radio." As a result, Warsaw could never maintain its information monopoly or eradicate dissent. "If you would close your Radio Free Europe," one official complained, "the underground would completely cease to exist."[134]

The offensive was taking a toll elsewhere, too. The Soviets were realizing, CIA officials reported, that Washington was determined to make the Kremlin a global pariah.[135] At home, RL and VOA amplified discontent among non-Russian populations. The distribution of dissident literature like *The Gulag Archipelago* came when dissatisfaction with the system was already increasing. Not least, although Reagan's rhetoric was sometimes deplored as Manichean by Western observers, it was just that quality that energized dissidents who met to discuss "Reaganite readings."[136] Within the Kremlin, Konstantin Chernenko fretted about Reagan's "especially strong anti-Soviet agitation."[137] The Reagan administration was morally isolating the Soviet government at home and abroad.

The economic impact of U.S. policy was subtler but still corrosive. Suspending Poland's most-favored-nation status cost Warsaw billions in trade. Efforts to discourage lending to Poland put the burden of stabilization squarely on Moscow. And although Reagan failed to stop the Siberian pipeline, the two-year delay cost the Soviets perhaps $15 billion in hard currency.[138] The West was exploiting "the growth of foreign debts, the food situation, our technological lag," General Secretary Yuri Andropov acknowledged. "For as long as these problems exist, our class enemies will try to turn them to their benefit."[139]

The broader Reagan offensive intensified these effects. The war in Afghanistan, the CIA assessed, was exacerbating "an array of pre-existing societal problems" within the Soviet Union itself, including military demoralization, drug abuse, and mistrust of a dishonest government.[140] Reagan Doctrine programs simultaneously heightened the burdens that Soviet foreign aid placed on the struggling domestic economy and the

political dissatisfaction those burdens caused at home. The "colonial regions are exploiting the Soviet Union!" one U.S. official joked.[141] Overall,
Reagan was making Moscow a weaker and less competitive adversary.

Where Reagan initially failed was in catalyzing reform. The president wanted not just to punish Moscow but also to foster internal
changes that might soften the Kremlin's stance over time. Yet the Soviet
Union intensified its crackdown during the early 1980s and even into the
early Gorbachev era. "Human rights and political dissent are more thoroughly suppressed in the USSR today than at any time since Stalin's
death," U.S. analysts reported in 1985.[142]

This outcome was not surprising. Totalitarian governments rarely
agree to reform themselves out of business. But by provoking fear and
hostility in Soviet ruling circles, Reagan's policies were actually encouraging the Soviet leadership to clamp down rather than loosen up. "The
leadership is convinced that the Reagan Administration is out to bring
their system down and will give no quarter," one Soviet commentator explained. "Therefore they have no choice but to hunker down and fight
back."[143] In striking at the very foundations of Soviet power, Reagan's
policies had inflamed the sensitivities of a congenitally insecure regime.

The events of the early 1980s thus showed that the enduring dilemmas of political warfare had hardly abated. Critics had long warned
against meddling too aggressively for fear of inciting repression and encouraging escalation. Proponents had long argued that America must run
risks to achieve anything. Both sides had a point. Reagan's offensive took
the fight to the enemy but also contributed to a more dangerous Cold
War. Escaping that quandary would require an adapted political warfare
strategy executed in partnership with a very different Soviet leader.

Looking back, Kennan called his role in Cold War political warfare "the
worst mistake I ever made in government."[144] Kennan deplored the rhetoric of liberation, even though he had earlier advocated something of the
sort. He deemed it wrong "for a great government such as ours to try to
. . . work internal changes in another country," even though this was where
his own strategy led.[145] Political warfare, Kennan alleged, was strategic
snake oil: it promised an easy remedy for a chronic disease. Yet this assessment is too harsh. Political warfare didn't win the Cold War on the cheap,
but it provided strategic value by targeting the asymmetric weaknesses of
totalitarian regimes.

Political warfare rested on the idea that America could help a repressive enemy defeat itself by exploiting the insecurity that its worst tendencies would create. Admittedly, Kennan's contemporaries would have been chastened by how tortuous the subsequent progress was. But if a seer had predicted, in the late 1940s, that U.S. political warfare would help split Moscow and Beijing, stoke persistent dissent and encourage periodic eruptions in Eastern Europe, intensify a grave crisis of legitimacy in the Soviet empire, and inflict severe pain on an adversary in distress, this would have seemed a very good outcome. In an extended struggle for mastery, Washington made the enemy pay for the deepest failures of its system.

Still, the lessons of this experience are somewhat ambiguous. There was, after all, no one formula for political warfare. U.S. administrations used everything from radio transmissions to paramilitary operations, from harsh pressures to subversive gifts. Some of the most useful tools were profoundly unorthodox, such as the Marshall Plan, or painstakingly incremental, such as RFE and RL. Some of the most spectacular initiatives, such as paramilitary operations, were spectacular failures. Nor was political warfare a linear phenomenon. Engagement could set the stage for coercion, but confrontation could also be a prelude to accommodation. Indeed, Reagan's strategy had such impact because it was, implicitly, a hybrid strategy: It exploited vulnerabilities created by an engagement strategy that Reagan had earlier derided. What all this indicates is not that U.S. political warfare was scattershot or random. U.S. political warfare was instead a cumulative discipline, one that encompassed multiple theories about how to hobble an adversary.

Cold War history also reminds us that political warfare demands as much patience and persistence as boldness and risk-taking. The very term "political warfare" conjures up imagines of daring. In reality, political warfare is more like interest that compounds over time. Slow but steady approaches gradually undercut repressive regimes and awkward alliances. The greatest breakthroughs, such as the opening to China, came only after years of preparation. The successes of the 1980s came after decades of waiting for Soviet weaknesses to reveal themselves. This meant, of course, that it was often difficult to tell whether American policy was working in real time. John Foster Dulles once invoked Saint Paul in this regard, explaining that "faith is the substance of things hoped for, the evidence of things not seen."[146] Political warfare was not always sexy. It was a long, grinding affair.

Successful political warfare equally required respecting the dynamics of authentic coalitions—especially because one of its goals was highlighting the perversities of Moscow's inauthentic coalition. Here, U.S.-allied tensions were the norm, both because America and its allies had differing levels of dependence on East-West trade and because the allies were more exposed to the perils that an aggressive strategy might bring. Waging political warfare required constantly balancing the imperatives of weakening and isolating the enemy against the imperatives of not isolating the United States. It also required, periodically, listening to the allies: it was the Europeans, for example, who first grasped the bloc-shaking potential of engagement and the Helsinki process. In the end, a multilateral policy proved smarter than a unilateral one. Here, as elsewhere, the United States benefited from the geopolitical wisdom of the crowd.

Yet it is essential to remember that political warfare was no panacea. Failures and disappointments were numerous. There was always the danger that political warfare might provoke an insecure regime or undermine East-West diplomacy. Not least, there were moral ambiguities—from inciting doomed unrest among captive populations to working with one oppressive Communist regime to contain another. These issues should not be sugarcoated. The moral costs of Washington's policy included Hungarians who were slaughtered after being inspired by RFE and victims of Chinese communism whom American leaders mostly forgot about once they toasted Mao and Zhou. Allen Dulles was right. Waging political warfare meant breaking lots of eggs.

CHAPTER SIX

Setting Limits

GREAT-POWER COMPETITIONS NEED not be unconstrained, zero-sum slugfests. Even bitter antagonists may have common interests; many—not all—states would prefer a tense peace to an all-out war. So how does a nation pursue cooperation without losing the competition? How does a nation limit a rivalry while prosecuting it effectively?

These were familiar questions for Cold War policymakers. As we have seen, hopes of bounding the struggle geographically didn't last long, and the Cold War's heady brew of ideology and geopolitics made the contest feel all-encompassing. Yet the very issue that made the Cold War so dangerous—the nuclear revolution—also created powerful incentives to establish rules of the road. The heavy costs of the rivalry gave policymakers reason to keep those costs under control. And the U.S.-Soviet competition was never fully zero-sum: scourges, whether geopolitical or epidemiological, that threatened both superpowers encouraged collaboration across the East-West divide.

In fact, efforts to limit the Cold War had a larger role in American statecraft than we often remember. It is simply not true that the beginning of containment marked the end of possibilities for meaningful diplomacy.[1] Every Cold War president met his Soviet counterpart at a summit. Cold War tensions did not preclude historic cooperation on important global challenges of the twentieth century. Moreover, the superpowers did eventually establish norms and agreements that allowed them to compete without catastrophe—to make the postwar era a "long peace."[2] Yet the quest to moderate the Cold War was itself full of dangers and quandaries, not least because the underlying conflict was so fundamental. So the real value of pursuing diplomacy with the Soviet Union lay not in transcending the competition, but in helping America win it.

In theory, the strategic rationale for setting limits on a rivalry is straightforward. Doing so may ease the strains that competition imposes on a country's wealth and well-being. It may allow rivals to address shared dangers. Periodic de-escalation may even aid effective competition: Because long-term rivalries are potentially exhausting, seeking pauses from time to time is useful. There is, not least, the need to prevent competition from spiraling into catastrophic conflict—an objective two antagonists may share even when they quarrel over everything else. These logics were all familiar to Cold War policymakers who viewed the Soviet Union as a villainous enemy but were nonetheless uneasy with the costs and potential cataclysms of unmitigated hostility.

In practice, however, limiting competition can be fraught. Negotiating with an adversary can help rally the home front by demonstrating that all possibilities for peace have been explored. Yet it can also lead to charges of appeasement as foreign policy becomes politically weaponized. Or it can produce a premature euphoria, a sense that a fundamental breakthrough has been achieved, that makes it tougher to keep the population mobilized. "Many dangerous problems were involved" in negotiations with the Soviets, Dean Rusk once said. "One was the tendency of democracies to disarm at the drop of a hat."[3]

The alliance politics were equally complex. During the Cold War, American allies wanted reassurance—which superpower détente could provide—that they would not be caught in the crossfire of undesired confrontation. It was always better for Washington to lead, rather than follow, its allies' efforts to moderate that conflict. Yet U.S. allies also worried that Washington might cut a superpower bargain behind their backs; at the same time, official Washington feared that a rush to negotiate would undermine the unity of the free world. If fear makes easy the task of diplomats, the easing of fear might make it harder to keep the West together.[4]

Negotiation could also have the wrong effect on the adversary. Ideally, a move toward de-escalation conveys an image of reasonableness but not weakness. In the nuclear age, high-level diplomacy could promote a shared understanding of the dangers of war. But a push for negotiations could also give the impression that the free world was weary; acknowledging a fear of nuclear war could encourage a ruthless opponent to push harder. Similarly, there is no guarantee that de-escalating a competition will pay strategic dividends, or even prove equally beneficial to both sides. In sparing itself from the pressures of rivalry, a country may also be sparing its adversary.

Timing matters, too. Ideally, diplomats would arrest a rivalry before it takes on unstoppable momentum. Yet it can be hard to address thorny issues until the rivalry has escalated dangerously and both sides have glimpsed the possibility of disaster. In the same vein, negotiating from weakness is unattractive, because it may result in lousy agreements. Yet once a nation develops greater strength, it may not feel inclined to negotiate.

During the Cold War, these problems were exacerbated by the extremely low level of U.S. trust in the Soviet Union. In any rivalry, there is the possibility that the opponent will negotiate in bad faith, violating agreements or using diplomacy to divide its adversaries. In the Cold War, that possibility was inescapable. America's adversary was dedicated to the destruction of the capitalist world; it treated negotiation as political warfare and lying and deception as arrows in its quiver.[5] Every Soviet leader believed in the "promotion of world revolution," Reagan argued in 1981. So long as the Soviets "reserve unto themselves the right to commit any crime, to lie, to cheat, in order to attain that," possibilities for accommodation were limited.[6]

Reagan's critique related to an even greater obstacle: the fundamental nature of the rivalry. From the start, Kennan held that the Soviet Union was not a normal regime or even a normal enemy. Rather, Moscow was pursuing an agenda that was antithetical to U.S. interests, and this agenda would not change until the regime changed. "This is no normal clash of national interests," Kennan wrote. "They are our enemies because their whole structure of power has been founded upon the theory of that enmity and would be unjustified—even criminal—without it."[7] The search for common ground could obscure the Manichean nature of the struggle. If the Kremlin was indeed "bent upon a policy of ruthless expansion aimed at world domination," as Truman's State Department put it, then seeking anything beyond the most tactical détente was a fool's errand.[8]

This judgment didn't cause American officials, including Kennan and Reagan, to reject the idea of managing the U.S.-Soviet competition. It did mean that U.S. officials constantly had to weigh the benefits of that endeavor against the risks. Efforts to moderate a rivalry are neither inherently good nor inherently bad. What matters is whether doing so improves one's ability to succeed.

The Truman administration mostly believed that it didn't. As the Cold War got under way, strategists inside and outside government looked for opportunities to tame it. Lippmann recommended a U.S.-Soviet deal on the future of Europe. Kennan thought America should ensure that "there is always an open door and an easy road to collaboration."[9] Through 1947, Washington hesitated to shut that door.

The year prior, the United States had proposed, unsuccessfully, a scheme for international control of atomic energy with the aim of averting a perilous arms race. As late as April 1947, George Marshall was still seeking Stalin's help in reviving Germany. Only when Stalin refused—ominously doodling wolves while remarking that the situation in Germany was "not tragic"—did the United States proceed on its own with the Marshall Plan.[10] Even then, Truman's aides made several proposals to check escalating superpower tensions. The reason Truman didn't pursue these proposals was fear that doing so would undermine the advantages necessary to win the Cold War.

The most telling examples came between 1948 and 1950. In 1948–1949, Kennan—appropriating Lippmann's earlier idea—proposed to negotiate the neutralization and reunification of Germany, along with mutual troop withdrawals from Central Europe. That idea was part political warfare: it would get the Red Army out of Eastern Europe. Yet the most important goal was to "avoid congealment of Europe along the present lines"—to prevent an unbreakable geopolitical stalemate.[11] Later, in 1949–1950, the administration initially hesitated to race to develop the hydrogen bomb after the first Soviet nuclear test. "Perhaps the best thing," Acheson allowed, "is an 18–24 month moratorium" in which the superpowers could try to "ease the international situation."[12]

The Truman administration never took up either proposal. An offer to neutralize Germany might or might not elicit Soviet agreement, yet it would almost certainly destroy the confidence of the fledgling Atlantic community. An H-bomb moratorium might head off a ghastly turn in the military competition, but it would expose America to tremendous dangers if the Soviets cheated and crossed the thermonuclear threshold first. "Sole possession by the Soviet Union of this weapon would cause severe damage not only to our military posture but to our foreign policy position," concluded a secret report to Truman. The search for de-escalation now could make it harder to deal effectively with a power-minded adversary over the long haul.[13]

By the time of the Korean War, U.S. policymakers were fully committed to the latter objective even at the expense of the former. Offers to negotiate with Moscow might be useful, NSC-68 stated, as a way of demonstrating Soviet intransigence.[14] But seeking a settlement of the Cold War now, when the U.S. military position seemed so weak, would be foolish. The thrust of U.S. policy should be building unassailable geopolitical positions, either as a prelude to successful negotiations or as a means of coercing the Kremlin. If Soviet behavior did change, Acheson asserted, "it will be only because of the rebuilding of Western strength and the repeated demonstration of the free world's will to defend its freedom."[15]

This policy drew criticism, at the time and later, from those who argued that America was shutting the door to diplomacy.[16] Yet U.S. diplomats did quietly engage their Soviet counterparts during the Berlin blockade and the Korean War, with the latter overture initiating armistice talks that culminated after Stalin's death. These episodes showed that Stalin was periodically willing to reduce tensions, but only after America had stabilized the battlefield by initiating the Berlin airlift or halting the Communist drive down the Korean Peninsula.[17] In other words, strength enabled diplomacy. And the stance on East-West negotiations that NSC-68 outlined was consistent with a deeper assessment of the enemy. When the Soviets offered to talk, Charles Bohlen concluded, it was not because they wanted "some constructive settlement." It was because "their sole objective is to try and disrupt what the West is doing for its own security and survival."[18]

This assessment was jaded but accurate. Stalin never envisioned any long-term accommodation with the West; he dismissed one entreaty with a simple "Ha ha."[19] The Soviets were, in fact, already building their hydrogen bomb by the time Truman decided to move ahead with development of that weapon. Had Washington held back to gain Soviet cooperation, Soviet scientist Andrei Sakharov later wrote, Stalin's response would have been "to exploit the adversary's folly at the earliest opportunity."[20] Even after the Korean armistice talks began, Stalin was happy to extend that conflict as a way of bleeding the United States and preparing for what he saw as a nearly inevitable military showdown.[21]

Building Western power while avoiding diplomatic traps was, in these circumstances, a reasonable policy. Admittedly, there were traps in this strategy, too. "There is always the danger," wrote Acheson's adviser

Philip Jessup, "that when we have a position of strength, we will say that we do not need to negotiate."[22] But Truman and his advisers understood that sequencing was critical, and that America must lay the geopolitical groundwork before it could make diplomacy succeed.

What happens, though, when avoiding negotiation is no longer possible or prudent? By 1953, Stalin's death had created hopes for a diplomatic thaw. U.S. llies were seeking to lower the nerve-wracking tensions that had accom nied the Korean conflict. Under the shadow of thermonuclear war, Churchill wrote, the superpower relationship must become something better "than a series of casual and dangerous incidents at the many points of contact between the two divisions of the world."[23] Around the globe, fears of nuclear war—and criticism of America's arsenal—were intensifying. "The world," Ike acknowledged, "was in a rather hysterical condition abo it the atomic bomb."[24] Talking to Moscow had become essential to preserving America's diplomatic position.

Ike himself wasn't averse to giving peace a chance. The president was appalled by nuclear weapons, even as he put them at the heart of his strategy. The infamous Castle Bravo nuclear test of 1954, which spread fallout over a large swath of the Pacific Ocean, intensified Ike's revulsion. "The nature of conflict has gotten beyond man," he remarked.[25] At the same time, Eisenhower believed that making the military struggle less financially onerous was essential to making American strategy bearable. The alternative to diplomacy, he warned, was a "life of perpetual fear and tension" and an intolerable "burden of arms." A generational approach to rivalry required an openness to negotiation.[26]

Sound strategy, however, also required avoiding a rush to the summit. Ike resisted Churchill's idea of an early meeting with Stalin's successors for fear of allowing Moscow to play divide-and-conquer before NATO had settled delicate debates on West German rearmament.[27] Additionally, the hope for progress was balanced by the desire to finish off a wounded enemy. The Soviets were desperate "to relieve the ever-increasing pressure upon their regime," Dulles said. "Accordingly, we must not relax this pressure unless the Soviets give promise of ending the struggle."[28] Underlying these concerns was a deeper one: that even though Stalin had died, the nature of the enemy was unchanged. Soviet policy, Ike remarked, remained one of "destroying the Capitalist free world by all means, by force, by deceit or by lies."[29]

It followed that negotiations must enhance, not undercut, the Western position in a long, bitter struggle. Washington must not make preemptive concessions, Ike's Basic National Security Policy stated; it must not "delay or reduce efforts to develop and maintain adequate free world strength."[30] Negotiations were a means of waging the Cold War, not ending it.

The policy that emerged was bold rhetorically and cautious in practice. In April 1953, Ike issued a stirring call for peace, with ringing denunciations of rivalry. "Under the cloud of threatening war," he declared, "it is humanity hanging from a cross of iron."[31] In December, he proposed an "Atoms for Peace" program wherein the nuclear powers would make atomic material available for the purposes of global development.[32] The next year, the key Western and Communist powers held an international conference on the fate of Indochina and Korea. In 1955, Ike met the Kremlin leadership at Geneva, proposing an Open Skies initiative that would reduce the danger of surprise attack by permitting overflights of U.S. and Soviet territory. During Eisenhower's second term, he held two additional summits with Khrushchev and sought to ban nuclear weapons tests. As Eisenhower left office, he still thought that hostility might yield to a more "sane and hopeful" future.[33]

Yet there was usually more—and less—than met the eye to these proposals. The president talked peace in 1953 but waited until 1955, once the debate over German rearmament was settled within NATO, to meet Soviet leaders. Dulles attended the Geneva foreign ministers' conference in 1954 but ostentatiously refused to shake Zhou Enlai's hand. The concrete proposals that Ike advanced were designed to be disproportionately favorable to Washington, which made them likely to be spurned by Moscow. Atoms for Peace, for instance, would isolate the Soviets in world opinion if they rejected the idea and would deplete their limited supply of fissionable material if they accepted.[34]

Finally, although Ike went to the Paris summit with Khrushchev in 1960 genuinely hoping for a breakthrough, he also approved, just beforehand, a fateful U-2 overflight that the Soviets shot down, leading to an angry blowup. Ike made no apologies, saying that the free world must have "information about the military capabilities of other powerful nations, especially those that make a fetish of secrecy."[35] The president desired a safer Cold War but was determined not to let America's guard down.

As the U-2 incident showed, the results of this approach were not always pretty. Dulles's refusal to shake Zhou's hand in 1954 made the United States look childish and ideologically prudish. Between 1955 and 1959, the administration struggled to overcome internal disagreements and present clear proposals for slowing or reversing the arms race; in some cases, U.S. diplomats put forward ideas only to back away when the Soviets showed interest. In fairness, the administration was working through complicated scientific issues regarding the detection of nuclear tests while also tending to the concerns of vulnerable allies and vigilant military advisers.[36] But the appearance conveyed was that Ike did not know what he wanted—and that Washington might be the stumbling block to East-West diplomacy.

A related problem was that Ike's cautious approach tended to postpone negotiations beyond when the Soviets were most desperate for them. Eisenhower and Dulles believed, rightly, that getting good deals required consolidating the Western alliance behind them.[37] Yet delaying the Geneva summit until 1955 allowed Moscow to improve its own position. By this point, the succession struggle was over. The Soviets were developing an intercontinental bomber fleet and ICBMs; there were tempting possibilities for Soviet expansion in the Third World. The purpose of interacting with Soviet leaders, Dulles said, was to see whether they would pay "the price to end the Cold War."[38] By the Geneva summit, however, the Soviets didn't want to pay much at all. Negotiations always reflect calculations of advantage and vulnerability. In the 1950s those calculations were shifting rapidly—and not always to America's benefit.

Ike was intensely frustrated that he failed to tame the Cold War. A presidency that had begun with talk of "a chance for peace" ended with nuclear arsenals and East-West tensions mushrooming. Eisenhower complained, in 1959, that he was "at his 'wits ends' " in thinking of "new subjects or possibilities on which to negotiate."[39] When the Joint Chiefs of Staff had earlier advised that it was better to run an "arms race than to enter an agreement with the Soviets," Ike snapped that he "wondered why they did not counsel that we go to war at once."[40] Yet Eisenhower was being unfair. His goal, after all, was not to end the Cold War quickly but make it more bearable. By that standard, he mostly succeeded.

The results of superpower diplomacy may not have been dramatic, but they weren't trivial, either. East-West negotiations brought the Korean War to a close and produced a compromise solution in Indochina after the French defeat there. The Western powers and the Soviets agreed to neutralize Austria in 1955. The failure of test ban negotiations did not prevent Moscow and Washington from observing unilateral moratoria for roughly three years. And in 1959, Ike used the carrot of a foreign ministers' meeting and then a summit with Khrushchev—in addition to the stick of U.S. military power—to deescalate the Berlin crisis. Talking to the Soviets, Eisenhower explained, "will have the great value of affording us time and of easing the tensions."[41] It also soothed British nerves and prevented a deeper rift within NATO. On balance, Ike's strategy modestly tamped down Cold War hostility without jeopardizing Western cohesion. His approach legitimized negotiations with the Soviets—a favor to future Cold War presidents—while orchestrating those negotiations so they did not jeopardize U.S. strengths.

Might a more forthcoming American position have led to better results? Probably not. Even a disarmament enthusiast like adviser Harold Stassen admitted that unless the Soviets agreed to foolproof inspections to enforce a test ban or other measures—an unlikely prospect—"it is better to have the United States under no restrictions whatsoever."[42] And although Stalin's successors wanted to reduce the danger of war, they hardly altered Moscow's long-run aims. Lavrentiy Beria—who at first appeared to win the post-Stalin struggle for leadership—was arrested and shot in part because he had advocated allowing the reunification of Germany. The man who betrayed him, Khrushchev, was determined to fragment NATO and take Soviet influence global. He linked arms control to Western concessions on European security; he saw negotiations as a way of splitting Washington from disaffected allies, like Paris, or worried ones, like London.[43]

The Eisenhower administration was not wrong, then, to treat negotiations as a "probing operation"—to see if Soviet attitudes had changed without naïvely hoping that they had.[44] It was not wrong to think that tending to Western solidarity was the best guarantee of successful negotiations. A case in point: the Soviets agreed to neutralize Austria in 1955 only after progress toward bringing West Germany into NATO made them fear that western Austria might be next.[45] As it turned out, America was better off waging an ongoing security competition than desperately seeking agreements.

In fact, the Eisenhower era offers a warning that negotiations can backfire. Churchill and Eisenhower had hoped that summitry would humanize the Cold War by allowing Soviet and Western leaders to get to know each other. "You have got to meet face to face the people with whom you disagree at times," Ike later said.[46] At Geneva, Eisenhower worked hard to persuade Khrushchev and his Soviet colleagues that he hated the idea of nuclear war. Yet Eisenhower succeeded too well, convincing Khrushchev that America was militarily strong but psychologically weak.

"Our enemies were afraid of us in the same way as we were afraid of them," Khrushchev concluded—which encouraged him to exploit that fear by brandishing his nascent missile capability in the late 1950s.[47] The crises that Ike confronted were partially a result of the diplomacy he pursued.

Kennedy quickly learned the same lesson. The president who pledged to pay any price, bear any burden, in waging the Cold War was also keen to control the competition. By closing off avenues for Soviet expansion, Kennedy calculated, the United States would demonstrate the futility of aggression. From this position of power, Washington could engage a chastened enemy to manage crises and develop—in Rostow's phrasing—"ground rules covering our competitions."[48] Here as elsewhere, Kennedy placed his faith in calibration: using a mixture of power and engagement to make the superpower conflict more predictable.

The maneuver worked poorly at first. When Kennedy met Khrushchev in Vienna in June 1961, the leaders did reach a loose (and ephemeral) agreement to neutralize Laos, sparing Kennedy the necessity of intervening military. On the whole, though, the summit had perverse results. The Bay of Pigs fiasco had already made Khrushchev doubt Kennedy's judgment and resolve. At Vienna, the Soviet premier battered the new president rhetorically. "I talked about how a nuclear exchange would kill seventy million people in ten minutes and he just looked at me as if to say, 'So what?' " Kennedy recalled.[49] And while Kennedy insisted that America would defend its rights in Berlin, his admission that the situation there was "not satisfactory" implied that it might not.[50] As had happened after Geneva, Khrushchev came away emboldened, not restrained: he soon escalated the Berlin crisis and sent missiles to Cuba. An effort to calm superpower relations helped produce the most dangerous year of the Cold War.

The resolution of the missile crisis—which itself featured a mixture of American strength and moderation—offered a reset. That episode answered any questions Khrushchev had about Kennedy's toughness. It also scared the devil out of both leaders. "There appear to be no differences between your views and mine regarding the need for eliminating war in this nuclear age," Kennedy wrote to Khrushchev in early 1963. "Perhaps only those who have responsibility for controlling these weapons fully realize the awful destruction their use would bring."[51] So the crisis helped crystallize, over the succeeding years, a set of norms aimed at making the Cold War less destructive.

First, there emerged a superpower consensus to begin limiting the arms competition and tempering the risk of war. Improving communication was imperative: For lack of a better channel, the Soviets had transmitted key messages through Western Union and Radio Moscow in October 1962. The superpowers now installed the Moscow-Washington "hotline," a dedicated teletype line meant to ensure, Dobrynin wrote, that leaders could "defuse another confrontation in time."[52] They concluded the Limited Test Ban Treaty of 1963, which prohibited nuclear tests in the atmosphere, underwater, or in outer space, and an agreement to prevent the arms race from spilling into the cosmos. Within a few years, arms control negotiations moved closer to the core of the military competition. The resulting agreements, admittedly, did little to address underlying geopolitical disagreements. "The armaments race," Ike had commented, "was a result rather than a cause."[53] But they did reduce the perils of Cold War rivalry.

Second, the superpowers committed to minimal strategic transparency. In 1958, the economist Thomas Schelling had written that "the reciprocal fear of surprise attack"—the danger that an adversary might go first in a crisis—could create a self-fulfilling prophecy.[54] The Soviets had batted down Ike's "Open Skies" solution to this problem, leading Eisenhower to employ the U-2. But during the 1960s, the superpowers implicitly agreed not to shoot down the orbital reconnaissance satellites now coming online, even as those satellites gathered all manner of sensitive military intelligence. Their willingness to do so reflected a mixture of mutual deterrence and mutual restraint, in that both sides (especially the United States) avoided trumpeting their espionage successes. "They are aware of what we are doing," CIA director Richard Helms noted in 1971, but "we draw no more attention than is necessary to this activity."[55] Above all, the agreement reflected a growing recognition that a total information blackout on one's own activities could be dangerous for both sides.[56]

Third, Moscow and Washington would go only so far in testing each other's spheres of influence. The Third World was still up for grabs, and both superpowers kept using economic, diplomatic, and covert tools to weaken each other's core alliances. But direct efforts by the superpowers to challenge the status quo militarily, or in ways that were likely to provoke a major crisis, became less frequent. The United States pledged not to invade Cuba and eventually quit trying to overthrow Castro; the Soviets stopped seeking to squeeze the West out of Berlin. The major military crisis of the 1970s—the October War of 1973—was triggered by third parties rather than the superpowers themselves. Intense, sometimes dangerous rivalry continued, yet there was, increasingly, a tacit pact to avoid the most frightening showdowns.

Finally, the period after the missile crisis saw more explicit cooperation to address global challenges. Beginning in 1965, the superpowers jointly spearheaded a campaign to eradicate smallpox, a disease then claiming 2 million lives per year. That program, powered by (mostly) American money and (mostly) Soviet serum, transformed public health conditions throughout the global south. Plenty of self-interest was at play, since both sides were looking to burnish their image in the Third World. Yet the initiative showed that U.S.-Soviet relations were not entirely zero-sum.[57]

Just as consequential as the smallpox campaign was the Nuclear Non-Proliferation Treaty. By the early 1960s, Kennedy feared that subsequent presidents might "face a world in which 15 or 20 or 25 nations" possessed nuclear weapons.[58] Observers in Washington and Moscow were realizing that neither power would benefit from rampant proliferation, which would dilute their influence and lead to a more volatile world. U.S. and Soviet officials were also united, albeit quietly, in their fear of what might happen if West Germany or China built the bomb. The superpowers, Rusk told Soviet diplomats, "have a common interest to prevent the proliferation of nuclear weapons regardless of the political or ideological systems of other states."[59]

The Limited Test Ban Treaty was a partial response to this danger: It was meant to create diplomatic obstacles to new nuclear arsenals. Through 1964, however, negotiations on a broad nonproliferation treaty were stalemated by disagreements over how to deal with the Chinese and German problems. China's first nuclear test in October provided the missing urgency by threatening to trigger a proliferation spiral throughout Asia and beyond. "If still other states gain access to nuclear weapons," the Soviet periodical *Izvestia* announced, "then a kind of chain reaction could arise among more and new states."[60] In late 1966, the superpowers set the terms of a treaty meant to inhibit the further spread of nuclear weapons. Over the next several years, both America and the Soviet Union pressured their respective allies to sign the accord—an unofficial division of labor to preserve a strict nuclear hierarchy.

These superpower accords had drawbacks. In the midst of the smallpox campaign, the Soviets embarked on, and blatantly lied about, a massive biological weapons program featuring smallpox and other deadly pathogens. The Kremlin thus used a good deed as cover for a very bad

one, engaging in precisely the duplicity that critics of engagement worried about.[61] With respect to the Nuclear Non-Proliferation Treaty,
America's willingness to cut a deal with its worst adversary to keep some
of its best allies from developing nuclear weapons led to real strain in the
Western coalition. Konrad Adenauer called the treaty "a Morgenthau
Plan squared"; Japanese officials worried "that the U.S. and USSR are
moving toward a kind of 'super-powers' club from which Japan will be
forever excluded."[62] Superpower bargains could test the very alliances
Washington needed to make containment work.

Overall, the 1960s nonetheless showed that patterns of restraint and
cooperation could emerge amid competition, that tacit bargains were
sometimes easier to establish than formal ones, and that the search for
common ground was facilitated by a realization of just how shaky the
strategic terrain had become. In other words, it was no coincidence that
efforts to limit the superpower competition gained real traction only
after the two rivals had seen, through searing experiences in Berlin and
Cuba, where a competition without limits might lead. The remaining
question was whether it was possible to parlay this incipient cooperation
into a wider rapprochement—to turn a bipolar rivalry into a fundamentally more stable, even normal, state of affairs.

Détente, as we have seen, was many things. It included arms control
agreements and expanded East-West commerce. It featured ambitious diplomacy and frequent high-level meetings. It involved efforts to moderate rivalry in the Third World and in the realm of ideas. All told, détente
was the most comprehensive effort to stabilize, and perhaps ultimately
transcend, the Cold War.[63]

A policy with many facets naturally had many motives. The American architects of détente—especially Kissinger and Nixon—were not
naïve about the Soviets; Kissinger called them "brutal bastards."[64] Yet
they were most worried about the United States. They believed that a
wounded American superpower needed to decrease the tempo of the
Cold War. They hoped that easing strains with the Kremlin would allow
America to extricate itself from Vietnam. More broadly, they judged that,
amid a changing balance of power, Washington would need a subtler
strategy of containment to decrease the intensity of crises and prevent
the Soviet Union from destabilizing the international system. The goal,
said Kissinger, was to lead Moscow "to a realization of the limitations of

both its physical strength and of the limits of its ideological fervor"—to calm Soviet behavior as Soviet capabilities grew.[65]

Détente thus had a strong competitive logic. Yet there was also a more transformative ethos, which became more pronounced as the policy matured. Détente was a path toward a more organic, cooperative order, Nixon wrote. It would "transform the U.S.-Soviet relationship so that a mutual search for a stable peace and security becomes its dominant feature and its dominant force."[66] The core of détente, Kissinger agreed, was to strengthen international peace by forging "habits of mutual restraint, coexistence, and, ultimately, cooperation."[67] In the short term, détente would prevent America from losing the Cold War. Over the long term, it might change the nature of that conflict.

Realizing either goal would require considerable diplomatic sophistication. Washington must provide the Soviet Union with incentives—expanded trade, recognition as a coequal superpower—to moderate its behavior. Yet it must also demonstrate that aggression carried a heavy price. America stood "ready to impose penalties for adventurism," Kissinger wrote, but was "willing to expand relations in the context of responsible behavior."[68] Tying this all together was "linkage"—the idea that there would be no progress on issues of interest to Moscow unless there was progress on issues of interest to Washington—namely, ending the Vietnam War, confirming Western rights in Berlin, freezing the Soviet buildup, and avoiding provocations in the Third World. The Soviets "cannot expect to reap the benefits of cooperation in one area while seeking to take advantage of tension or confrontation elsewhere," Nixon wrote.[69] A simultaneous opening to China would remind the Kremlin of the dangers of antagonizing Washington. Through creative diplomacy, the United States could confront the Soviets with powerful reasons for restraint. With time, Moscow might come to see that it had a stake in preserving the international order.

The plan worked brilliantly for a time. By mid-1972, Nixon and Brezhnev had inked the SALT and ABM treaties and finalized an accord enshrining Western rights in Berlin. Contacts across the Iron Curtain grew exponentially. Linkage seemed to pay dividends, as when Moscow defused crises in Cuba and Jordan in 1970 after Kissinger warned that Third World flare-ups might derail détente. The superpowers, Nixon declared, were forging a "generation of peace."[70]

Along these lines, the Moscow summit in 1972 produced a mutual declaration, known as the "Basic Principles" of détente. The superpowers would observe "normal relations" and seek "peaceful coexistence." They would forsake "efforts to obtain unilateral advantage." They would respect the legitimacy of each other's political system.[71] The Basic Principles, the administration explained, were a "code of conduct" for a changing Cold War.[72]

Aspects of this "code of conduct" survived through the 1970s. Superpower summitry became more frequent and productive than ever before. Arms control talks continued, with brief interruptions, through the end of the Cold War, producing increasingly precise rules about how many and what type of weapons the superpowers could deploy. The diplomatic atmosphere became more normal. Kissinger struck up a friendship with Dobrynin; Brezhnev memorably kissed Carter at the Vienna summit in 1979. At moments it was possible to imagine the East-West conflict evolving into a fundamentally safer—and better—state of affairs.

As early as the mid-1970s, though, détente was under fire. "The word is a disaster," Clare Booth Luce, a prominent conservative, told Ford.[73] By decade's end, the policy had broken down. The Soviets did not stay restrained in the Third World, and the military competition intensified as counterforce capabilities proliferated. Negotiations became more difficult and less rewarding; by the time Carter signed SALT II in 1979, political support for arms control was crumbling. Détente ended, not with a transformed superpower relationship but in a period of tensions more severe than any since the early 1960s. The policy, initially a political triumph for Nixon, became a political millstone for Ford and Carter.

Détente led back to a worsened Cold War for several reasons. Both the technical and the political challenges of arms control increased as military capabilities became more sophisticated and quantity became less important than quality. Meanwhile, Third World actors found ways of pulling the superpowers into showdowns, as Sadat did in the Middle East in 1973, or Castro did by intervening in Angola. "The situation in this area," Brezhnev complained after the former crisis, "is poisoning the general atmosphere of détente."[74] The untimely decline of key leaders also played a role. Although Leonid Brezhnev was no dove, his fading health gave ascent to a more aggressive, ideological coterie of officials.[75] In America, Nixon's fall removed a leader whose anticommunist credentials lubricated the political gears of détente. Fundamentally, however, détente failed because its core tenets were incompatible with the realities of U.S.-Soviet competition.

The Basic Principles of détente held that the superpowers would foreswear the search for unilateral advantage—but neither party was able to do so, in military competition or in the Third World, when holding back might lead to intolerable disadvantage. Similarly, détente sought to separate ideology from geopolitics; that is, bitter rivals should respect each other's systems and control their own passions. Yet that was not possible for Soviet leaders who believed in socialism's inevitable triumph and thrilled at revolutionary breakthroughs in the Third World. "Wherever colonialists imposed bloodshed on the African peoples, the victims are free to take the path of armed struggle and in this they deserve the support of the Soviet Union," Brezhnev declared.[76] Neither was it possible for U.S. observers who rejected a moral equivalency between America and a totalitarian power. A purely pragmatic policy, Kissinger acknowledged, would be "empty of vision and humanity"; it would offer "no standards to which the American people can rally."[77] The Cold War was a competition between rivals with fundamentally divergent views of the world's future. Not even the cleverest diplomacy could solve this problem.

Indeed, détente may have been doomed from the outset, because the superpowers disagreed irreconcilably on what it was meant to achieve. U.S. officials hoped that détente would reconcile the Soviets to a global status quo that remained favorable to Washington. Soviet officials believed the very opposite: "We do not conceal the fact that we see détente as a way to create more favorable conditions for peaceful socialist and communist construction," Brezhnev said.[78] What made this elemental conflict ever harder to obscure was the shifting power balance, which made Moscow more assertive and thus reduced the benefits of détente for the United States. "Frankly, the Soviet Union was quite amazed at how lightheartedly some corners of the world were being declared spheres of vital interests of the U.S.," Brezhnev told Carter.[79] This a surging Soviet superpower would not abide.

This dynamic touched on an equally fundamental problem: that détente was at odds with America's longstanding approach to superpower competition. Détente implied the acceptance of basic equality, in military and diplomatic terms, between the superpowers. This presumption was what made it attractive to Moscow. Yet containment was always based on U.S. superiority—the military superiority required to defend far-flung allies, the geopolitical superiority needed to check the Kremlin's Third World thrusts, the sense of ideological superiority required to mobilize Americans for a long contest of ideas. "The level of deterrence suitable for Brezhnev," Rumsfeld pointed out, "is not necessarily the level of deterrence suitable for us."[80] Détente thus sat on an unstable foundation. It encouraged Moscow to seek a parity that Washington could not accept.

Nixon and Kissinger were not fools. They understood these problems and had hoped to use intrepid statecraft to force moderation on Moscow until the Soviets realized that their vision of détente—and history—would not materialize. "Our strategy," Kissinger wrote in 1974, "has been to induce a prolonged period of restraint in Soviet international conduct."[81] But doing so would have required incredibly deft synchronization of carrots and sticks, giving Moscow enough to keep it chasing détente while preventing it from exploiting a relaxation of tensions. Unfortunately, neither sticks nor carrots materialized, for Congress slashed the defense budget, constrained covert action, and blocked Kissinger's economic diplomacy. "Our successes in foreign policy are because we have been able to tie things together through authority, decisiveness, quickness and courage," Kissinger said. "Now I am constantly having to say, 'We would like to, but.' "[82]

Nor did linkage work as well as Kissinger had hoped. The concept of holding hostage progress on some issues until the Soviets delivered on others was premised on the notion that Moscow needed détente more than Washington—that the White House could walk away from negotiations, whereas the Kremlin could not. But the U.S. needed arms control agreements at a time of defense austerity, and American politicians needed diplomatic successes for electoral purposes. So threats to stall détente quickly lost credibility, most notably when Moscow declined to prevent North Vietnamese troops armed with Soviet weapons from assailing South Vietnam in 1972 and overrunning it in 1975. By then, the Soviets could brush off indications that Third World interventions would endanger SALT II, because Kissinger was publicly admitting that America had no appetite for an "unrestrained strategic arms race."[83] Likewise, linkage required a nearly unchallenged executive, able to bestow rewards and punishments, but the collapse of executive authority in the mid-1970s, a result of Vietnam and Watergate, made this impossible. Containment worked well for decades because it was relatively simple. Détente required a complexity—and a diplomatic virtuosity—that democratic systems find hard to sustain.

Détente thus showed that efforts to limit the Cold War were themselves limited by the fundamental clash of interests and ideas that drove the U.S.-Soviet competition. It proved that transactional cooperation in one area—arms control—could not forever stabilize a relationship that remained competitive in so many others. Not least, the trajectory of détente revealed the inherent difficulty of trying to socialize the Soviet Union into a system predicated on American superiority. But was America better or worse off for having pursued détente? The truth is complicated.

Détente did sometimes create competitive drag. When Nixon and Kissinger argued that the superpowers had reached a "generation of peace," they probably made it harder to convince Americans that the struggle, and the need for harder measures, continued. Détente's reduced emphasis on ideological competition and economic denial gave Moscow a breather at a time when the system was struggling; it also obscured the fact that Soviet behavior was a product of the Soviet regime. America needed more "stress on the fundamental conflict between our values and those of the Soviets," one adviser wrote to Carter. "It is their *system* that generates an Afghanistan invasion or a Sakharov banishment."[84] Additionally, the intense focus on arms control did not stop the Soviets from cheating, sometimes egregiously, on détente-era agreements.[85] Yet détente did center the relationship on an issue—military power—where the Soviets were strong and not on issues where they were becoming weak.

Détente also developed a certain momentum—geopolitical and political —that made it tricky for policymakers to acknowledge its flaws. Kissinger was reluctant to admit any problems through the mid-1970s, even as aides concluded that "the line of most détente critics in the public and Congress is not far off target."[86] Carter, for his part, let his early commitment to détente numb him to Soviet expansion in the Third World. He and his secretary of state, Cyrus Vance, earnestly engaged Moscow on issues like conventional arms transfers to developing countries just as the Kremlin was aggressively using such transfers and other tools to advance its position.[87] The Carter administration was intent on arms control and cooperation, Dobrynin wrote in 1978. "It goes without saying that it is necessary to use this in our interest."[88]

The effect of détente on Soviet calculations also left something to be desired. Brezhnev viewed détente as a vindication of Soviet power. It was only possible, he explained, "because a new correlation of forces in the world arena has been established."[89] U.S. policy, then, seems to have had ironic results. The prestige, pageantry, and other benefits that détente brought the Kremlin reinforced the idea that Soviet strength would ultimately force the West to accept a new reality. For if, as the CIA reported, "Soviet leaders ascribe the progress of Moscow's policy of détente since the late 1960s in large measure to the growth of their military power," then what incentive was there for Moscow to stop expanding it?[90] Very little. The Soviets exploited détente by encouraging Western peace groups to inveigh against the arms race even as they deployed SS-20s and other instruments of coercion.

There were, then, real problems with détente. Yet it doesn't necessarily follow that the policy was a blunder. After all, détente was not the primary *cause* of America's waning energy for the Cold War; it was a *response* to that waning energy. And for all its flaws, détente did bring significant advantages.

We have already seen how détente aided America by making the arms race a qualitative contest and opening the Soviet bloc to subversive influences. There were other benefits, too. Détente reduced the danger of a truly grave international crisis at a time when the United States was ill suited for a showdown. When crises such as the October War did occur, close contact between U.S. and Soviet leaders arguably drove down the chances of matters getting truly out of control. Moreover, for all the handwringing about détente's impact on the defense budget, U.S. leaders periodically used international negotiations to avoid unilateral retreats.

In 1971, Nixon thwarted a Senate measure that would have unilaterally halved the U.S. troop commitment to NATO by seizing on a Soviet willingness to discuss mutual force reductions in Europe. And when the Pentagon secured funding for new weapons systems, it was often through the argument that these investments would give U.S. diplomats something to negotiate with. The United States, Nixon maintained, had to be "in a position to say, 'We've got something that you want to reduce, now what are you going to tell us?' "[91] Détente, in this sense, prevented further damage to America's strategic position.

Admittedly, when it came to U.S. alliances, the results were mixed. The French worried about a U.S.-Soviet deal to divide the world; the Germans feared that superpower arms control was leaving Europe exposed. The entire policy of détente, State Department officials wrote, was "weakening the rationale of NATO" by downplaying its motivating threat.[92] Yet the shift to diplomacy with Moscow probably prevented an even worse outcome: the fragmentation that would have occurred had America stood aside as the allies pursued bilateral détentes of their own. Kissinger summarized the strategic benefits in 1974: "We began détente in 1970 in an environment when we had to defend the budget for the

Vietnam War and fight constantly against the unilateral disarmers. Détente gave us: first, domestic maneuvering room; secondly, an opportunity to get control of our allies, and thirdly, to get into a position where
we would not get the blame for every confrontation that occurred."[93]
Some of this, admittedly, was after-the-fact rationalization. Yet it wasn't
all posturing, for détente eventually did have a constructive effect within
the United States.

By refusing to rush into the Cold War in the 1940s, the U.S. government had helped convince Americans that there was little alternative to
waging that conflict. Détente served a similar function. It showed Americans, disillusioned by Vietnam, that their leaders were willing to work for
peace, thus making it more likely that the population would support
stronger measures in the future. "If détente unravels in America," Nixon
had predicted, "the hawks will take over, not the doves."[94] Sure enough,
détente's erosion led to a distinctly hawkish turn. In 1976, nearly three-
quarters of Americans favored continuing détente, but by mid-1978, a
majority wanted a more assertive policy.[95] Two years later, Reagan rode
his critique of détente to the White House. A policy of negotiation in the
1970s made possible a policy of confrontation in the 1980s.

The Cold War, political scientist Robert Jervis reminds us, was not a
security dilemma—an essentially blameless situation in which two actors
are trapped in a spiral of unwanted hostility.[96] The Cold War was much
as Kennan diagnosed it: a struggle against an enemy that was paranoid,
deeply expansionist, and conditioned to seek the overthrow of the capitalist world. This competition was not "a normal clash of national interest." It was something more profound.

This cleavage made it all the more impressive that the superpowers
set any limits on the Cold War. That the two countries created rules to
regulate their rivalry showed that cooperation could prevail even within
heated competition. That Moscow and Washington succeeded in solving
shared problems proved that fierce rivals could find common ground.
The history of the Cold War is, in this sense, reassuring. It reminds us
that competition can be kept within bounds.

Yet that history also sounds notes of caution. The most important
steps taken to limit the Cold War came after the most dangerous moments in that contest: it took a glimpse of catastrophe for the superpowers to commit to avoiding it. Moreover, controlling the Cold War was so

hard because competitive diplomacy always comes with dilemmas. It can undermine alliances as well as strengthen them, weaken domestic resolve instead of solidifying it, tempt an adversary rather than reassuring it. During the Cold War, these concerns were hardly hypothetical. The Soviets did use negotiations to drive wedges between America and its allies; diplomacy did, at times, lead not to calm but to crisis.

All this placed a high premium on preventing the understandable desire for de-escalation from leading to a collapse of Western vigilance. The Truman administration's apparent indifference to diplomacy is more generously understood as a smart emphasis on sequencing—on maximizing free-world power before negotiating with Moscow. Ike's unsatisfying but prudent approach seems reasonable in retrospect. The American emphasis on negotiations gradually became more pronounced as the perils of an unconstrained Cold War increased. Yet the keenest observers understood that the search for stability must enhance, not weaken, the country's competitive position.

This was, in fact, where efforts to set limits ultimately paid off. Not every U.S. overture to the Soviet Union was a net strategic positive. But in general, the value of disciplined, careful diplomacy was in making the Cold War less onerous and dangerous for Americans—and thereby improving the odds that the country would stick with that conflict long enough to win it. This point applied even to détente. That policy's aspirations outstripped its achievements; it created competitive drawbacks of its own. But it also delivered sometimes-surprising benefits, not least that the travails of détente eventually convinced Americans to recommit to the Cold War.

Put differently, Kissinger probably didn't derive much satisfaction from watching Reagan rise to power by trashing his policies. But the repudiation of détente was, perhaps, an affirmation of its logic. Long-term rivalry demands commitment and a willingness to sacrifice, both of which must periodically be renewed. The vain search for cooperation can, ironically, remind a country of the importance of effective competition. Sometimes bids to ease tensions can, by failing, help a nation succeed.

CHAPTER SEVEN

Knowing the Enemy

L ONG-TERM COMPETITIONS PLAY out in arms races and diplomatic
dramas that rivet the world's attention. But such contests also
feature subtler, less-visible processes that occur in the background. Those processes rarely dominate the headlines. They
may, however, determine who dominates the competition.

One such behind-the-scenes struggle of the Cold War was the
decades-long effort to know the enemy—to understand Soviet intentions,
capabilities, and characteristics. What did the Kremlin ultimately want?
Would it wage war to achieve its goals? What was the true military balance? Was time on Washington's side or Moscow's? Answering such questions was critical to tailoring America's strategy. "The fate of the nation,"
according to one task force, "may well rest on accurate and complete intelligence data."[1]

Acquiring that information was a monumental challenge. No Cold
War asymmetry was starker than the contrast between American openness
and Soviet secrecy. Soviet observers could study America just by following
the news; U.S. analysts had to penetrate a system that made deception and
self-isolation an art form. Espionage came naturally to a party born in
clandestine struggle; it came less naturally to a democracy whose secretary
of state could remark, in the 1930s, that "gentlemen do not read each other's mail."[2] The United States, an intelligence panel noted in 1954, was
"relatively new at the game," and was "opposed by a police state enemy
whose social discipline and whose security measures have been built up

and maintained at a high level for many years."[3] Indeed, the Soviets were superior at collecting intelligence through traditional means, especially human sources, throughout the Cold War: Moscow penetrated Washington far more thoroughly than Washington ever penetrated Moscow. America had to close the intelligence gap by other means.

In the eyes of many critics, it failed miserably. Senator Daniel Patrick Moynihan was so disgusted by the CIA's performance that he proposed to abolish the agency.[4] Harvard historian Richard Pipes pronounced the entire field of Sovietology a boondoggle: "I do not believe that ever in history has so much money been lavished on the study of a foreign country with such appalling results."[5]

Yet these critiques missed just what a long road Washington faced in deciphering the Soviet Union and how far it got. From an inauspicious beginning, America eventually pieced together an impressive understanding of the enemy, one that was flawed but good enough to enable decent strategic choices. By the 1970s and 1980s, U.S. analysts sometimes knew more about the Soviet Union than Kremlin officials did. What is remarkable is not how poorly America did in the intelligence competition but how well. That achievement required a determined and eclectic approach to learning about the enemy, one that—like all good competitive strategies—overcame America's weaknesses by leveraging particular U.S. strengths.

"There is an urgent need to develop the highest possible quality of intelligence on the USSR in the shortest possible time," the director of the Central Intelligence Group announced in 1946.[6] Sound information—tactical and strategic—was a matter of life and death. Yet at first, U.S. intelligence managed to be very good and hideously bad at once.

To say that the U.S. government struggled to acquire detailed intelligence would be generous. Information on industrial facilities, military bases, and other potential targets was sketchy and outdated. Washington could only guess at the size of the Soviet economy or the timeline to the development of a Soviet atomic bomb.[7] American intelligence had hardly any agents behind the Iron Curtain; the State Department rarely knew the real biographies of Soviet officials until their obituaries appeared.[8] There were bright spots. The United States made good use of refugees that streamed out of the Soviet bloc after World War II, and signals intelligence (SIGINT), derived partially from captured German code-breaking capabilities, provided information on Soviet troop dispositions.[9] But into the 1950s, the United States was highly reliant on fragmentary or dubious information, and American intelligence failed to adequately predict key events such as the Berlin blockade, the Tito-Stalin split, the Soviet A-bomb test, and Chinese intervention in Korea. "In the beginning, we knew nothing," Helms wrote.[10]

This situation was partially a residue of the wartime Grand Alliance with the Soviet Union: Roosevelt had not spied on Stalin nearly as aggressively as Stalin had spied on Roosevelt. Institutional deficiencies were also a problem: in 1948, the CIA had only twelve analysts who spoke Russian.[11] The intelligence community's first major report on Soviet intentions was, a CIA higher-up wrote, "produced by one man over the weekend to meet an unanticipated and urgent requirement."[12] And, of course, the Soviets deserved credit. The Kremlin severely restricted contact with its population, and border controls made infiltration nearly impossible.[13] "A vast area of the world stretching from the Elbe River in Germany to the Yangtse in China is largely behind an iron curtain where the normal sources of information are partially or wholly lacking," an early government review of the CIA stated.[14]

It was all the more impressive, then, that America's broader understanding of the enemy was so astute. The Air Force may have used old *National Geographic* maps to plot bombing runs, but American officials nonetheless got the chief strategic judgments right. The CIA and the State Department accurately assessed that Stalin's Soviet Union was fundamentally hostile but not fanatically aggressive; that it would exploit weakness but respect strength; that it would not risk a third world war until it had recovered from the second.[15] This understanding provided the analytical backbone of containment. It also enabled Washington to move boldly, especially in Europe in the late 1940s, while avoiding a costly military buildup.

Even where analysts failed to precisely predict major shocks, the U.S. government sometimes got the basic strategic warning right. Kennan accurately forecast the Communist coup in Czechoslovakia; the CIA warned in 1949 that U.S. withdrawal from South Korea "would probably in time be followed by an invasion."[16] The best strategic intelligence—that knowledge, wrote longtime CIA official Sherman Kent, "upon which we base our high-level national policy"—did not always come from the sexiest sources.[17]

It came, rather, from an earlier investment in a small but able cadre of experts. Kennan, Bohlen, and a few State Department colleagues had studied the Soviet Union since the 1920s. They had lived there and knew its history. Not even they could surmount the wall of secrecy around Kremlin decision-making. But they understood what Kennan called "the mental world of the Soviet leaders" and could gauge how Moscow would react to key crises and challenges.[18] "They are power-minded to the greatest degree," Kennan explained, but "I don't think they will ever provoke a conflict with what they consider to be a superior force."[19]

This idea that the Soviets would "recognize situations, if not arguments," interacted with a second source of insight: an understanding of the "correlation of forces."[20] One need not read Stalin's mail to realize that World War II had devastated the Soviet Union, that the overall balance of power favored America, and that chaos in Western Europe provided copious opportunities for Soviet expansion without overt aggression. The CIA could assert, in 1948, that war was unlikely, based on available evidence and "the logic of the situation."[21]

This knowledge was good enough for the early Cold War, but not for a long Cold War. A small cadre of Sovietologists couldn't carry America through an extended global competition. By 1950, moreover, the balance of power was shifting so rapidly—and Moscow was behaving so assertively—that U.S. officials were losing confidence in their assessments of Soviet restraint. "We used to think we could take our time up to 1952," said Acheson, "but if we were right in that, the Russians wouldn't be taking such terrible risks as they are now."[22] America needed a clearer understanding of Soviet intentions; the advent of the thermonuclear age made a more precise view of the military balance imperative. As the Cold War escalated, so did the premium on knowing the enemy.

Meeting that challenge required building an intelligence capability worthy of a great power *and* a great democracy. In 1945, America had no peacetime history of centralized intelligence. The FBI, the military services, and the State Department ran their own operations, but their activities were uncoordinated and parochial. The shuttering of the wartime Office of Strategic Services in 1945 reflected the jealousy of these organizations, as well as fear that a democratic society might now require a secretive intelligence apparatus that could become an "incipient Gestapo."[23] The early setup of the intelligence community manifested this wariness. The Central Intelligence Group, created in 1946, was a bureaucratic pygmy—"a step-child of three separate departments," two officials noted—that never made its mark.[24]

The CIA, which superseded the Central Intelligence Group in 1947, wasn't initially much stronger. The military services refused to acknowledge that there was anything "central" about this agency; they fought to keep it bureaucratically marginalized. CIA covert action capabilities did grow quickly, but its analytical capabilities and utility to policymakers lagged. Amid crises in Berlin and other hot spots, Truman and Marshall wanted the CIA to provide tactical warning of a Soviet attack—an understandable request, but one that the agency was ill equipped to fulfill. The CIA, the *New York Times* commented, remained "one of the weakest links in our national security."[25]

That would change as an accelerating Cold War pulled U.S. intelligence along with it. By 1967, the CIA had 12,000 nonclerical staff.[26] The agency rapidly expanded its collection of intelligence, using human sources as well as overhead reconnaissance, satellite imagery, and other means. Under Walter Bedell Smith and Allen Dulles, the director of central intelligence (DCI) became a key presidential adviser and oversaw the larger intelligence community. The Board of National Estimates produced all-source assessments on the Soviet Union, and an Office of Current Intelligence monitored day-to-day developments. By the mid-1950s, the Office of Research and Reports had over five hundred analysts working on the Soviet economy; by the mid-1960s, the intelligence budget was 5 percent of federal outlays.[27] This was a massive investment in understanding America's competition.

The CIA, however, consumed only 15 percent of that investment, which meant that it had plenty of help. The U.S. intelligence establishment never resided in a single body; it retained a pluralistic, even competitive, feel.[28] The National Security Agency (NSA) ran signals intelligence and boasted 65,000 employees by 1960. The Defense Intelligence Agency served the Pentagon. The Bureau of Intelligence and Research served the nation's diplomats. The National Reconnaissance Office and National Photographic Intelligence Center coordinated major satellite programs. The U.S. community, in turn, anchored a global network of liaison relationships that linked America to its closest allies and eventually countries stretching from Sweden to Japan.[29]

This concentric-circles approach had its drawbacks. Liaison relationships could be vectors for vulnerability. The Soviets periodically stole American secrets through double agents within the British establishment; relying too heavily on foreign spies could make their blind spots America's own. Within the U.S. government, a decentralized intelligence

community sometimes struggled to share information or shake off parochial interests, as when the most alarmist assessments of Soviet bomber
and missile capabilities in the 1950s came from an Air Force looking to
expand its own forces.[30] The CIA itself had an elitist character that inhibited diversity; rapid growth during the 1950s led to sloppy management and security breaches. "Too much information is leaked at cocktail
party," one review scolded.[31]

Yet the U.S. approach also produced competitive advantages. "American intelligence analysts became encyclopedic in their knowledge," one assessment notes.[32] They studied Soviet canned goods to evaluate the
economy; they scrutinized the Soviet power structure by observing who
stood where at annual parades. They even learned the cynical jokes Soviet
citizens told each other.[33] By the 1970s, the CIA knew more about Soviet
weapons systems than some of Moscow's negotiators did. When America's
SALT delegation "set forth some details about Soviet ICBMs," Helms
commented, "eyebrows shot up on the other side of the table, and notes
were busily taken."[34] For all the travails with human sources, the CIA had
some significant successes, among them securing Warsaw Pact battle plans
that the Pentagon used to develop the competitive strategies of the 1980s.[35]

The concentric-circles design was also a net-positive. Liaison relationships had a tremendous multiplier effect. The United States and its Anglo-
sphere allies divided up the world for SIGINT; allies and partners allowed
Washington to set up listening posts around the Soviet periphery. Washington could trade its expertise in technical collection for access to human
sources and local expertise. Ties to the Western democracies were especially fruitful. America and the United Kingdom "shared more secrets than
any two independent powers had ever shared before." The United States
could not "unilaterally collect all the intelligence information we require,"
Secretary of Defense Weinberger explained. "We compensate with a variety of intelligence sharing agreements with other nations of the world."[36]

The greatest strengths of the U.S. intelligence community itself
were its decentralized nature, which produced a strong internal marketplace of ideas, and its emphasis on honest analysis and fierce debate.
Under Kent's direction, the Board of National Estimates produced National Intelligence Estimates (NIE), America's most authoritative assessments. The NIE process drew on inputs from across the community.
The goal was to produce consensus, but Kent encouraged dissent and
the NIEs explicitly flagged disagreements. Draft NIEs were scrutinized
by participating agencies and, in some cases, outside experts. The prod-

ucts that emerged set the gold standard for integration and assessment of intelligence, a capability the Soviets never had.[37]

Nor did the Soviets enjoy another feature of U.S. intelligence: its relatively apolitical nature. The CIA was headed by political appointees, but the community was overwhelmingly staffed by civil servants and military officials. Although Air Force or Navy intelligence sometimes advanced suspiciously self-serving positions, the CIA stood apart from any other bureaucratic interest. This ethos was a design feature. Back in 1945, Robert Lovett remarked that "the four top German Intelligence Officers had been executed for political reasons." It would be better to follow the British model, which aimed to "divorce the factual aspects of their findings from political creed."[38]

To be sure, the wall between intelligence and policy could be porous, and none of these arrangements guaranteed accuracy. The CIA compiled a long list of predictive and analytical failures, from falling for the myths of a "bomber gap" and a "missile gap" in the 1950s to underplaying Soviet fears of war in the early 1980s. As a result, certain policymakers doubted the community's wisdom, and analysts sometimes hedged their conclusions to avoid embarrassment if events went the other way. "Some products are written using a kind of Delphic writing," one Kissinger aide wrote; "the aim is to be not caught out rather than to clearly communicate."[39]

Indeed, the relationship between the intelligence establishment and the country it served was perpetually awkward. Some presidents, such as Eisenhower and Reagan, gave the CIA latitude. Others, such as Kennedy, Nixon, and Carter, distrusted it. Decision-makers periodically pressured the intelligence community to provide analysis that supported their policies, just as intelligence leaders occasionally censored their findings to avoid irritating the White House.[40] By the 1970s, after investigations revealed assassination plots, surveillance of Nixon's political enemies, and other malfeasance, the CIA itself was sometimes labeled a threat to democracy. "Abolish the CIA!" *Newsweek* declared.[41] The agency was not abolished, but Congress did impose curbs on covert action and create new oversight committees. The intelligence community was always the most controversial element of America's national security architecture, which made sense, given the tensions that its very existence created.

Yet these controversies revealed another attribute of the U.S. intelligence apparatus: that it remained responsive to democratic requirements. That some presidents trusted the CIA while others tried to ignore it showed, for better or worse, that elected civilians ran the show. Likewise,

Congress's bid to exert greater control over the CIA in the 1970s was evidence of an ongoing back-and-forth over how much power a democratic intelligence agency should have. That back-and-forth, in turn, made the existence of an intelligence agency more tolerable to Americans over the long run.

Not least, the greatest strengths of American intelligence—its apolitical ethos, its institutional pluralism and vigorous debate, its partnerships with genuine allies—flowed from the best characteristics of America's political system. "We are going to run an American intelligence service," DCI William Colby said in 1975. "It's going to reflect our country's attitudes; it's going to reflect our country's standards; and it's going to reflect our country's laws."[42] Perhaps the democratic approach to intelligence was not such a handicap after all.

A second aspect of U.S. strategy was using technology to conquer secrecy. The Kremlin's veil of isolation permitted it to either mask or exaggerate its military strengths. This could be a critical asset when assessing the military balance was vital and avoiding surprise attack was paramount. America could hardly emulate Soviet practices. "Thanks to our habit of publicizing everything," Ike said in 1953, "it was so much easier for the Soviets to find out what they needed to know about our capabilities."[43] Instead, America maximized its own asymmetric advantage. "What saved us," DCI James Schlesinger later remarked, "was our adoption of technology."[44]

This intelligence offset strategy was there from the start. During the early Cold War, when America's human intelligence capabilities were basically nonexistent, Washington used SIGINT—which capitalized on advantages in science, technology, and mathematics—to narrow the deficit. Under the VENONA program, Army codebreakers uncovered Soviet espionage in America. In 1946, SIGINT helped reveal how serious the Soviet threat to Turkey was. And in 1951, communications intercepts reassured Truman that the Soviets would not attack Western Europe while U.S. forces were bogged down in Korea. Thereafter, Truman and his successors aggressively expanded America's global SIGINT partnerships, marrying technological superiority to the benefits of genuine multilateralism.[45]

The NSA soon built an intelligence empire second to none. That agency employed more holders of advanced degrees in mathematics and electronics than any other entity. It developed a global network of ground intercept and monitoring stations. During the 1950s, specially equipped surveillance planes mapped Soviet air defenses; by the 1970s, a combination of SIGINT satellites, communications intercepts, and other tools allowed the NSA to track Moscow's most sophisticated military capabilities and detect signs of any major mobilization or attack.[46] Throughout the Cold War, SIGINT illuminated the dark interior of the Soviet bloc.

Yet the payoff from using technology to penetrate secrecy was greatest in the 1950s and 1960s. American knowledge of Soviet military programs was very limited then, creating severe analytical problems. The United States found itself vulnerable to cheap gimmicks, as when the same Soviet bombers repeatedly flew past the U.S. embassy on May Day, 1955, to create the impression that the overall fleet was several times its actual size.[47] The intelligence deficit also rendered Washington susceptible to worst-case analyses after unexpected shocks, such as the launch of *Sputnik*. When systematic information is lacking, nuggets of data—however misleading— take on outsized importance.

During the 1950s, Washington was thus gripped by fears of a bomber gap and then a missile gap. The Air Force warned that the Soviets might have 1,000 ICBMs by 1962; the CIA projected a lesser, but still terrifying, American inferiority.[48] "Strategic missiles will surely replace the manned bombers, as the longbow replaced the knights' swords," journalist Stewart Alsop warned. America would be like "the mounted French knights at Crécy, sword in hand, facing the skilled British bowmen killing them at will."[49] That prospect created psychological leverage for Khrushchev and left skeptics—namely Eisenhower—struggling to make the case that America was not headed for disaster.

Eisenhower tried to solve this problem through mutual transparency. But when the Soviets rejected his Open Skies proposal, he proceeded unilaterally. Allen Dulles had argued in 1954 that "no price would be too high to pay" for "systematic and repeated air reconnaissance over the Soviet Union itself."[50] By the time of the Geneva Conference in 1955, the United States was developing a high-altitude reconnaissance plane, the U-2, that could soar above Moscow's air defenses and use state-of-the-art cameras to surveil Soviet territory.

The U-2 soon showed that the bomber gap was a myth. It took longer to prove the absence of missile installations in a country covering 17 percent of the earth's landmass. Yet U-2 imagery did reinforce Ike's belief that Soviet strategic advantages were make-believe, allowing him to resist both Khrushchev's bullying and domestic calls for massive defense hikes. After a U-2 was shot down over the Soviet Union in 1960, Washington made another leap with the CORONA satellite, which provided far better coverage with far greater safety.[51] By 1961, the CIA assessed that Moscow had only 10–25 operational ICBMs, so Kennedy could handle Khrushchev from a position of strength in Berlin and Cuba.[52] Eyes in the sky helped America navigate the most perilous stretch of the Cold War.

Overhead imagery was not a cure-all. The U-2 was late to discover Soviet missiles in Cuba in October 1962, not because of technical limitations but because CIA analysts refused to believe that Khrushchev would take the risk of deploying them. The agency was also slow to understand the scope of the Soviet buildup that followed—not because it failed to accurately count Moscow's ICBMs but because it failed to realize that the Soviets aimed to achieve a strategic advantage and would keep on building. The problem, in both cases, was mirror-imaging: failing to recognize that Soviet leaders might not think like Americans. Even the best information has to be interpreted by humans who sometimes struggle to see the world through an enemy's eyes.[53]

By and large, however, Schlesinger was right to say that technology saved the United States. SIGINT and satellites yielded highly accurate information on Soviet forces, ensuring that—as Gates later wrote—"after the 1960s, there were virtually no Soviet military surprises of broad strategic importance."[54] That achievement protected the United States from fears of surprise attack or new smoke-and-mirrors bullying campaigns. It also protected America from exaggerated concerns that might have resulted in unsustainable defense burdens. "The key is knowledge," said Helms in 1967. "Without this knowledge there can be no rational planning of our own prodigiously costly defense effort."[55] America relied on what it did best—exploiting advanced technology—to overcome what the Soviets did best, keeping secrets from the world.

It wasn't just the U.S. government that tried to see the world through Soviet eyes. America also built an intellectual ecosystem focused on all things Soviet. This "whole of society" undertaking involved academics, think-tankers, and other intellectuals. Here, as elsewhere, the United States tapped distinctive features of its system—elite universities and well-endowed foundations, the climate of open inquiry and debate—to understand the enemy's.

The rise of academic Sovietology was remarkably rapid. In 1945, only a few dozen U.S. professors were studying the Soviet Union. That changed as the Cold War got under way. World War II had caused an explosion of cooperation between scholars and the state; the U.S.-Soviet struggle directed that blast toward a new enemy. In 1943, the OSS—the predecessor of the CIA—created its USSR Division, which led to Russian studies initiatives at Cornell and Columbia. By the late 1950s, thirteen prominent universities had programs offering Russian-language training and multidisciplinary coursework in history, economics, political science, literature, and other subjects to the next generation of Sovietologists.[56] The goal, one survey concluded, was to learn the "operating characteristics" of Soviet society, "the psychological traits of Soviet man," and "the balance of social strengths and weaknesses."[57]

If the momentum was impressive, that was because Sovietology linked some of America's most powerful institutions. Top universities conducted research and trained students, many of whom subsequently worked for the CIA or the State Department. Think tanks such as the RAND Corporation studied Soviet affairs, often in coordination with government sponsors. The Carnegie Corporation, Rockefeller Foundation, Ford Foundation, and other philanthropies provided generous funding—$47 million from the Ford Foundation in 1966 alone. The U.S. government arranged academic exchanges that gave American scholars access to the Soviet Union and enlisted academics as consultants and officials. By the 1970s, the CIA had relationships with more than 100 academic institutions. Not least, Uncle Sam helped bankroll the entire operation through research contracts and funding for Soviet studies programs.[58]

Sovietology was always meant to serve the needs of the state—as MIT and Harvard did in the 1950s by conducting a CIA-sponsored "Soviet Vulnerabilities Project."[59] But the presumption was that a mix of government sponsorship and intellectual freedom would produce the most useful results. Just as the logic of the market generated America's economic strength, the marketplace of ideas would maximize its intellectual strength.

The Soviet Vulnerabilities Project had CIA funding, but its conclusion contested the idea—still lingering in the political warfare community— that Washington might split Ukraine or other republics from Moscow's control. Similarly, the Air Force's "Refugee Interview Project" was meant to determine how Soviet citizens would react to nuclear war. Yet the principal resulting publication emphasized aspects of the system the Soviet population liked—welfare provisions, literacy programs—as well as control mechanisms it detested.[60] More broadly, the fact that there were lively, even vicious debates in the field belies the notion that anyone was pulling intellectual strings. By the 1980s, Sovietologists more commonly condemned U.S. policy than supported it. There was nothing remotely like this intellectual independence on the Soviet side.

Even so, the field went through peaks and valleys. The boom of the 1950s and 1960s gave way to the bust of the 1970s, when the Vietnam War pitted intellectuals against government and economic hardship took its toll. "The whole field of Soviet foreign policy ... is in rather sad shape," Stanford historian Alexander Dallin wrote. "The generation of Kennans and Bohlens is virtually gone."[61] The quality of the work was also uneven. During the early years, scholars such as Merle Fainsod produced groundbreaking studies on political conflict and control in the Soviet Union. Zbigniew Brzezinski highlighted dynamics of cooperation and discord within the bloc. Nathan Leites illuminated the worldview of Kremlin leaders.[62] Yet those in the field also compiled lots of work that was politicized, polemical, or simply wrong.

Some leading Sovietologists argued, into the 1980s, that Soviet citizens enjoyed high economic security. Others contended that the one-party Soviet system was pluralistic and inclusive or claimed that Moscow had won the loyalties of non-Russian nationalities.[63] Perhaps most damning, few Sovietologists foresaw the Soviet collapse, because they overestimated the stability of the system and underestimated the difficulties of successful reform. "The belief that the Soviet Union may disintegrate as a country contradicts all we know about revolution and national integration throughout the world," wrote one leading expert just months before that disintegration occurred.[64]

If anything, the quality of Sovietology declined as its scholarly "rigor" increased. In the 1940s and 1950s, key books were written by individuals who understood the despotic nature of Soviet power, in some cases because they were émigrés from the bloc. Breakthrough studies were based on refugee interviews or critical caches of records that revealed the inner workings of the regime.[65] By the 1970s, however, the field was dominated by social science. The search for hard data over softer sources sometimes left analysts reliant on misleading government statistics. Or it encouraged them to use quantifiable but trivial sources, such as counts of articles in Soviet journals, in hopes of somehow assessing the basic character of the system. Richard Pipes, a Polish émigré, argued that the obsession with "scientific" methods was his fellow Sovietologists' undoing. "They missed everything that was vital in that society and that, in the end, made it unworkable: human aspirations and human discontent."[66]

Yet blaming Sovietologists for missing something that Gorbachev himself failed to foresee seems uncharitable; predicting earth-shaking events that alter our sense of the possible is always difficult. The real question is whether Sovietology fostered knowledge and strategic insight. The answer is yes.

In the broadest sense, Sovietology provided America with a deeper, more diverse, and stronger bench of experts. Academics could do research in the Soviet Union more easily than their CIA colleagues; lacking access to classified data, they drew on sources their government counterparts might ignore. For example, Brzezinski's visits to the bloc during the 1950s illuminated for him how unhelpful, even irrelevant, Communist states had become to their citizens.[67] Where disagreements between Sovietologists occurred, the results were usually constructive. In the late 1970s and 1980s, experts from the CIA, the RAND Corporation, and other institutions debated the level of Soviet defense spending before Congress, exposing the members to multiple perspectives on a complex issue.[68] A larger intellectual ecosystem was a richer one. And even if the worst outputs of Sovietology were naïve and credulous, the best were quite astute.

Studies from the 1960s accurately forecast that a stultifying bureaucracy would impede the innovation needed to remain competitive.[69] In the 1970s and 1980s, RAND analysts demonstrated just how much Moscow's overseas commitments and multiplying enmities were burdening a weak economy.[70] Academic demographers were early to realize that Soviet infant mortality was rising and life expectancy was falling, sure signs of societal decay.[71] The sharpest academic students of the Soviet Union were among the first to see how grave its weaknesses were.

Indeed, if most Sovietologists didn't expect the Soviet collapse, they did warn that the system would not forever endure. As early as the 1950s, academics such as G. Warren Nutter pointed out that the "impressive façade" of the Soviet economy concealed a "hollow shell."[72] They argued that the Soviet growth model, which used brute-force inputs of capital and labor to compensate for extremely low efficiency, would produce declining results over time. In the 1960s and 1970s, academic (and CIA) economists concluded that productivity was slumping and consumer demands were going unmet. In 1983, Wellesley's Marshall Goldman predicted that the "ultimate day of reckoning" was approaching.[73] Predictions of where these trends would lead were, understandably, all over the place. Yet these Sovietologists, historian Marc Trachtenberg writes, identified the major problems and showed that "fundamental choices were going to have to be made."[74]

A final success of Sovietology was solving the "Kennan succession problem" by creating a pipeline of government experts. As national security adviser, Brzezinski advocated political warfare in Eastern Europe and efforts to inflame problems with Soviet nationalities because his work had convinced him that these were weak spots. In the 1980s, Pipes laid the intellectual foundation for Reagan's strategy with his argument—based on decades of studying the Soviet system—that "the Stalinist model . . . confronts at present a profound crisis caused by persistent economic failures and difficulties brought about by overexpansion."[75] Jack Matlock had trained in Russian studies at Cornell; as ambassador to a dying Soviet Union, he was one of the first Americans to sense the magnitude of the political earthquake Gorbachev had triggered.[76] By the late Cold War, the U.S. investment in Sovietology was paying dividends in administration after administration.

"The Americans beat us not because they had more tanks, but because they had more think tanks," one Soviet official later said.[77] Hyperbole, perhaps, but also a testament to how well America harnessed its intellectual strengths.

A final approach to overcoming the information asymmetry was learning through interaction. That asymmetry was greatest in the early Cold War, when Washington was poor in hard intelligence and the experiences through which it could comprehend a secretive competitor. The length of the Cold War afforded an opportunity to learn by doing and seeing— to decipher, through repeated interactions, the Soviet enigma.

U.S. officials certainly learned from their up-close interactions with Soviet leaders. During the 1970s, summits with Brezhnev revealed that his health was in stark decline—a visible manifestation of the system's advancing sclerosis. "Anyone who has dealt with Brezhnev recently must conclude that his life expectancy is limited," Kissinger noted.[78] In other cases, personal meetings yielded crucial policy insights. In 1959, Averill Harriman (an adviser to multiple Cold War presidents) had an hours-long discussion with Khrushchev, whose too-jaunty performance convinced him that the missile gap was a bluff. "The Soviets did not have much confidence in the present capability of their long-range missiles," he reported to Eisenhower's team.[79] Near the end of the Cold War, Reagan and George H. W. Bush used their meetings with Gorbachev to gauge whether his promises of diplomatic and political reform were real.[80] The value of summits could be as much in the information they revealed as in any agreements they produced.

Other East-West contacts were less rarefied but not less informative. Détente did not simply add to an understanding of how the Soviets negotiated. Expanded everyday contacts—East-West travel and cultural exchanges, trade and economic ties—constituted an intelligence treasure trove because they lowered the barriers Stalin had erected between the bloc and the world. For a time, détente also allowed a surge in emigration of Soviet Jews and dissidents to the West, where they conveyed a picture of economic shortages, political frustrations, and social malaise. CIA reporting on these issues soon became more perceptive. East-West exchanges allowed valuable information to escape the Soviet bloc as they let subversive ideas in.[81]

Learning through interaction also involved reconnaissance by fire—probing the Soviet system in ways that elicited informative responses. On multiple occasions, the United States flew aircraft near or even over Soviet territory, forcing Soviet air defenses to respond and thereby pinpointing gaps in the warning net.[82] Similarly, radio broadcasts triggered Soviet jamming and counterpropaganda that were themselves enlightening. If the Soviets furiously denied stories about the Katyn massacre of Polish officers in 1940, then Moscow must fear Eastern European nationalism. And if the Soviets were spending $70 million on jamming equipment and $17 million per year in operational costs—when America was spending just $22 million on its worldwide broadcasting program—then these vulnerabilities must be worth targeting.[83] Political warfare required knowing the enemy, but it could help acquire that knowledge as well.

The most valuable information revealed something fundamental about the competition and how it could be turned to American advantage. By the 1970s, Washington had a quarter-century of experience in the arms race. That experience helped dispel the hoary myth that the Soviets built new weapons only to keep pace with the Americans. "When we build they build; when we cut they build," quipped Harold Brown.[84] That experience also allowed analysts such as Marshall to see what threats—penetrating bombers, for instance—so concerned the Soviets that they consistently overinvested against them. Finally, it provided clues about how the Pentagon might game a Soviet defense complex that featured ponderous multiyear plans. The evolution of Soviet defense programs suggested "predictable patterns of behavior," Marshall wrote. "A superior understanding of the interaction process" could help Washington "steer Soviet posture choices."[85] The United States could not read Soviet minds. But it could read how Moscow had responded to stimuli in the past, and thereby forecast how it might behave in the future.

Indeed, the effort to know the Soviet way of war was a long-term endeavor. It required amassing copious information—including countless doctrinal publications and training manuals—on Soviet concepts of offense and defense.[86] It involved observing Soviet weaponry in proxy conflicts and scrutinizing major exercises to see how Moscow might employ its forces in Europe. Over time, this approach enabled the Americans to construct a clearer picture of what a superpower war might look like. Combined with secrets obtained through a heroic Polish mole within the Warsaw Pact hierarchy, it helped U.S. planners understand the Soviet emphasis on scripted maneuvers and rapid reinforcement, thus allowing the Pentagon to devise its devastating counters.[87] The competitive military strategies of the 1980s rested atop an intellectual breakthrough that was the product of both daring spycraft and the patient accumulation of knowledge.

Learning through interaction worked both ways, of course. Yet America benefited more than the Soviets did, since the marginal knowledge to be gained about a closed society was so much greater than the marginal knowledge to be gained about an open one. The protracted, iterative nature of the Cold War often seemed like a strategic burden. In this case, it was a blessing.

None of this solved all of America's intelligence problems. In the second half of the Cold War, the intelligence establishment was surprised by events it should have expected, like the Soviet invasion of Czechoslovakia, as well as by events that shocked everyone, like the opening of the Berlin Wall.[88] In between, there were times when American intelligence was in disarray. During the 1970s, the CIA was demoralized by budget cuts, embarrassing scandals, and a president (Nixon) who derided the agency as "muscle-bound bureaucracy."[89] Throughout the decade, acrimonious debates threw into question how much U.S. officials really knew.

One such debate involved what, precisely, the Soviets wanted in the Third World. Were they scooping up gains as chances arose? Or was there a "grand design" to attain hegemony? Defense Intelligence Agency analysts and hawkish officials advanced the latter thesis. The Soviets, they said, were seeking "overall dominance" by pursuing "the establishment of Soviet political, military, technological, and economic superiority world-wide."[90] Others, namely Cyrus Vance, argued that Moscow was merely engaged in "exploitation of opportunity," so America should not treat each crisis "as a local battle in a global East-West geopolitical struggle."[91] CIA assessments varied, often splitting the difference. Moscow was striving "to weaken Western military, economic, and political positions," one NIE stated, but was "highly opportunistic" in picking its moves. In retrospect, this nuanced assessment was about right.[92] Yet the unresolved debate created hesitance, even incoherence, in Carter's response well into 1979.

No less charged was the argument over whether the Soviets were striving for deterrence or dominance in the military competition. Pipes believed the Soviets were ruthlessly Clausewitzian—that they saw war as the continuation of political struggle—and were seeking nuclear superiority to prevail in any conflict with the West. "As long as the Soviets persist in adhering to the Clausewitzian maxim on the function of war, mutual deterrence does not really exist," he wrote.[93] Critics rejoined that Pipes was exaggerating the threat. A parallel internal debate raged from the beginning of détente to the end, with the CIA changing its view over the course of the 1970s. Having first attributed the Soviet buildup to a search for stability, the agency later concluded that Moscow was seeking nuclear advantage. The Soviets had "never accepted the concept of mutual assured destruction," the agency concluded in 1977, even if mutual deterrence was "a present reality that will be very difficult to alter."[94]

Even before this shift, the debate had caused a nasty fight. In 1974–1975, members of the President's Foreign Intelligence Advisory Board argued that recent NIEs were understating the Soviet buildup.[95] In response, Bush (then DCI) reluctantly blessed an exercise in competitive analysis, in which hawkish outsiders (Team B) would take on CIA analysts (Team A). Headed by the venerable national security official Paul Nitze and Richard Pipes, Team B argued that Soviet leaders were pursuing global hegemony through the accumulation of decisive military power. Team B also tore into a decade's worth of NIEs, charging the CIA with a litany of analytical sins, among them, downplaying Communist ideology and assuming that Soviet officials thought like their U.S. counterparts.[96] CIA analysts countered, correctly, that Team B had made worst-case assumptions about Soviet force development. They also rejoined, more disputably, that Team B itself had misjudged Soviet aims.[97] The experiment ended unhappily, with leaks of elements of the Team B report, allegations that critics of détente had politicized the intelligence process, and a lament from Bush that "I feel I have been had."[98]

Meanwhile, the CIA's reputation was tarnished by glaring analytical errors. Into the mid-1970s, the CIA argued that Moscow was spending 6–8 percent of its GNP on defense. Skeptics found the estimate absurd. How, Schlesinger wondered, "could the Soviets develop a military force roughly comparable to that of the United States if they were spending the same percentage of a GNP roughly half as big as that of the United States?"[99] It took an analytical crusade by Schlesinger and Marshall for the agency to concede that the Soviet defense burden was really 11–13 percent of GNP.[100] Yet even that estimate was wrong—the real number was at least 25 percent.[101]

To make matters worse, the CIA underestimated the Soviet defense burden because it overestimated the Soviet economy. The agency judged that Soviet GNP had reached 50–60 percent of American GNP in 1970. Yet that assessment overemphasized misleading official production measures and missed the appalling degree of waste and inefficiency in Soviet industry. In reality, the Soviet economy was one-sixth to one-third of the size of the U.S. economy. "The CIA considered the Soviet Union an economic power when it was actually an economic wreck," the *New York Times* later alleged.[102] The 1970s was a rough decade for American intelligence, just as it was a rough decade for America in the Cold War.

Fortunately, the United States wasn't as confused as it often looked. In some cases, debates were inconclusive because realities were complex—and the CIA did fairly well in parsing those complexities. Its assessment of Moscow's move into Afghanistan properly noted that the occupation was "a reluctantly authorized response" to the impending collapse of a friendly regime. But it also accurately noted that the Soviets "covet a larger sphere of influence in southwest Asia" and believed the occupation would "improve their access to . . . extremely lucrative targets."[103]

On other issues, such as the state of the military contest, intelligence debates were so polarized because they occurred amid heated policy disputes over arms control and détente. In still other cases, the underlying analytical problem was just extremely challenging. Top economists puzzled for years over how to measure investment and output in an economy without meaningful price mechanisms, how to accurately convert rubles (whose value was set by fiat) into dollars, and how to do all of this despite a smokescreen of Soviet obfuscation. "Even if the Soviets were a good deal more open than they are, we would still have problems of evaluation," RAND's Abraham Becker told Congress. But "the fact that the Soviets reveal virtually nothing" made matters harder.[104] And if the 1970s revealed shortcomings in American intelligence, that decade also affirmed the virtues of the U.S. approach.

Regarding the Soviet economy, the GNP estimates were off, but the assessment of trends and weaknesses was dead-on. In 1969, one NIE noted that "Soviet leaders face severe problems at home" and that "Marxism-Leninism is a dead ideology . . . a calcified scripture."[105] Throughout the 1970s, the CIA provided in-depth descriptions of worsening economic ills—shortages of consumer goods, unsustainable debt burdens, plummeting productivity.[106] In 1980, CIA briefers told President-elect Reagan that a "strategy of 'marking time' " would not keep Moscow competitive because "economic problems are too severe."[107] The CIA actually had a better understanding of Soviet economic problems than many Kremlin officials did. In one case, the agency's public reporting on the Soviet energy sector was so good that it helped Moscow address problems identified in the report.[108]

The intelligence community could so accurately describe the arc of the Soviet economy for a variety of reasons: because it had hundreds of analysts studying the issue; because it had built an enormous mass of data that revealed change over time; because it could exploit the work of leading academic economists; and because, in the 1970s and 1980s, parts of the U.S. government increasingly complemented economic figures with other revealing measures, such as rising infant mortality.[109] If U.S. reporting was fairly perceptive, it was because Washington had devoted so much energy to that endeavor.

The 1970s also showed how sophisticated U.S. appraisals of the balance of power had become. Under Carter, NSC aide and Harvard professor Samuel Huntington spearheaded a Comprehensive Net Assessment that compared the superpowers along multiple dimensions. That project utilized intelligence material as well as concepts from social science to compare the effectiveness of U.S. and Soviet political institutions, the dynamism of their economies, and the cohesion of their societies no less than their arsenals of ICBMs. The findings were debated in working groups and high-level meetings; the outstanding insight was just how narrowly based Soviet power was.[110] America "has a more creative technological and economic system," a flexible political system, and a retinue of "allies and friends who genuinely share similar aspirations." The Soviet Union was a military superpower with ghastly internal problems and "few genuinely committed allies."[111] The Soviets talked incessantly about the correlation of forces, but the Americans were measuring it in a serious way.

Most important, the debates of the 1970s confirmed that the intelligence community was capable of introspection and self-correction. After all, Marshall, Schlesinger, and others did successfully challenge the CIA on the Soviet defense burden by mustering evidence from defectors, classified data, and other sources. Even more remarkable, the CIA publicly admitted the error and explained why it had been wrong.[112] Likewise, in 1976 the CIA conducted a comprehensive review of NIEs produced over the last decade to understand why it had not foreseen "the degree to which the Soviets would not only catch up to the U.S. in number of ICBMs but keep right on going."[113] And while Bush was disgusted by the Team B exercise, it led to internal admissions that the CIA had too often dismissed the possibility that Moscow might want—and attain—a strategic advantage, and to refinements of the NIE process, such as paying greater attention to alternative scenarios and outside experts.[114] The episode was painful, but it showed the value of an environment in which orthodoxies could be challenged and mistakes scrutinized.

This sounds banal until we consider the Soviet approach. Moscow "had an inbuilt advantage" in collection, Christopher Andrew writes, but lacked reliable mechanisms for assessment. Pessimistic reports were suppressed, and intelligence agencies blamed setbacks on imperialist trickery rather than Soviet errors. The rule, one official admitted, was "blame everything on the Americans, and everything will be OK."[115] As Kremlin leaders became more decrepit and paranoid, Soviet bloc intelligence outfits had to adopt their obsessions. America could never compete with the Soviet Union in secrecy. What it could do was create a climate in which real analysis could occur.

The ultimate test of how well a country understands its antagonist is whether that knowledge can guide a winning strategy in a contest's crucial moments. As Washington turned the corner in the Cold War in the 1980s, Reagan's pressure campaign was based on a highly accurate map of enemy weaknesses.

Reagan's understanding of the Soviet Union was surprisingly strong and remarkably idiosyncratic. His gut told him that the Soviet experiment must eventually end, because perpetuating it required suppressing human freedom. His perceptions of Soviet policy and frailty came from many places: amateur Russia experts, quotes (often apocryphal) from Lenin's writings, information from dissidents, anecdotes about everyday life. Reagan had "heard reports of the fervor of the underground Church in the Soviet Union itself," he told Vatican officials in 1981. "He had heard stories of Bibles being distributed page-by-page among the believers."[116] Reagan's reliance on such impressionistic sources provoked ridicule from critics. Yet there was hard analysis behind his views.

During the 1980 campaign, Reagan consulted with leading Sovietologists. Pipes advised him that "there are regions of the Soviet Union where neither milk nor meat are even available in stores."[117] After the election, CIA briefings showed that economic problems would make it "increasingly difficult" for Moscow to keep pace.[118] Once in office, Reagan had access to a mountain of evidence that confirmed his instincts. Daily briefings "were revealing tangible evidence that Communism as we knew it was approaching the brink of collapse," he wrote.[119]

This reporting soon became even better. The U.S. intelligence budget roughly doubled between 1981 and 1988.[120] Under Casey, the CIA prepared detailed "vulnerability assessments" of the Soviet economy. Henry Rowen, head of the National Intelligence Council (NIC), highlighted signs of decay such as food lines, work stoppages, and surging crime. Defense Department intelligence reported growing "doubt that the Soviets can count on East European armies" in a conflict.[121] When Reagan argued that the Soviet system was headed for an existential crisis, he was basing that confidence on more than faith.

Herbert Meyer, vice chairman of the NIC, synthesized this analysis in a series of remarkable memos between 1983 and 1985. Meyer catalogued the problems afflicting the Soviet system. "At long last," he wrote, "history seems to be catching up with the world's last surviving empire."[122] He forecast that a declining superpower might become more erratic and "lash out dangerously."[123] And he identified the formidable roadblocks to revitalization. Reforms must "set free" economic sectors dominated by the state, which would require shattering the "Communist Party's stronghold on power." If that high-wire act failed, "then we are probably heading toward a major shift in the balance of global power, of a magnitude that happens only once or twice in a century."[124] It was a remarkably accurate roadmap for the rest of the Cold War.

There were still plenty of things the Reagan administration did not know. The CIA was reportedly unsure whether Yuri Andropov was married until his widow appeared at his funeral.[125] Yet what Reagan most lacked, into 1983, was a recognition of just how scared the Soviets might become as the Cold War slipped away from them. That realization would come sooner rather than later, setting the stage for a long drama's final act.

Assessments of U.S. intelligence during the Cold War have long been distorted by a myth—that America's spies missed the coming collapse of the Soviet Union because they overlooked the widening cracks in the system. The charge is misleading in several ways. Washington was not blind to Soviet decay. After all, Reagan's pressure strategies featured an acute appreciation of that weakness. Nor is it true, as the penultimate chapter shows, that American analysts never foresaw the possibility of a Soviet implosion. Finally, this interpretation of U.S. intelligence focuses excessively on whether the CIA predicted a single, profound historical discontinuity. It fails to take into account the decades-long campaign to know an enigmatic power.

Failure is an inherent part of any such effort. U.S. analysts, Gates wrote, were expected to "somehow perceive a change in policy between the time the decision is made in Moscow and the time when that change is manifested in action."[126] America nonetheless racked up impressive achievements. It built a vast repository of knowledge on Soviet capabilities and behavior. It found inventive ways of penetrating Soviet secrecy. Most important, the United States learned enough to avert irreparable surprises, keep the costs of competition manageable, and inform critical strategic judgments. America's performance was sound enough to see it through a decades-long rivalry with the ultimate intelligence hard target.

Still, that performance did not come easily. It required a remarkably broad approach to intelligence, one that drew insight from experience as well as espionage, from academics as well as cleared analysts. It took building not just a sprawling intelligence establishment, but a larger intellectual ecosystem of Sovietology. It involved generational investments in training and expertise. For all of America's ambivalence toward intelligence, U.S. officials recognized that competing effectively required knowing the competition intimately. The mobilization that America undertook—not just of financial resources, but of intellectual creativity—reflected that imperative.

Above all, the U.S. record shows that the logic of asymmetry applies to intelligence as much as to any other realm of strategy. At first glance, America suffered from crippling disadvantages. But it mitigated, even overcame, those weaknesses by building an intelligence establishment that reflected the strengths of American democracy; by tapping into a peerless network of allies and partners; by exploiting its technological superiority to overcome an asymmetry of transparency; by harnessing the capabilities of academic and philanthropic institutions; even by using the length of the Cold War to its advantage. When one faces a built-in competitive deficit, the only recourse is to mobilize offsetting strengths.

A few analysts had long understood the task. In 1949, Truman commissioned a review of a struggling intelligence establishment. Yet that scathing report, authored by, among others, Allen Dulles, argued that the country possessed underappreciated virtues. "America has the potential resources, human and material, for the best intelligence service in the world," the report stated. It possessed "loyal sons speaking every language," "the greatest reservoir of scientific and technical skills," and "allies abroad who are ready to join their knowledge to ours." Most critically, America enjoyed the "individual initiative, skill and ingenuity of a free people," which outweighed the "iron discipline" of "a slave system."[127] This passage may have read like patriotic puffery in the late 1940s. In retrospect, it seems rather prescient.

CHAPTER EIGHT

Organizing for Victory

OLICY IS MORE EXCITING than bureaucracy. But bureaucracy enables policy, because it is the mechanism through which a country organizes itself for action. "Organization cannot make a genius out of an incompetent," Eisenhower explained. Yet "disorganization can scarcely fail to result in inefficiency and can easily lead to disaster."[1]

U.S. officials understood the importance of organizing for victory during the Cold War. Creating a sophisticated intelligence apparatus was only part of a larger initiative: building the structures and processes America needed for a long global struggle. This task represented a historic departure for a country whose foreign policy bureaucracy was still scrawny and immature on the eve of World War II—and might well have reverted to its earlier state had the Cold War not intervened.

Winning that contest would require reinventing the American government for great-power rivalry. The United States would have to build a strong national security infrastructure, enable presidential command without destroying constitutional balance, develop new tools to address novel problems, and incubate long-term strategic thinking. America would need to do all this, moreover, within a political system in which power was fragmented and action was sluggish by design. The challenge, in short, entailed developing the bureaucratic sinews of a superpower without ruining the country's democratic soul.

————

Today, the existence of a powerful U.S. national security state seems eminently normal. It wasn't always that way. Distrust of diplomats and standing armies was inherent to the American experiment. Prior to World War II, America's ocean buffers kept rivals away and its foreign policy apparatus small and weak. Outside of wartime, the dominant departments were not State, War, and Navy, but Commerce, Agriculture, and Treasury; outside of the military, strategic planning remained a rarity. As late as 1938, there was no interagency process: FDR was the only integrator of foreign policy.[2]

World War II exposed the inadequacy of these arrangements and initiated a halting revolution in American government. Military leaders warily accepted interservice coordination. The State Department expanded dramatically. Interagency bodies took shape. Military and civilian staffs began looking over the horizon and planning for the peace. Entirely new organizations were created for covert action and propaganda. At the center was FDR, who balanced bureaucratic rivalries and provided a "world point of view."[3]

Yet America's national security institutions had expanded in wartime before and might again have contracted once the conflict ended. World War II had convinced many leaders that America needed a more unified defense establishment. There must be "one team with all the reins in one hand," Truman wrote in 1944.[4] Still, there was no straight line between World War II and the Cold War state. The fact that FDR was so devious in wielding presidential power had actually impeded the emergence of systematic decision-making structures. The Joint Chiefs of Staff remained an ad hoc, loosely organized body; there was strenuous opposition to unification within the services, particularly the Navy. Many wartime agencies were abolished after V-J Day. And since America's relationship with the Soviets remained ambiguous when World War II ended in 1945, so did the future of the national security establishment.[5]

The atmosphere of 1946–1947 was one of uncertainty and chaos. The intelligence establishment was a competitive mess. Debates between the military services were acrimonious. The State Department was dominated by parochially minded regional bureaus. "There has been a notable lack of any central planning on American policy," Forrestal (soon to be named secretary of defense) lamented. The world's greatest power, he wrote, lacked the governmental machinery for competition.[6] The growth and evolution of the American national security state would parallel the rise of the East-West contest. The U.S. government, one historian observed in 1992, was "a legacy of the Cold War."[7]

The first step was laying the basic institutional foundation; the key document was the National Security Act of 1947. That legislation preserved independent military services (and created an independent Air Force) but brought them under the authority of a civilian secretary of defense; it codified the Joint Chiefs of Staff as a standing body; and it brought forth the CIA and the National Security Council. The act resulted from long, rancorous debates; its institutional innovations were seminal.[8] Yet the National Security Act was both less and more than it appeared, because it embodied conflicting pressures inherent in remaking the government for global rivalry.

One pressure was the drive for centralization. The United States needed "something similar to the British system for coordinated and focused government action," Forrestal had earlier argued.[9] War Department leaders had repeatedly made the case for rationalizing America's military functions. The National Security Act was thus meant to close seams that had frustrated purposeful movement: seams between services that guarded their own distinctive cultures and ways of war, seams between military and civilian institutions, seams in intelligence and information-sharing that might prove fatal in the nuclear age. The newly created National Security Council would coordinate debate and action across the government and around the globe.

The act was less revolutionary than it might have been, though, because of a countervailing resistance to centralization. Truman fought the idea of a strong NSC, worrying that it might allow unelected cabinet heads to dictate policy. The military services blocked the drive for full unification; the civilian service secretaries—nominally subordinate to the secretary of defense—remained quite powerful as full members of the NSC. The Chairman of the Joint Chiefs of Staff was also weak by design, since he controlled no combat forces and had to rely more on persuasion than on command. Indeed, opponents of unification argued that naming a single uniformed commander might fatally undermine civilian authority. The idea, Truman himself conceded by 1946, reeked of a " 'man on horseback' philosophy."[10] What the Cold War required, in other words, might run counter to what the nation's traditions demanded.

The resulting legislation involved a clutch of awkward bargains and left a great deal unresolved. A basic framework for centralization had emerged, but key relationships remained ambiguous. The controversies that led to the National Security Act persisted after its passage.

The civil war within the Pentagon continued, with disputes over B-36s and supercarriers being exacerbated by zero-sum competition for dollars. The atmosphere, wrote Atomic Energy Commission chairman David Lilienthal, was one of "chaos and conflict and carnage confounded."[11] The State and Defense Departments regularly concealed information from each other. The combined stress of battling the Soviets and battling the services led Forrestal, who had become secretary of defense, to suffer a breakdown and kill himself. Through the 1950s, Ike found himself imploring the JCS to "work as a team, not fight among themselves."[12] Decades later, reformers were still trying to make the services cooperate and the interagency process work properly. In view of how frequently congressional critics and presidential commissions demanded redesigns of the foreign policy apparatus, its existing design might have seemed a flat-out failure. The system, however, was more intelligent than it looked.

For one thing, the National Security Act gave America the bedrock capability for competition. The bodies it created—an NSC to advise the president; a CIA to collect and analyze intelligence; a Department of Defense to oversee the military; a JCS to promote interservice cooperation—addressed, imperfectly, the need for coherent arrangements within government if Washington were to act effectively beyond its borders. Those bodies, along with the State Department, were the institutions on which America would most depend over the coming decades of rivalry; they constituted the foundation on which more issue-specific entities could be layered. That the country emerged from the Cold War with the same basic setup showed that the National Security Act got the building blocks of global influence mostly right.

In fact, the National Security Act endured *because* it was an awkward hybrid, one that balanced competitive requirements with political realities. The system of "coordinating pluralism" hardly ended bureaucratic rivalries.[13] But it provided mechanisms for arbitrating disagreements and encouraging cohesion without triggering the backlash a more dramatic centralization might have provoked. This reliance on coordination and persuasion, rather than ruthless discipline, could be a strength. It made consensus harder to come by but decreased the chances that terrible ideas would survive the bureaucratic gauntlet. Seemingly parochial feuds could also be healthy strategic debates. "How curious it is," quipped one naval officer, "that the Congress *debates*, the Supreme Court *deliberates*, but for some reason or other the Joint Chiefs of Staff just *bicker*."[14] If the American system was a set of unwieldy compromises meant to allow both pluralism and purposeful action, the Cold War state was its worthy descendant.

In the same vein, the persistence of independent military services ensured ongoing interservice rivalry, sometimes to the point of absurdity. But it also forced the services to compete and innovate against each other, and it helped the Pentagon develop the strategies and forces needed for Cold War rivalry. The emergence of a more robust nuclear triad (the three-legged deterrent consisting of strategic bombers, land-based missiles, and submarine-launched missiles) during the 1950s, for instance, was the result of interservice struggles for relevance as well as larger strategic concerns.

In the end, the relative ambiguity of the National Security Act framework was a virtue, because it left room for evolution and renegotiation. By 1949, the administration and the Congress were cooperating to clip the wings of obstructive service secretaries, strengthen the secretary of defense, and enhance the power of the JCS Chairman. Truman, meanwhile, was learning to tolerate the NSC. He appointed trusted aides like Averell Harriman to run it, and came to appreciate, amid crises in Berlin and Korea, the need for a central policymaking body over which he could preside.[15] These adjustments initiated a decades-long pattern of institutional change within the basic framework of the National Security Act; presidents used that construct while adapting it to suit their purposes. Like the U.S. Constitution, the National Security Act was a "living document." Like containment, it offered flexibility within an astute design.

That pattern of give-and-take was useful when facing a second challenge: strengthening presidential command without losing constitutional equilibrium. America's peacetime presidency had traditionally been rather weak, in part because government's primary business was managing domestic affairs. The Cold War, however, was an extended global emergency. It would require agile diplomacy, shadowy struggles for influence, and timely use of national power, all of which were tasks the American founders thought the executive best suited to perform. "Decision, activity, secrecy, and despatch will generally characterize the proceedings of one man," wrote Alexander Hamilton, not those "of any greater number."[16]

The Cold War made Hamilton look prescient. Truman took numerous crisis-driven actions—shipping arms to Europe, intervening covertly in France and Italy, joining the fight in Korea—unilaterally. By the early 1950s, the thermonuclear revolution had made it apparent that the president, or even his unelected subordinates, must be able to take the gravest, most irrevocable actions without congressional approval. For if victory in thermonuclear war truly hinged on a few precious moments, there would be no time for consultation, let alone legislation. And if U.S. strategy turned on the ability to threaten nuclear annihilation, the executive would need great latitude in quasi-peace as well as war. "When it comes to action risking war," said historian Richard Neustadt in 1963, "technology has modified the Constitution."[17]

By the time of Neustadt's observation, the tools of presidential power were truly awesome. U.S. nuclear command-and-control arrangements, initially cumbersome, were streamlined so that a presidential command to initiate the apocalypse could be carried out immediately. The rise of the Strategic Air Command, under General Curtis LeMay, created a capability to deliver death on a global scale. The president also wielded worldwide military and diplomatic capabilities, along with a global covert operations apparatus that allowed intervention with only modest oversight.[18]

The NSC provided the mechanism for presidential control. As Truman discovered, that body was not the enemy but the friend of presidential authority. Eisenhower took the NSC to the next level. The council met 366 times during his tenure, with Ike leading 90 percent of those meetings. He created a Planning Board meant to craft government-wide strategies; implementation was monitored by an Operations Coordinating Board. Ike insisted, moreover, that the NSC was *his* council—its members should speak in their capacity as presidential advisers, not as representatives of their home institutions.[19] The president used a structured deliberative process to consider key issues; he forced advisers to air their differences, providing space and information for presidential choice. Eisenhower "likes nothing better than the flashing interchange of views among his principal advisers," wrote Robert Cutler, his first national security adviser. "Out of the grinding of these minds comes a refinement of the raw material into valuable metal."[20]

Ike's successors argued that his NSC system had been stodgy and lethargic. "Too big, too formal, and too paperbound," Bundy wrote.[21] Kennedy deemphasized full-dress NSC meetings and long staff papers; Nixon and Kissinger bypassed the council to make decisions themselves. These adjustments solved some problems and created others. The price Kennedy paid for agility was sloppy decision-making. Nixon and Kissinger used extreme centralization to achieve creativity but alienated most of the government. Yet even presidents who disdained formal NSC meetings relied on the influence the council provided. The small but advantageously positioned NSC staff became a "little State Department" that offered the president his own sources of advice and initiative.[22] The NSC increasingly served, wrote Cutler's successor, as "the helm from which the President looks out toward the broad horizon ahead and charts the world course we are to follow."[23]

All this constituted what the historian and Kennedy adviser Arthur Schlesinger Jr. called the "imperial presidency"—an office whose prerogatives expanded with America's global interests.[24] The president increasingly spoke for the nation in foreign affairs, with Congress rarely checkmating major initiatives or intrusively managed crises. The postwar "American political contract," one State Department official later wrote, was "that unwritten arrangement ... under which the Executive was given considerable flexibility in the implementation of foreign policy."[25]

By the 1970s, Schlesinger deplored this arrangement, and with some cause. There was something incongruous about the idea that a democracy might find itself fighting a civilization-endangering war on the judgment of a single official. Over time, moreover, American presidents became less scrupulous in wielding their authority. Whether it was a Kennedy aide—ironically, Arthur Schlesinger Jr. himself—lying about plans for an exile invasion of Cuba, LBJ stretching the truth about the Gulf of Tonkin incident, or Nixon secretly expanding the Vietnam War, the trend of evading public and congressional scrutiny was clear.[26] By the 1970s, Nixon was carrying the habit of executive overreach to an alarming extreme. "If ... America is to become an empire," Senator J. William Fulbright had warned, "there is very little chance that it can avoid becoming a virtual dictatorship as well."[27]

The truth, fortunately, was more nuanced. An empowered presidency had offsetting advantages. These included the flexibility and decisiveness that proved crucial in crises in the Taiwan Strait, Berlin, and Cuba; the ability to undertake unseemly but productive covert interventions; and the diplomatic dexterity required to keep the Cold War from turning too hot. Kennedy's secret concession, assiduously concealed from Congress and the public, to remove Jupiter missiles from Turkey helped end the Cuban Missile Crisis. That, too, was the fruit of an imperial presidency. Likewise, the Nixon and Ford administrations used presidential secrecy to achieve worthy goals such as the opening to China and the signing of SALT. As Kissinger argued, "one cannot put a negotiation before forty-five members of the House Foreign Affairs Committee."[28]

If the domestic balance of power shifted, moreover, Congress was rarely quiescent. The Marshall Plan and NATO were significantly shaped by senatorial concerns; Kennan, for one, was aghast at the *executive* deference involved.[29] Legislative leaders played a key role in debates on strategy in Korea, Eisenhower's New Look strategy during the 1950s, and the foreign aid budget. Because a formal declaration of war might be impossible when a crisis climaxed, presidents also periodically turned to Congress for authorization beforehand. Ike did this in the Taiwan Strait affair of 1954–1955 and the Middle East crisis in 1957, just as Kennedy asked Congress to authorize emergency defense measures during the Berlin crisis.[30] Modes of congressional influence changed during long-term competition, but they hardly disappeared. In fact, the number of congressional staffers multiplied eightfold during the Cold War. There was an "imperial Congress" to rival an imperial presidency.[31]

Importantly, the balance between the branches was never static. Whatever deference the executive received was conditional; it could be withdrawn if the White House led the nation astray. By the late 1960s, Congress was already reclaiming its influence in response to executive deceptions and misjudgments in Vietnam. Over the next few years, Congress forced a drawdown in Southeast Asia, restricted defense spending and covert intervention, and constrained executive war powers. "None of us wants to restore an imperial Presidency," Ford lamented after leaving office. "But neither can we afford an imperiled Presidency."[32] The Cold War was not a time of unchecked presidential power. It was a time when the boundaries of executive and legislative power were contested and periodically redrawn.

These struggles could produce ugly results. In seeking to rein in ill-advised CIA operations, Congress hindered the agency's ability to carry out more useful ones. "We are both ineffective and scared in the covert action area," DCI Bush noted in 1977.[33] Congressional meddling in arms control negotiations in the 1970s made it harder for Kissinger and his

successors to replicate the balance of concessions that had produced
SALT I. When Kissinger and Ford reacted reflexively to the U.S. defeat
in Vietnam by directing the CIA to intervene in Angola, the Senate
reacted just as reflexively in ending that intervention. "Where the hell is
Angola?" one member of the world's greatest deliberative body asked.[34]

In other cases, however, clashes for influence were more constructive. The rise of human rights policy in the 1970s originated with a congressional critique of Kissinger's statecraft by what one official termed an
"unholy alliance" of liberals and neo-conservatives.[35] During the 1980s,
congressional demands that the United States seek far-reaching reforms
from repressive partners actually strengthened Washington's leverage.
Congressional support might collapse, Vice President George H. W.
Bush told Salvadoran officials in 1983, "if you are not able to help yourselves in this way."[36] White House officials still chafed at congressional
oversight, but that oversight probably improved their decision-making.
"Some awfully crazy schemes might well have been approved had everyone present not known and expected hard questions, debate, and criticism from the Hill," Gates wrote.[37] The Cold War required executive
decision and dispatch. Yet it also rewarded executive-legislative discord,
because no one—on either end of Pennsylvania Avenue—had a monopoly on foolishness or wisdom.

What about institutions that addressed the long-term aspects of U.S.-
Soviet rivalry? There was no guarantee that an expanded bureaucracy
would fare well here. As institutions become entrenched, they can become blinkered and parochial. As a country's responsibilities expand, crisis management can become all-consuming. To succeed in the Cold War,
Washington would need to find ways of making the government think
strategically and competitively.

One answer was to create specialized planning units within key organizations. That's what Marshall did in establishing Department of State's
Policy Planning Staff in 1947. The office was created, Acheson wrote, as
"the stimulator, and often deviser, of the most basic policies." A small and
agile team, under Kennan's elite leadership, would provide a long-term
global perspective that the regional bureaus lacked; it would ruthlessly
assess existing policies to ensure that they were not sustained by inertia
alone. The staff must resist the tyranny of the quotidian ("avoid trivia,"
Marshall instructed), but fuse its work to real policy debates. It must es-

cape the crush of events while helping America impose its will on them.[38] To this end, Kennan had a direct line to Marshall, who was Truman's most important adviser; Policy Planning Staff papers were often simply adopted as NSC directives with the force of national policy.

As Kennan's influence later faded, so did his enthusiasm for the PPS model. Yet in the crucial 1947–1948 period, the staff played exactly the role expected of it. PPS papers sorted out geographic priorities amid crises everywhere. They developed the strategic logic—empowering "local forces of resistance," prioritizing economic and political reconstruction—that guided U.S. policy.[39] Most important, the PPS identified inflection points at which a bold departure—support for Tito, massive aid for Europe—might alter the long-term trajectory of the Cold War.[40] The experiment showed that cultivating strategic thought was indeed worthwhile, particularly if that effort came early in a competition, when the scope for bold thinking was greatest.

Unfortunately, it was difficult to sustain the conditions that allowed the PPS to prosper: the high level of talent; the tight relationship between director, secretary, and president; the geopolitical plasticity that rewarded big ideas. In subsequent years, the staff churned out some very bad work—about the prospects of strategic bombing in Vietnam, for instance—and its products could sometimes seem academic or irrelevant.[41] At other points, though, Kennan's successors helped draft NSC-68, formulate the New Look, sharpen Kissinger's thinking during détente, and push George H. W. Bush to "dream big dreams" regarding the possibility of liberating Eastern Europe.[42] At its best, the PPS offered the strategic insight that a global superpower needs but officers deep in the bureaucracy often struggle to provide.

A second way the United States encouraged strategic thinking was through a multigeneration commitment to planning at the apex of government. The canonical example was Eisenhower, with his highly classified "Project Solarium" in 1953 and the series of Basic National Security Policy reports that flowed from it. Like much of Ike's statecraft, Project Solarium (so named because key meetings were held in the White House solarium) was somewhat deceiving. The president already knew, broadly, what he wanted, and he pushed the three task forces involved with the project to debate options—containment, massive retaliation, aggressive rollback—he intended to synthesize.[43] But by conducting a structured, competitive analysis, Ike forced his team to confront essential questions about the strategic utility of nuclear weapons and the country's prospects in an indefinite competition. He also ensured that the resulting policy was intensely scrutinized before being adopted. Eisenhower had "never attended a better or more persuasively presented staff job," he remarked.[44] The purpose of strategic planning, in Ike's administration, was to stress-test policies that would guide America in a long Cold War.

The Kennedy and Johnson administrations put less value on deliberate planning, which was one reason U.S. strategy so regularly jumped the tracks during the 1960s. But Nixon and Kissinger used "laboriously developed" reports on U.S. policy to systematically work out their ambitions for détente.[45] The Carter administration then used its Comprehensive Net Assessment to think holistically about superpower strengths and weaknesses.[46] And while the Reagan administration was at first a disorganized disaster, it eventually used the preparation of a classified national security strategy and a study on U.S.-Soviet relations in 1982–1983 to articulate a multiphase approach to ending the Cold War.[47] The modes and quality of American planning varied tremendously. But on balance, the pattern of high-level systematic thinking—whether about winning or about simply managing the superpower conflict—made U.S. statecraft sharper.

Third, the United States made the bureaucracy smarter by fostering institutions that were competitive at the core. The exemplar was the Pentagon's Office of Net Assessment. ONA had its antecedent in a 1950s-era body, the Net Evaluation Subcommittee, charged with estimating the damage both sides would suffer in a nuclear war. Its conclusions struck Kennedy-era policymakers as macabre and even absurd in an age of mutually assured destruction. Yet as U.S. strategic dominance waned, Nixon and Kissinger created a successor office tasked with finding advantage by mastering the interplay between the superpowers' military establishments.

Under Andrew Marshall, ONA sought a granular understanding of the military balance—not just counting weapons but also considering how bureaucratic dynamics and organizational cultures would influence a high-intensity showdown. It assessed what the Kremlin could ultimately bear in extended competition by studying subjects—demography, the Soviet economy—far more eclectic than those usually considered by Pentagon planners. Not least, ONA developed an unrivaled understanding of what made Soviet defense planners tick—of how history, bureaucracy, and other issues conditioned Moscow's response to America's capabilities.[48] ONA was slow by design: "My own view," Marshall wrote, "is that the production of really innovative net assessments will require a long-term and sustained intellectual effort."[49] The goal was to foster a competitive way of thinking—to identify insights that would give America greater control of the Cold War.

ONA succeeded in this task. By the 1980s, its ideas were shaping a punishing asymmetric approach to military competition. What made the office effective was a combination of organizational and intellectual factors. ONA was sufficiently distant from the daily grind to devote deep study to big issues, but it also had, through Marshall's relationship with a series of defense secretaries, the influence to make its ideas count. Because of its unique mission and relative independence, ONA had the luxury of thinking long-term—of asking where America should be a generation hence and working backward to identify key investments. To focus its thinking, ONA cultivated an aggressively strategic mindset. It prioritized challenging the status quo and seeking out asymmetries to exploit; it held that Washington could regain the high ground through intense intellectual effort.[50] Small but well-positioned government institutions thus had an outsized effect. If America achieved good strategy during the Cold War, it was because U.S. officials built a capacity for producing it into the national security state.

Institutional innovation was crucial to staying ahead in a long struggle. It was equally important to succeeding in a contest as broad as the Cold War. That contest confronted America with problems, from arms control to information warfare, that it had never before addressed on a sustained basis. It continually revealed competitive gaps to be filled. In response, American officials created an array of issue-specific institutions—bodies that would allow the U.S. government to keep pace with an evolving Cold War.

The Economic Cooperation Administration (ECA), for instance, oversaw the Marshall Plan. The focus on propaganda and psychological warfare during the 1950s produced the U.S. Information Agency, just as the intensifying struggle for the Third World birthed the Peace Corps and the United States Agency for International Development (USAID). The Arms Control and Disarmament Agency (ACDA) reflected the move toward détente in the 1960s and 1970s; the National Endowment for Democracy (technically a nongovernmental organization) highlighted the rise of democracy promotion in the 1980s.

In theory, these new entities would make government more effective. In practice, it wasn't always straightforward. Some institutions struggled and were disbanded—who, today, remembers the Foreign Operations Administration? In other cases, institutions formed to pursue a specific agenda came to see that agenda as an end in itself. ACDA officials, for example, sometimes showed a near-religious commitment to arms control, even at the expense of strategy.[51] Worse, the bigger the bureaucracy grew, the more labyrinthine it became. The creation of USAID and the Peace Corps had "most certainly strengthened the conduct of foreign affairs," Rusk wrote in 1964. But it also led to more turf wars and headaches "in a world where timely, well-considered action . . . has become a vital necessity."[52]

Fortunately, most second-tier institutions did add to America's arsenal. The ECA streamlined implementation of a historic foreign aid program and attracted top talent from academia, business, and labor to rebuild Western Europe.[53] The Peace Corps showed the friendlier face of U.S. power at a time when Washington was often resorting to blunter instruments in the Third World. The ACDA, for its part, ensured that Washington had a community of officials with deep knowledge of arcane technical issues—a value revealed when Kissinger made errors during the SALT process after shunting those officials aside.[54] The National Endowment for Democracy showed how even a small, underfunded entity could make a big difference. That institution united a diverse group of actors with a common interest in democracy promotion; established an enduring, nonpartisan framework for action; and filled a key competitive gap. America had "no institutions devoted to political training and funding," Secretary of State Alexander Haig wrote in 1982. "If we want democratic forces to win, they need practical training and financial assistance to become as effective as the communists in the struggle to take and maintain power."[55]

Then there was the United States Information Agency (USIA), the best example of an institution purpose-built for rivalry. The Cold War was "a struggle, above all else, for the minds of men," Truman remarked. Entire nations might be "lost to the cause of freedom, because their people do not know the facts."[56] The State Department, the ECA, the CIA, and other agencies ran propaganda programs as part of the Marshall Plan; funding for information operations surged along with Cold War tensions. Yet U.S. information warfare remained incoherent, with responsibility for propaganda programs scattered across the bureaucracy.[57]

In response, the USIA was established in 1953. The agency brought most of America's informational activities under a single roof and tightened the link between propaganda and policy. By the early 1960s, Director Edward R. Murrow, the legendary newsman, was conferring regularly with Kennedy. Meanwhile, the USIA rapidly scaled up its activities as the Cold War spilled into the Third World. In the first half of 1961, the USIA opened ten new posts in Africa alone.[58] By that point, the agency employed 11,000 people and had 202 posts in 85 nations, all for the cost of a Polaris submarine. America was creating a global communications empire, described by one former executive as a "full-service public relations organization, the largest in the world, about the size of the twenty biggest U.S. commercial PR firms combined."[59]

The roster of activities was enormous. The agency administered 101 radio stations, provided 4,000 additional ratio stations with information and programs, and helped publish magazines and books in dozens of languages.[60] Art displays and jazz exhibitions took American culture global; over 30 million people visited U.S.-funded overseas libraries annually by the late 1960s.[61] From the late 1950s on, the USIA mostly trafficked in "white" propaganda—accurate information attributed to the U.S. government. But "where the motives or the policies of the U.S. are suspect or are under heavy attack," one advisory commission noted, it might also use "unattributed activities"—in essence, working through friendly local mouthpieces.[62] Since U.S. officials generally believed that the truth was on the free world's side, the agency's overarching goals were to give foreign populations an accurate understanding of American life and policies while shedding light on the dark realities of Communist rule.

The USIA was never a magic weapon. It was hard pressed to put a positive spin on McCarthyism, racial injustice in America, or the Vietnam War.[63] Early programs in the Third World sometimes misfired owing to a relentless focus on the evils of communism rather than "legitimate aspirations for freedom, progress, and peace."[64] Later, amid the post-Vietnam backlash, Fulbright sought to abolish most of America's information-warfare capabilities; amid the austerity of the 1970s, capabilities and morale suffered. "USIA has been largely ignored by the Executive Branch and threatened by the Congress over the past decade," employees complained.[65]

Even so, the USIA was an irreplaceable asset in dealing with enemies that viewed propaganda as a deadly serious pursuit. The agency's work, one U.S. ambassador wrote, "provided more 'bang for the buck' than any other comparable program."[66] In the Third World and the Soviet bloc, USIA programs were often the primary way by which people came to know the United States. USIA-sponsored jazz tours were fabulously successful advertisements for American culture and freedom of expression, even with

audiences that hated American policy.[67] And if nothing could erase the
damage America suffered from its own failings, the USIA limited that damage by emphasizing the achievements of the civil rights movement and the
possibilities of peaceful change. In 1954, Voice of America flashed around
the world news of the *Brown v. Board of Education* decision banning racial
segregation in schools. "You may imagine what good use we are making of
the decision here in India," Ambassador George Allen cabled.[68]

The agency also held Communist regimes to account for their more
grievous shortcomings, such as crushing uprisings in Hungary in 1956 and
Tibet in 1959. The latter event "probably had a greater anti-Communist
impact than any event since the Hungarian revolution," the USIA reported.[69] Even relatively mundane offerings, such as the U.S. library in
East Berlin, discomfited Communist regimes by exposing their citizens to
otherwise-inaccessible ideas.[70] Not least, USIA could amplify indigenous
voices, such those of Europeans who favored the deployment of Pershing
II missiles in the 1980s.[71] The agency provided the bureaucratic underpin-
ning for a global information campaign.

When USIA was energetically led and adequately funded, it could be
potent indeed. Between 1981 and 1985, USIA's budget rose 74 percent.
The agency received new technology, including Worldnet, an early satellite
television network that could broadcast almost anywhere. Director Charles
Wick used that capability, as well as radio, print, and other media, to launch
a "coalesced massive assault of truth."[72] USIA programs revealed Kremlin
abuses in the Third World and contrasted the decrepit Soviet system with
a prosperous, resurgent West. After the Chernobyl nuclear accident, VOA
and Worldnet shredded the clumsy Soviet cover-up. "This is the end of the
Soviet monopoly on telling people what they want to tell them," Wick declared.[73] U.S. political warfare was so lethal in the 1980s because Washington could shoot information straight into the enemy camp.

If anything, the USIA was arguably too capable for its own good. By
helping America win the Cold War, the agency put itself out of a job: it
was abolished in 1999. The USIA had been a vital cog in a machine built
for great-power rivalry. It came to seem expendable in an age of great-
power peace.

Sometimes, though, it wouldn't do to build a new agency for a new task.
Since countless aspects of U.S.-Soviet rivalry reached across the government, rearranging the bureaucracy to address them was not always possi-

ble. In these instances, organizing for victory was less a matter of changing the organizational chart than better connecting its pieces.

The most successful example was the Active Measures Working Group (AMWG). Political warfare was part of the U.S. strategic toolkit, but disinformation was a Soviet specialty. The KGB and other agencies systematically used forgeries and other "active measures" to weaken American standing and divide the free world. Soviet agents spread "fake news" about America's alleged complicity in murdering foreign leaders, creating the AIDS virus to kill Africans, and harvesting the organs of Mexican babies. Moscow supported European "peace groups" that stridently opposed a strong NATO.[74] By the 1980s, the CIA estimated Soviet spending on active measures at $3–4 billion per year. "At no time in this century," Casey wrote, "have these techniques been used with more effect or sophistication than by the current Soviet state."[75]

These operations were especially insidious because they perverted the information environments of open societies. The Soviets laundered false information, such as charges that West German officials were former Nazis, through reputable sources. Disinformation campaigns might use a kernel of truth as the basis for outrageous lies. In the Third World, KGB officials stoked latent anti-Americanism to fuel raging infernos of anger. "A single press article containing sensational facts of a 'new American conspiracy' may be sufficient," one Soviet bloc intelligence operative reported. "Other papers become interested, the public is shocked and government authorities . . . have a fresh opportunity to clamour against the imperialists while demonstrators hasten to break American embassy windows."[76]

Through the late 1970s, the United States had trouble fighting back. An underfunded RFE struggled to keep up with the flood of falsehoods. High-level interest in exposing Soviet active measures faded during détente, and bureaucratic stovepipes kept information walled off from officials who needed it. The Reagan administration's response was the Active Measures Working Group.

AMWG was a small interagency forum. It included mid-level officials from the CIA, the Pentagon, the Departments of State and Justice, the USIA, and other entities. The State Department was nominally in the lead; the CIA and, to a lesser degree, the Justice Department provided much of the intelligence. The motto was RAP—report, analyze, publicize—and the objective was to quickly gather and publicize information on Soviet disinformation campaigns.[77] The group would produce, through the State Department and USIA, detailed reports that explained Soviet disinformation techniques and flagged specific forgeries. That work would allow U.S. diplomats and USIA offices to bring the weight of America's foreign policy machinery to bear. Speed and transparency were the only way to defeat disinformation. Active measures "are infections that thrive only in darkness, and sunlight is the best antiseptic," State Department official Lawrence Eagleburger wrote.[78]

On its own, AMWG could never compete with an industrial-scale Soviet disinformation program. But AMWG was supported by a president who was determined to "stop losing the propaganda war" and a bureaucracy energized by that determination.[79] What the group could do, then, was integrate American detection capabilities—FBI and CIA reporting, the knowledge of well-informed analysts and defectors—and connect them to the diplomatic and informational tools Washington possessed. Just as important, the group could mobilize the broader free world information environment. To that end, AMWG participants pushed information to friendly intelligence services. They sensitized journalists to the prevalence of forgeries and disinformation, making them less likely to act as Soviet dupes.[80]

The model worked remarkably well. The AMWG put a klieg light on practices that required opacity to succeed. It revealed, with forensic detail, the purposes, pervasiveness, and mechanisms of Soviet disinformation.[81] The group helped unravel potentially damaging Soviet plots, such as the effort to trigger a boycott of the 1984 Olympics by fanning fears that white supremacists would lynch Black athletes. Over time, its work made the information environment steadily less receptive to Soviet measures, flipping the cost curve in this domain of competition. "The group exposed Soviet disinformation at little cost to the United States," one study concluded, negating much of the "multibillion-dollar Soviet disinformation effort."[82]

The AMWG also empowered the rest of the U.S. government to confront the Kremlin by providing the information needed to make the allegations stick. In 1987, Secretary of State Shultz—armed with reporting derived from the group's work—publicly challenged Gorbachev over Soviet disinformation about AIDS. The KGB gradually wound down the campaign.[83] The AMWG accomplished a lot with a little by amplifying the effectiveness of a much larger bureaucracy. In doing so, it drove down the returns on a Soviet investment that had vexed the free world.

Neither the AMWG nor any other arrangement made the U.S. government a well-oiled machine. Through the late Cold War, rivalries between key players—Brzezinski and Vance, Shultz and Weinberger—were intense and sometimes damaging. The bureaucratic architecture periodically had to be reformed because of persistent shortcomings. The biggest overhaul of the Defense Department came with the Goldwater-Nichols Act of 1986, motivated in part because a war against Grenada, of all countries, showed that the services still struggled to fight as a team. Into the 1980s, chaos and conflict still characterized some U.S. decision-making. The Iran-Contra scandal, a tragicomedy that featured not one but two inept, illicit covert operations, was not what the National Security Act was meant to produce.

Yet no framework could have produced a seamless approach to competition. "Management of U.S. foreign affairs will never be tidy or easy," one presidential task force concluded in 1967. "It is beyond the power of any government, however manned and however organized, to foresee all events, to prepare for all contingencies, or even, in all situations, to see clearly its own best interests."[84] Many of the disputes that roiled the U.S. government reflected genuine policy disagreements. Nor would a structure that stifled these debates have served America well. Many of the country's worst blunders were failures of judgment as much as failures of process. And many of the challenges the U.S. government faced—rivalry between contending power centers, the messiness of decision-making—were baked into the nation's political tradition.

America did well enough in managing the resulting tension. It built a formidable national security bureaucracy that could turn the nation's raw power into global influence. It found ways of injecting strategic thinking into policy and crafted a framework for strengthened, but hardly limitless, presidential command. Washington forged institutions to close competitive gaps and solve pressing problems, as well as looser arrangements that pulled together parts of an expansive bureaucracy. To be sure, Cold War institutions and processes were flawed and unsatisfying. Yet they were ultimately good enough to win.

In assessing that effort, a few things stand out. First, organizing for competition was a complex, multilayered affair. It involved laying a solid foundation, by creating the basic instruments of the national security state, and then adding on entities that were tailored to the contours of a dynamic Cold War. It entailed establishing vast bureaucracies at the core of the system, less prominent agencies along the periphery, and smaller offices and outposts that made the entire corpus more cohesive. It involved combining hard institutions with the softer routines of cooperation and planning. Creating a government equipped for competition required building an entire bureaucratic ecosystem.

Second, imperfection was the price of sustainability. Critics never tired of pointing out that the U.S. government was plodding and inefficient. There were, certainly, ways that America might have maximized discipline and speed in decision-making—for example, by creating a single military service or a European-style general staff, or by strengthening presidential power far more dramatically than it did. But because foreign policy is hard and a more robust debate is generally a better one, doing so might not have produced superior strategy over a long Cold War. It might, instead, have activated the country's deep-seated aversion to an overweening state, leading more Americans to question whether the competition was worth waging. In this sense, the imperfections of the U.S. government were rational because they kept the country's political culture and geopolitical needs in rough equilibrium.

Third, small entities could pack a big bureaucratic punch. The entire U.S. national security apparatus would not have fared as well in the late 1940s without the strategic concepts fashioned by the Policy Planning Staff. U.S. military strategy would not have been as devastatingly asymmetric in the 1980s absent the intellectual inputs of ONA. The modestly sized AMWG raised the performance of disparate pieces of the bureaucracy; the NSC and its staff provided the integration that any large undertaking requires. Mobilizing for competition meant getting the best out of a vast bureaucracy. Here, limited investments had a powerful multiplier effect.

In the end, organizing for victory was a matter of evolution as much as design. The United States never finished orienting the government for rivalry: It began overhauling the national security bureaucracy almost as soon as that bureaucracy took form. One of the virtues of the American system, in fact, was that it was flexible enough to change along with the Cold War or simply in response to its own failures. Those failures sometimes made it seem that America couldn't get organizational matters right. In reality, Washington got its national security architecture right enough because it kept at it for decades. Organizing for victory was an ongoing, iterative affair—just like long-term competition itself.

CHAPTER NINE

Winning the Contest of Systems

"THE CENTRAL ISSUE OF our time is this," declared Senator Henry Jackson in 1959. "Can a free society so organize its human and material resources as to outperform totalitarianism? Can a free people continue to identify new problems ... and respond, in time, with new ideas?"[1] Indeed, a fundamental challenge of the Cold War was whether American democracy could generate the power and stamina to compete with Soviet tyranny—and which model would better appeal to people around the globe. The Cold War was a contest of systems as much as a contest of strategies: it would test the attractiveness and efficacy of the American way.

Looking back, we might assume that America was fated to pass this test—that the totalitarian Soviet system never had a chance. Yet the outcome wasn't obvious for a generation that had seen ruthless authoritarians mount deadly challenges to global stability. During the early Cold War, Americans were haunted by a fear that the country's democracy might not meet the challenge of competition or, even worse, that competition might be the undoing of democracy. After all, the stresses of war with Sparta had debased the politics of Athens; America's founders had warned that continual conflict was toxic to liberty. The price of rivalry might be the militarization of America's economy and society; in defending freedom overseas, the United States might crush it at home. "We could lick the whole world ... if we were willing to adopt the system of Adolph Hitler," Eisenhower said, but that victory would be Pyrrhic in the extreme.[2]

Ike wasn't wrong to worry. The Cold War touched nearly all aspects of American life, and the effects weren't always benign. Competition with Moscow empowered demagogues and made anticommunist taunts a mainstay of U.S. politics. It led to a frenzied search for subversives and egregious violations of civil liberties. It produced a "military-industrial complex" whose weight, Ike warned, might "endanger our liberties or democratic processes."[3] The Cold War, in Eisenhower's view, was a warning about what prolonged rivalry can do to a democratic system.

Fortunately, this isn't the whole story—or even half of it. America never became an illiberal garrison state, thanks to the strength of its political traditions and the vigilance of leaders like Eisenhower. And rather than simply corrupting American society, the Cold War mostly strengthened it. Because the Cold War was a long, ideological rivalry, it created pressure for America to live up to the image it portrayed to the world. Because the contest required the United States to mobilize so much power, it spurred economic and intellectual investments that produced more dynamism than decay. These steps made America a fiercer competitor; they ensured that the contrast of systems remained distinctly, and fatally, disadvantageous to the Soviet Union. The Cold War had its deplorable effects. But it also revealed a hidden virtue of competition: the opportunity it offers a country to become a better version of itself.

There was a striking duality in how Americans thought about the connection between democracy and Cold War strategy. On the one hand, Washington put the ideological dimensions of the contest front and center from the moment Truman announced that the world faced a choice between two ways of life. For the most part, U.S. leaders evinced confidence that this moral asymmetry was the greatest guarantee of America's success. "In the long run the strength of our free society, and our ideals, will prevail over a system that has respect for neither God nor man," Truman declared.[4]

On the other hand, that confidence was hardly complete. The moral superiority of a free system wouldn't matter if America failed to summon the discipline needed in a long struggle for supremacy. "A free and undirected economy," Lippmann had warned, could not win the Cold War. And if U.S. officials sometimes feared what democracy might do to the quality of Cold War policy, they were even more concerned about what Cold War policy might do to the quality of American democracy.[5]

"Of all the enemies to public liberty," James Madison had written, "war is, perhaps, the most to be dreaded, because it comprises and develops the germ of every other."[6] Likewise, mobilizing the country for a cold war was sure to profoundly change American life. It would presumably empower government at the expense of the individual and compel far greater taxes and expenditures on military preparations. A long cold war could invite mass conscription, restrictions on personal freedoms, and an obsessive fear of fifth columnists. The result might be the garrison state that political scientist Harold Lasswell contemplated—a society in which the requirements of security destroy liberty.[7] As Hanson Baldwin, the *New York Times* correspondent, wrote, "It would be easy, in preparing for total war, to lose the very things we are trying to defend."[8]

What made the problem even knottier was that not one but two roads led to the garrison state. The United States could get there by overexerting itself—by so aggressively containing Soviet influence that it perverted its own values. Yet it could also get there by underexerting itself—by not doing enough to check Moscow's momentum. If key regions fell to communism, America would eventually find itself alone and insecure. The demands of autarky might then make a free-market system unworkable; the demands of survival might make the militarization of society unavoidable. Once the Soviets dominated Eurasia, Truman warned, "we would have to . . . change our way of life so that we couldn't recognize it as American any longer."[9]

The United States was thus confronted with a cruel paradox—the paradox, Eisenhower said, of "trying to meet the threat to our values and institutions by methods which themselves endangered those institutions."[10] The entire Cold War, then, was a balancing act. It required fighting a twilight struggle overseas while maintaining the vibrancy of the American model at home. If the United States could do so, it would take a giant step toward winning the superpower contest. If it failed, it might lose everything.

The dark scenario wasn't so implausible. If competition is often taxing for liberal societies, competition in the age of total war looked especially onerous. "Total war means total effort," Baldwin wrote, "and the peacetime preparations for it must be as comprehensive . . . as the execution of it."[11] If nuclear devastation could come in a heartbeat, and if Washington must now defend faraway allies rather than liberate them after they were conquered, America would require standing military capabilities as never before. The country might also need to fundamentally alter its domestic affairs—where people and factories were located, which powers the federal government exercised—to compete in peace and survive in war. "We must initiate radical changes in the character of our national life," the journalists Joseph and Stewart Alsop wrote in 1946.[12]

This wasn't science fiction: The early Cold War saw numerous steps toward a more regimented society. The Truman administration repeatedly sought universal military service or training. The National Security Resources Board was created to harness industry and science to the demands of the state. Serious observers called for the government to take charge of producing key weapons and construct a nationwide system of civil defenses.[13] During the 1950s, there was strong support in the Pentagon and Congress for significantly higher military spending, which would have required far more fiscal compulsion. Even Truman's post-1950 buildup was insufficient "to meet the military needs of this nation and its allies in the hour of our gravest crisis," wrote Secretary of the Air Force Stuart Symington.[14]

The country got a taste of where this might lead during the Korean War. Skyrocketing military spending caused higher taxes and economic controls. The Truman administration engaged in large-scale industrial planning, encouraged the geographic dispersal of factories, and severely restricted production of consumer items. Crucially, many of these steps were expected to be part of a new normal. "There may be serious danger for several years," wrote economic adviser Leon Keyserling. There was "no certain end in sight and never a full peace to be seen ahead."[15] Yet just as the push for centralization within government had not gone unchallenged, neither did the move toward a society permanently mobilized for conflict.

A broad coalition including pacifists, labor leaders, and old-school conservatives fought universal military training as contrary to U.S. traditions. "The army cannot teach democratic values," one labor spokesman declared, "because it is in practice the most undemocratic of our institutions."[16] Efforts to disperse industries provoked cries of "socialism." During the Korean War, the Supreme Court struck down Truman's effort to nationalize the steel mills. "We are embarked on a voyage" that "may wreck the greatest adventure in freedom the human race has ever known," Senator Robert Taft thundered.[17] The resulting backlash helped end Truman's presidency. Even Keyserling warned that hostility to the administration's defense program could "grow into hostility to the basic international policy of the Government"—it might undo America's commitment to waging cold war.[18]

What thus took shape, mostly during the 1950s, was an American "strategic synthesis"—an approach that fused the country's antistatist traditions with its new geopolitical responsibilities.[19] Instead of universal military training, America ended up with the looser Selective Service System. By the 1970s, America was fighting with an all-volunteer force. Similarly, U.S. military strategy emphasized technology over manpower; defense spending gradually receded from the highs of the early 1950s and mostly fell, as a percentage of GNP, over the rest of the Cold War. The government invested vast sums in scientific research and the development of weapons, but did so mostly through universities and private firms. All told, the United States extracted more effort and money from the citizenry than it had ever done outside of major war. But as adviser Robert Bowie noted in 1958, "The threshold of the garrison state is far beyond what we are spending today."[20]

The American synthesis was a compromise that didn't make anyone (least of all Eisenhower) happy. Even limited forms of compulsion could prove enormously controversial, as the backlash against the Vietnam-era draft showed. But mutual dissatisfaction aside, this approach ultimately yielded enough power to stymie the Soviets without also stymieing American democracy. The United States avoided catastrophic failures of deterrence or a limp version of containment that allowed Moscow to run wild. It also avoided a scenario in which the demands of American strategy were so onerous, and for so long, that the American system became alien to its original nature or the American people gave up on the Cold War. If the government was to focus on procuring guns when war came, one official wrote, it had to ensure that "there is enough butter in the hands of the American people" to make peacetime competition bearable.[21] The danger of the garrison state had to be vanquished if containment was to survive.

In one sense, this resistance to the garrison state was the natural response—the allergic reaction—of America's political culture. A country in which power was purposefully divided, and for whose citizens distrust of concentrated authority was second nature, proved averse to radical change even in an extended crisis.[22] Yet the balance within the American system was not entirely self-regulating, and the country might have gone down a dangerous road if not for the vigilance of key leaders. Whatever Truman's other failings, he protected the authority of elected officials as the U.S.

government mobilized in the late 1940s. And if the Eisenhower years produced a synthesis that allowed effective competition while protecting the American way of life, that was in no small part because Ike never forgot that imperative.

It was Eisenhower's White House that fought dramatically higher military spending. It was Ike who opposed "wild-eyed schemes of every kind," such as centralized economic planning or a nationwide system of bomb shelters after *Sputnik*.[23] Not least, it was Ike who continually insisted—in classified documents and public remarks—that "we must not destroy what we are attempting to defend."[24] America didn't avoid the garrison state purely because of its innate exceptionalism. It took strenuous efforts to protect the American system from the excesses that global competition can bring.

Excesses did happen, unfortunately. If America escaped the militarization of its society, it didn't escape a search for internal enemies that became far more destructive than the threat it was meant to counter. McCarthyism was one of the most shameful episodes of America's Cold War. It underscored a possibility that Alexander Hamilton had identified: that a "state of continual danger" might convince citizens to "run the risk of being less free."[25]

McCarthyism became so powerful because it drew on so many interwoven themes. First, there was a legacy of fierce anticommunism dating to the 1920s and particularly the 1930s, when fears of subversion infused domestic battles over race relations and the New Deal. Second, the United States did confront plausible internal security threats in the 1940s, from Soviet agents who pilfered atomic secrets and from Communists, who were well represented in the nation's strategic industries. Third, the ominous turn of the Cold War in the late 1940s prepared the political ground by provoking recriminations over who was to blame. Finally, anticommunism was powerful politics, a truth that Harry Truman had helped demonstrate.

Truman was no demagogue, and he loathed the "Red Scare" mentality of the time. The president vetoed, unsuccessfully, heavy-handed internal security legislation; he quipped that the House Un-American Activities Committee was "more un-American than the activities it is investigating." Yet Truman initiated the federal Employee Loyalty Program, which gave J. Edgar Hoover's FBI broad and easily abused authority to purge the government of suspected security risks.[26] He also relied on stark ideological language to rally support for his policies and to position himself for reelection in 1948. "There is considerable political advantage to the Administration in its battle with the Kremlin," advisers Clark Clifford and James Rowe counseled. "In times of crisis the American citizen tends to back up his President."[27] If Truman could harness anticommunism in a worthy cause, others could harness it in an unworthy one.

So showed McCarthy. By alleging, without evidence, that the top levels of government were infested with traitors, McCarthy capitalized on a real but receding problem—the danger of treachery within—and provided a deceptively simple explanation for the country's misfortunes. "How can we account for our present situation unless we believe that men high in this government are concerting to deliver us to disaster?" he asked.[28] Yet McCarthyism caught fire because McCarthy energized what historian Ellen Schrecker calls "a concerted campaign" by those "who had been working for years to drive Communism out of American life"—namely, Hoover's FBI, the House Un-American Activities Committee, and state and local leaders.[29] This network translated the sensational accusations that McCarthy and others made into investigations and economic sanctions, using a frenzied national climate to prevail in localized struggles. All this was possible because Cold War fears made a still larger group of Americans willing to subordinate civil liberties to the perceived imperatives of security.

America's more responsible leaders understood that McCarthy was playing on the country's most destructive impulses. The whole episode, Eisenhower wrote, was a "sorry mess; at times one feels almost like hanging his head in shame." Yet Republican congressional leaders found McCarthy a useful ally in ending twenty years of Democratic dominance. Eisenhower himself shirked a confrontation for fear of handing McCarthy a bigger megaphone or earning his wrath.[30] Not until 1954, when McCarthy targeted George Marshall and the U.S. Army, did he discredit himself, leading his Senate colleagues—with Ike's quiet encouragement—to censure him.[31] Viewed positively, the outcome showed that American democracy proved stronger than McCarthy's demagoguery. Viewed negatively, it showed that the Cold War could create a toxic climate that too many U.S. leaders either exploited or declined to resist.

The wreckage McCarthyism left behind was considerable. Hundreds of individuals were jailed or deported; over 10,000 people were blacklisted or fired. The FBI and CIA used anticommunism as a pretext to surveil an array of activists and reformers; opportunists deployed anticommunism to destroy political rivals or business competitors. Fear of persecution narrowed the country's political culture and discouraged dissent through much of the 1950s.[32] Whatever protection America purchased from subversion, it more than paid for in damage inflicted upon itself. "Fear is an enemy within ourselves," Truman had warned, "and if we do not root it out, it may destroy the very way of life we are so anxious to protect."[33]

It is important to keep McCarthyism in perspective. The repression that characterized the American system at its worst moment during the Cold War was an order of magnitude less than the repression that characterized the Soviet system at its best moment. By the mid-1950s, the fever had broken and the United States was learning how to wage Cold War without destroying itself. By the raucous 1960s, American pop culture, music, and dissident intellectuals were creating a language of mobilization and dissent at home and abroad.[34] Nor is it unusual that a country—even a great democracy—would respond to foreign perils by restricting civil liberties.

But this was precisely the problem. McCarthyism revealed that America was not immune to the weaponization of fear, hypersensitivity to internal threats, and other corrosive impacts of competition. Persistent rivalry can bring out the worst in a society. Fortunately, it can also bring out the best.

Because the Cold War was a struggle for the allegiance of peoples around the globe, the decisions of smaller powers would determine which superpower would triumph. From the beginning, American presidents argued that the world should choose the United States not because its arms were mightier but because its society was more just. "Communism is based on the belief that man is so weak and inadequate that he is unable to govern himself, and therefore requires the rule of strong masters," Truman declared. "Democracy is based on the conviction that man has the moral and intellectual capacity, as well as the inalienable right, to govern himself with reason and justice."[35] Yet nothing made this claim seem more ridiculous than the subjugation of large parts of the country's Black population by state-sponsored discrimination and political repression.

Since the end of Reconstruction, this system had been held in place by the southern states and abetted by federal acquiescence. The Cold War quickly revealed that this moral obscenity came at a steep competitive cost. The lynching of Black World War II veterans, the fierce resistance to integrating schools and other institutions, the exclusion of African Americans from the democratic process, and the use of shocking violence to maintain white supremacy constituted a serious injury to America's global image. In the Third World, the wound might prove fatal. How could Washington convince entire continents of people of color, who were now throwing off one form of racial hierarchy, to align with a country that was practicing another? Segregation was "ruining our foreign policy," John Foster Dulles exclaimed in 1957. "The effect of this in Asia and Africa will be worse for us than Hungary was for the Russians."[36]

The Cold War did not, alas, create some universal American awakening, a realization that segregation was unjust and diplomatically self-defeating. In some cases, segregationists added anticommunism to their political arsenal. State and local governments used anti-subversive legislation to target civil rights reformers. In response, the National Association for the Advancement of Colored People (NAACP) and other mainstream civil rights organizations purged their ranks of Communists and fellow travelers who had previously been vital allies. Even so, the FBI hounded Martin Luther King Jr. and other civil rights leaders on the grounds that the nation was threatened "with a form of social revolution." That harassment could be extreme: it included illegal wiretaps and threats to expose King's extramarital affairs unless he committed suicide.[37]

Yet defenders of the status quo were losing the argument. The superpower contest focused international attention on the glaring contrast between what America said and what it did. It thereby created opportunities to argue that the success of U.S. foreign policy required racial progress. "What is done here has immediate and far-reaching effect upon the fortunes and aspirations of the two-thirds of the world's people whose skins are colored," said Walter White, the NAACP executive secretary, in 1947.[38] Third World countries were "moving with jetlike speed toward the goal of political independence," King wrote 16 years later, "and we still creep at horse and buggy pace toward the gaining of a cup of coffee at a lunch counter."[39] This argument eventually convinced a critical mass of voters that white supremacy was incompatible with American supremacy. By 1963, most (78 percent) of those surveyed believed discrimination hurt Washington's diplomatic position.[40] Even more pertinently, the Cold War motivated the only entity that could break down state-sponsored segregation—the federal government—to get serious about the task.

Truman justified his reforms—banning segregation in Washington, D.C., eliminating discriminatory federal hiring, integrating the U.S. military—on the grounds of geopolitical as well as moral necessity. "The support of desperate populations of battle-ravaged countries must be won for the free way of life," he declared. "We can no longer afford the luxury of a leisurely attack upon prejudice and discrimination."[41] When the Supreme Court struck down school segregation in 1954, the Cold War connections were obvious. "Our American system ... is on trial both at home and abroad," Chief Justice Earl Warren believed.[42] Eisenhower himself opposed using federal power to compel desegregation. What forced his hand, in sending troops to integrate Little Rock schools in 1957, was his dismay that state governments were ignoring the law and his realization that inaction would be diplomatically crippling. "Our enemies are gloating over this incident and using it everywhere to misrepresent our whole nation," he said.[43]

When President Kennedy introduced a landmark civil rights bill or sent federal forces to integrate interstate travel and southern universities, he likewise highlighted the global dimensions of the issue: "Are we to say to the world, and much more importantly, to each other that this is a land of the free except for the Negroes; that we have no second class citizens except Negroes; that we have no class or cast [*sic*] system, no ghettoes, no master race except with respect to Negroes?"[44] And when LBJ pushed through two federal laws—the Civil Rights Act of 1964 and the Voting Rights Act of 1965—that dramatically weakened segregation and race-based political exclusion, he struck similar notes. "Today is a triumph for freedom as huge as any victory that has ever been won on any battlefield," he declared.[45]

The Cold War was hardly the only reason the United States made major, if incomplete, breakthroughs on civil rights. The superpower contest simply tipped the balance of political forces by making it less tolerable for America to continue failing to honor its own ideals.[46] Here the extended nature of the competition was critical, because it ensured that there was no waiting out the virtuous pressures that rivalry generated. An intense but relatively short hot war against totalitarianism had not sufficed to end segregation and push America toward racial equality. A less intense, but much longer, Cold War helped make the reality of an imperfect America more compatible with the image it portrayed to the world.

Long-term competition was also a force for positive change in other areas, including the nation's economy. The United States might not have stifled its free-market system, but critics, notably Eisenhower, alleged that the Cold War still drained its prosperity. "Every gun that is made, every warship launched, every rocket fired signifies, in the final sense, a theft from those who hunger and are not fed, those who are cold and are not clothed," he declared in 1953.[47] As Ike left office, he warned that the military-industrial complex—a perverse symbiosis between powerful arms manufacturers and powerful military and congressional interests— had "grave implications" for the country's economy and politics.[48]

Eisenhower wasn't entirely off base. The contracting system used to develop and procure arms could indeed be a source of waste and patronage—and corruption. Money spent on arms was not spent, strictly speaking, on social programs or other priorities. Fortunately, the idea of a pernicious military-industrial complex was still more myth than reality.

For one thing, unless Washington abandoned the Cold War, it needed some system for procuring the means of deterrence and defense. "So long as such an unmistakable, self-confirmed threat to our freedom exists," Ike acknowledged, America would carry the hated burden of heavy armaments "with dedication and determination."[49] In these circumstances, the military-industrial complex was the best of bad alternatives. Other approaches, in which the government itself made weapons or controlled the means of production, would have distorted the economy far more severely and led to even greater concentrations of political influence. Such approaches would have produced less efficiency and innovation than a system that required private firms to compete in order to survive.[50] But perhaps the best reason to defend the military-industrial complex is that the Cold War provided tremendous stimulus to America's postwar growth.

The superpower competition spurred infrastructure projects that might otherwise have gone nowhere. The construction of the Saint Lawrence Seaway eased transport between the Great Lakes and the Atlantic and thus trade between the Midwest and the world. The federal government supported that project because it was vital to securing the flow of iron ore needed to produce munitions and moving those munitions to overseas bases. The building of the interstate highway system in the 1950s and 1960s, at a cost of over $100 billion, improved domestic travel and shipping. That, too, was a Cold War innovation. A conservative president used a strategic argument—that America needed good roads to evacuate major cities in wartime—to cut through longstanding resistance.[51]

Meanwhile, the military-industrial complex was reshaping the economy, mostly in a welcome way. Cold War spending hardly impoverished

Americans, given that the period of greatest military spending as a percentage of GNP (the 1950s and 1960s) was also the period when growth was highest and inequality decreased most rapidly.[52] In fact, federal spending supported industries—such as aerospace—that invigorated entire regions. Over $50 billion in defense dollars flowed into California during the 1950s; the rise of Orange County was a by-product of the Cold War. Federal funding allowed private firms to push the frontiers of innovation. In 1959, nearly 85 percent of American research and development in electronics was government-funded.[53] These investments led to fearsome military breakthroughs. They also led to commercial spinoffs—computers, semiconductors, the internet—that would position America at the forefront of the information age.

In the same vein, Cold War spending catalyzed the rise of Silicon Valley by providing consistent demand for high-performance electronics. Fairchild Semiconductor began by making silicon chips for missiles; production for government clients eventually drove down costs to the point where the chips could be marketed commercially.[54] Not least, the expansion of the peacetime military and the construction of bases across the country injected a semipermanent stimulus—and millions of high-quality jobs—into state and local economies. Combined with the expansion of the American welfare state and working-class unionization after World War II, Cold War military spending led to an overall affluence beyond anything the Communist world could offer.

Might the United States have been even more prosperous had it fed government dollars directly into civilian industries? Perhaps, in theory. "If you want the by-product, you should develop the by-product," one physicist quipped.[55] But a one-for-one trade between military spending and other stimuli was never politically feasible, because defense was one of the few issues on which conservatives supported a large federal role in the economy—it was, as economist John Kenneth Galbraith put it, "the greatest of all exceptions to the general constraint on public expenditure."[56] The Cold War required massive American investments in global security. It also enabled America to invest, massively, in itself.

One reason the U.S. economy had such a good Cold War was that the American university had an ever better one. Prior to World War II, American higher education was good but not great; the U.S. system lagged behind the best European ones. Half a century later, American universities were unparalleled, which had everything to do with the country's long crisis of national security.

The change began in the 1930s, thanks to the flight of Jewish intellectuals from Hitler's Germany. The momentum accelerated in World War II. That conflict devastated Europe and many of its universities. It led to the GI Bill, an unprecedented American commitment to give returning service members access to higher education. Most critically, the war itself was a lethal, high-stakes competition in innovation. From the Manhattan Project to the development of the proximity fuse, World War II made the pursuit of knowledge a matter of life and death. "Time and again," argued Vannevar Bush, who headed the Office of Science Research and Development, "the margin which separated victory from disaster was the margin afforded by our scientific and technical advantages."[57]

The Cold War consummated the marriage between government and academia. America's technology-centric strategy staked the nation's security on innovation. "Our safety lies in being farther ahead scientifically and productively than the Russians," nuclear physicist Ernest O. Lawrence said.[58] Congress established the National Science Foundation to support basic research. The Office of Naval Research funded 1,131 projects in 200 institutions during the late 1940s. The Atomic Energy Commission built a national laboratory system to ensure America dominated the nuclear revolution.[59] By the early 1950s, elite schools such as Stanford, MIT, and Harvard were being transformed by government-sponsored research and graduate education on electronics and other key technologies. Cold War competition was creating the Cold War university.[60]

Yet it was a Soviet satellite that truly launched the American university to greatness. *Sputnik* evoked a fear that America's critical advantage was slipping away. "If we lost repeatedly to the Russians," one adviser warned, "the accumulated damage would be tremendous."[61] The crisis made winning the space race and the missile race overriding national priorities. It also produced, beginning with the National Defense Education Act (NDEA) of 1958, a concerted effort to ensure that America remained the world's intellectual superpower.

Federal support for academic research rose from $254 million in 1958 to $1.447 billion in 1970, with the focus on science, technology, engineering, and mathematics—the disciplines required to master the missile age. Yet the NDEA encompassed a broad view of intellectual preparedness, including social science, area studies, and language training. By 1961, 77 out of 90 academic departments at the University of Wisconsin, one of the

country's top public universities, were involved in federally funded programs. At the same time, the act funded college loans for working and
middle-class families and channeled federal dollars into primary and secondary education.[62] "Our schools are strongpoints in our national defense," Ike had remarked, "more important than our Nike batteries, more
necessary than our radar warning nets, and more powerful even than the
energy of the atom."[63] Although Ike had envisioned the NDEA as a stop-
gap measure, his successors, LBJ especially, extended and expanded its
writ. "Next to defense," a CIA report concluded in 1968, "education is the
biggest business of the modern state."[64]

This expansion was only possible in the context of the Cold War.
And all of this added up to what sociologist Jonathan Cole has rightly
described as a historically enlightened education policy.[65] University en-
rollments shot up from 2.8 million in 1955 to 8.6 million in 1970.[66] Generously funding research with federal money, while forcing applicants to
compete for that funding, turned good universities into world-class institutions. America's universities produced the graduates and knowledge a
superpower needed; they fostered the innovation that would sustain U.S.
economic leadership into the next century. Federal aid to universities had
"helped greatly in meeting national needs," University of California
president Clark Kerr wrote in 1963, and it had "greatly assisted the universities themselves."[67]

It wasn't all roses. There was always a tension between the ideal of the
academy and the needs of the state. The goal of open inquiry fit awkwardly
with the pursuit of classified, Pentagon-sponsored research. Many universities compiled a less-than-sterling record in protecting academic freedom
during the McCarthy era. The number of faculty fired for their beliefs and
associations was small, but the number affected by intimidation was surely
larger. Academia, a *New York Times Magazine* article claimed in 1951, was
afflicted by "a subtle, creeping paralysis of thought and speech."[68]

Yet the Cold War university mostly maintained its liveliness and intellectual integrity. The government was a research patron with a relatively light touch, because biased science was not useful science.[69] If
universities were condemned as havens of conformity in the 1950s, by
the 1960s they were incubators of protest. Colleges and universities
birthed organizations like Students for a Democratic Society. As the U.S.
government noted, "students supplied much of the manpower and inspi-
ration for the Civil Rights Movement" and the movement to end the
Vietnam War.[70] By decade's end, students were driving the upheaval,

sometimes bordering on violent revolt, occurring across America and much of the world. "Student unrest is indeed a significant factor now in upwards of thirty countries and a potentially active element in at least thirty more," a government Student Unrest Study Group reported in 1969.[71] Investing in education meant investing in dissent.

At its peak, that dissent sometimes seemed to be tearing the country apart. After the shooting of 13 unarmed students by National Guardsmen at Kent State in 1970, one university president wondered "whether these institutions will even hold together 'til Monday without more people getting killed."[72] Yet the turmoil was nonetheless a reminder that the American system permitted a political spontaneity that Soviet citizens could only dream of. And if the United States generally took the Cold War as an opportunity to improve that system, doing so helped it win the competition in the end.

Progress on racial issues was a necessary if not sufficient condition of winning the Cold War in the Third World, if only because state-sponsored racism had so tarnished America's image. Similarly, an America that became a stale, heavily regimented garrison state would have had far greater difficulty maintaining bonds of deep affection with other democracies. University exchanges exposed rising foreign leaders to one of America's most attractive features: a higher-education system that promoted free expression and intellectual curiosity. If U.S. public diplomacy was relatively effective during the Cold War, it was because the underlying material was relatively appealing.

By improving the vitality of the American model, the United States also subverted the Soviet model. Maintaining a vibrant, free-market economy was a prerequisite to outpacing the Soviets geopolitically and militarily. America's Cold War–driven prosperity was also critical in the effect it exerted on the Soviet sphere.

Nikita Khrushchev may have derided U.S. consumer goods as capitalist gadgets. But those gadgets fascinated the nearly three million Soviet citizens who thronged to an exhibition of American cars, cosmetics, and appliances in Moscow in 1959.[73] Throughout the postwar decades, the ability of the American economy to supply guns and butter was a rebuke to a Soviet economy that delivered the former only at the expense of the latter. And as USIA exhibitions, East-West travel, and Hollywood films revealed the disparity between how people lived in two very different worlds, the Soviet model lost credibility with its citizens. Ronald Reagan was only half joking when he proposed dropping "a few million typical mail order catalogs on Minsk & Pinsk & Moscow."[74] A free-market economy, stimulated by Cold War spending, was a potent psychological weapon.

America's popular culture proved equally deadly, for its pervasiveness behind the Iron Curtain testified to the inadequacies of Communist regimes. Western jeans and music became markers of status in the late-stage Soviet Union. East-bloc dissidents used rock-and-roll to peacefully challenge the system.[75] The end of the Cold War showed just how influential American culture had become. In late 1989, a Soviet official remarked that the Brezhnev Doctrine had given way to the "Sinatra Doctrine": the states of Eastern Europe could do it their way.[76] The Cold War constricted dissent in the United States during the 1950s. But the country ultimately preserved a climate in which creativity could flourish, which contributed enormously to U.S. influence within the Soviet bloc.

The appeal of the American system even reached the Soviet elite. The Daughters of the American Revolution once warned that academic and cultural exchanges with the enemy were dangerous, and they were— to the Soviet Union. Some of the Soviet reformers who took power in the 1980s had earlier visited or studied in America; their glimpse of what a freer society could be informed their disgust with what Soviet society had become. When one such reformer, Boris Yeltsin, visited an American supermarket in 1989, the quality of the offerings left him "sick with despair for the Soviet people" and more determined than ever to change the system from within.[77]

The Cold War left scars on America, just as it left scars on the world. In the end, however, a long ideological rivalry served more to spur self-improvement than self-destruction. That dynamic, in turn, helped America maintain its strategic edge; it helped the country appeal to some of its foes along with many of its friends. "As the free world grows stronger, more united, more attractive to men on both sides of the Iron Curtain," Truman had predicted, "then there will have to come a time of change in the Soviet world."[78] Strengthening the American system was important in its own right. It also encouraged historic transformations across the East-West divide.

CHAPTER TEN

Managing the Endgame

Those changes within the Soviet bloc were long in coming, but they arrived with devastating finality and speed. Into the mid-1980s, the Cold War seemed as deadlocked as ever—more likely to end in "a hail of fiery atoms," in Ronald Reagan's phrase, than a sublimely satisfying Western victory.[1] By the end of Reagan's presidency, the superpower conflict was fading fast. Gorbachev was retreating in the arms race, and the Third World, working *with* Reagan to reform the Soviet system, was otherwise abandoning the competition. Within a year of George H. W. Bush taking office, the Soviet empire had disintegrated; less than two years later, the Soviet state was gone. The Cold War lasted longer and cost more than Kennan and most of his contemporaries had imagined. It ended more suddenly, peacefully, and decisively than almost anyone expected.[2]

What can that denouement teach us about long-term competition? The answer might seem to be "nothing." The Cold War's conclusion was historically extraordinary. Every major issue was settled on American terms. The international system was transformed without a shot being fired. The Cold War endgame thus vindicated America's containment strategy, even as its rapidity astounded some of the strategy's ablest practitioners. If the resolution of the Cold War was simply a geopolitical miracle, then it reveals little about the patterns of protracted struggle.

Yet the end of the Cold War didn't just happen, and once-in-a-lifetime breakthroughs can still speak to timeless challenges. All competitions conclude eventually. Most competitors would prefer to win peacefully rather than violently. The question of how a competitor handles the endgame—how one steers a stubborn rivalry toward a successful conclusion—is just as important as building a position of advantage in the first place.

The Reagan and Bush administrations set a high standard: No aspect of the rivalry did U.S. officials manage more expertly. But doing so required America to come through one last frightening spike in tensions and find ways of making a wounded adversary back down rather than lash out. Above all, it required framing the Cold War endgame as something other than it was—a negotiated Soviet surrender under crushing pressure from within and without. The key to waging the Cold War was building situations of strength that made Soviet victory impossible and Western victory achievable. The key to winding down the long, bitter struggle was showing enough magnanimity to make a ruthless policy effective.

Ending the Cold War first required looking beyond it. This was not as easy as it sounds. The Cold War had lasted so long that it seemed to be a permanent feature of the international landscape. The logic of rivalry was so strong that it repeatedly ensnared leaders who tried to escape it.

Ironically, a leader often considered the inveterate Cold Warrior was the one who began moving the conflict to a conclusion. Reagan authored the largest peacetime military buildup in U.S. history; he escalated the competition with nearly every tool at hand. Yet his long-held revulsion for the arms race convinced him that the Cold War should not go on forever. "Our policy of MAD could get us both killed," he remarked.[3] At the same time, his understanding of Moscow's serious, accumulating weaknesses convinced him that it need not go on forever—that a system so "incompetent and ridiculous" must eventually change or collapse.[4] These two ideas put Reagan at odds with the prevailing orthodoxy. They also informed a strategy meant to first intensify and then de-escalate the Cold War.

Even before becoming president, Reagan had promised to wage a multipronged offensive—in the arms race, the Third World, Eastern Europe, and even by attacking the stability of the Soviet regime. Yet the purpose was not to entrench a perpetual Cold War, much less provoke a hot one. The purpose was to put the Kremlin in such dire straits that it would have to begin reducing tensions on American terms. "We could threaten the Soviets with our ability to outbuild them," Reagan said in 1981, and then "invite the Soviets to join us in lowering the level of weapons on both sides."[5] A worsening Cold War might bring about a better peace.

That peace, however, could not be a simple détente, a relaxation of tensions that left fundamental issues unresolved. Reagan had attacked détente in the 1970s because he believed aggression was baked into Soviet Communism, so political change in Moscow had to precede the geopolitical change that might end the Cold War. And Reagan was keen on political warfare because he believed it would drive home the failures of communism and invigorate those challenging the system from within. "The more we focus attention on internal Soviet repression," Reagan wrote, "the better chance that over the years Soviet society will lose its cruelty and secrecy." Peace would follow "because they no longer wish to blot out all who oppose them at home and abroad."[6] Adviser Max Kampelman explained the logic more bluntly. Reagan "really wants the totalitarian Soviet system to end, but not by war."[7]

This strategy made for a complex and sometimes-contradictory mix. The president attacked Soviet power relentlessly while composing handwritten appeals for peace to his ailing Kremlin counterparts.[8] Alongside an across-the-board military buildup, Reagan made revolutionary arms control proposals to eliminate intermediate-range nuclear forces (INF) in Europe and make deep cuts in strategic missiles. His administration sought to empower Soviet dissidents, which enraged Moscow, on the theory that doing so would mellow Moscow over the long term. Soviet officials were baffled by the discrepancies. There was a "contradiction between words and deeds that greatly angered Moscow," Dobrynin wrote, "the more so because Reagan himself never seemed to see it."[9]

But Reagan knew where he was going. In two landmark strategy documents, his administration spelled out a sequenced carrot-and-stick approach. National Security Decision Directive (NSDD)-32, finalized in 1982, outlined interlocking policies to "contain and reverse the expansion of Soviet control and military presence," "discourage Soviet adventurism, and weaken the Soviet alliance system by forcing the USSR to bear the brunt of its economic shortcomings," as well as "encourage long-term liberalizing and nationalist tendencies within the Soviet Union and allied countries." This was precisely the multidimensional campaign the administration was undertaking.[10] NSDD-75, signed in January 1983, linked this onslaught to a phased agenda for transforming the Cold War. America would seek:

1. To contain and over time reverse Soviet expansion by competing effectively on a sustained basis with the Soviet Union in all
international arenas. . . .
2. To promote, within the narrow limits available to us, the process of change in the Soviet Union toward a more pluralistic
political and economic system. . . .
3. To engage the Soviet Union in negotiations to attempt to
reach agreements which protect and enhance U.S. interests.

Washington must convince Moscow that "unacceptable behavior" would
not pay, but that "genuine restraint . . . might bring important benefits."[11]
The goal, NSDD-32 had stated, was to achieve "a fundamentally different East-West relationship by the end of this decade"—to make the
Soviets see that ending the Cold War was their only option.[12]

Through the mid-1980s, stage one of Reagan's strategy was succeeding
spectacularly. The United States was retaking the geopolitical and ideological initiative; Soviet positions were crumbling from the military
competition to the fight for the Third World. America was leading the
West into the information age, while the Soviet system was falling deeper
into obsolescence and decay. The multiple offensives Washington had
launched in the late 1970s and 1980s—along with its generational investments in the free world—were all coming together. "We are facing one of
imperialism's most massive attempts to slow down the process of social
change in the world, to stop the advance of socialism or even to push it
back in some places," Andropov lamented.[13] America, Reagan could declare in 1984, had taken "its strongest position in years."[14]

Which made it all the more perplexing that stage two—winding down
the Cold War—was not working. Soviet leaders mocked Reagan's arms
control proposals and broke off negotiations after the Pershing II ballistic
missile deployments in 1983. Foreign Minister Andrei Gromyko wondered,
in one conversation with Shultz, "what sort of simpletons did the U.S. side
take the Soviet leadership for." Moscow yielded no ground in Third World
conflicts from Central America to Southwest Asia, either, and rather than
loosening up against dissenters it cracked down harder at home.[15] The diplomatic climate was worse than any time since the early 1960s; the Kremlin
even compared Reagan to Hitler and alleged he was "fanning the flames of
war."[16] The Soviets were digging in rather than giving up.

This resistance was partially a function of age. A senescent leadership in Moscow, held by one dying man after another, was in no position to fundamentally reevaluate Soviet policy. It was partially a function of hope—that Reagan might not be reelected, or that the Western peace movement might derail his buildup. But it was also a function of fear. Reagan's offers to negotiate hardly registered when he was battering the Soviets; the force of his assault convinced some Kremlin officials that accommodation was suicidal. "If we begin to make concessions," Andropov remarked in 1983, "defeat would be inevitable."[17]

Internal disorder made the problem worse. Even as Reagan set the overall direction of policy, hard-liners (led by Weinberger) and moderates (led by Shultz) warred over whether and how to engage Moscow. Their disputes made it impossible to send the coherent signals that coercive diplomacy required. Worse, Weinberger and his allies periodically made provocative comments about "winning" a nuclear war. Digging backyard bomb shelters was the trick, one official remarked. "If there are enough shovels to go around, everybody's going to make it."[18] Reagan's strategy required carefully shaping Moscow's incentives, but his administration gave an impression of careless belligerence instead.

The spiral of tension climaxed in 1983. In March, Reagan unveiled SDI, the Strategic Defense Initiative, and called Moscow an "evil empire." In April, U.S. air and naval forces aggressively probed Soviet defenses. In September, Soviet interceptors shot down a South Korean airliner that strayed into Soviet airspace, killing everyone on board; Reagan called the incident a "massacre" and a "crime against humanity."[19] October saw U.S. forces liberate Grenada; by November, fast-flying Pershing II missiles were arriving in Europe. It is hard to imagine a worse time for Soviet early warning systems to malfunction, but during the fall they did, mistakenly showing U.S. missiles inbound. "Many in the Soviet public are asking if war is imminent," one U.S. observer reported.[20]

This was the backdrop to the quietest nuclear crisis of the postwar era. In November, NATO held Able Archer 83, an exercise that included rehearsing a full nuclear strike. Able Archer featured new communications codes and coincided with a spike in high-level traffic between Washington and London. Soviet officials, who already feared Reagan and were worriedly monitoring adverse trends in the nuclear balance, scrambled to determine whether the exercise might be something more sinister. Top military officials moved into hardened bunkers; some Soviet nuclear forces went on higher alert. Casey later reported a "rather stunning array of indicators" of Soviet alarm, including costly measures, such as terminating support for the fall harvest, that would not have been taken lightly.[21]

Fortunately, the Kremlin eventually confirmed that Able Archer was an exercise, which passed without further incident. Historians have subsequently debated just how severe the danger of war was.[22] But a detailed U.S. intelligence review concluded that there had been "a genuine belief on the part of Soviet leaders that U.S. was planning a nuclear first strike." Indeed, Soviet fears of war were far more acute in 1983 than Reagan or the CIA realized.[23] As this crisis passed, the Kremlin was responding to the U.S. buildup by secretly deploying the closest thing to a real-world doomsday device—a system meant to ensure nuclear retaliation even if the leadership was wiped out.

The crisis of 1983 dramatized the risks of Reagan's policies—the trade-offs between advantage and stability, the chance that pressure could provoke a fearful adversary—and focused them into a moment of subtle but serious peril. It demonstrated that Reagan's understanding of the enemy was incomplete. The Soviets, he now realized, "feared us not only as adversaries but as potential aggressors who might hurl nuclear weapons at them in a first strike."[24] Not least, it showed that coercion alone would not produce diplomatic breakthroughs. "We must persuade the Soviets ... that we have no aggressive intentions," Shultz would argue in 1984.[25] Its dangers notwithstanding, the 1983 crisis thus played a critical role in the Cold War endgame. It provided the missing intellectual pieces of a visionary strategy.

The crisis led, in particular, to a defter blending of conciliation with compulsion—to an approach that used a velvet glove to conceal an iron fist. This was not a dramatic "Reagan reversal." The president had always understood the importance of diplomacy.[26] What Reagan concluded, rather, was that the balance of positive and negative incentives needed adjusting: strategic leverage would produce accommodation only if Moscow did not equate accommodation with suicide. "I feel the Soviets are so defense minded, so paranoid about being attacked, that without being in any way soft on them we ought to tell them no one here has any intention of doing anything like that," Reagan wrote.[27]

Lowering the diplomatic temperature was equally important to preserving key coalitions at home and abroad. The battle over INF deployments had severely tested NATO, causing street demonstrations and political crises. Even staunch allies were now urging Reagan to reduce the danger. "We all had to live in the same planet," Thatcher remarked.[28] As the 1984 election approached, Reagan also had to face the fact that nearly half of Americans believed his policies were "increasing the chances of war." "We must strongly position the President on the 'peace' side of the formula—'peace through strength,' " one adviser wrote.[29]

In response to these concerns, Reagan undertook a diplomatic offensive during 1984. He told a joint session of Congress that military conflict was unthinkable: "A nuclear war cannot be won and must never be fought."[30] He emphasized his desire for productive diplomacy. "Living in this nuclear age," he explained in a televised speech, "makes it imperative that we do talk."[31] After Andropov died in February, Reagan assured General Secretary Konstantin Chernenko that "neither I nor the American people hold any offensive intentions toward you or the Soviet people."[32] Reagan had shown the Soviets the costs of competition. Now he had to convince them, he told French president François Mitterrand, that they might benefit if they "joined the family of nations."[33]

Doing so also meant sharpening U.S. negotiating strategy. Reagan gradually elevated Shultz at the expense of his bureaucratic rivals. Shultz's State Department, in cooperation with Jack Matlock and other NSC officials, developed a fourfold approach to superpower diplomacy, focusing on arms control, Third World conflicts, human rights and political reform, and economic and cultural issues. The agenda was comprehensive by design; the goal was meaningful change across the superpower relationship and even within the Soviet Union. That ambitious approach would be effective only if Washington firmly but nonprovocatively kept the pressure on. "The strategic reality of leverage," Shultz concluded, "comes from creating facts in support of our overall design."[34]

No major breakthroughs came in 1984. But the Soviets did agree to rejoin the strategic arms reduction talks and INF negotiations—a small step that showed how the Western buildup had shifted the negotiating landscape. And time was now doing America's work. Shultz believed that the diplomatic window would truly open only after the pathetic final stages of the Brezhnev era reached a close. That transition seemed imminent. The Kremlin might soon be run by "younger men who have a significantly different outlook," Shultz told Reagan. "It will pay dividends to treat them with civility." Within months, Chernenko had died, Gorbachev had taken charge, and Shultz had traveled to Moscow with a message. "President Reagan told me to look you squarely in the eyes and tell you: 'Ronald Reagan believes that this is a very special moment in the history of mankind.' "[35]

There is a strategic concept known as the golden bridge—the idea that an enemy surrounded on all sides will fight to the death, but one that is overmatched on three sides will retreat. Reagan had cornered the Soviets in his first term. Now he would show Moscow how it could escape a competition that was becoming unbearable.

The strategy wouldn't have worked with a different Soviet interlocutor. The new general secretary was a "somewhat different breed," Reagan would find—a committed Communist who was nonetheless willing to discard the dogmas of the past.[36] Having spent time in the West, Gorbachev realized just how desperately Moscow needed rejuvenation. He also knew that a relaxation of tensions was a prerequisite to tackling the accumulating domestic problems.[37] Indeed, Gorbachev had absorbed the lesson that Reagan was trying to impart: that a wheezing Soviet system couldn't sustain an all-out race. America was building " 'Tridents,' 'Minutemen,' arms in space," Gorbachev remarked. This onslaught threatened "the deterioration of our ecological, strategic and political security, the loss everywhere, but above all exhausting our economy."[38]

Yet Gorbachev wasn't ready to admit defeat. He distrusted Reagan at the outset. "You want to take advantage of the Soviet Union," he charged at their first meeting.[39] More important, Gorbachev's strategy aimed to reinvigorate Soviet power, not dismantle it. He initially refused to discuss human rights issues and intensified the war in Afghanistan, even allowing strikes into Pakistan, in hopes of breaking the resistance.[40] He demanded that Reagan kill SDI and made arms control proposals meant primarily to undercut the U.S. military buildup.[41] Gorbachev "seeks to relax East-West hostility ... not to suspend the competition but to put the USSR in an improved long-term position," the CIA reported.[42] Moscow couldn't win an all-out race, but perhaps it could slow down Washington.

That strategy would fail, for several reasons. The principal cause was that Soviet power was collapsing too fast. The weaknesses of the Soviet system reflected its very essence, so Gorbachev's reforms often turned chronic problems into acute catastrophes. His early campaign to "accelerate" industrial production through deficit spending could hardly correct the structural flaws of the Soviet economy, but it did, along with falling oil prices, deepen a budgetary hole the Kremlin could not escape. Gorbachev then undertook political reforms to create space for more thoroughgoing economic change; the result was to destabilize a system held together only by the Communist Party's iron grip. The building tensions took several years to explode in climactic crisis. But along the way, Gorbachev would find himself ever more eager for détente—his path to accessing trade and technology, cutting defense spending, and winning diplomatic support as his political base eroded—and willing to pay ever more to get it. The cruel reality, Foreign Minister Eduard Shevardnadze recalled, was that "we would achieve nothing without normalization of Soviet-American relations."[43]

In part because the Soviet system was failing, Gorbachev's thinking also became more radical. The general secretary was "a true believer," the U.S. ambassador in Moscow wrote, yet he blended Marxism-Leninism with an abhorrence of war and an interest in social democracy.[44] With the aid of several advisers, Gorbachev synthesized these influences into his "New Political Thinking," which emphasized opening the Soviet Union and pursuing a positive-sum vision of global security. In some ways, the New Political Thinking was a façade for policies born of desperation. But it nonetheless shook up the status quo in Moscow by easing the xenophobic, zero-sum mentality separating the Soviet Union from the world.[45]

Finally, Gorbachev's strategy was defeated by Reagan's strategy. Throughout the second term, Reagan denied Moscow maneuvering room. The Reagan Doctrine really got rolling, with a new front in Angola and an intensified effort to expel the Soviets from Afghanistan, and Reagan remained as committed as ever to SDI.[46] The president also made clear that Moscow wouldn't get what it needed—arms control and East-West trade—without progress on human rights and Third World conflicts. The United States, Reagan wrote, was "just hanging back until we get some of the things we want."[47] Indeed, the administration set high standards for agreement. The bottom line, as National Security Adviser Frank Carlucci put it, was that "we want accommodation on our terms."[48]

Yet it would take more than blunt objects to move Gorbachev. Reagan quickly invited the Soviet leader to a conference in hopes of making a personal connection; he repeatedly assured him that he had no desire for hot war or perpetual cold war. And although Reagan continually pushed Gorbachev to give ground, he did so politely and discreetly. "You shouldn't back your adversary into a corner, embarrass him, or humiliate him," Reagan wrote.[49] In short, Reagan was seeking to build the trust that would make concessions tolerable while maintaining the strength that would make them necessary. "Our interest is to keep the Russians well behind us but not so far behind that they become desperate and dangerous," Shultz summarized.[50] This U.S. strategy was a delicate balancing act, for political and bureaucratic reasons as much as for diplomatic ones. Over the course of the 1980s, it delivered three historic breakthroughs.

The first breakthrough was de-escalating the arms race on American terms. Reagan worked doggedly at this objective, starting at the Geneva summit in 1985. That meeting produced no major agreements; the discussions became quite animated. But it did result in a joint statement that "a nuclear war cannot be won and must never be fought."[51] More important, it initiated the sustained personal diplomacy that Reagan was banking on. The meeting confirmed for Reagan that Gorbachev was nothing like his predecessors. "You could almost get to like the guy," he noted.[52] For Gorbachev, it showed that Reagan was at least "not as hopeless as some believed."[53]

The pace of the superpower dialogue soon quickened. In January 1986, Gorbachev broached a big idea—ridding the world of nuclear weapons by 2000. The proposal was probably a propaganda ploy, meant to expose Reagan and his buildup as barriers to peace. But Reagan turned the gambit to his advantage. He endorsed, in a letter to Gorbachev, the basic goal of nuclear abolition. He then offered to work toward eliminating offensive ballistic missiles—the weapons that were most destabilizing and in which Moscow had invested the most. The proposal, he wrote, "should open the door to some real arms negotiations if [Gorbachev] is really interested."[54] Adding to Gorbachev's sense of urgency, and Reagan's sense of opportunity, was the Chernobyl disaster in April. That tragedy humiliated the Soviet regime and illustrated, in Gorbachev's words, "what nuclear war can be."[55] It convinced Reagan that the "time is right for something dramatic."[56]

There was drama aplenty at the Reykjavik summit in October. Gorbachev now urgently sought to lighten the Soviet military burden and needed diplomatic victories to sustain his political capital at home. In Iceland, he offered to destroy all INF-range forces in Europe and reduce superpower strategic arsenals by half. Reagan responded by mooting the elimination of offensive ballistic missiles. What followed was a virtuous spiral of proposals to eliminate strategic weapons and even abolish superpower nuclear arsenals. But the talks collapsed because Gorbachev insisted on severe restrictions on SDI, which Reagan believed was vital to deterrence in a world without MAD.[57] The summit broke up with anger on both sides. Reagan thought that Gorbachev had come to Iceland to embarrass him. Gorbachev told the Politburo that Reagan "exhibited extreme primitivism, a caveman outlook, and intellectual impotence."[58]

Western reactions weren't much kinder. U.S. allies and some of Reagan's own advisers were horrified that the president had nearly given up the nukes that shielded the free world. But Reagan's position in Iceland wasn't so nonsensical. U.S. and NATO conventional capabilities were reaching the point where the alliance could plausibly defend itself without going nuclear. Rapid reductions in nuclear weapons, especially fast-flying missiles, could thus improve strategic stability without destroying America's ability to compete. Besides, the United States was clearly winning the Cold War everywhere, so radical cuts would vitiate Soviet strength in the only area where Moscow's influence was still imposing. "Without an arsenal of nuclear weapons," Shultz had said, "the Soviets are not a superpower."[59]

Reykjavik showed, in fact, that Reagan's strategy was working. The president got the personal connection he wanted: Despite the initial recriminations, the intense negotiations ultimately convinced Gorbachev that Reagan really desired to tame the nuclear beast. After Iceland, Dobrynin wrote, Gorbachev decided "that he could and would work with Reagan."[60] But this would mean working on American terms, because the one-two punch of U.S. pressure and Soviet decline was forcing Gorbachev ever closer to Reagan's position. At Reykjavik, Gorbachev had agreed to the "zero option" for Europe (the idea of removing all intermediate-range missiles from that continent, a proposal that Soviet officials had long ridiculed), agreed to exclude British and French systems from the agreement, and made key concessions on strategic arms reductions. "We may have made some truly historic breakthroughs," wrote National Security Adviser John Poindexter.[61] The dynamics of the negotiation were working inexorably in Reagan's favor.

The payoff came in 1987. After a last-gasp Soviet bid to kill SDI failed, Gorbachev relented, and he and Reagan soon signed the most ambitious—and asymmetrical—superpower arms control treaty of the Cold War. The INF Treaty eliminated an entire class of nuclear weapons from superpower arsenals and resolved the Euromissile dilemma that had vexed NATO since the 1970s. It did all this while requiring the Soviets to destroy 1,500 deployed missiles, as opposed to 350 U.S. missiles—and leaving America with a vast arsenal of sea- and air-launched cruise missiles, which Moscow mostly lacked.[62] "U.S. policy is one of extorting more and more concessions," Gorbachev griped amid the negotiations. "I'm weeping for you," Shultz replied.[63]

The terms of the treaty bruised Soviet feelings, but Reagan worked hard to ease any embarrassment. The administration balanced substantive Soviet concessions with symbolic American ones, such as persuading West Germany to scrap a few dozen obsolete missiles. At the Washington summit in December, Reagan gave Gorbachev all the honors due a world statesman. The president and general secretary joked like old friends about Reagan's arms control credo—"trust but verify"—and Gorbachev gave a ringing statement calling the treaty a triumph of visionary diplomacy over "old thinking."[64] The summit, which provided Gorbachev with badly needed prestige and political capital, was part of a deliberate U.S. strategy that used kindness to mask cunning. "So far," wrote Shultz before the summit, "we have brilliantly allowed Gorbachev to posture as the innovator and take the credit for moves that come in our direction and follow our agenda."[65] Treating a declining competitor as an equal was the key to extracting profoundly unequal concessions.

The same playbook was enabling a second breakthrough: ending the Cold War in the Third World. Gorbachev knew that the Soviets could not remain in Afghanistan forever. Chernyaev, his close adviser, griped that Moscow was stuck with "a shitload of Marxists, in Africa too."[66] Yet the general secretary was reluctant to surrender Moscow's global influence. His solution was to combine tactical escalations—meant to help Moscow resolve longstanding conflicts without admitting defeat—with demands for parity in Third World retrenchment. "They should find a balance of concessions," Gorbachev told Reagan in 1987. The Soviets would quit Afghanistan once Washington quit supporting the rebels.[67]

Gorbachev's gambit was fruitless. By holding out for wins or even draws in the Third World, the Soviet Union was mostly punishing itself. Subsidies to Marxists in Nicaragua and El Salvador were becoming more economically oppressive. The war in Afghanistan was blackening Moscow's global reputation and taking a rising domestic toll. "At home," the CIA reported, the war was causing "pockets of social unrest . . . the diversion of energies from pressing economic problems, and dissatisfaction in the political hierarchy."[68] Afghanistan was the mirror-image of Vietnam: Prolonging a peripheral conflict here cost Washington little but taxed Moscow severely.

Reagan's strategy ensured that the pain wouldn't stop until the interventions did. Covert U.S. campaigns in Angola and Nicaragua made it impossible for Soviet clients to defeat their rivals. In Afghanistan, U.S. support—particularly Stinger missiles—made an insurgent victory conceivable. "The Stinger missile," one assessment concluded, "has changed the course of the war" by holding Soviet airpower at bay.[69] Meanwhile, the president pushed Gorbachev relentlessly. He reminded the world that the Soviets "are still waging a war of indiscriminate bombing and civilian massacre against a Moslem people whose only crime is to love their country and their faith."[70] Yet he also offered Gorbachev a path toward international legitimacy if he withdrew. The Soviets could "win accolades from people of good will everywhere ... by grounding their helicopter gunships, promptly withdrawing their troops, and permitting the Afghan people to choose their own destiny."[71]

By the late 1980s, Gorbachev was taking that path. Soviet diplomats asked for U.S. help in ending conflicts in southern Africa. They pushed their Central American clients to make peace. And in May 1988, Soviet troops began leaving Afghanistan, even though Reagan refused to cease supporting the rebels.[72] To soften the blow, the administration blessed diplomatic accords that provided the fiction of a multilateral settlement. The Soviets had lost, Chernyaev wrote, but the withdrawal would "be easier and more graceful to do ... within the framework of an agreement."[73] In the Third World as in the military competition, America was winning by practicing coercion with a smile.

This balancing act enabled a third breakthrough: transforming the Soviet regime. Human rights and political reform were "literally at the heart of the U.S.-Soviet relationship," Reagan said: Only a Soviet government at peace with its people could be at peace with the world.[74] Throughout Reagan's second term, U.S. officials kept the price of repression high, slamming Soviet human rights violations at meetings of the Conference on Security and Cooperation in Europe. Reagan himself made clear that liberalization was a prerequisite to easing East-West tensions. He and Shultz urged the Soviets to release political prisoners, permit dissent, and allow more emigration and freedom of religion.[75] Quietly but unambiguously, Reagan was making the Soviet system a matter of superpower negotiation.

Yet Reagan trod carefully. Even as he applied pressure, he avoided public confrontations that might make it impossible for Gorbachev to say yes. "If the Soviets loosened up, we would not exploit it," he promised at Reykjavik. "We would simply express our appreciation."[76] Likewise, Shultz recognized that changes Gorbachev embraced would prove more durable than those accepted under duress. The secretary thus sought to convince Gorbachev that reform was in his own best interest. "Closed and compartmented societies cannot take advantage of the information age," he explained at one "seminar" in the Kremlin. "People must be free to express themselves, move around, emigrate and travel if they want to, challenge accepted ways without fear."[77]

Gorbachev often bridled at these suggestions. He certainly didn't need Reagan and Shultz to tell him that perestroika would fail without glasnost, that economic reform required political relaxation. Yet American diplomacy did make a difference. The mix of pressure and engagement strengthened liberalizers such as Shevardnadze, whose aides eventually began asking American diplomats to push harder.[78] Gorbachev himself, who knew the system had to change but didn't know how, would hardly have tolerated Shultz's tutorials had he not learned something from them. Most important, by putting internal reform at the center of the relationship, Reagan prodded Gorbachev to liberalize more aggressively than he might have intended. "Our policy did not change until Gorbachev understood that there would be no improvement and no serious arms control until we admitted and accepted human rights, free emigration, until glasnost became freedom of speech, until our society and the process of perestroika changed deeply," Chernyaev acknowledged.[79]

The changes began in earnest in 1987. Arrests for political crimes fell; the jamming of VOA ceased; emigration rose from 2,000 individuals in 1986 to nearly 78,000 in 1987. Political issues were fair game, Shevardnadze told Shultz; Moscow would discuss "any proposal that emerges in the humanitarian area."[80]

Reagan kept the pedal down. He visited West Berlin in 1987, acknowledging Gorbachev's reforms while calling on him to free Eastern Europe: "Tear down this wall!"[81] The CIA increased distribution of subversive books, magazines, and other materials, an "enhanced program" to "exploit the current Soviet policy of 'glasnost.' "[82] U.S. officials urged Gorbachev to go beyond scattered, easily reversible improvements—to free all political prisoners; enshrine freedom of speech, religion, and emigration; and begin deconstructing authoritarian political controls.[83] Even Reagan's

jokes about the Soviet system—which he conveyed, at summits, to an an-
noyed Gorbachev—were political weapons. They illustrated that a decrepit Soviet regime had become an object of ridicule before the world.[84]

Still, none of this would have worked had Reagan not combined
sticks with carrots—had he not shown that Washington would respect
and reward political reform. The success of this calibrated approach became clear with the Moscow summit in 1988.

By this point, Soviet reform was accelerating as Gorbachev maneuvered to reinvigorate a flagging economic program through an unprecedented political opening. He introduced measures to strengthen the
judiciary, enhance individual rights, institute real elections for certain positions, and otherwise weaken one-party rule. As this daring agenda
evoked rising opposition in Moscow, Gorbachev looked for support
abroad. The general secretary passed a message asking if Reagan "still
thinks of the USSR as an evil empire whose social and political positions
have placed it on the ash heap of history." If not, perhaps Reagan could
say so publicly; the Soviets would happily take "concrete steps ... to
prompt such a statement."[85] Gorbachev was now courting Reagan's en-
dorsement of his reforms.

Reagan would give it, at a price. What exactly Gorbachev was up to
remained a matter of debate in Washington. But by late 1987, Reagan
believed Gorbachev was "serious about introducing major economic and
political reforms." By 1988, he and other officials thought Soviet officials
might find it impossible to control the forces they were unleashing. Gorbachev's changes, the CIA wrote, were "placing tremendous pressure on
the system."[86] By pushing Gorbachev to go further, the administration
was exacerbating those pressures. By supporting Gorbachev diplomatically, Reagan was helping him break totalitarian rule. Reagan was still
waging political warfare against the Soviet *system*, but he was doing it in
cooperation with a Soviet *leader* who was challenging that system as
never before.

In Moscow, the president urged Gorbachev to undertake faster, more
fundamental reforms regarding freedom of religion, freedom of speech,
and other areas.[87] In remarks at Moscow State University, Reagan declared
that "democracy is the standard by which governments are measured":
The Soviet Union could not fully join the world until it left authoritarianism behind.[88] But Reagan also praised Gorbachev's vision and reforms.
The Soviet Union was no longer an "evil empire," he said; that remark
was from "another time, another era." Reagan's approval invigorated

Gorbachev before a critical Party Congress.[89] And it sealed a historic bargain: Gorbachev would keep changing the system, and America would support him. The Soviet Union, Gorbachev affirmed at a final summit in New York in December, "would never go back to what it had been."[90]

The promise wasn't hollow. In a speech at the United Nations the same day, Gorbachev delivered what Daniel Patrick Moynihan later called "the most astounding statement of surrender in the history of ideological struggle."[91] Gorbachev announced that the Soviet military would unilaterally cut 500,000 troops and withdraw 50,000 soldiers and 5,000 tanks from Eastern Europe. He endorsed "freedom of choice" for all nations. The Kremlin, he said, had no claim "to be in possession of the ultimate truth"—the antithesis of what Soviet leaders had argued since 1917. Reagan had no direct role in shaping the speech, but it reflected the relationship he had built. Gorbachev realized that Moscow could no longer wage a global struggle—and did not need to—"because politically we have entered a new situation in our relations with the United States."[92]

When Reagan left office, the Cold War was receding rapidly because the Kremlin was giving up in place after place. The U.S.-Soviet relationship had become shockingly amiable. It was Gorbachev's misfortune to preside over a country whose decline was so steep that he had to sue for peace while portraying historic retreats as triumphs of enlightened statecraft. It was Reagan's genius to help Gorbachev conclude that doing so was possible and necessary.

The Reagan years hadn't resolved the fate of Europe, the central theater of the Cold War. Resolution, however, was not long in coming. When 1989 began, the satellite regimes were still intact. By year's end, those regimes littered history's graveyard. The landmark event was the opening of the Berlin Wall in November; the landmark non-event was the Soviet military intervention that never came. Changes that had eluded policymakers for decades were now coming in months or weeks. "A tidal wave of history," as Gates put it, was sweeping away what remained of the superpower competition.[93]

If anyone got that wave rolling, it was Gorbachev. The general secretary had meant to revive, not euthanize, troubled Warsaw Pact regimes. "We clearly have to draw boundaries," he told Hungarian officials. "The limit . . . is the safekeeping of socialism and assurance of stability."[94] Calls for reform in Eastern Europe backfired, however, by confirming for many citizens just how bankrupt their governments had become. Because Gorbachev signaled, privately and then publicly, that the Kremlin would no longer violently suppress political change, the pace of that change became unmanageable. "The total dismantling of socialism as a world phenomenon has been proceeding," Chernyaev wrote. "And a common fellow from Stavropol set this process in motion."[95]

Yet if anyone ensured that this cascading change ended favorably for America, it was George H. W. Bush. Bush had been Reagan's vice president, but his policies were initially rooted in a critique of Reagan's statecraft. In particular, Bush and National Security Adviser Brent Scowcroft believed that Reagan's focus on arms control had led him to neglect the persistent reality of Soviet power in Europe. "The Cold War began with the division of Europe," Bush declared in May 1989. "It can only end when Europe is whole."[96] Bush and Scowcroft were concerned that Reagan had gotten too chummy with Gorbachev, who—Scowcroft feared—might yet prove a wolf in sheep's clothing.[97] Most of all, they worried that prematurely declaring an end to the Cold War might destroy the leverage that had brought the free world so close to triumph. "Once you say the Cold War is over," Scowcroft said, "you can never take it back."[98]

Bush's Soviet policy was thus very deliberate and very ambitious. Deliberate, in that the administration announced a diplomatic "pause" in early 1989, so it could determine what it would take to conclusively end the Cold War. And ambitious, in the answer it delivered. "We are approaching the conclusion of an historic postwar struggle between two visions," Bush declared in May 1989, "one of tyranny and conflict and one of democracy and freedom." For the Soviet Union to move "beyond containment" and rejoin "the community of nations," Moscow must take historic steps: markedly reduce its armed forces, allow real democratization at home, and get out of the Third World. Not least, Moscow must liberate Eastern Europe. "Tear down the Iron Curtain," Bush exhorted. If the Soviet Union fundamentally changed its policies, it could go from being a pariah state to being a member of the civilized world.[99]

Bush's speech was panned by critics, because Gorbachev was already doing much of what he asked. But the address was important because it explicitly laid out maximalist terms for a Soviet surrender. It called on Moscow to abandon its global influence, its claim to military parity, its security buffer in Eastern Europe, even its system of one-party rule. It showed that Washington would support Gorbachev's reforms while pushing him to do more: "Don't stop now!"[100] And it signaled, subtly, that Bush's strategy involved engaging Gorbachev in order to exploit him: The United States would encourage a friendly leader to make changes that even a hard-line successor could not easily roll back. "Our policy is not designed to help a particular leader or set of leaders," a classified directive stated. "We seek, instead, fundamental alterations in Soviet military force structure, institutions, and practices which can only be reversed at great cost."[101]

Even before late 1989, Eastern Europe was the focus of U.S. policy. In May, Bush publicly urged Gorbachev to allow true freedom in the heart of Europe: "Let Berlin be next!"[102] The same month, Bush proposed to slash Western and Warsaw Pact forces in Europe, with the Soviets making disproportionate cuts. "Our aim is nothing less than removing war as an option in Europe," Bush said. More subversively, the proposal would create space for political reform by moving Red Army units out of the region.[103] Over the summer, Bush visited Poland and Hungary, observing negotiated transitions under way and promising U.S. support if reforms continued. Mindful of the recent massacre of dissidents by the Chinese Communist Party in response to the Tiananmen Square protests, and unsure whether Moscow's forbearance would last, Bush took care not to be provocative. "Americans . . . do not want to see people crushed under tanks, as in 1956," he had said.[104] But he openly aligned himself with actors remaking the bloc from within. "America stands with you," he declared in Poland. "It is in your power to help end the division of Europe."[105]

Bush was sometimes knocked for not more quickly declaring the Cold War over. But he refused to do so because he wanted to ensure that America won that conflict decisively. By mid-year, the administration had laid out terms for a new U.S.-Soviet relationship. It was seeking to end Moscow's dominance of Eastern Europe without risking bloody upheaval. By fall, Bush was even wondering whether the Warsaw Pact might disintegrate. "That may seem naïve," he said, "but who predicted the changes we are seeing today?"[106] Bush had spent 1989 preparing for the Cold War endgame. That preparation would help him dominate the fluidity created by surprise.

The Bush administration saw that Europe was on the verge of a new dawn. But it hadn't predicted the opening of the Berlin Wall in November 1989, an event that was essentially an accident caused by fumbling

East German functionaries. "We've imagined it," Bush admitted, "but I can't say that I foresaw this development at this stage."[107] That development sped up history dramatically, dooming a regime that had survived only by imprisoning its citizens. Within weeks, Helmut Kohl, the West German chancellor, had seized the initiative with a ten-point plan for re-unification. The possibility of a wholesale reordering of Europe was at hand. "It seems like the world is changing overnight," Bush said.[108]

Yet the reordering that occurred—peaceful reunification of Germany within NATO—was hardly guaranteed. The French were wary of a reuni-fied Germany and Thatcher was vehemently hostile. "Such a develop-ment," she had told Gorbachev, "could undermine the stability of the entire international situation."[109] Gorbachev felt the same way. He had tolerated unprecedented change in Eastern Europe, but he had not recon-ciled himself to the total loss of Soviet influence there, much less to the idea that the outcome of the Cold War might undo the outcome of World War II. Moscow thus issued ominous warnings. Reunification, Gorbachev told Western leaders, would cause "not only the destabilization of the situation in Central Europe, but also in other parts of the world."[110]

The only global leader, beyond Kohl, who was unambiguously for reunification was Bush. The president was outwardly cautious at first, for fear of provoking Gorbachev and his 400,000 troops in East Germany. Escalating upheaval in East Germany, an interagency planning group had warned, "is among the World War III scenarios for which U.S. and NATO planners have been preparing for decades."[111] But behind the scenes, Bush saw opportunity.

The United States now had an epic chance to end the division of Europe and, in Scowcroft's words, "rip the heart out of the Soviet secu-rity system."[112] It could show that Moscow's socialist allies were now in-tegrating into the democratic world. And critically, if the United States could keep a reunified Germany tied to NATO, it could ensure that the end of the Cold War did not release the historical demons America's presence had suppressed. After Kohl unveiled his ten-point plan, the president told him, "I'm with you completely."[113] At a summit in Malta in December, he gently informed Gorbachev, "You cannot expect us not to approve of German reunification."[114]

The question was how hard to push. At Malta, Gorbachev had objected more to the pace than the principle of reunification. Kohl was "in too much of a hurry," he griped. Bush's takeaway was that a measured approach, playing out over years, might gain Moscow's acquiescence in the end. "We need a formulation which doesn't scare him, but moves forward," Bush told Kohl.[115] Yet events were moving too rapidly for a gradual approach to work. The East German regime was bleeding money, legitimacy, and people by the day. By early 1990, Kohl was seeking to arrange an economic union; reunification might occur, or trigger a grave crisis, in months, not years.[116]

The potential for tragedy was real. Even as the Soviet Union became more pliant, U.S. officials could not know, in real time, what the exact limits of Moscow's flexibility were. A rush to reunification over Kremlin objections might still cause a harsh Soviet reaction or perhaps a military coup in Moscow. If Germany reunified, Gorbachev had warned, "a Soviet marshal will be sitting in my chair."[117] The general secretary also had other cards to play. He could make common cause with Thatcher and other opponents of reunification, splitting NATO down the middle. Or he could offer to support reunification in exchange for German neutrality—a proposal that, if accepted, would drastically weaken U.S. influence in Europe. Scowcroft "doubted whether Kohl wanted to leave NATO," he told British officials, "but if Gorbachev made the offer . . . he would be very tempted."[118]

In early 1990, the administration took control of events with an interlocking three-pronged strategy for winning the Cold War endgame. First, Bush established a quid pro quo with Kohl: ironclad American support for reunification in exchange for ironclad German commitment to NATO. The administration now encouraged Kohl to go fast rather than slow, because doing so would make it harder for Gorbachev, or any hard-liners plotting against him, to mount effective resistance. "As absorption of the GDR [German Democratic Republic] into the FRG [Federal Republic of Germany] becomes a fait accompli," Scowcroft wrote, "Soviet leverage to reshape the new FRG will decline."[119] What Bush sought—and got—in return was an explicit promise that a reunified Germany would not go its own way. "The concept of Germany being in NATO is absolutely crucial," he told Kohl.[120]

Second, Bush used Germany's commitment to NATO to build consensus within Europe. Bush eventually won Thatcher's approval by pledging that he would make sure Kohl kept Germany in the alliance. He would, he said, "get it from the horse's mouth and in the clearest and most specific terms."[121] Washington also struck a bargain with Paris, pledging to support deeper European unity in exchange for French backing of reunification. At the same time, Bush soothed the fears of Germany's eastern neighbors. He pushed Kohl to guarantee the post–World War II border with Poland and told Czechoslovakia's Václav Havel that American commitment was the best protection against German revisionism.[122] By mid-spring, European resistance to reunification was fading and Soviet opportunities for mischief were narrowing.

The third prong of U.S. strategy was to bring Moscow to terms. Reunification, Scowcroft acknowledged, would be a "bitter pill for Gorbachev to swallow."[123] Bush tried to sweeten it by treating Moscow with respect. The United States established a diplomatic forum, the "two-plus-four," that gave Moscow, Washington, London, and Paris formal roles in the diplomacy surrounding reunification while the two German states handled the internal aspects. Secretary of State James Baker offered assurances on Germany's future—that it would not develop nuclear weapons, for example—while reminding Gorbachev that a nonaligned, embittered Germany might actually be more dangerous than a NATO-aligned one. "It could very well decide to create its own nuclear potential," Baker pointed out.[124] Bush also encouraged Kohl to buy Gorbachev off with billions of marks in loans and credits. "You've got deep pockets," he remarked.[125] The administration even floated (but didn't commit to) limiting future NATO expansion in exchange for Soviet acquiescence.[126] The Soviets would never be enthusiastic about reunification, but they might accept it. "Gorbachev has to be provided with face, with standing," Bush explained.[127]

The president went a long way to win that acceptance. In early 1990, Bush responded delicately to a blowup in the Baltic when Lithuania declared independence from the Soviet Union and Gorbachev responded with economic sanctions. Rather than issue fiery statements in favor of Baltic self-determination, the president urged both sides to negotiate. When Gorbachev balked, Bush applied pressure quietly, informing him that Moscow could not receive most-favored-nation trade status until the crisis eased.[128] In June and July, moreover, Bush pushed through a major reform of NATO meant to deemphasize nuclear weapons and show that the West was demilitarizing its relationship with the East. "What we tried to do," he told Gorbachev, "was to take account of your concerns."[129] The Soviets needed to feel that their weakness was not being exploited.

Yet because Bush was so scrupulously polite, it was easy to forget that this was exactly what was happening. Negotiations over Germany were never a dialogue between equals. Bush subtly pressured Moscow by helping Kohl move rapidly ahead. The administration also ensured that the diplomacy surrounding reunification provided the Soviets with face but little else. America, France, Britain, and West Germany coordinated closely in a "one-plus-three," so Moscow was always outnumbered in the two-plus-four. The latter group was really a "two by four," one State Department official joked, "because it represents ... a lever to insert a united Germany in NATO whether the Soviets like it or not."[130]

Not least, the administration threatened Gorbachev with diplomatic isolation, which would have destroyed his foreign policy, his hopes for desperately needed economic support, and his domestic legitimacy, if he refused to cooperate. "Events in Europe will not stand still," was the message Baker carried to Gorbachev and Shevardnadze in May, "and you risk leaving yourselves out with your current position."[131] At every juncture, Bush and Baker patiently listened to Soviet concerns while refusing to let those concerns determine Germany's future. "We are going to win the game," Bush remarked, "but we must be clever while we are doing it."[132]

That game was still tense and difficult. But eventually the collection of inducements, pressures, and accumulating realities left Gorbachev with the options of conceding gracefully or refusing and making himself irrelevant. "Germany will be in NATO and you will again miss the train," Chernyaev warned.[133] High-level meetings in June and July sealed the key agreements and payoffs. East and West Germany reunified in October, and the Warsaw Pact disintegrated not long thereafter. Bush was magnanimous. "Forty-five years of conflict and confrontation between East and West are now behind us," he said.[134] One Soviet general thought differently. "We have lost World War III without a shot being fired."[135]

They had indeed. German reunification shattered the bipolar system in Europe and showed that a successful free world was now absorbing a failed communist world. But if reunification marked a historic rupture, it also marked the culmination of critical policies that had carried America to victory.

The United States could bring its allies along on reunification because it had built, over four decades, the credibility it now used to ask them to take a leap of faith. Similarly, Bush could convince the Soviets that reunification within NATO was not the worst outcome, because Washington had proven so effective in taming German power. A neutral Germany that was not allied to Washington, Shevardnadze admitted, "would be a big problem."[136] Furthermore, America could so effectively exploit Soviet decline because it had developed, during the 1980s, an approach that Bush now appropriated: using a soft touch to gain acceptance of a very hard line.

Not much was left of the Cold War after German reunification. Soon, little was left of the Soviet Union. If the stresses that had been building for years were sure to cause a grave crisis eventually, the severity of the turmoil that engulfed the country in 1990–1991 owed much to Gorbachev's efforts at revival.[137]

Gorbachev's policy of perestroika was never ambitious enough to move the Soviet Union to a market economy, but by 1990 it had destroyed the old command model. Likewise, Gorbachev's democratization program failed to provide renewed legitimacy, yet it did fatally divide the Communist Party and set off a whirlwind of pent-up grievances. "Gorbachev has yet to fashion a coherent system of legitimate power around new state institutions to replace the old party-dominated, Stalinist one he has extensively dismantled," reported Matlock, the U.S. ambassador.[138] Nationalism surged in the republics; political and economic chaos spread; Gorbachev's popularity plunged amid challenges from leaders like Russia's Boris Yeltsin. As the general secretary zigzagged between liberalization and efforts to appease Soviet hard-liners, he alienated both sides and found himself clinging to his one remaining group of supporters: Western countries. Reform proved deadly to a system predicated on repression.

As in Eastern Europe, bids to save the system sealed its demise. Gorbachev's most admirable quality was his reluctance to use widespread violence. His preference was that "a renewal take place in Russia without blood, without civil war."[139] Yet his effort to create a looser union among the republics faltered, thanks to the same centrifugal forces that Gorbachev had encouraged. And because the proposed union treaty would have weakened the Soviet state, it provoked hard-liners to attempt a last-ditch coup in August 1991. That rebellion collapsed thanks to popular resistance, international condemnation, and internal divisions, taking with it any remaining legitimacy of the system. Gorbachev's authority crumbled and the state fragmented; by year's end, Gorbachev was signing the Soviet Union out of existence. With epic understatement, he lamented that "the debate in our union ... took a different track from what I thought right."[140]

This outcome was what U.S. policymakers had always wanted: the mellowing and breakup of Soviet power. Yet American officials were ambivalent about the events of 1990–1991.

The challenge wasn't that U.S. leaders were poorly informed. Diplomats had reported that Gorbachev was destroying Soviet institutions without fashioning new ones. CIA analysts had warned, as early as late 1990, that previously unimaginable changes were becoming more likely: "The old Communist order is in its death throes" amid a "historical transformation that threatens to tear the country apart."[141] The challenge, rather, was that the terminal crisis of Soviet power presented a set of competitive dilemmas. Some officials, principally Gates and Secretary of Defense Dick Cheney, wished to intensify the crisis by supporting nationalism in the republics and cultivating Yeltsin at Gorbachev's expense. "I believed that the breakup of the Soviet Union was a good thing," Cheney later said, because it would kill off a powerful rival once and for all.[142] Yet actively seeking to destroy the Soviet Union could also backfire.

Gorbachev was, by 1990, giving America everything it wanted. Why ditch him for Yeltsin, an erratic drunk whose intentions remained unclear?[143] Indeed, if Washington appeared to be subverting the Soviet state, it might inadvertently trigger the hard-line restoration it hoped to avoid. "If Gorbachev is thrown out," Canadian prime minister Brian Mulroney warned Bush, "We could go back to Stalin."[144] Nor would smaller necessarily be better. The prospect that a Soviet collapse could trigger violence between nuclear-armed successor states loomed large, particularly after another multinational communist empire, Yugoslavia, fragmented into chaos. If a smooth, peaceful breakup of the Soviet Union was desirable, a far more frightening scenario was plausible. The consequent U.S. strategy was carefully measured and coldly unsentimental. It was less about supporting one leader than supporting America's interest in a defanged Soviet Union.

In the first instance, this meant reducing any chance of a totalitarian revival. To this end, Washington protected Gorbachev by warning him of coup plots and arranging modest economic support. "You are our man," Bush told him.[145] The administration praised Gorbachev for his reforms and his reluctance to hold the union together with force. "Your place in history is assured if you don't change course," Baker assured him.[146] Yet it also quietly threatened him with economic sanctions and diplomatic abandonment on those few occasions when he did resort to coercion.[147] The president simultaneously explained that larger assistance packages would come only if Gorbachev fully committed to a free-market democracy—a change that would, not incidentally, require demolishing the Soviet military-industrial complex.[148] America's objective, Scowcroft summarized, "is to keep Gorby in power for as long as possible, while doing what we can to head them in the right direction—and doing what is best for us in foreign policy."[149]

Second, the administration wrapped up remaining diplomatic business. "Our window of opportunity appeared to be closing," Scowcroft believed. "It was time to consolidate our gains."[150] U.S. and Soviet negotiators finalized the Conventional Forces in Europe Treaty, which locked in asymmetric Soviet reductions; the Strategic Arms Reduction Treaty, which brought major Soviet cuts in heavy missiles; and the presidential nuclear initiatives of 1991, which slashed tactical nuclear weapons. Each initiative lowered the military danger; each exploited a moment of Soviet cooperativeness to secure agreements that could be reversed only at high cost.[151]

Third, the administration began reaching beyond Gorbachev while discouraging destabilizing forms of change. Bush worried that an outright collapse of the Soviet state might be violent; he believed that the system needed some central authority, preferably Gorbachev, to prevent chaos. So he opposed the republics simply making a rush for the exits. "Americans will not support those who seek independence in order to replace a far-off tyranny with a local despotism," he warned the Ukrainian parliament. "They will not aid those who promote a suicidal nationalism based on ethnic hatred."[152] The administration simultaneously hedged its bets, however, by forging ties to Yeltsin and other liberals. "We will not do anything to undermine [Gorbachev]," Bush told Yeltsin. "But that does not mean that we cannot do business with you."[153]

Bush misread the room with his cautionary remarks in Ukraine—the "Chicken Kiev" speech, columnist William Safire mocked.[154] But his policy was more purposeful and predatory than it looked. Bush continually pushed Gorbachev to make reforms that would weaken the Soviet Union geopolitically. He exploited Gorbachev's diplomatic dependence to conclude agreements that accentuated the collapse of Soviet military power. He tried to keep in power as long as possible a leader who was, as Scowcroft put it, "doing our work for us" while also reaching out to those who might succeed him.[155] And he subtly undermined Soviet authority by pushing Gorbachev to accommodate rather than confront elements that sought the breakup of the state. "Behind the scenes," Gates wrote, "there was constant pressure . . . to avoid the use of force in the Baltics and elsewhere."[156] Bush was not protecting Gorbachev; he was protecting a process of change that was overwhelmingly favorable to the United States. He might not have been trying to kill off the Soviet Union, but he was trying to kill off the Soviet threat.

As Soviet decay advanced, U.S. policy became more aggressive. After some early equivocation, Bush and his aides strongly opposed the August coup against Gorbachev. "They should have no legitimacy at home," Baker told the NATO allies. "They should have no legitimacy abroad."[157] Once the coup failed, Bush recognized the independence of the Baltic states and concluded that the "best arrangement" would be the emergence of "many different states, none of which would have the awesome power of the Soviet Union."[158] When the union collapsed, Bush quickly established ties with the successor states to underscore the end of the empire.

"What you have done will live in history," Bush assured Gorbachev as the Soviet Union collapsed around him.[159] But Gorbachev might have been forgiven for wondering whether he had gotten along so well with American leaders only because he was helping them end the superpower rivalry on their terms. "Bush manipulated and used Mikhail Gorbachev" to obtain concessions the West had sought for decades, Gates wrote.[160] Amid all the smiles and summitry, the United States never stopped treating the Cold War as a competition.

The Cold War lasted so long because the antagonisms that drove it were so basic and sharp. It persisted because there wasn't much overlap—beyond avoiding nuclear war—in what the superpowers wanted for the world. As time passed, aspects of the conflict became self-reinforcing; decades of rivalry created inertia that was enormously difficult to break. Without the decline of Soviet vitality, the rise of an unorthodox leader, and the cascading crises he set off, the Cold War might well have kept on going. As Kennan had anticipated, it took fundamental changes—in Moscow's power, in its international behavior, in the Soviet system—for the competition to end.

Yet Kennan also anticipated that America would play an important role in ending the Cold War, and there have long been two opposing narratives about what that role was. The first is that strength and pressure were crucial—that U.S. leaders, particularly Reagan, brought the empire to its knees by exhausting the Soviet economy, overmatching the Soviet military, and rallying forces of liberation within the Communist bloc.[161] The second is that empathy and understanding mattered most.[162] In this view, confrontation produced only a more dangerous Cold War; it took a deliberate turn toward dialogue and cooperation to help Gorbachev reach for peace. Neither argument is entirely wrong. But neither fully captures what happened or what that history can tell us about the challenges of ending a rivalry as intractable as the Cold War.

The Cold War never would have ended so decisively had the United States not built a position of such towering advantage. The creation of a free world strong enough to resist Soviet pressure and give the lie to Soviet promises; the patient accumulation of leverage across multiple domains; the counterattacks that brutally punished Soviet overextension—all of these factors made it possible for Reagan to imagine an American victory. In this sense, the end of the Cold War was the moment when Washington cashed in on strategic investments it had made over decades. Moreover, it took the maximum pressure campaign of the 1980s to drive home the Kremlin's terrible predicament; it took a coldly calculating diplomacy to ensure that Gorbachev could get the peace he wanted only by giving America everything it wanted. The Cold War ended in a blowout, not a draw; it required tremendous coercion to secure that result. The warmth that emerged between Gorbachev and the American leaders who accepted his surrender concealed a more cut-throat reality.

But that concealment was important, because the Cold War would not have ended had American policy been purely predatory. Breaking the superpower deadlock required Gorbachev to believe that the Soviet Union could benefit from revolutionizing its approach to the world. It required him to make historic retreats that would have been unthinkable had Kremlin officials still feared the worst about the United States. The diplomatic achievements of the period were usually quite one-sided, but those achievements were still only possible in a climate of at least minimal reassurance. Gorbachev would not have gone as far as he did if Reagan and Bush had not cultivated him, supported him, and helped him portray himself as a visionary statesman rather than the desperate chief of a collapsing despotism. Making the most of Moscow's decline meant showing some deference to Soviet sensitivities. Untangling an entrenched, protracted rivalry required strength and subtlety alike.

Lessons of a Twilight Struggle

THUCYDIDES WROTE THAT HIS account of the Peloponnesian War was a "possession for all time."[1] His claim, immodest and accurate, was that the story of one great rivalry could reveal elemental truths that applied to others. The Cold War is no less timeless. Like the Peloponnesian War, the Cold War had many never-to-be-repeated features. Like the Peloponnesian War, it nonetheless reveals deep insights that can help policymakers under very different circumstances.

Today's circumstances are different, of course. America's competitions with China and Russia could shape the balance of power and the fate of freedom as profoundly as the Cold War did. Cold War strategists would recognize many aspects of these rivalries: the blend of geopolitical and ideological tension, the challenge of managing fractious coalitions, the painful dilemmas of deterrence and defense. But the dissimilarities are also obvious.

Xi Jinping isn't Stalin (not yet, anyway), even though he practices neo-totalitarianism at home and pursues determined expansion abroad. Vladimir Putin doesn't rule the Soviet Union, which combined revolutionary ideology with imperial ambition, even though he would clearly like to recapture its power.[2] The world is not nearly as broken as it was in 1945; some crucial areas of competition, such as the struggle over communications networks, have no clear Cold War parallel. America's rivalries with China and Russia can probably be called cold wars—long-running, smoldering competitions over world order—but they are not *the* Cold War. Add in the inherent difficulty of learning from the past—knowing what actually happened, determining which lessons to heed or discard—and it is tempting to ignore history altogether.

Yet forgetting the Cold War would be just as calamitous as slavishly following the Cold War playbook. The whole point of studying history is that we can garner useful insights from eras that do not precisely resemble our own. We search for patterns in the past because phenomena like great-power rivalry have certain enduring features, even though one contest is never just like another. And the reason for studying the Cold War is not that it exemplifies immaculate, virtuoso competition. Rather, that history is so rich because it reveals failures and tragedies as well as triumphs. Learning how Washington won that competition can help strategists prepare for coming trials. History can never reveal a detailed blueprint for victory, but it can sharpen the judgment of policymakers as they confront a new generation of challenges.

The United States particularly needs such sharpening right now. In part, this is because America is still in the early stages of what could be long rivalries—the time when big-picture, high-level thinking can deliver outsized rewards. In part, it is because America's intellectual and bureaucratic aptitude for competition atrophied after the Cold War. And in part, it is because the country has, at times, followed such a confused approach.

To its credit, the Trump administration declared that from 2017 on, America was revving up for rivalry. The Pentagon devised a defense strategy focused squarely on Beijing and Moscow; other parts of the bureaucracy began slowly rebuilding competence in competition.[3] Yet the president's behavior—his laceration of U.S. alliances, his indifference to the ideological clash between democracy and authoritarianism, his odd personal solicitude for Putin and Xi, his sowing of disunity at home—revealed an administration that was talking competition but often making the country less competitive. These contradictions revealed a country that was touting a "new Cold War" while ignoring the old Cold War's lessons.

The United States needs, in the post-Trump era, a steadier, more serious approach. It needs a deeper familiarity with its own history of great-power competition, lest it embrace a superficial understanding of an idealized past. What follows are 12 lessons the Cold War can teach as America engages in contests that will require all the insight it can summon.

———

First, *long-term competition requires navigating between unacceptable extremes.* The choice to wage a risky geopolitical rivalry implies that the stakes are worth a war. U.S. officials believed that about the Soviet threat. But the choice of competition also implies a desire to avoid outright conflict. If the first task of long-term competition is choosing the right strategy, then good strategy should offer an alternative to disastrous escalation as well as disastrous retreat.[4]

This was a prime virtue of containment. That strategy didn't always look like a winner. It required abandoning a beautiful dream—collective security and global integration—for the ugly reality of rivalry. It often seemed to combine perpetual danger with perpetual indecision. Yet containment is now seen as one of history's great strategies because its key traits were well suited to protracted struggle.

Containment responded to the transformative aims and insatiable insecurity that made Moscow dangerous, but also to the deep-seated weaknesses that made it manageable. It offered a way to attack the Kremlin's theory of victory by using America's distinct advantages to strengthen a fragile, frightened free world. The strategy was simple enough in concept (a political virtue in a democracy) but supple enough in its specifics to evolve with changing geopolitical realities. Most important, containment made clear that time was on America's side so long as it took the Soviet menace seriously. It thus allowed Washington to work toward a radical end— the breakup or mellowing of Kremlin power—through relatively patient policies that avoided both capitulation and annihilation. Containment blended audacity with caution. It succeeded, not despite, but because of its slow and steady nature.

Not all aspects of containment transfer to other challenges. Yet its record does suggest basic requirements of an effective approach: the need to combine clarity of conception with flexibility of application, the need to recognize the severity of a rival's challenge without underselling one's own strengths, the need to speak to America's democratic ideals as well as its geopolitical interests. Containment reminds us that we can reject an unachievable universalism—in this case, the one-worldism of the post–Cold War era—without succumbing to the fatalism of believing that authoritarian revisionists are destined to dominate. And as we saw in the Cold War, a gradualist, primarily defensive policy can produce transformative strategic breakthroughs: holding the line while exerting selective counterpressures can eventually moderate the ambitions and reveal the weaknesses of even formidable foes. Today, as in the past, this will be a tense, dangerous process. But as the Cold War also reminds us, the alternative to competition may be something much worse.

The efficacy of containment also rested on another attribute—that Washington never approached the U.S.-Soviet duel as a purely bilateral affair. Wars and diplomatic struggles have often been determined by which participant better orchestrates support from other nations—in other words, by which country masters the multilateral context. During the Cold War, what Washington built with its friends was central to what it achieved against its enemy. The creation of a vibrant, historically cooperative free world denied Moscow its best bet for victory; it generated the geopolitical strength and ideological pressure that made Western triumph possible. A lesson is that *an enlightened inside game can make a hardnosed outside game more lethal.*

During the Cold War, a lot went into making that inside game work. The United States tirelessly cultivated allies and partners, no matter how tiresome that endeavor was. It made unprecedented and unequal investments in the well-being of the noncommunist world. Indeed, America even had to change the way it calculated gain and loss in world affairs, because a narrowly self-interested approach would leave the country strategically impoverished in the end. Achieving U.S. interests vis-à-vis the Communist world meant shifting the arc of history within the capitalist world, which meant that Washington could most ruthlessly coerce its rivals by showing generosity toward its friends.

This history could hardly be more relevant. After 2017, the Trump administration combined an overdue emphasis on great-power competition with an overwrought disdain for the liberal order America had built.[5] What resulted was a policy of pressures and threats toward America's friends as well as its rivals, overseen by a president who generally seemed hostile to the very idea of democratic solidarity and mutual advantage. During the Cold War, America retreated from one world to two worlds: it fused competition with the Communist powers to unprecedented cooperation with the democracies. The danger the Trump era revealed was that America might retreat from one world to no worlds—that competition with Russia and China might be undermined by an omnidirectional antagonism that fragments the democratic community.

The implication for the Biden administration and its successors is not that America should never play hardball with its allies. The implication, rather, is that the consistent pursuit of narrow self-interest or the consistent practice of irresponsible leadership will make it harder to deal with competitors. Today, only deeper cooperation—in security, trade, technology—can generate a *collective resilience* against authoritarian coercion and the *collective pressure* that may eventually force those rivals to change course. "On any issue that matters to the U.S.-China relationship," President-elect Joe Biden declared just before taking office, "we are stronger and more effective when we are flanked by nations that share our vision for the future of the world." The precise contours of collaboration and the membership of key coalitions will doubtless be different today than they were during the Cold War, because the geography and some of the core issues of competition are different, too.[6] Yet holding the free world together is still the key to resisting the autocratic world. Without an enlightened inside game, America's outside game won't prosper.

The free world could not have thrived without a strong military shield. Throughout the Cold War, the military balance shaped risk-taking and decision-making; deterrence required continually updating concepts and capabilities amid an evolving nuclear rivalry. The strategy that America ultimately developed helped convince an exhausted rival that it could no longer run a full-throttle race. The military contest thus revealed that *dominating a dynamic interaction requires exploiting asymmetric strengths and imposing asymmetric costs*. It also revealed, however, that dominating a competition and stabilizing it are not the same thing.

To be sure, the logic of asymmetry and cost-imposition was ubiquitous during the Cold War. Washington relied on its economic and technological advantages to rebuild Western Europe; it employed asymmetric strengths in areas from political warfare to intelligence competition. Cost-imposition, too, underpinned key policies. By exploiting a new wave of national liberation movements, the Reagan Doctrine used small investments to drive up Soviet losses in the Third World. In long struggles, imposing disproportionate costs is vital to making an enemy's strategy unsustainable. In rivalries between vastly different competitors, exploiting distinct advantages is essential to gaining the upper hand.

The same principles governed the military competition. Since America could not match the Kremlin tank for tank, it used technological prowess to offset Soviet numbers. A global network of allies gave America peerless geopolitical influence, but Washington could only defend those allies by reaping the asymmetric leverage that nuclear weapons provided. This was why tit-for-tat interventions on the periphery frequently back-fired: they allowed the enemy to bleed America more easily than vice versa. And it was why the Soviet buildup of the 1960s and 1970s was so daunting: it threatened to rip away the shield of U.S. strategic superiority, leaving the West naked before Moscow's conventional power. Salvation came when the overstressing of the Soviet economy, along with crisis-driven creative thinking, birthed an aggressive new strategy. Washington steered the arms race into high-tech areas where the Kremlin was hope-lessly disadvantaged, thereby depreciating massive Soviet investments dating back decades. Ruthless asymmetric cost-imposition made competi-tion unaffordable for a cash-strapped enemy.

There was a downside: the strategic advantage that Washington needed to win the Cold War was sometimes at odds with the strategic stability it might need to escape that contest alive. In the nuclear age, sta-bility might come from accepting the perversely reassuring logic of MAD. But doing so might destroy a U.S. defense posture that could not work in a situation of true nuclear stalemate. This was why U.S. policy-makers who loathed nuclear weapons designed strategies built around them, and why American officials tried so persistently to escape the con-straints and contradictions of MAD. "Stability is a U.S. goal," Andrew Marshall wrote, "but not the only one." Washington needed advanta-geous instability to defend its allies and coerce its enemies.[7]

America is relearning this lesson today. In recent years, U.S. compet-itors have shrewdly employed cost-imposition and asymmetry—for ex-ample, by using a combination of favorable geography and anti-access/area-denial capabilities to make it far too expensive for America to proj-ect decisive military power. Russia is using low-price tools such as disin-formation and cyberattacks to impose high costs, in political rancor and instability, on its adversaries.[8] America is rich, but not rich enough to overcome a perpetually unfavorable cost-exchange ratio. America is pow-erful, but not powerful enough to win if it is consistently wrong-footed by asymmetric strategies.

Washington has options, as long as intense challenges are once again a spur to creative thinking. In East Asia, it can use the natural barrier cre-ated by the First Island Chain, running from Japan to Taiwan to the Phil-ippines, along with cheap and expendable defensive capabilities to make it far more expensive for China to project power into the Pacific.[9] By strengthening its foremost geopolitical advantage—its network of allies

and partners—it can present Beijing and Moscow with threats from unexpected directions, preserve a free-world overbalance of power, and ensure that authoritarian aggression simply produces self-defeating
strategic encirclement. There will also be chances to impose heavy costs
on authoritarian regimes by manipulating their internal weaknesses or
exploiting the local resentments they may encounter as their influence
expands. Remember, the Cold War shows that expansion can create vulnerabilities that must be defended at a very high price. All this may prejudice near-term stability. So Washington must again accept that no
strategy can optimize safety and advantage all at once.

Nor can any strategy offer comprehensive protection against every
threat. In 1948, Kennan urged the United States to compete heartily—to
embrace the "perpetual rhythm of struggle."[10] Yet Kennan's phrasing implied that competitions are marathons, which means that *excelling in extended rivalry requires setting a steady pace.*

Washington struggled with this during the Cold War. Metering
American military efforts—maintaining global deterrence while responding to local challenges—was a recurring problem. Distinguishing peripheral from vital interests in the Third World was devilishly tricky. The
calm effort to cultivate long-term forces of resistance often gave way to
hyperactivity when near-term dangers were intense. These issues quickly
carried Washington into commitments it had never wanted to make. All
of these problems merged in Vietnam, a conflict that was so shattering
because it showed that U.S. strategy had become unsustainable.

The fact that the Cold War was a competitive slog created a set of
strategic imperatives. Timing was important in knowing when to push:
not until the Soviets left themselves dangerously exposed, and the ideological landscape shifted, could Washington retake the offensive. Tactical
retrenchment, whether from Vietnam or Lebanon, was sometimes the
price of strategic sustainability. Accepting weakness in certain areas, as
Ike did during the 1950s, was often a prerequisite to preserving strength
in more important ones. American audacity had to be tempered with a
certain humility about the limits of U.S. power. Above all, the extended
nature of the Cold War placed a high value on recovering from mistakes.

Washington did fairly well in this last area, and not just because it had
lots of practice. The grievous errors that Moscow committed during the
1970s were compounded by the structure and stagnation of Kremlin poli-

tics, which made it hard for the Soviet Union to correct course until it was too late. The relative responsiveness of the American system made it easier to shift when things went awry. The intelligence community learned from its analytical mistakes in the 1960s and 1970s through self-scrutiny that made it better at assessing the enemy. In the military competition, the strategic dead-end of the 1970s stimulated new ideas about how to restore U.S. advantage. A series of presidents also gradually rebuilt a broken strategy in the Third World with innovations that limited Washington's liability while throwing the Soviets on the defensive. Here, America surged at the right moment by punishing Soviet overreach while avoiding its own.

Setting a steady pace is admittedly easier said than done. Adversaries often expand into spaces left undefended; nonvital interests may no longer seem nonvital when attacked. The line between exertion and excess is always clearer in hindsight than in foresight. Yet understanding the basic need for pacing is nonetheless vital because the price of exhaustion is so high. Overreach anywhere can end up weakening a superpower everywhere. In long-term competition, restraining your enemies may also require restraining yourself.

Sustainability involves morale as well as matériel, so a fifth lesson is that *values are an imperfect but essential weapon in a great-power struggle.* An enduring myth of U.S. foreign policy is that values and interests are typically at odds; a resilient misconception is that contestants in great-power rivalry must check their principles at the door.[11]

These views are not entirely wrong: the Cold War did show that a puritanical policy cannot succeed. If there had been a perfect alignment between interests and values, Washington wouldn't have felt compelled to back brutal authoritarians and bloody coups. It wouldn't have supported nasty "freedom fighters" or cut sordid deals with Tito and Mao. There was always the prospect, additionally, that ideological messianism might obliterate distinctions between vital and secondary interests, between tolerable outrages and intolerable dangers. "Anyone who wants to join a missionary organization should wait for the next Secretary of State," Kissinger remarked. "That's not what we're doing foreign policy for."[12] Yet Kissinger soon discovered a reality that realists ignore—that over the long term, effective competition requires keeping American values near the heart of American statecraft.

In part, valuing values was pure political realism. Calls to wage an amoral struggle over dots on a map never would have rallied Americans to the cause for decades. No ideological fervor, no Cold War consensus. In part, focusing on values also was a matter of moral balance. When Washington departed too egregiously from its values, as many Americans perceived it to have done by the 1970s, it raised doubts about whether the desired geopolitical end was worth the use of such dubious means. Fundamentally, however, the issue was one of cold-eyed strategic efficacy.

Promoting democratic values in Western Europe and Japan created lasting ideological cohesion in the free world; it helped hold that community together when rancorous disputes were threatening to pull it apart. Taking up the cause of human rights and democratic reform in the 1970s and 1980s allowed Washington to seize the ideological high ground. Not least, highlighting the ideological contest also highlighted the fundamental moral asymmetry—the contrast between freedom and totalitarianism—that ultimately served as one of America's key strategic assets. Ethical absolutism was a nonstarter in a contest as desperate as the Cold War, but an arid realism would have surrendered one of the best weapons America possessed.

The basic proposition still holds. Today's struggles will demand effort, perseverance, and sacrifice. Mobilizing Americans means activating the passion for defending freedom that has long coursed through the body politic.[13] Moreover, the U.S. competitions with China and Russia are inescapably ideological, and Washington should not evade this reality. Highlighting the clash of political values illuminates, for global audiences, the difference between a world led by a democratic superpower and one led by aggressive authoritarians. It reminds democratic allies in Europe and Asia of the moral ties that bind them to the United States. Above all, it keeps the focus on an asymmetric weakness of the Russian and Chinese governments—their abuse and fear of large swaths of their own populations—and may eventually put Washington in position to align itself with forces of change within these societies. For what America and its competitors are truly engaged in, Biden has correctly argued, is "an historic and fundamental debate about the future direction of our world."[14]

America will still make compromises that blur the moral lines. Working with friendly autocrats in Southeast Asia or the Middle East is a reasonable price to pay for containing unfriendly autocrats in Beijing and Moscow. Washington will surely find itself relying on expedients, from covert action to outright coercion, it would never sanction at home. Yet now as before, the requirements of a flexible morality cannot become an excuse for blanket amorality. A strategy that regularly ignores American values would hardly be realistic.

Moral asymmetries were certainly central to U.S. political warfare. Containment involved myriad efforts to weaken the Soviet Union, fracture its empire, and dissipate its energies. Washington won the Cold War by making the free world function better—and by making the Communist world function worse. *Political warfare is indispensable in great-power rivalry, even if it invites grim dilemmas.*

Political warfare was indispensable because it weaponized—for American benefit—the most repugnant features of totalitarian regimes. Some initiatives involved attraction and others involved coercion; some aimed to trigger near-term shocks while others aimed to subtly increase strains over time. Yet all drew on the idea that the nature of the enemy created exploitable vulnerabilities. In a contest where imposing costs, splitting allies, and stoking discontent were central to the final outcome, political warfare proved its worth.

It was also dirty, dangerous, and painstakingly deliberate. Political warfare featured the moral clarity that came from exposing Communist repression, but also the moral ambiguity that came from inciting captive populations and toasting monsters like Mao. It threatened to inflame tensions with Moscow and even with American allies. Even when the endeavor worked well, which wasn't always the case, progress could be excruciatingly slow and the path to success could be tortuous. Political warfare was no shortcut to victory. It was an endeavor that often delivered its payoff only over long stretches of time.

Both sides of political warfare loom large today. Washington will need more than a static defense against Russia and, especially, China: Diverting their energies and throwing them on the defensive will be critical in holding the line. Now as before, regimes that invest massive sums in controlling their populations make attractive targets. So political warfare—whether it involves attacking the cohesion of the Sino-Russian alignment, retarding China's growth and innovation through technological denial, or raising the economic and diplomatic costs of authoritarian governance—will be central to twenty-first-century competition.[15] Given how aggressively Beijing and Moscow are attacking Western societies, anything less would be unilateral disarmament.

Yet political warfare is no magic weapon. At best, it works slowly and in hard-to-forecast ways. Perhaps Washington can, for example, pull Moscow away from Beijing, but that will require Russia to become more convinced of Western strength and more worried about Beijing's rise, a process that will take years to unfold. En route, U.S. officials should expect all the problems—the concerns of allies, the awkward moral questions, the fury of insecure autocrats—that their Cold War predecessors faced. An improved defense, in the form of measures to harden democratic societies against autocratic meddling, must therefore accompany an active offense.[16] The basic premise of democratic political warfare—that competition requires punishing authoritarian weaknesses—is as valid as ever. So are the difficulties that have long accompanied that endeavor.

One reason political warfare was so fraught was the chance that it might undercut superpower diplomacy. Competition and negotiation are often seen as polar opposites, but that wasn't true in the Cold War. Shared threats, such as smallpox and nuclear anarchy, united geopolitical antagonists; the superpowers periodically tempered the destructiveness and dangers of their rivalry. During détente, U.S. officials sought a fundamentally tamer, more stable Cold War. The effort to impose limits was a central feature of the superpower contest because the perils of unlimited rivalry were so appalling. A seventh lesson is to *treat negotiation as an integral part of competition.*

To be sure, superpower diplomacy was never an unalloyed good. Reaching out to the Soviets might have weakened Western resolve or made Moscow think that Washington was fearful. Indeed, some of the worst Cold War crises flowed, in part, from U.S. efforts to engage the Soviets. Anyone who hopes to use the Cold War as a model for limiting today's competitions should recall that only after that contest nearly turned deadly was there meaningful progress toward managing it.[17] And anyone who hopes that energetic diplomacy can bridge fundamental ideological and geopolitical divides should remember the unfulfilled hopes of détente.

The true value of superpower diplomacy lay, not in overcoming the Cold War, but in helping America triumph. Negotiation was most useful when it tempered competition at moments of American weakness, shifted the rivalry into areas of U.S. advantage, or exposed the Kremlin to subversive influences. Diplomacy paid dividends when it allowed Washington to turn carefully cultivated strengths into concrete political achievements or prevented rifts with nervous allies. One of the lasting achievements of détente, ironically, was that its failure reminded the West of what it was up against in the first place. Most important, negotiation made the Cold War somewhat more tolerable for America and thus made it more likely that Americans would see the competition to a decisive finish.

Now as before, the onset of rivalry need not imply the death of diplomacy. Transnational issues, from climate change to pandemic prevention, demand collaboration among competitors. In a number of areas, from nuclear weapons to the regulation of emerging technologies, the dangers of unlimited antagonism remain severe.[18] Policymakers must always be wary of the dreaded spiral into outright conflict, so realistic cooperation and the search for periodic de-escalation should again be a key part of great-power rivalry. Yet the emphasis must again be on "realistic."

It is fanciful to expect transformative diplomatic breakthroughs before Moscow and Beijing are convinced that competition will not pay. It is important to remember that these regimes have previously used the lure of transnational cooperation to extract geopolitical concessions or to undercut America's competitive posture.[19] If Washington treats diplomacy as an end in itself, or chases after unrealistic agreements, it will end up in a world of trouble. If, however, Washington treats diplomacy as a tool of competition—as a way of creating enough stability to permit the determined pursuit of advantage—it can position itself well for contests that won't end anytime soon.

Eighth, *long-term competition rewards a strategic understanding of time*. Time is a crucial dimension of any extended rivalry. The best competitors use a sophisticated grasp of time to gain strategic leverage.

Containment writ large was a time-based competition: Since the clock favored the free world, there was no need to rush into an unwise settlement or precipitate an ill-judged showdown. Some of America's most calculated initiatives also rested on temporal logic.

During the late 1940s, Washington deliberately used a narrow moment of advantage to undertake bold initiatives—the Marshall Plan, the revival of Japan, the creation of NATO—that produced lasting patterns of strength. In the 1970s, Kissinger and Nixon tried, with mixed results, to use diplomatic wizardry to decelerate the race until a wounded America could once again run at top speed. A few years later, Reagan turned up the tempo dramatically, thereby showing the Soviets that their predicament would only worsen the longer an unconstrained Cold War continued. When windows of opportunity opened, America moved quickly; when windows of vulnerability threatened, it went slowly. America even put time to its benefit in the intelligence competition by using the gradual accumulation of superpower interactions to better know a secretive enemy.

During the 1990s and 2000s, it was Beijing that best managed the clock. It kept Washington hooked on the near-term benefits of economic cooperation in order to develop the long-term power potential to reach for dominance.[20] America must relearn how to view time through a strategic lens.

Understanding to what degree time favors America or its rivals over the long haul is vital to knowing how urgently Washington needs to be impairing those rivals' potential right now. Similarly, understanding how U.S. rivals perceive time can offer clues regarding their behavior. A challenger that believes it is currently well positioned, but has only a few years before crippling internal pathologies set in, may be more dangerous than a challenger that thinks the future looks bright.[21] The same knowledge can generate opportunities for action. If Beijing believes that its moment will come but has not yet arrived, then initiatives that demonstrate U.S. staying power in the Western Pacific or in military-technological competition can make Chinese leaders question their own revisionist designs.[22] If the United States shows it can react quickly to Chinese or Russian military thrusts, it can spoil enemy theories of victory that are premised on American lethargy. Finally, adjusting the tempo of the competition—knowing when a flurry of moves can set an opponent on its heels and when it is better to retard the rivalry—can help Washington adapt to the ups and downs of protracted duels. One way or another, U.S. officials will rediscover a Cold War truth: the clock is never neutral in the clash for global power.

America cannot manipulate time horizons or exploit weaknesses without knowing the competition intimately. It cannot compete holistically without mobilizing the bureaucracy for rivalry. These aspects of competition are less visible than diplomatic showdowns and military crises but are no less important. A ninth lesson is, *don't neglect the hidden dimensions of rivalry.*

The United States largely avoided this mistake during the Cold War. It made generational investments in knowing the enemy by building a rich Sovietological ecosystem and using distinct U.S. advantages to penetrate Kremlin secrecy. It constructed an entire national security state meant to provide the bureaucratic brawn and brainpower for rivalry. That, too, was a generational task. The contours and capabilities of the American government evolved along with a shifting Cold War.

Studying the hidden aspects of competition reveals the hidden virtues of democracies. It sometimes seemed that the nature of the American system contradicted the requirements of good intelligence and organization. But hindsight shows that it was often the democratic aspects of U.S. intelligence that saved the day. What a liberal America lost in secrecy and subterfuge, it made up for with authentic analysis and debate, partnerships with world-class academic institutions and private foundations, and other attributes that were unavailable to an authoritarian competitor.

In the same vein, a system that emphasized imperfect coordination between contending centers of power helped ensure that the national security state never veered too far out of alignment with America's political traditions. It also probably produced better decision-making—or, at least, fewer catastrophic mistakes—over time. Policymakers in democracies sometimes envy authoritarian decisiveness. Yet in a protracted rivalry, the inefficiency that pluralism produces can be a strength.

Today, America need not start from scratch in the hidden dimensions of rivalry: it already has a sophisticated intelligence and national security apparatus. But there is still plenty to do. Because America again faces secretive authoritarian rivals, and because it currently has nowhere near the same intellectual capital it once developed in dealing with Moscow, it will take another national mobilization to build the body of expertise the country requires.[23] (It will also take another national effort to master new technologies that may revolutionize intelligence no less thoroughly than space satellites did.)[24] Washington will need, for example, more granular understanding of Russian and Chinese theories of military victory to develop effective counters; it will require better mechanisms for gathering and assessing geoeconomic intelligence; it must have a clearer picture of how Moscow and Beijing operate in the murky space short of violent conflict.

Similarly, Washington will have to rebuild bureaucratic capability where it has languished or vanished since the Cold War, especially in areas such as information rivalry and political warfare. It will have to reinvest in strategic planning and competitive-minded institutions, and perhaps create new bodies or coordinating mechanisms to handle political meddling, global supply chains, advanced dual-use technologies, and other problems no one existing agency can master.[25] The U.S. government can bring impressive energy and effectiveness to difficult issues. But first it must be oriented—and continually reoriented—to the task.

Mobilizing the bureaucracy was part of a larger challenge: winning the contest of systems. Long-term competition ruthlessly reveals whose domestic model can best withstand the rigors of geopolitical strife. A tenth lesson of the Cold War is that *winning the contest of systems requires resisting the forces of democratic self-destruction while exploiting the pressures for democratic self-improvement.*

The Cold War could have gone very badly for America. The United States let vigilance turn into paranoia during the McCarthy era; it glimpsed, during the Korean War, the garrison state. Only determined leadership from the likes of Eisenhower, plus the strong defense mechanisms of America's political culture, defeated the latter threat. And if the country mostly thrived during the superpower contest, it was because Americans used that contest to drive investments and reforms that might otherwise have gone wanting. By demanding that America improve its image and power, the Cold War created virtuous pressure for progress on issues from race relations to higher education. Here, domestic uplift assisted political warfare: in enhancing its democratic dynamism, America accelerated the enemy's decay.

Can the United States repeat the feat? There have recently been signs of the pathologies that long-term competition can bring, such as calls to ban Chinese students from U.S. universities and race-laden descriptions of Sino-American rivalry.[26] There have been, of late, too many policies and proposals that represent competitive self-harm—for example, restrictions on immigration that would undermine America's economic and demographic health, insufficient investment in education at all levels, a long-term decline in government funding for research and development, the profligate spending down of the country's soft power.[27] Historian Paul Kennedy's description of imperial Spain's decline comes to mind:

> The expulsion of the Jews, and later the Moriscos; the closing of contacts with foreign universities . . . ; the sale of monopolies

which restricted trade; the heavy taxes upon wool exports, which made them noncompetitive in foreign markets; the internal customs barriers between the various Spanish kingdoms, which hurt commerce and drove up prices—these were just some of the ill-considered decisions which, in the long-term, seriously affected Spain's capacity to carry out the great military role which it had allocated to itself in European (and extra-European) affairs.[28]

The better method is to use a new era of rivalry to launch a new era of self-improvement. Competition can alter the domestic balance of power. Initiatives that seem politically difficult—revamping immigration policy to attract more high-skilled workers, reinvesting in education and basic research, pursuing political reforms to mitigate deepening dysfunction—can become more feasible when external dangers loom. Bold projects that are important in their own right—tackling corruption, improving America's cyber and physical infrastructure, catalyzing technological innovation, designing a twenty-first-century industrial policy—take on added import amid intensifying competition.[29] Authoritarian powers will mercilessly exploit America's shortcomings and exacerbate its internal divisions. The best defense is to build a stronger, more cohesive society to confront the challenges that high-stakes rivalry makes too damaging to ignore.

Great-power rivalries can last a long time, but they don't last forever. The purpose of waging them is to achieve a better peace. Even if Washington plays its cards masterfully, its current rivalries probably won't culminate as decisively, triumphantly, and bloodlessly as the Cold War did. Yet Cold War history does offer useful guidance.

The Reagan and Bush years remind us that thinking about how a competition might end—what it would take to establish a different relationship—can help orient a country's statecraft as the conclusion comes into view. That era shows that the shrewdest Cold War policymakers were coldblooded: they never forgot the competitive dynamics of a rivalry even if they muted those dynamics once the possibility of a settlement emerged. More important still, the Cold War endgame illustrates that *ending an entrenched competition peacefully requires ruthlessly blocking an opponent's way forward—but not its way out.*

By the 1980s, Moscow's vitality was bleeding away. Still, it took prodigious U.S. coercion under Ronald Reagan to break the East-West impasse. Because that coercion initially made the Cold War more dangerous, intensive engagement—along with a leadership change in Moscow—was also required to move the competition toward a close. Under George H. W. Bush, the story was similar. Elaborate displays of solicitude for a collapsing rival were a crucial part of a relatively remorseless diplomacy. Winding down a bitter struggle without violence is not a matter of pressure alone. In the nuclear age especially, it requires providing a path for a semi-dignified retreat.

How, when, or whether Washington will be able to wrap up today's competitions on favorable terms is impossible to know. No one should count on a near-cinematic collapse of China or Russia anytime soon. What is clear, though, is that any positive resolution will require consistent U.S. pressure and resistance to disabuse Russia and China of their visions of victory and to increase the strains that authoritarian rule often provokes. There is no path to success that doesn't involve making China and Russia pay exorbitantly for aggressive policies. Yet it will also be critical not to back a desperate, nuclear-armed regime all the way into a corner. It will be equally essential to convince future generations of leaders in Moscow and Beijing that more constructive behavior, and less repressive governance, will be rewarded. For all the uncertainties ahead, it seems prudent to assume that winning a long-term rivalry will once again demand strength and sophistication alike.

Implicit in these lessons is a final point: *the need to see competition as a way of life.* The United States did not, thankfully, destroy its institutions during the Cold War. Yet the patterns of American policy, government, and society did change remarkably. This is not surprising. The Cold War forced Americans to understand that the hardships of competition were the alternative to the greater misery of a world in which hostile ideologies and hostile powers were once again ascendant.

Over two generations, the United States geared its statecraft to an unceasing struggle for influence and position; it took on burdens and sacrifices that would have seemed appalling in any prior "peacetime" era. America reoriented the federal government and reconsidered domestic challenges in the light of the Cold War. Above all, the country accepted, albeit fitfully and warily, that competition in the space between war and peace was the natural state of global affairs, and that security, let alone triumph, would come only through extraordinary effort over an extraordinary time span. Americans might complain that "we have been carrying this burden for 17 years; can we lay it down?" as John Kennedy remarked in late 1962. But "we can't lay it down, and I don't see how we are going to lay it down in this century."[30]

Present-day competitions could conceivably require far less time and effort than the Cold War. Authoritarian systems in China and Russia could soon mellow or become benign. Yet if American leaders should hope for that outcome, they'd be fools to plan on it.

They should plan, rather, on rivalries that will expose America and its allies to high costs and real dangers and that will be won only through the persistent accumulation of advantage. They should understand that defending U.S. interests will require an encompassing approach to increasingly encompassing competitions. They should thus revive Kennan's ethos of "holding our own world together" and "increasing the disruptive strains" on the opponent's world for as long as it takes to succeed. To be sure, an indefinite struggle to protect the gains America and its allies achieved through their victory in the Cold War may sound depressing. But it is the best way to contain the new authoritarian challenges and prevent the emergence of a darker future. Today's competitions are bound to differ, sometimes dramatically, from the Cold War. Yet America won't prosper unless it refamiliarizes itself with the history of that contest—and once again accepts competition as a way of life.

Abbreviations

CH	*The Cambridge History of the Cold War*, edited by Melvyn Leffler and Odd Arne Westad
CIAFOIA	Freedom of Information Act Electronic Reading Room, Central Intelligence Agency
CON	Conference Files
CREST	CIA Records Search Tool
CWIHP	Cold War International History Project
DDEL	Dwight D. Eisenhower Presidential Library
DDRS	Declassified Documents Reference System
DNSA	Digital National Security Archive
DOSB	*Department of State Bulletin*
EBB	Electronic Briefing Book
EIE	*Emergence of the Intelligence Establishment*
ESF	Executive Secretariat File
FRUS	*Foreign Relations of the United States* (with year, volume, and document number)
GFKP	George Kennan Papers
GFL	Gerald R. Ford Presidential Library
GHWBL	George H. W. Bush Presidential Library
HAK	Henry A. Kissinger
Hoover	Hoover Institution Archives
HSTL	Harry S. Truman Presidential Library
JCL	Jimmy Carter Presidential Library
JCS	Joint Chiefs of Staff
JFP	James Forrestal Papers, SMML

LBJL	Lyndon Baines Johnson Presidential Library
LC	Library of Congress
MemCon	Memorandum of Conversation
NARA	National Archives and Records Administration
NIE	National Intelligence Estimate
NSA	National Security Archive
NSAF	National Security Adviser Files
NSC	National Security Council
NSDD	National Security Decision Directive(s)
PPS	Policy Planning Staff
PSF	President's Secretary's Files
RAC	Remote Archives Capture (Program)
RG	Record Group
RRL	Ronald Reagan Presidential Library
SF	Subject File
SMML	Seeley Mudd Manuscript Library, Princeton University
ZBDM	Zbigniew Brzezinski Donated Material

Notes

Introduction. Twilight Struggles, Then and Now

1. This chapter draws on some ideas first expressed in my contribution to the Center for a New American Security's second Michael J. Zak Grand Strategy lecture series, *New Voices in Grand Strategy*, Washington, DC, 4/2/2019.
2. Larry Bland, Mark Stoler, Sharon Ritenour Stevens, and Daniel Holt, eds., *The Papers of George Catlett Marshall*, vol. 6 (Baltimore, 2013), 49.
3. David Larter, "White House Tells the Pentagon to Quit Talking about 'Great Power Competition' with China," *Navy Times*, 9/26/2016.
4. U.S. Department of Defense, *Summary of the 2018 National Defense Strategy of the United States of America: Sharpening the Military's Competitive Edge*, https://www.defense.gov/Portals/1/Documents/pubs/2018-National-Defense-Strategy-Summary.pdf.
5. World Bank, "GDP (constant 2010 US$)," https://data.worldbank.org/indicator/NY.GDP.MKTP.KD; and Stockholm International Peace Research Institute, Military Expenditure Database, "Data for All Countries from 1988–2019 in Constant (2018) USD," https://www.sipri.org/sites/default/files/1_Data%20for%20all%20countries%20from%201988%E2%80%932017%20in%20constant%20%282016%29%20USD.pdf, accessed March 2019.
6. Ankit Panda, "China Creates New 'Asia for Asians' Security Forum," *The Diplomat*, 9/15/2014.
7. Daniel Tobin, "How Xi Jinping's 'New Era' Should Have Ended U.S. Debate on Beijing's Ambitions," Center for Strategic and International Studies, 2020; Aaron Friedberg, "Competing with China," *Survival* 60, 3 (2018), 7–64.
8. Hal Brands, "Democracy vs. Authoritarianism: How Ideology Shapes Great-Power Conflict," *Survival* 60, 5 (2018), 61–114.
9. Howard French, *Everything Under the Heavens: How the Past Shapes China's Push for Global Power* (New York, 2017).

10. David Shlapak and Michael Johnson, *Reinforcing Deterrence on NATO's Eastern Flank* (Santa Monica, CA, 2016).

11. Molly McKew, "The Gerasimov Doctrine," *Politico*, 9/5/2017.

12. Joel Gehrke, "Russia: 'We Are in the Post-West World Order,' " *Washington Examiner*, 6/29/2018.

13. Thomas Mahnken, ed., *Competitive Strategies for the 21st Century: Theory, History, and Practice* (Stanford, 2012).

14. George Kennan, "Measures Short of War (Diplomatic)," 9/16/1946, George Kennan Papers [hereafter GFKP], Seeley Mudd Manuscript Library [hereafter SMML], Princeton University.

15. Frank Hoffman, "Grand Strategy: The Fundamental Considerations," *Orbis*, Fall 2014, 482.

16. John F. Kennedy, "Inaugural Address," 1/20/1961, American Presidency Project [hereafter APP], University of California, Santa Barbara, https://www.presidency.ucsb.edu/.

17. Melvyn Leffler, *For the Soul of Mankind: The United States, the Soviet Union, and the Cold War* (New York, 2007).

18. Odd Arne Westad, "The Sources of Chinese Conduct," *Foreign Affairs* 98, 5 (2019), 86–95; also Melvyn P. Leffler, "China Isn't the Soviet Union. Confusing the Two Is Dangerous," *Atlantic*, 12/2/2019. For an opposing view, see Robert Kaplan, "A New Cold War Has Begun," *Foreign Policy*, 6/2/2019; Hal Brands and Charles Edel, "The Real Origins of the U.S.-China Cold War," *Foreign Policy*, 6/2/2019; Niall Ferguson, "The New Cold War? It's with China, and It Has Already Begun," *New York Times*, 12/2/2019.

19. Robert Jervis, *Perception and Misperception in International Politics* (Princeton, 2017), 239.

20. Odd Arne Westad, *The Cold War: A World History* (New York, 2017); John Lewis Gaddis, *The Cold War: A New History* (New York, 2005); Lorenz M. Lüthi, *Cold Wars: Asia, the Middle East, Europe* (New York, 2020). This book is based on extensive primary and secondary research, but owing to space constraints, the citations are extremely selective.

21. Richard Neustadt and Ernest May, *Thinking in Time: The Uses of History for Decision-Makers* (New York, 1986).

Chapter One. Forging a Strategy

1. Carl von Clausewitz, *On War*, ed. and trans. Michael Eliot Howard and Peter Paret (Princeton, 1984), 579.

2. Charles Bohlen Memo, 4/14/1949, *Foreign Relations of the United States, 1949*, Office of the Historian, U.S. Department of State, I: 113 [hereafter *FRUS*, followed by year, volume, and document number].

3. Leslie Gelb, *Power Rules: How Common Sense Can Rescue American Foreign Policy* (New York, 2009), 103.

4. Robert Patterson, "Four Planks for Peace," *Collier's*, 11/24/1945, 15.

5. Franklin D. Roosevelt Address, 7/4/1941, APP.

6. Walter Lippmann, *U.S. Foreign Policy: Shield of the Republic* (Boston, 1943), 94.

7. Joseph Grew, *Turbulent Era: A Diplomatic Record of Forty Years, 1904–1945* (Boston, 1952), II: 1446.

8. Franklin D. Roosevelt, Address to Congress, 3/1/1945, APP.

9. John Morton Blum, ed., *The Price of Vision: The Diary of Henry A. Wallace, 1942–1946* (Boston, 1973), 490.

10. Stalin Speech, 2/9/1946, Cold War International History Project, Woodrow Wilson International Center for Scholars, Washington, DC [hereafter CWIHP].

11. Robert H. Ferrell, ed., *Off the Record: The Private Papers of Harry S. Truman* (Columbia, MO, 1997), 80.

12. *Bretton Woods Agreements Act*, Hearings before Committee on Banking and Currency, United States Senate (Washington, DC, 1945), 19.

13. Walter Bedell Smith to Secretary, 6/21/1946, *FRUS 1946*, VI: 517; John Lewis Gaddis, *We Now Know: Rethinking Cold War History* (New York, 1997).

14. Robert Lovett Oral History, 7/7/1971, Harry S. Truman Presidential Library [hereafter HSTL].

15. Harry S. Truman, Message to Congress, 3/12/1947, APP.

16. Charles Bohlen, *Witness to History: 1929–1969* (New York, 1973), 176–177; Wilson Miscamble, *From Roosevelt to Truman: Hiroshima, Potsdam, and the Cold War* (New York, 2008).

17. Kennan to Secretary, 3/20/1946, *FRUS 1946*, VI: 487.

18. Kennan to Secretary, 2/22/1946, *FRUS 1946*, VI: 475.

19. Kennan to Secretary, 2/22/1946, *FRUS 1946*, VI: 475.

20. Kennan to Secretary, 2/22/1946, *FRUS 1946*, VI: 475.

21. Douglas to Lovett, 4/17/1948, *FRUS 1948*, II: 536.

22. "X" (George F. Kennan), "The Sources of Soviet Conduct," *Foreign Affairs* 25, 4 (1947), 576.

23. "X," "Sources," 582.

24. Kennan to Secretary, 2/22/1946, *FRUS 1945*, VI: 475.

25. Dean Acheson, *Present at the Creation: My Years in the State Department* (New York, 1969), 3; Melvyn Leffler, *A Preponderance of Power: National Security, the Truman Administration, and the Cold War* (Stanford, 1992).

26. Cabinet Meeting, 3/7/1947, Box 1, Matthew Connelly Papers, HSTL.

27. JCS 1769/1, in JCS to SWNCC, 5/12/1947, *FRUS 1947*, I: 386. [JCS is used hereafter for Joint Chiefs of Staff.]

28. Forrestal Diary, 5/21/1948, James Forrestal Papers [hereafter JFP], SMML.

29. Kennan, "Where Are We Today?" 12/21/1948, Box 299, GFKP, SMML; PPS-13, 11/6/1947, *FRUS 1947*, I: 393. [PPS is used hereafter for Policy Planning Staff.]

30. Forrestal to Gurney, 12/8/1947, *The Forrestal Diaries*, ed. Walter Millis (New York, 1951), 350–351; CIA, "Threats to the Security of the United States,"

9/28/1948, Freedom of Information Act Electronic Reading Room, Central Intelligence Agency [hereafter CIAFOIA].

31. PPS-23, 2/24/1948, *FRUS 1948*, I, Part 2: 4.
32. Kennan, "Planning of Foreign Policy," 6/18/1947, Box 298, GFKP, SMML; Kaeten Mistry, *The United States, Italy and the Origins of Cold War: Waging Political Warfare, 1945–1950* (New York, 2014).
33. News Conference, 1/29/1948, APP.
34. Acheson to Jessup, 7/18/1949, Box 5, Charles Bohlen Records, Record Group [hereafter RG] 59, National Archives and Records Administration [hereafter NARA].
35. NSC-68, "United States Objectives and Programs for National Security," 4/12/1950, President's Secretary's Files [hereafter PSF], HSTL. [NSC is used hereafter for National Security Council.]
36. Meeting with Congressional Leaders, 12/13/1950, Box 142, PSF, HSTL.
37. Forrestal Diary, 1/16/1948, JFP, SMML.
38. Bruce to State, 6/26/1950, *FRUS 1950*, VII: 99.
39. Philip Jessup, "The United States Goal in Tomorrow's World," *Department of State Bulletin* [hereafter *DOSB*], 2/27/1949, 246.
40. Tony Judt, *Postwar: A History of Europe Since 1945* (New York, 2006), 145–149.
41. Meeting of Secretary of Defense and Service Chiefs with Secretary of State, 10/10/1948, Box 147, JFP, SMML.
42. Truman Statement, 6/27/1950, APP; William Stueck, *The Korean War: An International History* (Princeton, 1995), 30–36.
43. Kennan, "Preparedness as Part of Foreign Relations," 1/8/1948, Box 299, GFKP, SMML.
44. Forrestal Diary, 2/12/1948, JFP, SMML.
45. Memo for Truman, 10/2/1950, Box 187, NSC, HSTL; Marc Trachtenberg, *A Constructed Peace: The Making of the European Settlement, 1945–1963* (Princeton, 1999), 87–90.
46. George Kennan, *Memoirs, 1925–1950* (Boston, 1967), 356.
47. Thomas Paterson, *On Every Front: The Making and Unmaking of the Cold War* (New York, 1992).
48. Terry Anderson, *The United States, Great Britain, and the Cold War, 1944–1947* (Columbia, MO, 1981), 106; Lawrence Kaplan, *The United States and NATO: The Formative Years* (Lexington, KY, 2014), 31.
49. Cabinet Meeting, 3/7/1947, Box 1, Matthew Connelly Papers, HSTL.
50. Message to Congress, 3/12/1947, APP.
51. George Marshall, "Assistance to European Economic Recovery," *DOSB*, 1/18/1948, 71, 77.
52. Address to Congress, 3/17/1948, *FRUS 1948*, III: 48.
53. Message to Congress, 3/12/1947, APP.
54. State of the Union, 1/9/1952, APP; William Inboden, *Religion and American Foreign Policy, 1945–1950: The Soul of Containment* (New York, 2008), 105.

55. Kennan, *Memoirs*, 323–324.
56. "Notes on White House Meeting," 2/27/1947, Truman Doctrine Collection, HSTL.
57. Paterson, *On Every Front*, 101.
58. Harry S. Truman, *Years of Trial and Hope* (Garden City, NY, 1956), 105; Eric Goldman, *The Crucial Decade—and After: America, 1945–1960* (New York, 1960), 59
59. Acheson, *Present at the Creation*, 375.
60. State-Defense Policy Review Group, 3/16/1950, *FRUS 1950*, I: 70.
61. Joseph Jones, *The Fifteen Weeks, February 21–June 5, 1947* (New York, 1964), 152.
62. Benn Steil, *The Marshall Plan: Dawn of the Cold War* (New York, 2018), 198–201.
63. Kennan, *Memoirs*, 405.
64. *Congressional Record*, 3/13/1948, 2763, https://www.govinfo.gov/content/pkg/GPO-CRECB-1948-pt2/pdf/GPO-CRECB-1948-pt2-17.pdf.
65. Scowcroft Oral History, 11/12–13/1999, Presidential Oral Histories Project, Miller Center for Public Affairs, University of Virginia.
66. Thomas Christensen, *Useful Adversaries: Grand Strategy, Domestic Mobilization, and Sino-American Conflict, 1947–1958* (Princeton, 1997), 190–191.
67. Julian Zelizer, *Arsenal of Democracy: The Politics of National Security—From World War II to the War on Terrorism* (New York, 2012), 120.
68. Arthur Krock, "New Emphasis on Divisions in the Government," *New York Times*, 9/13/1946.
69. Walter Lippmann, *The Cold War: A Study in U.S. Foreign Policy* (New York, 1947), 18, 23.
70. Joseph Kennedy, "Present Policy Is Politically and Morally Bankrupt," *Vital Speeches of the Day*, XVII, 6 (1951), 170–173.
71. State-Defense Policy Review Group, 2/27/1950, *FRUS 1950*, I: 64.
72. Truman-Auriol Meeting, 3/29/1952, Box 142, Subject File [hereafter SF], PSF, HSTL.
73. Republican Platform, 7/7/1952, APP.
74. Harry S. Truman, Farewell Address, 1/15/1953, APP.
75. Jones, *Fifteen Weeks*, 225.
76. Telegram from Nikolai Novikov, 9/27/1946, CWIHP.
77. Walter Russell Mead, *Special Providence: American Foreign Policy and How It Changed the World* (New York, 2001), 33–34.

Chapter Two. Creating Situations of Strength

1. Adapted from Arnold Wolfers, *Discord and Collaboration: Essays of International Politics* (Baltimore, 1962), 73–76.
2. Dean Acheson, *Present at the Creation: My Years in the State Department* (New York, 1969), 378.

3. Dean Acheson, "The Pattern of Leadership—A Pattern of Responsibility," *DOSB*, 9/22/1952, 427.

4. Truman Address, 6/26/1945, APP.

5. Wilson Address, 1/22/2017, APP.

6. Truman Statement, 2/6/1946, APP.

7. Winston S. Churchill, "The Sinews of Peace," Westminster College, Fulton, MO, 3/5/1946, NATO Archives Online, https://www.nato.int/docu/speech/1946/s460305a_e.htm.

8. Bohlen Notes, 8/25/1947, Box 5, Charles Bohlen Records, NARA.

9. Acheson, *Present at the Creation*, xvii.

10. Annual Report of Supreme Allied Commander Europe, 4/2/1952, Box 278, Averill Harriman Papers, Library of Congress [hereafter LC].

11. Truman Address, 3/6/1947, APP.

12. Harold James, *International Monetary Cooperation since Bretton Woods* (New York, 1996).

13. William Clayton, "The European Crisis," 5/27/1947, Box 33, Policy Planning Staff Records, RG 59, NARA.

14. G. John Ikenberry, *Liberal Leviathan: The Origins, Crisis, and Transformation of the American World Order* (Princeton, 2011), 199.

15. PPS-1, 5/23/1947, Box 7, Charles Bohlen Records, NARA.

16. British Embassy to State, undated, *FRUS 1947*, III: 11.

17. Robert Pollard, *Economic Security and the Origins of the Cold War, 1945–1950* (New York, 1985), 156.

18. Daniel Yergin and Joseph Stanislaw, *The Commanding Heights: The Battle for the World Economy* (New York, 2002), 13.

19. Truman Address, 6/11/1947, APP.

20. Acheson-Adenauer Discussions, 11/13/1949, Box 2, Conference Files [hereafter CON], RG 59, NARA; Geir Lundestad, *Empire by Integration: The United States and European Integration, 1945–1997* (New York, 1998).

21. Douglas Irwin, *Clashing over Commerce: A History of U.S. Trade Policy* (Chicago, 2017), 484; Census Bureau, *Statistical Abstract of the United States, 1954* (Washington, DC, 1955), 902.

22. Dean Acheson, "The Requirements of Reconstruction," *DOSB*, 5/18/1947.

23. Acheson, "Requirements."

24. Kaysen to Kennedy, 9/18/1962, *FRUS 1961–1963*, IX: 60; Francis Gavin, *Gold, Dollars, and Power: The Politics of International Monetary Relations, 1958–1971* (Chapel Hill, NC, 2004).

25. Richard Bissell, Statement to House Foreign Affairs Committee, 2/19/1948, Box 238, Averill Harriman Papers, LC.

26. John Harper, *American Visions of Europe: Franklin D. Roosevelt, George F. Kennan, and Dean G. Acheson* (New York, 1996), 99.

27. Hickerson to Marshall, 1/19/1948, *FRUS 1948*, III: 4.

28. *Foreign Relief Assistance Act of 1948, Hearings Held in Executive Session before the Committee on Foreign Relations, United States Senate* (Washington, DC, 1973), 242.

29. Tim Kane, "Global U.S. Troop Deployments, 1950–2003," Heritage Foundation, 2004, https://www.heritage.org.

30. Memorandum for Files, 1/22/1951, Box 14, Records of Dean Acheson, Lot 53D444, RG 59, NARA.

31. Paraphrase of Telegram from Ernest Bevin, 4/9/1948, *FRUS 1948*, III: 67.

32. Kennan to Lovett, 4/29/1948, *FRUS 1948*, III: 84.

33. Paraphrase of Telegram from Bevin.

34. Editorial Note, *FRUS 1955–1957*, XIX: 41.

35. Acheson, "Pattern of Leadership," 426–427.

36. George Kennan, "Problems of U.S. Foreign Policy after Moscow," 5/6/1947, Box 298, GFKP.

37. Second Meeting of Washington Exploratory Talks, 7/6/1948, *FRUS 1948*, III: 113.

38. Douglas MacArthur letter, 1/24/1948, in Supreme Commander of the Allied Powers, *Political Reorientation of Japan: September 1945 to September 1948*, Volume II (Washington, DC, 1949), 780.

39. JCS to Commander-in-Chief of U.S. Occupation Forces, 7/11/1947, in *Documents on Germany, 1944–1985* (Washington, DC, 1985), 134.

40. Walter LaFeber, *The Clash: U.S.-Japanese Relations throughout History* (New York, 1997), 265; Tony Smith, *America's Mission: The United States and the Worldwide Struggle for Democracy* (Princeton, 2012), 155–167.

41. Robert Kagan, *The Jungle Grows Back* (New York, 2018).

42. Harry S. Truman, Message to Congress, 12/19/1947, APP.

43. James Dunn to Secretary, 2/7 and 6/16/1948, *FRUS 1948*, III: 511, 543.

44. Harry S. Truman, Farewell Address, 1/15/1953, APP.

45. Elliott Abrams, *Realism and Democracy: American Foreign Policy after the Arab Spring* (New York, 2017), 1–91.

46. Memorandum of Conversation [hereafter MemCon], 1/21/1948, Box 9, Charles Bohlen Records, NARA.

47. Kissinger Address, 3/11/1976, *FRUS 1969–1976*, XXXVIII, 1: 71.

48. Truman Address, 3/6/1947, APP.

49. Peter Peterson, "The United States in the Changing World Economy: Statistical Background Material," 12/27/1971, Box 31, James Schlesinger Papers, LC; Wilfried Loth, "The Cold War and the Social and Economic History of the Twentieth Century," in Melvyn Leffler and Odd Arne Westad, eds., *The Cambridge History of the Cold War*, Volume II (New York, 2010), 512, hereafter *CH*.

50. Hal Brands, *Making the Unipolar Moment: U.S. Foreign Policy and the Rise of the Post–Cold War Order* (Ithaca, NY, 2016), 44.

51. MemCon, 9/11/1972, *FRUS 1969–1976*, III: 100; Daniel Sargent, *A Superpower Transformed: The Remaking of American Foreign Relations in the 1970s* (New York, 2014).

52. MemCon, 10/30/1956, *FRUS 1955–1957*, XVI: 435.

53. Thomas Schwartz, *Lyndon Johnson and Europe: In the Shadow of Vietnam* (Cambridge, MA, 2003), 103.

54. MemCon, 3/6/1974, National Security Adviser Files [hereafter NSAF], MemCons, Box 3, Gerald R. Ford Presidential Library [hereafter GFL].

55. Acheson to Schuman, 2/4/1952, *FRUS 1952–1954*, V, Part 1: 15.

56. MemCon, 10/21/1955, Box 3, White House Memoranda Series, John Foster Dulles Papers, Dwight D. Eisenhower Presidential Library [hereafter DDEL].

57. MemCon, 1/8/1974, Box 3, NSAF, MemCons, GFL; MemCon, 2/3/1973, *FRUS 1969–1976*, E-15, Part 2: 6.

58. Jimmy Carter, *White House Diary* (New York, 2010), 172, 335.

59. Schwartz, *Lyndon Johnson*, 35.

60. Kennedy Remarks, 1/22/1963, *FRUS 1961–1963*, XIII: 168.

61. MemCon, 6/1/1961, *FRUS 1961–1963*, XIII: 107.

62. Harold Brown, "National Security 1977–1980," 12/18/1980, Box 740, Council on Foreign Relations Sound Recordings, SMML.

63. Leon Fuller Memo, 9/10/1954, *FRUS 1952–1954*, V, Part 2: 39.

64. Timothy Sayle, *Enduring Alliance: A History of NATO and the Postwar Global Order* (Ithaca, NY, 2019), 139.

65. "Global Economic Forces," 1/22/1982, CIA Records Search Tool [hereafter CREST], NARA; Michael Mastanduno, "System Maker and Privilege Taker: U.S. Power and the International Political Economy," *World Politics* 61, 1 (2009), 121–154.

66. Bator to Johnson, 3/7/1966, *FRUS 1964–1968*, XIII: 138.

67. Senior Interdepartmental Group for International Economic Policy Minutes, 12/5/1984, Declassified Documents Reference System [hereafter DDRS].

68. John Foster Dulles, "Developing NATO in Peace," *DOSB*, 4/30/1956, 708.

69. Editorial Note, *FRUS 1952–1954*, V, Part 1: 462.

70. NIE-20-1-69, 12/4/1969, *FRUS 1969–1976*, XLI: 27. [NIE is used hereafter for National Intelligence Estimate.]

71. INR Memo, 11/24/1973, *FRUS 1969–1976*, E-15, Part 2: 39.

72. "Global Economic Forces," 1/22/1982, CREST, NARA.

73. "Overall Statement of Problem Involved," December 1950, Box 297, Averill Harriman Papers, LC.

74. G. John Ikenberry, *After Victory: Institutions, Strategic Restraint, and the Rebuilding of Order after Major Wars* (Princeton, 2001), chapter 6.

75. Carter, *White House Diary*, 206; Robert Putnam and Nicholas Bayne, *Hanging Together: Cooperation and Conflict in the Seven-Power Summits* (Cambridge, 1987), esp. 73–92.

76. Helga Haftendorn, *NATO and the Nuclear Revolution: A Crisis of Credibility, 1966–1967* (New York, 1996).

77. Caffery to State, 7/3/1947, *FRUS 1947*, III: 182.

78. NSC Meeting, 12/21/1954, *FRUS 1952–1954*, II, Part 1: 143; Mira-Rapp Hooper, *Shields of the Republic: The Triumph and Peril of America's Alliances* (Cambridge, 2020).

79. Kennan, "Problems of U.S. Foreign Policy."

80. Giovanni Arrighi, "The World Economy and the Cold War," *CH*, III: 28.

81. Meyer to Casey, 6/28/1984, CIAFOIA.

82. British Embassy to State, 3/11/1948, *FRUS 1948*, III: 37.

Chapter Three. Competing in the Nuclear Shadow

1. NSC Meeting, 1/26/1956, *FRUS 1955–1957*, XX: 103.

2. CIA, "The Possibility of Direct Soviet Military Action during 1949," 5/3/1949, CIAFOIA.

3. Joint Strategic Survey Committee Report, 4/29/1947, *FRUS 1947*, I: 386.

4. Carl von Clausewitz, *On War*, ed. and trans. Michael Eliot Howard and Peter Paret (Princeton, 1984), 603.

5. Truman Remarks, 4/4/1952, APP.

6. Bernard Brodie, ed., *The Absolute Weapon* (New York, 1946), 74.

7. Joint Intelligence Committee Report, 4/1/1948, *FRUS 1948*, I, Part 2: 14.

8. Forrestal to Gurney, 12/8/1947, *Forrestal Diaries*, 350–351, JFP, SMML.

9. NSC-30, 9/10/1948, Box 177, PSF, NSC, HSTL.

10. David Holloway, *Stalin and the Bomb: The Soviet Union and Atomic Energy, 1939–1956* (New Haven, 1994).

11. "Outlays by Superfunction and Function: 1940–2024," White House, Office Management and Budget, Historical Tables, 50–51, Table 3.1, https://www. whitehouse.gov/omb/historical tables.com.

12. *First Report of the Secretary of Defense* (Washington, DC, 1948), 7; David Rosenberg, "American Atomic Strategy and the Hydrogen Bomb Decision," *Journal of American History* 66, 1 (1979), 64–73.

13. Bohlen to Voorhees Group, 4/3/1950, Box 272, Averill Harriman Papers, LC.

14. ORE 32–50, 6/9/1950, Digital National Security Archive [hereafter DNSA]; Marc Trachtenberg, *A Constructed Peace: The Making of the European Settlement, 1945–1963* (Princeton, 1999), 87–99.

15. Marc Trachtenberg, *History and Strategy* (Princeton, 1988), 119.

16. Memo for Truman, 1/25/1951, Box 187, Meetings File, NSC, PSF, HSTL.

17. "Estimated U.S. and Soviet/Russian Nuclear Stockpiles, 1945–94," *Bulletin of the Atomic Scientists*, December 1994, 59; Allan Millett, Peter Maslowski, and William Feis, *For the Common Defense: A Military History of the United States* (New York, 2012), 460–467.

18. Memo for Truman, 10/11/1951, Box 136, Paul Nitze Papers, LC.

19. Vojtech Mastny, *The Cold War and Soviet Insecurity: The Stalin Years* (New York, 1996), 106; Trachtenberg, *History and Strategy*, 149–152.

20. Dean Acheson, "Soviet Reaction to Free World's Growing Strength," *DOSB*, 10/20/1952, 596.

21. "Outlays," 50; Aaron Friedberg, *In the Shadow of the Garrison State: America's Anti-Statism and Its Cold War Grand Strategy* (Princeton, 2000), 123.

22. NSC 141, 1/19/1953, Box 136, Nitze Papers, LC.

23. John Foster Dulles, "Evolution of Foreign Policy," 1/12/1954, Box 80, John Foster Dulles Papers, SMML.

24. "Strategic Concept," 2/21/1954, Box 80, John Foster Dulles Papers, SMML; Robert Bowie and Richard Immerman, *Waging Peace: How Eisenhower Shaped an Enduring Cold War Strategy* (New York, 1998).

25. "Estimated Nuclear Stockpiles," 59.

26. Campbell Craig and Fredrik Logevall, *America's Cold War: The Politics of Insecurity* (Cambridge, 2009), 169–172.

27. NSC Meeting, 12/3/1954, *FRUS 1952–1954*, II, Part 1: 138; MC 14/2, Final Decision, 5/23/1957, DNSA.

28. News Conference, 2/10/1954, APP.

29. "Outlays," 51–52.

30. MemCon, 5/24/1956, DNSA.

31. David Holloway, "Nuclear Weapons and the Escalation of the Cold War," *CH* I: 391–393; Vladislav Zubok, *A Failed Empire: The Soviet Union in the Cold War from Stalin to Gorbachev* (Chapel Hill, NC, 2009), 102, 127–130, 141.

32. John Lewis Gaddis, *We Now Know: Rethinking Cold War History* (New York, 1997), 221–259.

33. Memorandum for Herter, 8/13/1958, DNSA.

34. Gregory Treverton, *America, Germany, and the Future of Europe* (Princeton, 2014), 138.

35. Eisenhower Diary, 1/23/1956, *FRUS 1955–1957*, XIX: 53.

36. MemCon, 3/6/1959, DNSA; Richard Betts, *Nuclear Blackmail and Nuclear Balance* (Washington, DC, 1985), 86.

37. Campbell Craig, *Destroying the Village: Eisenhower and Thermonuclear War* (New York, 1998), 86; Robert Watson, *The Joint Chiefs of Staff and National Policy, 1953–1954* (Washington, DC, 1998), 266.

38. NSC Meeting, 1/11/1957, *FRUS 1955–1957*, XIX: 105.

39. *Deterrence and Survival in the Nuclear Age: Report to the Joint Committee on Defense Production, Congress of the United States* (Washington, DC, 1976), 28.

40. Radio-Television Report, 3/16/1959, APP.

41. Cabinet Meeting, 8/5/1954, DNSA.

42. David Rosenberg, "The Origins of Overkill: Nuclear Weapons and American Strategy, 1945–1960," *International Security* 7, 4 (1983), 8.

43. NSC Meeting, 2/18/1960, DNSA.

44. Draft PPC Paper, 6/22/1962, *FRUS 1961–1963*, VIII: 93.

45. Dulles, "Evolution of Foreign Policy"; Message to Congress, 3/28/1961, APP.

46. McGeorge Bundy, *Danger and Survival: Choices about the Bomb in the First Fifty Years* (New York, 1988), 375; John Lewis Gaddis, *Strategies of Containment: A Critical Appraisal of American National Security Policy during the Cold War* (New York, 2005), 205–206, 213–219; Lawrence Freedman, *The Evolution of Nuclear Strategy* (Princeton, 1983), 225–255.

47. McNamara Address, 5/5/1962, *FRUS 1961–1963*, VIII: 82.

48. William Taubman, *Khrushchev: The Man and His Era* (New York, 2003), 537; Lawrence Freedman, *Kennedy's Wars: Berlin, Cuba, Laos, and Vietnam* (New York, 2002).

49. Richard Ned Lebow and Janice Gross Stein, *We All Lost the Cold War* (Princeton, 1994), 37.

50. Taylor to Lemnitzer, 9/19/1961, and Kaysen to Taylor, 9/5/1961, both at EBB 56, National Security Archive [hereafter NSA].

51. Minutes 60A, 10/22/1962, Kremlin Decision-Making Project, Miller Center for Public Affairs, University of Virginia.

52. McNamara Address, 12/14/1962, *FRUS 1961–1963*, VIII: 120.

53. Steven Rearden, *Council of War: A History of the Joint Chiefs of Staff* (Washington, DC, 2012), 216–217; Aleksandr Fursenko and Timothy Naftali, *One Hell of a Gamble: Khrushchev, Castro, and Kennedy, 1958–1964* (New York, 1998), 244–245; Craig, *Destroying the Village*, 160–161.

54. Scott Sagan, *The Limits of Safety: Organizations, Accidents, and Nuclear Weapons* (Princeton, 1993).

55. MemCon, 12/27/1962, *FRUS 1961–1963*, VIII: 121.

56. State to Ankara and Other Posts, 12/23/1964, Electronic Briefing Book [hereafter EBB] 31, NSA.

57. Scott Sagan, *Moving Targets: Nuclear Strategy and National Security* (Princeton, 1990), 40–41.

58. Walter Poole, *The Joint Chiefs of Staff and National Policy, 1965–1968* (Washington, DC, 2012), 17–30.

59. Meeting Notes, 12/6/1966, *FRUS 1964–1968*, X: 150.

60. Text of McNamara Speech, *New York Times*, 9/19/1967.

61. Rearden, *Council of War*, 259.

62. McNamara and Rusk to Johnson, 5/28/1966, *FRUS 1964–1968*, XIII: 171.

63. MemCon, 6/1/1961, *FRUS 1961–1963*, XIII: 107.

64. Marc Trachtenberg, *The Cold War and After: History, Theory, and the Logic of International Politics* (Princeton, 2012), 167.

65. James Cameron, *The Double Game: The Demise of America's First Missile Defense System and the Rise of Strategic Arms Limitation* (New York, 2017), 81; Bundy, *Danger and Survival*, 546.

66. Sagan, *Moving Targets*, 41.

67. Anatoly Dobrynin, *In Confidence: Moscow's Ambassador to America's Six Cold War Presidents* (New York, 1995), 165.

68. Laird to Nixon, 12/8/1971, in *Melvin Laird and the Foundation of the Post-Vietnam Military, 1969–1973*, Documentary Supplement, ed. Richard A. Hunt, Secretaries of Defense Historical Series, Volume VII, Office of the Secretary of Defense (Washington, DC, 2016), https://history.defense. gov/Portals/70/Documents/secretaryofdefense/Laird%20Document %20Supplement.pdf.

69. Marc Trachtenberg, "The Influence of Nuclear Weapons in the Cuban Missile Crisis," *International Security* 10, 1 (1985), 160.

70. Jonathan Haslam, *Russia's Cold War: From the October Revolution to the Fall of the Wall* (New Haven, 2011), 304.

71. BDM Corporation, *Soviet Intentions, 1965–1985*, Volume I: *An Analytical Comparison of U.S.-Soviet Assessments during the Cold War*, 4, EBB 285, NSA; Gordon Barrass, *The Great Cold War: A Journey through the Hall of Mirrors* (Stanford, 2009), 212–214.

72. MemCon, 3/8/1976, *FRUS 1969–1976*, XXXV: 73.

73. Census Bureau, *Statistical Abstract of the United States, 1998* (Washington, DC, 1998), 358; Millett, Maslowski, and Feis, *Common Defense*, 568.

74. MemCon, 8/5/1971, *FRUS 1969–1976*, XXXIV: 190.

75. MemCon, 8/13/1971, *FRUS 1969–1976*, I: 96.

76. William Wohlforth, *The Elusive Balance: Power and Perceptions during the Cold War* (Ithaca, NY, 1993), 187.

77. Richard Nixon, "U.S. Foreign Policy for the 1970's," *DOSB*, 3/22/1971, 342.

78. MemCon, 11/6/1973, *FRUS 1969–1976*, E-15, Part 2: 275.

79. Nixon Address, 11/4/1972, *FRUS 1969–1976*, I: 123.

80. Special NIE 11-4-73, 9/10/1973, DNSA.

81. NSC Meeting, 2/11/1971, *FRUS 1969–1976*, XXXIV: 174.

82. NSC Meeting, 2/14/1969, EBB 173, NSA.

83. John Maurer, "The Purposes of Arms Control," *Texas National Security Review* 2, 1 (2018).

84. Kissinger to Walsh, 2/21/1969, *FRUS 1969–1976*, XII: 20.

85. Francis Gavin, *Nuclear Statecraft: History and Strategy in America's Atomic Age* (Ithaca, NY, 2012), 113–116.

86. MemCon, 5/7/1974, Box 7, Records of Henry A. Kissinger [hereafter HAK], RG 59, NARA.

87. Victor Israelian, "Nuclear Showdown as Nixon Slept," *Christian Science Monitor*, November 3, 1993; Matthew Kroenig, *The Logic of American Nuclear Strategy: Why Strategic Superiority Matters* (New York, 2018), 104.

88. Defense Posture Review, 7/28/1970, EBB 173, NSA.

89. NSC Meeting, 4/12/1973, Box 1, MemCons, NSAF, GFL.

90. William Burr, "The Nixon Administration, the 'Horror Strategy,' and the Search for Limited Nuclear Options, 1969–1972: Prelude to the Schlesinger Doctrine," *Journal of Cold War Studies* 7, 3 (2005), 34–78.

91. Memo in Lord to Kissinger, 12/3/1973, EBB 173, NSA.

92. Henry Kissinger, *Years of Upheaval* (Boston, 1982), 1175.

93. Jimmy Carter, *Keeping Faith: Memoirs of a President* (Fayetteville, AR, 1995), 220.

94. Brzezinski to Carter, 6/3 and 8/2/1977, Box 22, SF, Zbigniew Brzezinski Donated Material [hereafter ZBDM], Jimmy Carter Presidential Library [hereafter JCL].

95. Special Coordinating Committee Meeting, 11/24/1980, Box 23, SF, ZBDM, JCL.

96. Norman Friedman, *The Fifty-Year War: Conflict and Strategy in the Cold War* (Annapolis, 2007), 418.

97. Mikhail Gorbachev, *Memoirs* (New York, 1995), 444.

98. Svetlana Savranskaya and David Welch, eds., *Global Competition and the Deterioration of U.S.-Soviet Relations, 1977–1980*, 38–39, Carter-Brezhnev Documents, Global Competition Collection, NSA.

99. Rumsfeld to Ford, 11/30/1976, *FRUS 1969–1976*, XXXV: 113.

100. MemCon, 8/10/1971, *FRUS 1969–1976*, XXXII: 190.

101. A. W. Marshall, "Long-Term Competition with the Soviets: A Framework for Strategic Analysis," RAND Corporation, R-862-PR, April 1972.

102. Marshall, "Long-Term Competition."

103. Barrass, *Great Cold War,* 210–211.

104. "Precision-Guided Munitions and Collateral Damage," undated, Box 58, James Schlesinger Papers, LC.

105. Vitalii Leonidovich Kataev Interview, 6/23/1993, EBB 285, NSA; Brendan Green, *The Revolution That Failed: Nuclear Competition, Arms Control, and the Cold War* (New York, 2020).

106. Goodby and Lord to Kissinger, 11/16/1976, *FRUS 1969–1976*, XXXV: 109.

107. State to NATO Capitals, 6/11/1980, EBB 390, NSA; PD/NSC-59, 7/25/1980, EBB 390, NSA (PD is Presidential Directive); Zbigniew Brzezinski, *Power and Principle: Memoirs of the National Security Adviser* (New York, 1983), 457–459.

108. BDM Corporation, *Soviet Intentions 1965–1985, Volume II: Soviet Post-Cold War Testimonial Evidence*, 188, EBB 285, NSA.

109. *Department of Defense Annual Report, Fiscal Year 1982*, x, https://history. defense.gov/Portals/70/Documents/annual_reports/1982_DoD_AR. pdf?ver=2014-06-24-150904-113.

110. Gordon Barrass, "U.S. Competitive Strategy during the Cold War," in Thomas Mahnken, ed., *Competitive Strategies for the 21st Century: Theory, History, and Practice* (Stanford, 2012), 85; Robert Tomes, *U.S. Defense Strategy from Vietnam to Operation Iraqi Freedom: Military Innovation and the New American Way of War, 1973–2003* (New York, 2007), 39–96.

111. Brown-Deng MemCon, 1/8/1980, DDRS; Jesus Velasco, *Neoconservatives in U.S. Foreign Policy under Ronald Reagan and George W. Bush: Voices behind the Throne* (Baltimore, 2010), 111.

112. Ronald Reagan, *An American Life* (New York, 1990), 547.

113. Reagan, "World Challenges, 1979," 1/12/1979, Box 3, Ronald Reagan Subject Collection, Hoover Institution Archives [hereafter Hoover].

114. Paul Lettow, *Ronald Reagan and His Quest to Abolish Nuclear Weapons* (New York, 2005), 35.

115. "Outlays," 54–55.

116. National Security Planning Group Meeting, 1/13/1983, Box 91683, NSC Executive Secretariat File [hereafter ESF], Ronald Reagan Presidential Library [hereafter RRL].

117. Richard Halloran, "Pentagon Draws Up First Strategy for Fighting a Long Nuclear War," *New York Times*, 5/30/1982; "MX Missile Deployment," Fall 1982, Part III: Box 3, Caspar Weinberger Papers, LC.

118. David Walsh, *The Military Balance in the Cold War: U.S. Perceptions and Policy, 1976–1985* (New York, 2008), 126, 145–150.

119. NSDD-13, 10/19/1981, Federation of American Scientists, Intelligence Resources Program, National Security Decision Directives [hereafter NSDD], http://www.fas.org/irp/offdocs.nsdd/; George Wilson, "Preparing for Long Nuclear War Is Waste of Funds, Gen. Jones Says," *Washington Post*, 6/19/1982.

120. Seth Jones, *A Covert Action: Reagan, the CIA, and the Cold War Struggle in Poland* (New York, 2018), 70–71.

121. Reagan Address, 3/23/1983, APP.

122. NSC Meeting, 11/30/1983, Box 91303, NSC ESF, RRL.

123. Christopher Ford and David Rosenberg, "The Naval Intelligence Underpinnings of Reagan's Maritime Strategy," *Journal of Strategic Studies* 28, 2 (2005), 393–394; Barrass, "U.S. Competitive Strategy," 85; Thomas Mahnken, *Selective Disclosure: A Strategic Approach to Long-Term Competition* (Washington, DC, 2020).

124. NSC Meeting, 1/13/1983, Box 91306, NSC ESF, RRL; Austin Long and Brendan Green, "Stalking the Secure Second Strike: Intelligence, Counterforce, and Nuclear Strategy," *Journal of Strategic Studies* 38, 1 (2015), 38–73.

125. Reagan Remarks, 11/18/1981, APP.

126. Ustinov Statement, 10/20/1983, CWIHP; Dima Adamsky, "The 1983 Nuclear Crisis—Lessons for Deterrence Theory and Practice," *Journal of Strategic Studies* 36, 1 (2012), 4–41.

127. "Dinner with Andrei Grachev," 5/27/1990, Box 1, Don Oberdorfer Papers, SMML.

128. Leslie Gelb, "Foreign Affairs; Who Won the Cold War?" *New York Times*, 8/20/1992.

129. Shultz-Gromyko MemCon, 1/7/1985, Box 8, Jack Matlock Files, RRL.

130. Anatoly Chernyaev, *My Six Years with Gorbachev* (University Park, PA, 2000), 84.

131. Vojtech Mastny and Malcolm Byrne, eds., *A Cardboard Castle? An Inside History of the Warsaw Pact, 1955–1991* (Budapest, 2006), 466.

132. John Lewis Gaddis, *The Long Peace: Inquiries into the History of the Cold War* (New York, 1986).

133. Albert Wohlstetter, *The Delicate Balance of Terror* (Santa Monica, CA, 1958).

134. Robert Jervis, "Why Nuclear Superiority Doesn't Matter," *Political Science Quarterly* 94, 4 (1979–1980), 617–633.

Chapter Four. Contesting the Periphery

1. Odd Arne Westad, *The Global Cold War: Third-World Interventions and the Making of Our Times* (New York, 2005); Paul Chamberlain, *The Cold War's Killing Fields: Rethinking the Long Peace* (New York, 2018).

2. "Declaration of Independence of the Democratic Republic of Vietnam," 9/2/1945, at American Social History Project and Center for History and New Media, *History Matters: The U.S. Survey Course on the Web*, http://historymatters.gmu.edu/d/5139/.

3. Dinner Meeting, 1/5/1952, Box 15, CON, RG 59, NARA.

4. Walter Lippmann, *The Cold War: A Study in U.S. Foreign Policy* (New York, 1947), 21–23.

5. PPS-23, 2/24/1948, *FRUS 1948*, I, Part 2: 4.

6. Kennedy Address, 5/25/1961, APP.

7. Qiang Zhai, *China and the Vietnam Wars, 1950–1975* (Chapel Hill, NC, 2000).

8. Lloyd Gardner, *Pay Any Price: Lyndon Johnson and the Wars for Vietnam* (Chicago, 1995), 56.

9. Hal Brands, *Latin America's Cold War* (Cambridge, 2010), 23.

10. Peter Rodman, *More Precious Than Peace: Fighting and Winning the Cold War in the Third World* (New York, 1994), 73.

11. *Analysis of the Khrushchev Speech of January 6, 1961* (Washington, DC, 1961), 52–78.

12. Joseph Jones, *The Fifteen Weeks, February 21–June 5, 1947* (New York, 1964), 262–263.

13. *Reviews of the World Situation: 1949–1950, Hearings Held in Executive Session before the Committee on Foreign Relations, United States Senate* (Washington, DC, 1974), 87.

14. Inaugural Address, 1/20/1949, APP.

15. MemCon, 8/31/1959, Box 193, CON, RG 59, NARA; Matthew Connelly, *A Diplomatic Revolution: Algeria's Fight for Independence and the Origins of the Post–Cold War Era* (New York, 2002).

16. Dulles-Malik MemCon, 4/9/1955, Box 3, Secretary's and Undersecretary's Memorandums of Conversation, RG 59, NARA.

17. NSC Meeting, 6/28/1956, Box 8, NSC, DDEL.

18. Douglas Little, *American Orientalism: The United States and the Middle East since 1945* (Chapel Hill, NC, 2009), 179; Salim Yaqub, *Containing Arab Nationalism: The Eisenhower Doctrine and the Middle East* (Chapel Hill, NC, 2004).

19. MemCon, 7/1/1958, Box 151, CON, RG 59, NARA.

20. Nick Cullather, *The Hungry World: America's Cold War Battle against Poverty in Asia* (Cambridge, 2011).

21. NSC Meeting, 1/3/1957, Box 8, NSC Series, DDEL; Robert McMahon, *The Cold War on the Periphery: The United States, India, and Pakistan* (New York, 1996).

22. Fredrik Logevall, *Embers of War: The Fall of an Empire and the Making of America's Vietnam War* (New York, 2012), xiii.

23. Ogburn to Rusk, 8/18/1950, *FRUS 1950*, VI: 552.

24. George Herring, *America's Longest War: The United States and Vietnam, 1950–1975* (New York, 2014), 70.

25. NSC Meeting, 3/4/1953, *FRUS 1952–1954*, X: 312; Lindsey O'Rourke, *Covert Regime Change: America's Secret Cold War* (Ithaca, NY, 2018).

26. Richard Bissell Oral History, 11/9/1976, DDEL.

27. Cabinet Meeting, 11/6/1959, *FRUS 1958–1960*, X, Part 1: 137.

28. James Doolittle et al., "Report on the Covert Activities of the Central Intelligence Agency," September 1954, CIAFOIA.

29. Piero Gleijeses, *Conflicting Missions: Havana, Washington, and Africa, 1959–1976* (Chapel Hill, NC, 2003), 21.

30. NIE 1–61, 11/17/1961, *FRUS 1961–1963*, "Estimate of the World Situation," https://static.history.state.gov/frus/frus1961-63v07-09mSupp/pdf/d229.pdf; Michael Latham, *Modernization as Ideology: American Social Science and "Nation Building" in the Kennedy Era* (Chapel Hill, NC, 2000).

31. Inaugural Address, 1/20/1961, APP.

32. CIA, "Instability in Latin America," 5/20/1965, CIAFOIA.

33. Kennedy Address, 3/13/1962, APP.

34. Arthur Schlesinger Jr., *A Thousand Days: John F. Kennedy in the White House* (New York, 2002), 774.

35. Kennedy to McNamara, 10/4/1963, DDRS.

36. NIE 80/90-68, 3/28/1968, Box 8, NIE File, National Security File, Lyndon Baines Johnson Presidential Library [hereafter LBJL].

37. Summary Minutes, 11/29/1961, *FRUS 1961–1963*, XII: 35.

38. Goodwin to Kennedy, 9/10/1963, *FRUS 1961–1963*, XII: 63.

39. Kennedy Address, 11/18/1963, APP.

40. CIA, "Survey of Latin America," 4/1/1964, Box 1, Latin America, Country File, NSF, LBJL.

41. TelCon, 11/18/1964, PNO3, WH6411.23, LBJL; Stephen Rabe, *The Most Dangerous Area in the World: John F. Kennedy Confronts Communist Revolution in Latin America* (Chapel Hill, NC, 1999).

42. Hughes to Rusk, 10/23/1967, EBB 32, NSA.

43. Hughes to Rusk, 10/23/1967, EBB 32, NSA; David Schmitz, *Thank God They're on Our Side: The United States and Right-Wing Dictatorships, 1921–1965* (Chapel Hill, NC, 1999), 290.

44. Nixon Remarks, 10/31/1969, APP.

45. Fredrik Logevall, *Choosing War: The Lost Chance for Peace and the Escalation of the War in Vietnam* (Berkeley, 1999); Mark Atwood Lawrence, *The Vietnam War: A Concise International History* (New York, 2010); Lien-Hang T. Nguyen, *Hanoi's War: An International History of the War for Peace in Vietnam* (Chapel Hill, NC, 2012).

46. News Conference, 7/28/1965, APP.

47. TelCon, 5/27/1964, *FRUS 1964–1968*, XXVII: 52.

48. Johnson Address, 4/7/1965, APP.

49. Johnson Remarks, 8/12/1964, APP.

50. McGeorge Bundy, "A Policy of Sustained Reprisal," 2/7/1965, from *The Pentagon Papers*, Gravel edition, Volume 3, pp. 687–691, in Documents Relating to American Foreign Policy: Vietnam, Mount Holyoke College, https://www.mtholyoke.edu/acad/intrel/pentagon3/doc250.htm.

51. Mark Moyar, *Triumph Forsaken: The Vietnam War, 1954–1965* (New York, 2006).

52. Rostow to Kennedy, 5/10/1961, *FRUS 1961–1963*, I: 51.

53. Lawrence, *Vietnam War*, 91, 99, 103.

54. White House Meeting, 9/9/1964, *FRUS 1964–1968*, I: 343.

55. Lodge to Nixon, 2/12/1969, *FRUS 1969–1976*, VI: 20.

56. Laird to Nixon, 12/8/1971, in *Melvin Laird and the Foundation of the Post-Vietnam Military, 1969–1973*, Documentary Supplement, ed. Richard A. Hunt, Secretaries of Defense Historical Series, Volume VII, Office of the Secretary of Defense (Washington, DC, 2016), https://history.defense.gov/Portals/70/Documents/secretaryofdefense/Laird%20Document%20Supplement.pdf; Herring, *America's Longest War*, 185.

57. Robert McNamara with Brian VanDeMark, *In Retrospect: The Tragedy and Lessons of Vietnam* (New York, 1996), 378; Jeffrey Kimball, *Nixon's Vietnam War* (Lawrence, KS, 1998), 51.

58. Mansfield to Johnson, 7/27/1965, *FRUS 1964–1968*, III: 96.

59. Henry Kissinger, *White House Years* (Boston, 1979), 64.

60. Secretary's Staff Meeting, 1/7/1974, DNSA.

61. Hartsman to Kissinger, 4/1/1976, Box 19, HAK.

62. Odd Arne Westad, "Moscow and the Angolan Crisis, 1974–1976: A New Pattern of Intervention," *CWIHP Bulletin* 8–9 (1996/97): 21; Vladislav Zubok, "Soviet Foreign Policy from Détente to Gorbachev," *CH* III: 101.

63. Honecker-Castro Meeting, 4/3/1977, *CWIHP Bulletin* 8–9 (1996/97): 61.

64. Robert Gates, *From the Shadows* (New York, 2006), 65.

65. MemCon, 12/18/1975, Box 17, MemCons, NSAF, GFL.

66. Brzezinski to Carter, 1/3/1980, Box 17, Geographic File, ZBDM, JCL.

67. Nixon notes, 7/7/1968, Box 1, Nixon Papers, Hoover.

68. Editorial Note, *FRUS 1969–1976*, I: 29.

69. MemCon, 12/7/1971, EBB 71, NSA.

70. MemCon, 8/17/1974, Box 5, MemCons, NSAF, GFL.

71. Editorial Note, *FRUS 1969–1976*, XI: 256.

72. Jonathan Haslam, *The Nixon Administration and the Death of Allende's Chile: A Case of Assisted Suicide* (London, 2005).

73. Report to Congress, 2/18/1970, *FRUS 1969–1976*, I: 60.

74. MemCon, 10/13/1973, Box 2, *MemCons, NSA, GFL;* Craig Daigle, *The Limits of Détente: The United States, the Soviet Union, and the Arab-Israeli Conflict, 1969–1973* (New Haven, 2012).

75. Secretary's Staff Meeting, 10/1/1973, Box 1, Secretary's Staff Meetings, RG 59, NARA; Kissinger-Pinochet MemCon, 6/8/1976, DNSA.

76. Buenos Aires to State, 10/19/1976, Box 4, Patricia Derian Papers, Duke University; Jakarta to State, 12/6/1975, DNSA.

77. Barbara Keys, "Congress, Kissinger, and the Origins of Human Rights Diplomacy," *Diplomatic History* 34, 5 (2010), 823–851.

78. Lipshutz to Carter, 12/7/1977, Box 18, White House Counsel Files, JCL.

79. Address at Notre Dame, 5/22/1977, APP.

80. Address at Notre Dame, 5/22/1977, APP.

81. Samuel Huntington, *The Third Wave: Democratization in the Late Twentieth Century* (Norman, OK, 1993); Michael Morgan, "The Seventies and the Rebirth of Human Rights," in Niall Ferguson et al., eds., *The Shock of the Global: The 1970s in Perspective* (Cambridge, 2010), 237–250.

82. Brzezinski Remarks, 12/20/1978, Box 139, Hedrick Smith Papers, LC.

83. Draft of Carter Address, 3/15/1976, Box 17, 1976 Presidential Campaign Files, JCL.

84. Brown Remarks, 2/28/1978, Box 27, N-S Files, NSAF, JCL.

85. Anthony Lake, *Somoza Falling: A Case Study of Washington at Work* (Boston, 1989), esp. 273.

86. Kirkpatrick Remarks, 3/10/1981, Box 740, CFR Digital Sound Recordings, SMML.

87. National Foreign Assessment Center, "Impact of the U.S. Stand on Human Rights," 4/20/1977, NLC-28-0-3-2-5, JCL.

88. Pastor to Brzezinski, 1/18/1981, Box 34, SF, ZBDM, JCL; INR, "Current Reports," 9/26/1978, NLC-SAFE 17 B-13-72,12-8, JCL.

89. Mondale to Carter, 1/22/1979, DDRS.

90. Hartsman to Kissinger, 4/1/1976, Box 19, HAK.

91. Svetlana Savranskaya and David Welch, eds., *Global Competition and the Deterioration of U.S.-Soviet Relations, 1977–1980*, 59, Carter-Brezhnev Documents, Global Competition Collection, NSA.

92. National Intelligence Council, "The USSR and the Vulnerability of Empire," 11/27/1981, CREST.

93. INR, "Afghanistan: 18 Months of Occupation," August 1981, DNSA.

94. Brzezinski to Carter, 3/18/1980, Box 12, Geographic File, ZBDM, JCL.

95. NSC Meeting, 2/11/1981, Box 91282, NSC ESF, RRL.

96. NSC Meeting, 2/6/1981, Box 91282, NSC ESF, RRL.

97. "Reuters News Dispatch," 3/18/1981, Box 46, Richard Allen Papers, Hoover.

98. James Scott, *Deciding to Intervene: The Reagan Doctrine and American Foreign Policy* (Durham, NC, 1996), 40–81.

99. NSC Meeting, 11/10/1981, Box 91283, NSC ESF, RRL.

100. Herbert Meyer, "What Should We Do about the Russians?" 6/28/1984, CIAFOIA.

101. Draft Presidential Address, 9/24/1987, OA 18965, Robert Schmidt Files, RRL.

102. Christopher Dickey, "Haig's Emissary, in Guatemala, Discounts Charges of Rights Abuse," *Washington Post*, 5/14/1981.

103. Question-and-Answer Session, 12/4/1982, APP.

104. Kathryn Sikkink, *Mixed Signals: U.S. Human Rights Policy and Latin America* (Ithaca, NY, 2004), 150–159.

105. "Excerpts from State Department Memo on Human Rights," *New York Times*, 11/5/1981.

106. "Response to NSSD 11-82: U.S. Relations with the USSR," late 1982, NSC 00070, NSC Meetings, NSC ESF, RRL; Reagan Remarks, 10/8/1983, APP.

107. Radio Address, 3/24/1984, APP.

108. National Endowment for Democracy, Annual Report 1985, 5, DNSA; Tony Smith, *America's Mission: The United States and the Worldwide Struggle for Democracy* (Princeton, 2012), chapter 10.

109. Kirkpatrick Remarks, 3/21/1981, Box 45, Richard Allen Papers, Hoover.

110. William LeoGrande, *Our Own Backyard: The United States in Central America, 1977–1992* (Chapel Hill, NC, 1996), 582–583.

111. Remarks to Interim Committee, 4/9/1987, Box 153, James A. Baker Papers, SMML.

112. NSC Meeting, NSC 00142, 3/13/1987, RRL; Hal Brands, *Making the Unipolar Moment: U.S. Foreign Policy and the Rise of the Post-Cold War Order* (Ithaca, NY, 2016), 119–171.

113. Robert Pastorino, "Outline of Strategy for Peace and Democracy in Central America," undated, Box 92348, Pastorino Files, RRL.

114. Vojtech Mastny and Malcolm Byrne, eds., *A Cardboard Castle? An Inside History of the Warsaw Pact, 1955–1991* (Budapest, 2006), 467.

115. CIA, "The Costs of Soviet Involvement in Afghanistan," February 1987, DNSA.

116. NSC Meeting, 3/4/1953, *FRUS 1952–1954*, X: 312.

Chapter Five. Taking the Fight to the Enemy

1. George Kennan, "Meeting of Joint Orientation Conference," 11/8/1948, Box 299, GFKP.

2. "The World Position and Problems of the United States," 8/30/1949, Box 299, GFKP.
3. State of the Union, 2/2/1953, APP.
4. PPS Memo, 5/4/1948, *FRUS 1949–1950, Emergence of the Intelligence Establishment* [hereafter *EIE*]: 269.
5. George Kennan, "Measures Short of War (Diplomatic)," 9/16/1946, GFKP, SMML.
6. CIA, "Political Alignments and Major Psychological Warfare Vulnerabilities in the Event of War before July 1951," 5/9/1950, CIAFOIA.
7. Kohler to Acheson, 2/24/1949, *FRUS 1949*, V: 130.
8. Republican Platform, 7/7/1952, APP.
9. NSC-20/4, 11/23/1948, *FRUS 1948*, I, Part 2: 60.
10. NSC-68, "United States Objectives and Programs for National Security," 4/12/1950, PSF, HSTL.
11. Giles Harlow and George Maerz, eds., *Measures Short of War: The George F. Kennan Lectures at the National War College, 1946–47* (Washington, DC, 1991), 37; PPS-38, 8/18/1948, Box 54, Policy Planning Staff Records, NARA.
12. Office of the Secretary of Defense, Historical Office, "Almost Successful Recipe: The United States and East European Unrest Prior to the 1956 Hungarian Revolution," February 2012, EBB 581, NSA.
13. CIA, "Observations on the Unrest in All Satellite Countries," 6/14/1949, CIAFOIA.
14. NSC-58/2, 12/8/1949, *FRUS 1949*, V: 17.
15. John Lewis Gaddis, *Strategies of Containment: A Critical Appraisal of American National Security Policy during the Cold War* (New York, 2005), 44.
16. News Conference, 4/23/1948, APP.
17. PPS-35, 6/30/1948, *FRUS 1948*, IV: 702; H. W. Brands, *The Specter of Neutralism: The United States and the Emergence of the Third World, 1947–1960* (New York, 1989); Census Bureau, *Statistical Abstract, 1954*, 900.
18. Alan Dobson, *U.S. Economic Statecraft for Survival, 1933–1991: Of Sanctions, Embargoes, and Economic Warfare* (New York, 2002), 83–108.
19. Conclusions of London Conference, 10/24–26/1949, *FRUS 1949*, V: 13.
20. Wisner to Deputy Director of Central Intelligence, 11/22/1950, CWIHP.
21. Cord Meyer, *Facing Reality: From World Federalism to the CIA* (New York, 1980), 114; Arch Puddington, *Broadcasting Freedom: The Cold War Triumph of Radio Free Europe and Radio Liberty* (Lexington, KY, 2000), 20–88, esp. 34.
22. Lay to Hillenkoetter, 6/7/1948, *FRUS 1945–1950, EIE*: 285. OPC was originally labeled "Office of Special Projects."
23. David Rudgers, "The Origins of Covert Action," *Journal of Contemporary History* 35, 2 (2000), 257.
24. NSC-68.
25. Office of the Secretary of Defense, "Almost Successful Recipe."
26. Dobson, *U.S. Economic Statecraft*, 108.

27. Stephen Dorril, *MI6: Inside the Covert World of Her Majesty's Secret Intelligence Service* (New York, 2000), 489; Peter Grose, *Operation Rollback: America's Secret War behind the Iron Curtain* (New York, 2001), 188.

28. "Role of Psychological Strategy Board under 4/4/51 Presidential Directive," 9/28/1951, CIAFOIA.

29. Beatrice Heuser, "Covert Action within British and American Concepts of Containment," in Richard Aldrich, ed., *British Intelligence, Strategy and the Cold War, 1945–51* (New York, 1992).

30. Office of the Secretary of Defense, "Almost Successful Recipe," 17.

31. Norman Naimark, "The Sovietization of Eastern Europe, 1944–1953," *CH* I: 189.

32. George Kennan, "GFK Notes for Secy. Marshall," 7/21/1947, Box 33, Policy Planning Staff Records, NARA.

33. CIA, ORE-44-49, 6/20/1949, CIAFOIA.

34. On that consideration, see William Stueck, *The Korean War: An International History* (Princeton, 1995), 5, 147, 196.

35. Wilbur Schramm, "An Estimate of the Effectiveness of Radio Liberation," 9/1/1955, CWIHP; Report by Committee on International Information Activities, 6/30/1953, *FRUS 1952–1954*, II, Part 2: 370.

36. Vojtech Mastny, *The Cold War and Soviet Insecurity: The Stalin Years* (New York, 1996), 118; Meyer, *Facing Reality*, 120.

37. Conclusions of London Conference; State Report to NSC, undated, in *FRUS 1950*, IV: 140; Report by Committee on International Information Activities, 6/30/1953, *FRUS 1952–1954*, II, Part 2: 370.

38. Mastny, *Cold War*, 80–84, 121.

39. Gregory Mitrovich, *Undermining the Kremlin: America's Strategy to Subvert the Soviet Bloc, 1947–1956* (Ithaca, NY, 2000), 109, 127.

40. Republican Platform; John Foster Dulles, "A Positive Foreign Policy," 5/15/1952, Box 63, John Foster Dulles Papers, SMML.

41. Cutler to Dulles, 9/3/1953, *FRUS 1952–1954*, II, Part 1: 87.

42. MemCon, 12/21/1954, *FRUS 1952–1954*, II, Part 1: 143.

43. Psychological Strategy Board, "Interim U.S. Psychological Strategy Plan for Exploitation of Unrest in Satellite Europe," 6/29/1953, CIAFOIA.

44. NSC Meeting, 6/18/1953, CWIHP.

45. Office of the Secretary of Defense, "Almost Successful Recipe," 31–36.

46. NSC 162/2, 10/30/1953, *FRUS 1952–1954*, II, Part 1: 101.

47. Draft from Wisner to Dulles, 1/8/1954, *FRUS 1950–1955, The Intelligence Community*: 167.

48. MemCon, 5/17/1956, *FRUS 1955–1957*, XXV: 58; Puddington, *Broadcasting Freedom*, 92.

49. MemCon, 7/5/1955, *FRUS 1955–1957*, V: 148.

50. Hagerty Diary, 3/4/1955, *FRUS 1955–1957*, XXV: 8.

51. Dulles-Yey MemCon, 2/10/1955, Box 3, Lot 64D199, RG 59, NARA.

52. "Phone Calls, 11/9/56," Box 19, DDE Diary Series, DDEL.

53. "Stenographic Notes of Conversation," 7/21/1956, CIAFOIA.
54. NSC Meeting, 6/18/1953, CWIHP.
55. NSC-5608/1, 7/18/1956, EBB 76, NSA.
56. State Department Public Services Division, *Highlights of Foreign Policy Developments—1956*, March 1957, 2, CIAFOIA.
57. Charles Gati, *Failed Illusions: Moscow, Washington, Budapest, and the 1956 Hungarian Revolt* (Stanford, 2006), 163.
58. MemCon, 10/26/1956, *FRUS 1955–1957*, XXV: 116.
59. NSC Meeting, 11/8/1956, *FRUS 1955–1957*, XXV: 175.
60. "Policy Review of Voice for Free Hungary Programming, October 23–November 23, 1956," 12/5/1956, EBB 76, NSA; NSC Meeting, 7/12/1956, CWIHP.
61. Fritz Hier, "A Hungarian Diary," 1956, CWIHP.
62. *Reviews of the World Situation: 1949–1950*, Hearings Held in Executive Session before the Committee on Foreign Relations, United States Senate (Washington, DC, 1974), 273.
63. Chen Jian, "The Myth of America's 'Lost Chance' in China: A Chinese Perspective in Light of New Evidence," *Diplomatic History* 21, 1 (1997), 77–86; Warren Cohen, *America's Response to China: A History of Sino-American Relations* (New York, 2000), 164–169.
64. U.S. Minutes, 12/7/1953, *FRUS 1952–1954*, V, Part 2: 353.
65. Editorial Note, *FRUS 1955–1957*, II: 77.
66. NSC Meeting, 8/18/1954, *FRUS 1952–1954*, XIV, Part I: 256.
67. John Lewis Gaddis, *The Long Peace: Inquiries into the History of the Cold War* (New York, 1986), 187.
68. U.S. Minutes, 12/7/1953, *FRUS 1952–1954*, V, Part 2: 353.
69. Lorenz Luthi, *The Sino-Soviet Split: Cold War in the Communist World* (Princeton, 2008), 99–113; Sulmaan Khan, *Haunted by Chaos: China's Grand Strategy from Mao Zedong to Xi Jinping* (Cambridge, 2018), 88–90.
70. NSC 166/1, 11/6/1953, *FRUS 1952–1954*, XIV, Part 1: 149.
71. Editorial Note, *FRUS 1961–1963*, XXII: 162.
72. MemCon, 5/22/1974, Box 4, MemCons, NSAF, GFL.
73. Report by Chinese Marshals, 9/17/1969, CWIHP.
74. Davidov-Stearman MemCon, 8/18/1969, DNSA.
75. Henry Kissinger, *White House Years* (Boston, 1979), 184–191.
76. MemCon, 12/20/1971, Box 1025, Presidential-HAK MemCons, Richard Nixon Presidential Library.
77. Kissinger, *White House Years*, 190–191, 698–703.
78. Nixon-Kissinger TelCon, 4/14/1971, DNSA.
79. Nixon-Zhou MemCon, 2/23/1972, DNSA; Gary Bass, *The Blood Telegram: Nixon, Kissinger, and a Forgotten Genocide* (New York, 2014).
80. Kissinger to Nixon, 2/5/1972, EBB 70, NSA.
81. Kissinger-Pompidou MemCon, 5/18/1973, DNSA.
82. Henry Kissinger, *Years of Renewal* (New York, 1999), 138.

83. Evelyn Goh, "Nixon, Kissinger, and the 'Soviet Card' in the U.S. Opening to China, 1971–1974," *Diplomatic History* 29, 3 (2005), 489.
84. MemCon, 8/3/1973, *FRUS 1969–1976*, XXXVIII, Part 1: 15.
85. Dobrynin to Foreign Ministry, 3/8/1972, *FRUS, Soviet-American Relations: The Détente Years*, Document 267.
86. Odd Arne Westad, "The Great Transformation: China in the Long 1970s," in Niall Ferguson et al., eds., *The Shock of the Global: The 1970s in Perspective* (Cambridge, 2010), 77.
87. Reagan Remarks, 5/31/1988, APP; Chris Miller, *The Struggle to Save the Soviet Economy: Mikhail Gorbachev and the Collapse of the USSR* (Chapel Hill, NC, 2016).
88. Jeffery Engel, "Of Fat and Thin Communists," *Diplomatic History* 29, 3 (2005), 466–467.
89. Julia von Dannenberg, *The Foundations of Ostpolitik: The Making of the Moscow Treaty between West Germany and the USSR* (New York, 2008).
90. State to European Posts, 2/1/1976, Box 3, Presidential Name File, NSAF, GFL; Douglas Selvage, "Transforming the Soviet Sphere of Influence? U.S.-Soviet Détente and Eastern Europe, 1969–1976," *Diplomatic History* 33, 4 (2009), 671–687.
91. Kissinger-Zhou MemCon, 6/21/1972, DNSA.
92. Henry Kissinger, *Years of Upheaval* (Boston, 1982), 243.
93. Jussi Hanhimaki, "Détente in Europe, 1962–1975," *CH* II: 215.
94. Michael Jensen, "Soviet Grain Deal Is Called a Coup," *New York Times*, 9/29/1972.
95. TelCon, 1/15/1975, DNSA.
96. Cabinet Meeting, 10/18/1973, *FRUS 1969–1976*, XXXVIII: 20.
97. Kissinger-Shultz MemCon, 3/29/1973, Box 24, HAK Records, RG 59, NARA.
98. Barbara Keys, *Reclaiming American Virtue: The Human Rights Revolution of the 1970s* (Cambridge, 2013), 121–122.
99. Cheney to Rumsfeld, 7/8/1975, Rumsfeld Papers, http://papers.rumsfeld.com/.
100. Michael Morgan, *The Final Act: The Helsinki Accords and the Transformation of the Cold War* (Princeton, 2018), 67.
101. Kissinger-Kraft TelCon, 8/5/1975, DSNA.
102. Kissinger, *Years of Renewal*, 643.
103. Kissinger-Kraft TelCon.
104. Stephen Kotkin, "The Kiss of Debt: The East Bloc Goes Borrowing," in Ferguson et al., *Shock of the Global*, 80–84.
105. CIA, "The Next Two Years: Brezhnev, or a Succession?" September 1977, NLC-6-79-1-23-3, JCL.
106. Chernyaev Diary, 5/1/1972 and 4/3/1972, EBB 379, NSA.
107. Kotkin, "Kiss of Debt," 86–89.
108. Andropov Memo, 1/5/1977, EBB 387, NSA.

109. CIA, "Dissident Activity in East Europe: An Overview," March 1977, EBB 391, NSA; Sarah Snyder, *Human Rights Activism and the End of the Cold War* (New York, 2011).

110. Vladislav Zubok, "The Soviet Union and Détente of the 1970s," *Cold War History* 8, 4 (2008), 438–442.

111. Chernyaev Diary, 10/26/1974, EBB 471, NSA.

112. Matthew Ouimet, *The Rise and Fall of the Brezhnev Doctrine in Soviet Foreign Policy* (Chapel Hill, NC, 2003), 234–235.

113. Henze to Brzezinski, 4/17/1980, EBB 391, NSA; Robert Gates, *From the Shadows* (New York, 2006), 94–95, 117.

114. MemCon, 9/23/1977, Box 35, SF, ZBDM, JCL.

115. INR, "Soviet-U.S. Relations: A Six-Month Perspective," 8/15/1977, DNSA.

116. Kiron Skinner, Annelise Anderson, and Martin Anderson, eds., *Reagan, in His Own Hand: The Writings of Ronald Reagan That Reveal His Revolutionary Vision for America* (New York, 2001), 42.

117. Ronald Reagan, "Communism, the Disease: Viewpoint with Ronald Reagan," 1975, Box 1, Ronald Reagan Radio Commentary, Hoover.

118. Skinner et al., *Reagan, in His Own Hand*, 150.

119. Richard Pipes, "A Reagan Soviet Policy," October 1981, Box 3, Richard Pipes File, RRL.

120. News Conference, 6/16/1981, APP.

121. Reagan to Brezhnev, 4/3/1981, Box 38, Head of State File, NSC ESF, RRL.

122. Benjamin Fischer, "Solidarity, the CIA, and Western Technology," *International Journal of Intelligence and Counterintelligence* 25, 3 (2012), 427–469; Reagan, *American Life*, 304.

123. NSC Meeting, 5/24/1982, Box 91284, NSC ESF, RRL; State to Bonn, Paris, and London, 1/2/1982, DDRS.

124. Gregory Domber, *Empowering Revolution: America, Poland, and the End of the Cold War* (Chapel Hill, NC, 2014), chapters 1–2.

125. "TV Interview for BBC," 9/1/1982, Margaret Thatcher Foundation: Archive, https://www.margaretthatcher.org/archive.

126. NSC Meeting, 11/9/1982, Box 91284, NSC ESF, RRL.

127. National Intelligence Council, "The Soviet Bloc Financial Problem as a Source of Western Influence," April 1982, DNSA; Peter Schweizer, *Victory: The Reagan Administration's Secret Strategy That Hastened the Collapse of the Soviet Union* (New York, 1994), esp. 72–74.

128. Reagan Remarks, 3/8/1983; Reagan Address at Notre Dame, 5/17/1981, APP.

129. "East-West Policy Study," in Paul Wolfowitz et al. to Haig, 6/4/1981, *FRUS 1981–1988*, III: 62.

130. Kimmitt to Hill and others, 12/12/1983, Remote Archives Capture [hereafter RAC] Box 7, Raymond Walter Files, RRL; General Accounting Office,

U.S. Information Agency: Options for Addressing Possible Budget Reductions (Washington, DC, 1996), 18–19.

131. Puddington, *Broadcasting Freedom*, 253–286.

132. NSDD-54, 9/2/1982, Box 1, NSDD File, RRL; NSDD-75, 1/17/1983, Box 91287, NSC ESF, RRL.

133. "Response to NSSD 11-82: U.S. Relations with the USSR," undated, NSC 00070, Meeting Files, NSC ESF, RRL.

134. Fischer, "Solidarity," 429; Domber, *Empowering Revolution*, 111; Arch Puddington, "The Summer of Solidarity," *Weekly Standard*, 8/8/2005.

135. CIA, "Conference on Security and Cooperation in Europe: The Madrid Meeting Resumes," November 1982, CREST.

136. John Arquilla, *The Reagan Imprint: Ideas in American Foreign Policy from the Collapse of Communism to the War on Terror* (Chicago, 2006), 150.

137. Politburo Meeting, 6/4/1981, CWIHP.

138. Schweizer, *Victory*, 265; Domber, *Empowering Revolution*, 42–43; Warren E. Norquist, "How the United States Used Competition to Win the Cold War," 2001, http://www.angelfire.com/geek/mafstuff/temp.html.

139. Vojtech Mastny and Malcolm Byrne, eds., *A Cardboard Castle? An Inside History of the Warsaw Pact, 1955–1991* (Budapest, 2006), 472–473.

140. CIA, "Domestic Costs to the Soviet Regime of Involvement in Afghanistan," 10/25/1984, Box 34, Country File, NSC ESF, RRL.

141. Odom to Army Secretary, 5/11/1984, Box 14, Odom Papers, LC.

142. NIE 11-18-85, November 1985, CIAFOIA.

143. MemCon, 10/11/1983, Box 2, Jack Matlock Papers, RRL.

144. *The Kennan Diaries*, ed. Frank Costigliola (New York, 2014), xxix.

145. Kissinger-Kennan TelCon, 9/13/1973, DNSA.

146. Dulles-Yey MemCon.

Chapter Six. Setting Limits

1. Fredrik Logevall, "A Critique of Containment," *Diplomatic History* 28, 4 (2004), 473–499.

2. John Lewis Gaddis, *The Long Peace: Inquiries into the History of the Cold War* (New York, 1986).

3. Meeting of Principals, 3/2/1961, *FRUS 1961–1963*, VII, Microfiche Supplement, https://history.state.gov/historicaldocuments/frus1961-63v07-09mSupp/d4.

4. John Foster Dulles, "Developing NATO in Peace," *DOSB*, 4/30/1956, 708.

5. "X" (George F. Kennan), "The Sources of Soviet Conduct," *Foreign Affairs* 25, 4 (1947), 573.

6. News Conference, 1/29/1981, APP.

7. Kennan to Lippmann (unsent), 4/6/1948, Box 299, GFKP.

8. State Department Memo, 1/5/1951, *FRUS 1951*, III, Part 1: 214.

9. Walter Lippmann, *The Cold War: A Study in U.S. Foreign Policy* (New York, 1947); George Kennan, *Memoirs, 1925–1950* (Boston, 1967), 303.

10. Larry Bland, Mark Stoler, Sharon Ritenour Stevens, and Daniel Holt, eds., *The Papers of George Catlett Marshall*, vol. 6 (Baltimore, 2013), 103.

11. Kennan to Marshall and Lovett, 8/12/1948, *FRUS 1948*, II: 719.

12. Meeting Notes, 11/3/1949, *FRUS 1949*, I: 212.

13. Report by NSC Special Committee, 1/31/1950, *FRUS 1950*, I: 162.

14. NSC-68, "United States Objectives and Programs for National Security," 4/12/1950, PSF, HSTL.

15. Dean Acheson, "Soviet Reaction to Free World's Growing Strength," *DOSB*, 10/20/1952, 597.

16. Henry Kissinger, *Diplomacy* (New York, 1994), 462–468.

17. William Stueck, *The Korean War: An International History* (Princeton, 1995), esp. 205–206.

18. Charles Bohlen, "Soviet Policy," 3/13/1951, Box 6, Charles Bohlen Records, NARA.

19. John Lewis Gaddis, *George F. Kennan: An American Life* (New York, 2011), 313–314.

20. Andrei Sakharov, *Memoirs* (New York, 1992), 99.

21. Vojtech Mastny, *The Cold War and Soviet Insecurity: The Stalin Years* (New York, 1996), chapters 7–10.

22. Jessup to Matthews, 1/16/1951, *FRUS 1951*, IV, Part 2: 295.

23. Churchill to Eisenhower, 3/11/1953, *FRUS 1952–1954*, VIII: 564.

24. MemCon, 12/4/1953, Box 28, CON, RG 59, NARA.

25. NSC Meeting, 8/5/1955, Box 7, NSC Series, DDEL.

26. Eisenhower Address, 4/16/1953, APP.

27. Eisenhower to Churchill, 3/11/1953, *FRUS 1952–1954*, VIII: 565.

28. NSC Meeting, 3/31/1953, *FRUS 1952–1954*, II: 53.

29. MemCon, 12/4/1953, Box 28, CON, RG 59, NARA.

30. NSC-162, 9/30/1953, *FRUS 1952–1954*, II: 93.

31. Eisenhower Address, 4/16/1953, APP.

32. Eisenhower Address, 12/8/1953, APP.

33. Radio and Television Report, 5/25/1960, APP; Robert Divine, *Blowing on the Wind: The Nuclear Test Ban Debate, 1954–1960* (New York, 1978).

34. Ira Chernus, *Eisenhower's Atoms for Peace* (College Station, TX, 2002), 80.

35. Radio and Television Report, 5/25/1960, APP.

36. Benjamin Greene, *Eisenhower, Science Advice, and the Nuclear Test-Ban Debate, 1945–1963* (Stanford, 2007).

37. MemCon, 4/7/1953, Box 1, Box 22, CON, RG 59, NARA.

38. MemCon, 8/29/1955, Box 3, Lot 64D199, Secretary's and Undersecretary's Memorandums of Conversation, RG 59, NARA.

39. Eisenhower Address, 4/16/1953, APP; MemCon, 6/15/1959, DNSA.

40. NSC Meeting, 6/30/1955, *FRUS 1955–1957*, XX: 45.

41. MemCon, 3/6/1959, DNSA.

42. *Executive Sessions of the Senate Foreign Relations Committee (Historical Series)*, Volume III: Eighty-Fourth Congress, Second Session, 1956 (Washington, DC, 1978), 125.

43. Vladislav Zubok, *A Failed Empire: The Soviet Union in the Cold War from Stalin to Gorbachev* (Chapel Hill, NC, 2009), 105–106; Hope Harrison, *Driving the Soviets Up the Wall: Soviet–East German Relations, 1953–1961* (Princeton, 2003), 27–28, 47.

44. *Executive Sessions of the Senate Foreign Relations Committee (Historical Series)*, Volume XI: Eighty-Sixth Congress, First Session, 1959 (Washington, DC, 1982), 337.

45. Jonathan Haslam, *Russia's Cold War: From the October Revolution to the Fall of the Wall* (New Haven, 2011), 157.

46. News Conference, 1/30/1957, APP.

47. Zubok, *Failed Empire*, 107–109; William Taubman, *Khrushchev: The Man and His Era* (New York, 2003), 351–352.

48. "Basic National Security Policy: Short Version," 8/2/1962, National Security File, John F. Kennedy Presidential Library.

49. Taubman, *Khrushchev*, 500.

50. MemCon, 6/4/1961, *FRUS 1961–1963*, XIV: 32.

51. Kennedy to Khrushchev, 12/28/1962, *FRUS 1961–1963*, VI: 87.

52. Anatoly Dobrynin, *In Confidence: Moscow's Ambassador to America's Six Cold War Presidents* (New York, 1995), 96.

53. TelCon, 6/15/1957, Box 6, White House Memoranda Series, John Foster Dulles Papers, DDEL.

54. T. C. Schelling, *The Reciprocal Fear of Surprise Attack* (Santa Monica, CA, 1958).

55. Richard Helms, "Strategic Arms Limitation and Intelligence," 10/13/1971, Federal Depository Library Program Electronic Collection Archive, https://permanent.access.gpo.gov/gpo15410/helms/pdf/salt_intel.pdf.

56. Gaddis, *Long Peace*, 195–214.

57. Erez Manela, "A Pox on Your Narrative: Writing Disease Control into Cold War History," *Diplomatic History* 34, 2 (2010), 299–323.

58. News Conference, 3/21/1963, APP.

59. MemCon, 11/30/1962, *FRUS 1961–1963*, VII, https://static.history.state.gov/frus/frus1961-63v07-09mSupp/pdf/d154.pdf.

60. Hal Brands, "Non-Proliferation and the Dynamics of the Middle Cold War," *Cold War History* 7, 3 (2007), 406.

61. Milton Leitenberg and Raymond Zilinskas, *The Soviet Biological Weapons Program: A History* (Cambridge, 2012).

62. Rostow to Johnson, 3/6/1967, *FRUS 1964–1968*, XIII: 239; Tokyo to State, 3/1/1967, *FRUS 1964–1968*, XXIX: 84.

63. Raymond Garthoff, *Détente and Confrontation: American-Soviet Relations from Nixon to Reagan* (Washington, DC, 1994); Jeremi Suri, *Power and Protest: Global Revolution and the Rise of Détente* (Cambridge, 2003).

64. MemCon, 3/29/1974, Box 7, HAK Records.

65. Background Briefing, 8/14/1970, *FRUS 1969–1976*, I: 69.
66. Report to Congress, 2/9/1972, APP.
67. "The Permanent Challenge of Peace: U.S. Policy toward the Soviet Union," *DOSB*, 2/23/1976, 204.
68. Henry Kissinger, *White House Years* (Boston, 1979), 128.
69. Nixon to Rogers, 2/4/1969, *FRUS 1969–1976*, XII: 10.
70. Nixon Address, 3/29/1973, *FRUS 1969–1976*, XXXVIII, Part 1: 6; Robert Litwak, *Détente and the Nixon Doctrine: American Foreign Policy and the Pursuit of Stability, 1969–1976* (New York, 1986), 101–102.
71. Text of Nixon-Brezhnev Declaration, *New York Times*, 5/30/1972.
72. Report to Congress, 5/3/1973, APP.
73. MemCon, 2/25/1976, Box 18, MemCons, NSAF, GFL.
74. MemCon, 11/24/1974, Box 1, Kissinger Reports on USSR, China, Middle East, GFL.
75. Odd Arne Westad, *The Cold War: A World History* (New York, 2017), 206.
76. Carter-Brezhnev MemCon, 6/17/1979, Box 37, SF, ZBDM, JCL.
77. Kissinger Address, 10/8/1973, *FRUS 1969–1976*, XXXVIII, Part 1: 19.
78. Extracts from Brezhnev Speech, 2/24/1976, Box 51, James Schlesinger Papers, LC.
79. Carter-Brezhnev MemCon, 6/17/1979.
80. Steven Rearden, *Council of War: A History of the Joint Chiefs of Staff* (Washington, DC, 2012), 385.
81. Kissinger to Ford, undated, *FRUS 1969–1976*, XVI: 36.
82. Kissinger-Ford MemCon, 9/27/1975, Box 15, MemCons, NSAF, GFL.
83. Kissinger News Conference, *DOSB*, 2/2/1976, 125.
84. Donovan to Carter, 4/12/1980, Box 22, Plains File, SF, JCL.
85. Aleksandr' Savel'yev and Nikolay Detinov, *The Big Five: Arms Control Decision-Making in the Soviet Union* (Westport, CT, 1995), 99–106.
86. Thornton to Lord, 11/19/1975, *FRUS 1969–1976*, XVI: 218.
87. MemCon, 3/29/1977, *FRUS 1977–1980*, XXVI: 267.
88. Dobrynin to Gromyko, 7/11/1978, CWIHP.
89. Garthoff, *Détente and Confrontation*, 46.
90. NIE 11-4-78, May 1978, Carter-Brezhnev Project, NSA.
91. MemCon, 3/20/1973, *FRUS 1969–1976*, XXXV: 13; Kissinger to Nixon, undated (1972) EBB 60, NSA.
92. Thornton to Lord, 11/19/1975, *FRUS 1969–1976*, XVI: 218.
93. MemCon, 3/11/1974, *FRUS 1969–1976*, XXXVIII, Part 1: 29.
94. Julian Zelizer, *Arsenal of Democracy: The Politics of National Security—From World War II to the War on Terrorism* (New York, 2012), 249.
95. Olav Njolstad, "Key of Keys? SALT II and the Breakdown of Détente," in Odd Arne Westad, ed., *The Fall of Détente: Soviet-American Relations during the Carter Years* (Oslo, 1997), 50.
96. Robert Jervis, "Was the Cold War a Security Dilemma?" *Journal of Cold War Studies* 3, 1 (2001), 36–60.

Chapter Seven. Knowing the Enemy

1. Report by Task Force on Intelligence Activities, May 1955, *FRUS 1950–1955, The Intelligence Community*: 220.
2. Stephen Kinzer, *The Brothers: John Foster Dulles, Allen Dulles, and Their Secret World War* (New York, 2013), 21.
3. Report on CIA Covert Activities, September 1954, CIAFOIA.
4. "Moynihan Bill Would Abolish CIA, Shift Functions to State," *Washington Post*, 1/23/1991.
5. Richard Pipes, *Vixi: Memoirs of a Non-Belonger* (New Haven, 2003), 233.
6. Souers Memo, 4/29/1946, *FRUS 1945–1950, EIE*: 148.
7. Hillenkoetter to Truman, 7/6/1948, Box 19, William Leahy Papers, RG 218, NARA; Gregg Herken, *The Winning Weapon: The Atomic Bomb in the Cold War, 1945–1950* (Princeton, 2014).
8. Kennan to State, 2/2/1945, *FRUS 1945*, V: 617.
9. James Bamford, *Body of Secrets: Anatomy of the Ultra-Secret National Security Agency* (New York, 2007), 11–24.
10. Tim Weiner, *Legacy of Ashes: The History of the CIA* (New York, 2007), 9.
11. Richard Immerman, *The Hidden Hand: A Brief History of the CIA* (New York, 2014), 35–38.
12. Montague to Babbit, 11/12/1947, *FRUS 1945–1950, EIE*: 329.
13. Report on CIA Covert Activities.
14. "The Central Intelligence Agency and National Organization for Intelligence," Memorandum for the National Security Council, January 1949, Federal Depository Library Program Electronic Collection Archive, https://permanent.access.gpo.gov/gpo15410/helms/pdf/dulles_correa.pdf.
15. Willard Matthias, *America's Strategic Blunders: Intelligence Analysis and National Security Policy, 1936–1991* (University Park, PA, 2001), 46.
16. ORE 3-49, 2/28/1949, CIAFOIA; PPS-13, 11/6/1947, *FRUS 1947*, I: 393.
17. Sherman Kent, *Strategic Intelligence for American World Policy* (Princeton, 2015), 3.
18. "X" (George F. Kennan), "The Sources of Soviet Conduct," *Foreign Affairs* 25, 4 (1947), 570.
19. Lecture by Kennan and Llewellyn Thompson, 9/17/1946, Box 298, GFKP.
20. PPS-38, 8/18/1948, Box 54, Policy Planning Staff Records, NARA.
21. ORE 22-48, 4/2/1948, CIAFOIA.
22. Matthew Connelly et al., " 'General, I Have Fought Just as Many Nuclear Wars as You Have': Forecasts, Future Scenarios, and the Politics of Armageddon," *American Historical Review* 117, 5 (2012), 1439–1440.
23. Memo for Record, 6/19/1947, *FRUS 1945–1950, EIE*: 218.
24. Memo for File, 7/17/1946, *FRUS 1945–1950, EIE*: 197.
25. Amy Zegart, *Flawed by Design: The Evolution of the CIA, JCS, and NCS* (Stanford, 1999), 190.

26. Milo Jones and Philippe Silberzahn, *Constructing Cassandra: Reframing Intelligence Failure at the CIA, 1947–2001* (Stanford, 2013), 38.

27. Brent Durbin, *The CIA and the Politics of U.S. Intelligence Reform* (New York, 2017), 106; Rhodri Jeffreys-Jones, "The Rise and Fall of the CIA," in Loch Johnson, ed., *The Oxford Handbook of National Security Intelligence* (New York, 2010), 126.

28. Kissinger and Shultz to Nixon, in Haig to Kissinger, 3/27/1971, *FRUS 1969–1976*, II: 229.

29. Richard Aldrich, *The Hidden Hand: Britain, America, and Cold War Secret Intelligence* (London, 2001); Matthew Aid, "The National Security Agency and the Cold War," in Matthew Aid and Cees Wiebes, eds., *Secrets of Signals Intelligence during the Cold War and Beyond* (London, 2001), 36.

30. Michael Petersen, *Legacy of Ashes, Trial by Fire: The Origins of the Defense Intelligence Agency and the Cuban Missile Crisis Crucible* (Washington, DC, 2011), 3.

31. MemCon, 10/19/1954, *FRUS 1950–1955, The Intelligence Community:* 193.

32. Sherman Kent, *Sherman Kent and the Board of National Estimates—Collected Essays* (Washington, DC, 1994), xv.

33. Jack Anderson, "Foreign Outlook: Intelligence Failures," July 1986, CIA-FOIA.

34. Richard Helms, "Strategic Arms Limitation and Intelligence," 10/13/1971, Federal Depository Library Program Electronic Collection Archive, https://permanent.access.gpo.gov/gpo15410/helms/pdf/salt_intel.pdf.

35. Seth Jones, *A Covert Action: Reagan, the CIA, and the Cold War Struggle in Poland* (New York, 2018), 70–71.

36. Jeffrey Richelson, "The Calculus of Intelligence Cooperation," *International Journal of Intelligence and Counterintelligence* 4, 3 (1990), 311; Christopher Andrew, "Intelligence in the Cold War," *CH* II: 418.

37. Kent, *Sherman Kent.*

38. Meeting Minutes, 11/14/1945, *FRUS 1945–1950, EIE:* 45.

39. Marshall to Haig, 9/6/1972, *FRUS 1969–1976*, II: 282.

40. Richard Helms, *A Look over My Shoulder: A Life in the Central Intelligence Agency* (New York, 2004), 386–392.

41. A. J. Langguth, "Abolish the CIA!" *Newsweek*, 4/7/1975, 11.

42. Colby Remarks, 6/18/1975, *FRUS 1969–1976*, XXXVIII, Part 2: 43.

43. Michael Gallagher, "Intelligence and National Security Strategy: Reexamining Project Solarium," *Intelligence and National Security* 30, 4 (2015), 471.

44. Schlesinger Remarks, March 2001, in CIA, Center for the Study of Intelligence, *Watching the Bear: Essays on CIA's Analysis of the Soviet Union* (Langley, VA, 2004), 255.

45. John Lewis Gaddis, "Intelligence, Espionage, and Cold War Origins," *Diplomatic History* 13, 2 (1989), 199; Eduard Mark, "The War Scare of 1946 and Its Consequences," *Diplomatic History* 21, 3 (Summer 1997), 383–415.

46. Aid, "National Security Agency," 36–46; Bamford, *Body of Secrets*, 32–36.

47. CIA, "Post-Mortem of NIE 11-6-54, 'Soviet Capabilities and Probable Programs in Guided Missiles,' " 10/4/1954, CIAFOIA; Donald Steury, ed., *Intentions and Capabilities: Estimates on Soviet Strategic Forces, 1950–1983*, Center for the Study of Intelligence, 1983, esp. 5–7.
48. NIE 11-8-59, 2/9/1960, CIAFOIA; Robert Divine, *The Sputnik Challenge: Eisenhower's Response to the Soviet Satellite* (New York, 1993), 33.
49. Stewart Alsop, "How Can We Catch Up?" *Saturday Evening Post*, 12/14/1957, 27.
50. Dulles Memo, 11/24/1954, *FRUS 1950–1955, The Intelligence Community*: 198.
51. Lawrence Freedman, *U.S. Intelligence and the Soviet Strategic Threat* (Princeton, 1977), passim; Leonard Parkinson and Logan Potter, "Closing the Missile Gap," 1975, CIAFOIA.
52. NIE 11-8/1-61, 9/21/1961, CIAFOIA.
53. For example, see CIA, "Cuba 1962: Khrushchev's Miscalculated Risk," CIAFOIA.
54. Robert Gates, *From the Shadows* (New York, 2006), 562.
55. Helms, "Intelligence in American Society," April 1967, Federal Depository Library Program Electronic Collection Archive, https://permanent.access.gpo.gov/gpo15410/helms/pdf/intl_in_amer.pdf.
56. Victoria Bonnell and George Breslauer, "Soviet and Post-Soviet Area Studies," Berkeley Program in Soviet and Post-Soviet Studies Working Paper, 1998, esp. 1–4.
57. Department of State, "Soviet Studies in the United States: A Survey of American Social Science Research on Soviet Russia, 1947–1957," 1/15/1958, Box 3, Alexander Dallin Papers, Stanford.
58. "The CIA and Academe," undated, CIAFOIA; David Engerman, *Know Your Enemy: The Rise and Fall of America's Soviet Experts* (New York, 2009), 35; Bonnell and Breslauer, "Soviet and Post-Soviet Studies," 9–10.
59. The result was published as W. W. Rostow, *The Dynamics of Soviet Society* (Cambridge, 1952).
60. Raymond Bauer, Alex Inkeles, and Clyde Kluckholm, *How the Soviet System Works: Cultural, Psychological, and Social Themes* (Cambridge, 1956).
61. Dallin to Geer and Schoettle, 1/23/1981, Box 3, Alexander Dallin Papers, Stanford.
62. Merle Fainsod, *Smolensk under Soviet Rule* (Cambridge, 1958); Fainsod, *How Russia Is Ruled* (Cambridge, 1964); Zbigniew Brzezinski, *The Soviet Bloc: Unity and Conflict* (Cambridge, 1960); Nathan Leites, *The Operational Code of the Politburo* (Santa Monica, CA, 1951).
63. Ed Hewett, *Reforming the Soviet Economy: Equality vs. Efficiency* (Washington, DC, 1988); Stephen Cohen, *Rethinking the Soviet Experience* (New York, 1986); Jerry Hough and Merle Fainsod, *How the Soviet Union Is Governed* (Cambridge, 1979).
64. Paul Hollander, *Political Will and Personal Belief: The Decline and Fall of Soviet Communism* (New Haven, 1999), 7–8; Martin Malia, "From Under the Rubble, What?" *Problems of Communism* 41, 1–2 (1992), 100–101.

65. Justin Vaisse, *Zbigniew Brzezinski: America's Grand Strategist* (Cambridge, 2018), 27–32.

66. Richard Pipes, "Misinterpreting the Cold War: The Hard-Liners Had It Right," *Foreign Affairs* 74, 1 (1995), 160; Peter Rutland, "Sovietology: From Stagnation to *Perestroika*?" Woodrow Wilson International Center for Scholars, October 1990, 7.

67. Vaisse, *Zbigniew Brzezinski*, 56–58.

68. *CIA Estimates of Soviet Defense Spending*, Hearings before Subcommittee on Oversight of the Permanent Select Committee on Intelligence, 9/3/1980 (Washington, DC, 1980).

69. George Breslauer, "In Defense of Sovietology," *Post-Soviet Affairs* 8, 3 (1992), 215.

70. Charles Wolf et al., *The Costs of the Soviet Empire* (Santa Monica, CA, 1983); John Despres, "Extraordinary Cost of the Soviet Buildup against China," WN-9187-OSD, July 1975, Box 59, James Schlesinger Papers, LC.

71. Christopher Davis and Murray Feshbach, "Life Expectancy in the Soviet Union," *Wall Street Journal*, 6/20/1978.

72. G. Warren Nutter, "The True Story of Russia's Weakness," *Newsweek*, 3/1/1957, 46.

73. Marshall Goldman, *The USSR in Crisis: The Failure of an Economic System* (New York, 1983), 61.

74. Marc Trachtenberg, "Assessing Soviet Economic Performance during the Cold War: A Failure of Intelligence?" *Texas National Security Review* 1, 2 (2018), 85–88, 99; CIA, "The Soviet Economy in 1978–79 and Prospects for 1980," June 1980, NLC-29-12-2-1-4, JCL.

75. Richard Pipes, "A Reagan Soviet Policy," October 1981, Box 3, Richard Pipes File, RRL.

76. Jack Matlock, *Autopsy on an Empire: The American Ambassador's Account of the Collapse of the Soviet Union* (New York, 1996), 125–133.

77. Gordon Barrass, *The Great Cold War: A Journey through the Hall of Mirrors* (Stanford, 2009), 410.

78. NSC Meeting, 8/9/1975, NSC Meetings, GFL.

79. MemCon, 7/10/1959, *FRUS 1958–1960*, X: 77.

80. Briefing Book for Malta Summit, December 1989, EBB 298, DNSA.

81. CIA, "Dissident Activity in East Europe: An Overview," 4/1/1977, NLC-7-17-5-4-7, JCL.

82. Ben Fischer, "The 1983 War Scare in U.S.-Soviet Relations," 1996, 65, EBB 426, NSA.

83. Walter Hixson, *Parting the Curtain: Propaganda, Culture, and the Cold War, 1945–1961* (New York, 1997), 50–51.

84. Press Release, "SALT II," 8/1/1979, Office of Staff Secretary, Presidential Files, JCL, https://www.jimmycarterlibrary.gov/digital_library/sso/148878/138/SSO_148878_138_12.pdf.

85. A. W. Marshall, "Long-Term Competition with the Soviets: A Framework for Strategic Analysis," RAND Corporation, R-862-PR, April 1972.

86. For example, Intelligence Report, "Soviet Naval Strategy: Concepts and Forces for Theater War against NATO," January 1975, CIAFOIA.

87. Barrass, *Great Cold War*, 198, 211–214; Christopher Ford and David Rosenberg, "The Naval Intelligence Underpinnings of Reagan's Maritime Strategy," *Journal of Strategic Studies* 28, 2 (2005), 382.

88. Memorandum for Director of Central Intelligence, "Post Mortem on Czech Crisis," 11/22/1968, CIAFOIA.

89. Nixon to Haldeman, 5/18/1972, *FRUS 1969–1976*, II: 273.

90. Defense Intelligence Agency, "Détente in Soviet Strategy," 9/2/1975, *FRUS 1969–1976*, XVI: 184.

91. Cyrus Vance, *Hard Choices: Four Critical Years in Managing America's Foreign Policy* (New York, 1983), 91.

92. NIE 11-10-76, 10/21/1976, CIAFOIA.

93. Richard Pipes, "Why the Soviet Union Thinks It Could Fight and Win a Nuclear War," *Commentary*, July 1977, 34.

94. NIE 11-4-77, 1/12/1977, in *FRUS 1969–1976*, XXXV: 173; Special National Intelligence Estimate 11-4-73, 9/10/1973, DNSA.

95. Anderson to Nixon, 4/30/1974, *FRUS 1969–1976*, XXXV: 144.

96. Team B, "Soviet Strategic Objectives: An Alternative View," December 1976, *FRUS 1969–1976*, XXXV: 171; "Paper Prepared by Team B," January 19, 1977, *FRUS 1969–1976*, XXXV: 174.

97. Documents in Vice Chairman, National Intelligence Council to Deputy Director of Central Intelligence, 11/16/1982, CIAFOIA; Joshua Rovner, *Fixing the Facts: National Security and the Politics of Intelligence* (Ithaca, NY, 2011), 127–129.

98. NSC Meeting, 1/13/1977, *FRUS 1969–1976*, XXXV: 172.

99. Andrew Marshall and Abram Shulsky, "Assessing Sustainability of Command Economies and Totalitarian Regimes: The Soviet Case," *Orbis*, Spring 2018, 240.

100. CIA, SR-76-10121U, May 1976, *FRUS 1969–1976*, XXXV: 164.

101. Norman Friedman, *The Fifty-Year War: Conflict and Strategy in the Cold War* (Annapolis, 2007), 418; Barry Watts and Andrew Krepinevich, *The Last Warrior: Andrew Marshall and the Shaping of Modern American Defense Strategy* (New York, 2015), 150–151.

102. "Economic Espionage," *New York Times*, 10/22/1995; James Noren, "CIA's Analysis of the Soviet Economy," in CIA, *Watching the Bear*, chapter 2; CIA, "A Comparison of Soviet and U.S. Gross National Products, 1960–83," August 1984, CREST.

103. Stansfield Turner, "Soviet Union and Southwest Asia," January 1980, NLC-6-82-7-14-3, JCL.

104. *CIA Estimates of Soviet Defense Spending*, 33.

105. NIE 11-69, 2/27/1969, *FRUS 1969–1976*, XII: 21.

106. Douglas MacEachin, "CIA Assessments of the Soviet Union: The Record Versus the Charges," Center for the Study of Intelligence, May 1996; CIA, "Investment and Growth in the USSR," March 1970, CIAFOIA.

107. Agenda for Briefing of President-Elect, 12/11/1980, CIAFOIA.

108. Stansfield Turner, *Burn before Reading: Presidents, CIA Directors, and Secret Intelligence* (New York, 2006), 168–169.

109. Robert Gates, "The Prediction of Soviet Intentions," 1974, CIAFOIA; Marshall and Shulsky, "Assessing Sustainability," 242.

110. Presidential Review Memorandum (PRM)/NSC-10, "Comprehensive Net Assessment: The Current Balance and Trends," NLC-15-105-4-14-0, JCL.

111. PD/NSC-18, 8/24/1977, NLC-132-42-4-3-1, JCL (PD is Presidential Directive).

112. CIA, "Estimated Soviet Defense Spending in Rubles, 1970–1975," SR 76-10121U, May 1976.

113. "The Track Record in Strategic Estimating," 2/6/1976, in *FRUS 1969–1976*, XXXV: 163.

114. "Estimate of Team B Assessment," 1/27/1977, CIAFOIA; Robert Vickers, "The History of CIA's Office of Strategic Research, 1967–1981," Center for the Study of Intelligence, August 2019, 105–107.

115. Andrew, "Intelligence," 430–433.

116. MemCon, 12/15/1981, Box 49, SF, NSC ESF, RRL.

117. Pipes, Foreign Policy Statement, 6/12/1980, Box 14, Fred Iklé Papers, Hoover.

118. Agenda for Briefing of President-Elect, 12/11/1980, CIAFOIA.

119. Ronald Reagan, *An American Life* (New York, 1990), 237–238.

120. Marshal Erwin and Amy Belasco, *Intelligence Spending and Appropriations: Issues for Congress* (Washington, DC, 2013), 5.

121. Leningrad to State, 11/17/1981, in Rowen Memo, 11/18/1981, CIAFOIA; Peter Schweizer, *Victory: The Reagan Administration's Secret Strategy That Hastened the Collapse of the Soviet Union* (New York, 1994), 102–105; Bruce Berkowitz and Jeffrey Richelson, "The CIA Vindicated: The Soviet Collapse Was Predicted," *The National Interest* 41 (1995), 40–41; Odom to Chief of Staff et al., 9/5/1984, Box 14, Odom Papers.

122. Herbert Meyer to Director of Central Intelligence, 6/28/1984, CREST.

123. Herbert Meyer, "The View from Moscow, 1983," EBB 426, NSA.

124. Herbert Meyer, "Can Gorbachev Pull It Off?" 5/17/1985, CREST.

125. John Prados, *How the Cold War Ended: Debating and Doing History* (Lanham, MD, 2011), 171.

126. Gates, "Prediction."

127. "The Central Intelligence Agency and National Organization for Intelligence."

Chapter Eight. Organizing for Victory

1. Dwight Eisenhower, *The White House Years: Mandate for Change, 1953–1956* (Garden City, NY, 1963), 114.

2. Richard Best, "The National Security Council: An Organizational Assessment," *Congressional Research Service*, 6/9/2009, 1–2.

3. George Herring, *From Colony to Superpower: American Foreign Relations since 1776* (New York, 2011), 545.

4. *Congressional Record—Senate*, 3/14/1947, 2066.

5. Douglas Stuart, *Creating the National Security State* (Princeton, 2008).

6. Forrestal Diary, 4/26/1947, JFP, SMML.

7. Ernest May, "The U.S. Government, a Legacy of the Cold War," *Diplomatic History* 16, 2 (1992).

8. Michael Hogan, *A Cross of Iron: Harry S. Truman and the Origins of the National Security State, 1945–1954* (New York, 1998).

9. Forrestal Diary, 11/23/1944 and 7/26/1947; *Unification of the War and Navy Departments and Postwar Organization for National Security: Report to Hon. James Forrestal, Secretary of the Navy* (Washington, DC, 1945).

10. Forrestal Diary, 5/13/1946.

11. David Lilienthal, *The Journals of David E. Lilienthal: The Atomic Energy Years, 1945–1950* (New York, 1964), 493.

12. "Major Meetings at Which Interservice Rivalries Discussed," undated, Box 9, Whitman Diary Series, DDEL.

13. Richard Betts, "Don't Retire the National Security Act," *The American Interest*, 2/9/2017.

14. Samuel Huntington, *The Common Defense: Strategic Programs in National Politics* (New York, 1961), 170.

15. Anna Nelson, "President Truman and the Evolution of the National Security Council," *Journal of American History* 72, 2 (1985).

16. "The Federalist Papers: No. 70," Avalon Project, Yale University.

17. *Administration of National Security: Staff Reports and Hearings Submitted to the Committee on Government Operations, United States Senate, by Its Subcommittee on National Security Staffing and Operations* (Washington, DC, 1965), 77.

18. Michael Hunt, *American Ascendancy: How the United States Gained and Wielded Global Dominance* (Chapel Hill, NC, 2007), 140–149.

19. Peter Rodman, *Presidential Command: Power, Leadership, and the Making of Foreign Policy from Richard Nixon to George W. Bush* (New York, 2010), 24–29.

20. Robert Cutler, "The Development of the National Security Council," *Foreign Affairs* 34, 3 (1956), 443.

21. Bundy to Kennedy, 1/24/1961, *FRUS 1961–1963*, XXV: 4.

22. David Rothkopf, *Running the World: The Inside Story of the National Security Council and the Architects of American Power* (New York, 2005).

23. Dillon Anderson, "The President and National Security," *Atlantic Monthly*, January 1956.

24. Arthur Schlesinger Jr., *The Imperial Presidency* (New York, 1973).

25. Charles Robinson to Kissinger, 4/17/1975, Box 7, Charles Robinson Records, RG 59, NARA.

26. "Schlesinger Backs Cuba 'Cover Story,' " *New York Times*, 11/29/1965.

27. Schlesinger, *Imperial Presidency*, 299.

28. MemCon, 1/28/1975, Box 22, HAK.

29. George Kennan, *Memoirs, 1925–1950* (Boston, 1967), 409–410.

30. Robert David Johnson, *Congress and the Cold War* (New York, 2005); Report to American People, 7/25/1961, APP.

31. Amos Jordan, William Taylor Jr., and Lawrence Korb, *American National Security: Policy and Process* (Baltimore, 1993), 131.

32. Marjorie Hunter, "Ford Says That Congress Hobbles President by Foreign Policy Action," *New York Times*, 12/14/1978.

33. NSC Meeting, 1/13/1977, *FRUS 1969–1976*, XXXVIII, Part 2: 83.

34. Robert David Johnson, "The Unintended Consequences of Congressional Reform: The Clark and Tunney Amendments and U.S. Policy toward Angola," *Diplomatic History* 27, 2 (2003), 224.

35. Scowcroft Memo, 7/11/1975, *FRUS 1969–1976*, XVI: 163.

36. "Vice President Bush's Meetings with Salvadoran Officials," 12/14/1983, DNSA.

37. Robert Gates, *From the Shadows* (New York, 2006), 559.

38. Kennan, *Memoirs*, 326; Dean Acheson, *Present at the Creation: My Years in the State Department* (New York, 1969), 214–215.

39. PPS-13, 11/6/1947, *FRUS 1947*, I: 393.

40. PPS-1, 5/23/1947, Box 7, Charles Bohlen Records, NARA; PPS-35, June 30, 1948, *FRUS 1948*, IV: 702.

41. David Milne, *America's Rasputin: Walt Rostow and the Vietnam War* (New York, 2008), 131–157.

42. Ross to Baker, 12/16/1988 and 2/21/1989, Box 1, Zelikow-Rice Files, Hoover.

43. Paper by Directing Panel of Project Solarium, 6/1/1953, *FRUS 1952–1954*, II, Part 1: 69.

44. NSC Meeting, 7/16/1953, *FRUS 1952–1954*, II, Part 1: 79; Paul Miller, "Organizing the National Security Council: I Like Ike's," *Presidential Studies Quarterly* 43, 3 (2013), esp. 598–599.

45. "Interview with Harold H. Saunders," 11/24/1993, Foreign Affairs Oral History Collection, LC.

46. "Comprehensive Net Assessment: The Current Balance and Trends," NLC-15-105-4-14-0, JCL.

47. NSDD-32, 5/20/1982, and NSDD-75, 1/17/1983, both in Box 91287, NSC ESF, RRL.

48. Thomas Mahnken, ed., *Net Assessment and Military Strategy: Retrospective and Prospective Essays* (Amherst, MA, 2020).

49. Marshall to Kissinger, 3/15/1972, *FRUS 1969–1976*, II: 266.

50. A. W. Marshall, "Long-Term Competition with the Soviets: A Framework for Strategic Analysis," RAND Corporation, R-862-PR, April 1972.

51. Haig to Kissinger, 10/29/1969, *FRUS 1969–1976*, II: 85.

52. Rusk to LBJ, 12/1/1964, *FRUS 1964–1968*, XXXIII: 14.

53. Greg Berhman, *The Most Noble Adventure* (New York, 2008).

54. Raymond Garthoff, *Détente and Confrontation: American-Soviet Relations from Nixon to Reagan* (Washington, DC, 1994), 181–185.

55. Haig to Reagan, 3/8/1982, Box 90304, Robert Kimmitt Files, RRL.

56. Truman Address, 4/20/1950, APP.

57. Kenneth Osgood, *Total Cold War: Eisenhower's Secret Propaganda Battle at Home and Abroad* (Lawrence, KS, 2006), 43.

58. Murrow to Dutton, 7/13/1961, *FRUS 1917–1972*, VI: 41.

59. Alvin A. Snyder, *Warriors of Disinformation: American Propaganda, Soviet Lies, and the Winning of the Cold War* (New York, 1995), xi; Nicholas Cull, *The Cold War and the United States Information Agency* (New York, 2009), 187–188; Gregory Tomlin, *Murrow's Cold War: Public Diplomacy for the Kennedy Administration* (Lanham, MD, 2016), xxiv.

60. Reinhold Wagnleitner, *Coca-Colonization and the Cold War: The Cultural Mission of the United States and Austria after the Second World War* (Chapel Hill, NC, 1994), 60–61; Sorensen to Kennedy, 4/16/1962, *FRUS 1917–1972*, VI: 78.

61. Address by the Director, 4/23/1966, *FRUS 1917–1972*, VII: 87.

62. "The Roles of Attributed and Unattributed Information and the Division of Responsibility between USIA and CIA," undated (1960), DDRS.

63. Report by Task Force on USIA, 12/31/1960, *FRUS 1917–1972*, VI: 5.

64. Jason Parker, *Hearts, Minds, Voices: U.S. Cold War Public Diplomacy and the Formation of the Third World* (New York, 2016), 111.

65. Petition by USIA Employees, 11/3/1976, *FRUS 1977–1980*, XXX: 1.

66. Helsinki to USIA, 9/15/1988, Folder 4, Carton 18, Tom Korologos Papers, University of Utah.

67. Penny von Eschen, *Satchmo Blows Up the World: Jazz Ambassadors Play the Cold War* (Cambridge, 2006).

68. Mary Dudziak, "Brown as a Cold War Case," *Journal of American History* 91, 1 (2004), 37.

69. "The USIA Program, Status on June 30, 1959," DDRS.

70. East Berlin to Feulner, 8/24/1988, Tom Korologos Papers, University of Utah.

71. Jock Shirley to Wick, 2/2/1983, DDRS.

72. Wick to Gergen, 8/7/1981, DDRS; Wagnleitner, *Coca-Colonization*, 60–61.

73. Wick to Budget Review Board, 12/8/1982, DDRS; Cull, *Cold War*, 417–418, 457.

74. State Department, "Active Measures: A Report on the Substance and Process of Anti-U.S. Disinformation and Propaganda Campaigns," August 1986; Thomas Rid, *Active Measures: The Secret History of Disinformation and Political Warfare* (New York, 2020).

75. Bill Gertz, "U.S. Begins New Offensive on Soviet Disinformation," *Washington Times*, 10/6/1986; Seth Jones, "Going on the Offensive: A U.S. Strategy to Combat Russian Information Warfare," Center for Strategic and International Studies, October 2018, 3.

76. Christopher Andrew and Vasili Mitrokhin, *The World Was Going Our Way: The KGB and the Battle for the Third World* (New York, 2005), 19; State Department, "Soviet 'Active Measures': Forgery, Disinformation, Political Operations," October 1981, CIAFOIA.

77. Fletcher Schoen and Christopher Lamb, *Deception, Disinformation, and Strategic Communications: How One Interagency Group Made a Major Difference* (Washington, DC, 2012), 12–19, 39.

78. Lawrence Eagleburger, "Unacceptable Intervention: Soviet Active Measures," *DOSB*, August 1983, 49.

79. Kiron Skinner, Annelise Anderson, and Martin Anderson, eds., *Reagan: A Life in Letters* (New York, 2003), 376.

80. Department of State, "Soviet Influence Activities: A Report on Active Measures and Propaganda, 1986–87," August 1987.

81. Department of State, "Soviet Influence Activities"; State Department, "Soviet 'Active Measures.' "

82. Schoen and Lamb, *Deception*, 3, 52–53.

83. Thomas Boghardt, "Soviet Bloc Intelligence and Its AIDS Disinformation Campaign," *Studies in Intelligence* 53, 4 (2009), 16.

84. Report of Task Force on Foreign Affairs Organization, 10/1/1967, *FRUS 1964–1968*, XXXIII: 127.

Chapter Nine. Winning the Contest of Systems

1. Henry Jackson, "How Shall We Forge a Strategy for Survival?" 4/16/1959, CIAFOIA.

2. NSC Meeting, 10/7/1953, Box 4, NSC, DDEL.

3. Eisenhower, Farewell Address, 1/17/1961, APP.

4. Truman, Farewell Address, 1/15/1953, APP.

5. Walter Lippmann, *The Cold War: A Study in U.S. Foreign Policy* (New York, 1947), 16–17.

6. James Madison, "Political Observations," 4/20/1795, National Archives, Founders Online, https://founders.archives.gov/documents/Madison/01-15-02-0423.

7. Harold Lasswell, *Essays on the Garrison State* (New Brunswick, NJ, 1997).

8. Hanson Baldwin, *The Price of Power* (New York, 1948), 325–326.

9. Truman Address, 3/6/1952, APP.

10. NSC Meeting, 9/24/1953, *FRUS 1952–1954*, II, Part 1: 91.

11. Baldwin, *Price of Power*, 18–19.

12. Joseph Alsop and Stewart Alsop, "Your Flesh Should Creep," *Saturday Evening Post*, 7/13/1946, 49.

13. Aaron Friedberg, "Why Didn't the United States Become a Garrison State?" *International Security* 16, 4 (1992), 109–142.

14. Paper in Symington to Truman, 12/10/1951, DDRS.

15. Keyserling Statement, 10/16/1951, *FRUS 1951*, I: 56.

16. *Full Committee Hearings on Universal Military Training*, House of Representatives, Committee on Armed Services, 6/11/1947, 4341, Hathi Trust Digital Library, https://babel.hathitrust.org/cgi/pt?id=umn.31951p011425204&view=1up&seq=8.

17. Robert Taft, *A Foreign Policy for Americans* (Garden City, NY, 1951), 5.

18. Keyserling Statement, 10/16/1951, *FRUS 1951*, I: 56.

19. Aaron Friedberg, *In the Shadow of the Garrison State: America's Anti-Statism and Its Cold War Grand Strategy* (Princeton, 2000).

20. Planning Board Meeting with Consultants, 3/7/1958, DDRS.

21. Office of Defense Mobilization Memorandum, 2/20/1951, DDRS.

22. Michael Hogan, *A Cross of Iron: Harry S. Truman and the Origins of the National Security State, 1945–1954* (New York, 1998), 475.

23. Eisenhower to Arthur Burns, 3/12/1958, Box 1, Arthur Burns Papers, Duke University.

24. News Conference, 11/11/1953, APP; NSC-162, 9/30/1953, *FRUS 1952–1954*, II, Part 1: 93.

25. Alexander Hamilton, "Federalist No. 8," 11/20, 1787, The Avalon Project, Yale Law School, https://avalon.law.yale.edu/18th_century/fed08.asp.

26. Robert David Johnson, *Congress and the Cold War* (New York, 2005), 10; Benjamin Fordham, *Building the Cold War Consensus: The Political Economy of U.S. National Security Policy, 1949–1951* (Ann Arbor, MI, 1998).

27. Clifford-Rowe Memorandum, 11/19/1947, Box 22, Clark Clifford Files, HSTL.

28. Richard Hofstadter, *The Paranoid Style in American Politics: And Other Essays* (New York, 1965), 7.

29. Ellen Schrecker, *Many Are the Crimes: McCarthyism in America* (Princeton, 1998), xiii.

30. Eisenhower to Bullis, 5/18/1953, Box 317, Official File, DDEL.

31. William Hitchcock, *The Age of Eisenhower: America and the World in the 1950s* (New York, 2017), 115–146.

32. Philip Jenkins, *The Cold War at Home: The Red Scare in Pennsylvania, 1945–1960* (Chapel Hill, NC, 1999); Schrecker, *Many Are the Crimes*, xiii, 178.

33. State of the Union, 1/7/1953, APP.

34. Jeremi Suri, *Power and Protest: Global Revolution and the Rise of Détente* (Cambridge, 2003).

35. Truman, Inaugural Address, 1/20/1949, APP.

36. TelCon, 9/24/1957, *FRUS 1955–1957*, IX: 208.

37. Taylor Branch, *Pillar of Fire: America in the King Years, 1963–1965* (New York, 1998), 151.

38. Address Given by Walter White at the Lincoln Memorial, 6/29/1947, Clark Clifford Files, HSTL, https://www.trumanlibrary.gov/library/research-files/address-given-walter-white-lincoln-memorial?documentid=NA&pagenumber=2.

39. Martin Luther King Jr., "Letter from a Birmingham Jail," 4/16/1963, Online King Records Access, Martin Luther King, Jr., Research and Education Institute, Stanford University, http://okra.stanford.edu/transcription/document_images/undecided/630416-019.pdf.

40. Mary Dudziak, *Cold War Civil Rights: Race and the Image of American Democracy* (Princeton, 2011), 187.

41. Truman Address, 6/29/1947, APP.

42. Mary Dudziak, "*Brown* as a Cold War Case," *Journal of American History* 91, 1 (2004), 37.

43. Eisenhower Address, 9/24/1957, APP.

44. Report to American People, 6/11/1963, APP.

45. Johnson Remarks, 8/6/1965, APP.

46. Thomas Borstelmann, *The Cold War and the Color Line: American Race Relations in the Global Arena* (Cambridge, 2003), esp. 269–271.

47. Eisenhower Address, 4/16/1953, APP.

48. Eisenhower, Farewell Address, 1/17/1961, APP.

49. News Conference, 4/30/1953, APP.

50. Friedberg, *In the Shadow*, 292–295.

51. H. W. Brands, *The Strange Death of American Liberalism* (New Haven, 2001), 77–78.

52. Judith Stein, *Pivotal Decade: How the United States Traded Factories for Finance in the 1970s* (New Haven, 2013), chapter 1.

53. Lisa McGirr, *Suburban Warriors: The Origins of the New American Right* (Princeton, 2002), 26; Melvyn Leffler, *Safeguarding Democratic Capitalism: U.S. Foreign Policy and National Security, 1920–2015* (Princeton, 2017), 231.

54. Margaret O'Mara, *The Code: Silicon Valley and the Remaking of America* (New York, 2019), 50–51.

55. Walter McDougal, *The Heavens and the Earth: A Political History of the Space Age* (New York, 1985), 438.

56. John Kenneth Galbraith, *The Culture of Contentment* (Princeton, 2017), 97; Diane Kunz, *Butter and Guns: America's Cold War Economic Diplomacy* (New York, 1997).

57. *Hearings on Science Legislation*, Committee on Military Affairs, United States Senate (Washington, DC, 1945), 199.

58. State-Defense Policy Review Group, 3/20/1950, *FRUS 1950*, I: 71.

59. Roger Geiger, "Science, Universities, and National Defense, 1945–1970," *Osiris*, 2nd Series, 7 (1992), 37.

60. Rebecca Lowen, *Creating the Cold War University: The Transformation of Stanford* (Stanford, 1997).

61. NSC Meeting, 10/10/1957, Box 9, NSC Series, DDEL.

62. Geiger, "Science," 44; Matthew Levin, *Cold War University: Madison and the New Left in the Sixties* (Madison, WI, 2013), 36.
63. Eisenhower Address, 4/4/1957, APP.
64. CIA, "Restless Youth," September 1968, DDRS.
65. Jonathan Cole, *The Great American University: Its Rise to Preeminence, Its Indispensable National Role, Why It Must Be Protected* (New York, 2012).
66. Suri, *Power,* 269.
67. Clark Kerr, *The Uses of the University* (Cambridge, 1963), 68–69.
68. "College Freedoms Being Stifled by Students' Fear of Red Label," *New York Times,* 5/10/1951.
69. David Engerman, "Rethinking Cold War Universities," *Journal of Cold War Studies* 5, 3 (2003), esp. 82–83.
70. CIA, "Restless Youth."
71. Report of Student Unrest Study Group, 1/17/1969, DDRS.
72. Memorandum for President's File, 5/7/1970, *FRUS 1969–1976,* I: 66.
73. Laura Belmonte, *Selling the American Way: U.S. Propaganda and the Cold War* (Philadelphia, 2010), 88.
74. Kiron Skinner, Annelise Anderson, and Martin Anderson, eds., *Reagan, in His Own Hand: The Writings of Ronald Reagan That Reveal His Revolutionary Vision for America* (New York, 2001), 147.
75. Stephen Kotkin, *Armageddon Averted: The Soviet Collapse* (New York, 2008), 42–43.
76. Bill Keller, "Gorbachev, in Finland, Disavows Any Right of Regional Intervention," *New York Times,* 10/26/1989.
77. Archie Brown, *The Rise and Fall of Communism* (New York, 2009), 472; Yale Richmond, *Cultural Exchange and the Cold War: Raising the Iron Curtain* (University Park, PA, 2004), esp. 22–34; Emily Rosenberg, "Consumer Capitalism and the End of the Cold War," *CH* III: 506–509.
78. Truman, Farewell Address, 1/15/1953, APP.

Chapter Ten. Managing the Endgame

1. Reagan Address, 6/8/1982, APP.
2. See, as relatively recent accounts, Philip Zelikow and Condoleezza Rice, *To Build a Better World: Choices to End the Cold War and Create a Global Commonwealth* (New York, 2019); Jeffrey Engel, *When the World Seemed New: George H. W. Bush and the End of the Cold War* (Boston, 2017); Kristina Spohr, *Post Wall, Post Square: Rebuilding the World after 1989* (New Haven, 2020).
3. National Security Planning Group Meeting, 12/10/1984, Box 91307, ESF, RRL.
4. Kiron Skinner, Annelise Anderson, and Martin Anderson, eds., *Reagan, in His Own Hand: The Writings of Ronald Reagan That Reveal His Revolutionary Vision for America* (New York, 2001), 30–31.
5. MemCon, 12/15/1981, Box 49, SF, ESF, RRL.

6. "Détente," 1975, Box 1, Ronald Reagan Radio Commentary.

7. Max Kampelman, "The Madrid Agreement," 1/3/1984, Box 4, Max Kampelman Papers, Minnesota Historical Society.

8. Message to Brezhnev, April 1981, Box 38, Head of State File, RRL.

9. Anatoly Dobrynin, *In Confidence: Moscow's Ambassador to America's Six Cold War Presidents* (New York, 1995), 527.

10. NSDD-32, 5/20/1982, Box 91287, NSC ESF, RRL.

11. NSDD-75, 1/17/1983, Box 91287, NSC ESF, RRL.

12. NSDD-32.

13. Vojtech Mastny and Malcolm Byrne, eds., *A Cardboard Castle? An Inside History of the Warsaw Pact, 1955–1991* (Budapest, 2006), esp. 473.

14. Reagan Address, 1/16/1984, APP.

15. MemCon, 9/8/1983, *FRUS 1981–1988*, IV: 105; Max Kampelman, "At the East-West Divide," *Freedom at Issue*, March–April 1985, 12–14.

16. Ben Fischer, "The 1983 War Scare in U.S.-Soviet Relations," 1996, 61, EBB 426, NSA.

17. Vladislav Zubok, *A Failed Empire: The Soviet Union in the Cold War from Stalin to Gorbachev* (Chapel Hill, NC, 2009), 275.

18. Robert Scheer, *With Enough Shovels: Reagan, Bush, and Nuclear War* (New York, 1983).

19. Reagan Address, 9/5/1983, APP.

20. MemCon, 10/11/1983, Box 2, Jack Matlock Papers, RRL.

21. Casey Memorandum, 6/19/1984, EBB 428, NSA.

22. For skepticism, see Vojtech Mastny, "How Able Was 'Able Archer'? Nuclear Trigger and Intelligence in Perspective," *Journal of Cold War Studies* 11, 1 (2009), 108–123. The best analysis remains Dima Adamsky, "The 1983 Nuclear Crisis—Lessons for Deterrence Theory and Practice," *Journal of Strategic Studies* 36, 1 (2012).

23. Interview with U.S. Official, 5/22/1990, EBB 428, NSA.

24. Ronald Reagan, *An American Life* (New York, 1990), 588.

25. George Shultz, "Managing the U.S.-Soviet Relationship over the Long Term," 10/18/1984, Box 128, Charles Hill Papers, Hoover.

26. Beth Fischer, *The Reagan Reversal: Foreign Policy and the End of the Cold War* (Columbia, MO, 1997).

27. Douglas Brinkley, *The Reagan Diaries* (New York, 2007), 199.

28. Reagan-Thatcher Meeting, 9/29/1983, Box 51, SF, ESF, RRL.

29. "Draft Reagan Campaign Action Plan," 10/27/1983, Box 136, James A. Baker Papers, SMML.

30. Reagan, State of the Union, 1/25/1984, APP.

31. Reagan Address, 1/16/1984, APP.

32. Kiron Skinner, Annelise Anderson, and Martin Anderson, *Reagan: A Life in Letters* (New York, 2003), 743.

33. MemCon, 3/22/1984, DDRS.

34. Shultz, "Managing"; Jack Matlock, *Reagan and Gorbachev: How the Cold War Ended* (New York, 2004), 73–85.
35. George Shultz, *Turmoil and Triumph: My Years as Secretary of State* (New York, 1993), 478, 531–532.
36. Reagan to Loeb, 11/25/1985, Skinner et al., *Reagan: A Life in Letters*, 414.
37. Archie Brown, *The Gorbachev Factor* (New York, 1996).
38. Andrei Grachev, *Gorbachev's Gamble: Soviet Foreign Policy and the End of the Cold War* (Cambridge, 2008), 84.
39. "Summit Notes—11/20/85—Second Day," Box 215, Donald Regan Papers, LC.
40. Gorbachev to Reagan, 6/10/1985, EBB 172, NSA.
41. Gorbachev to Reagan, 12/24/1985, Box 214, Donald Regan Papers, LC; Dobrynin, *In Confidence*, 570.
42. SNIE, "Gorbachev's Policy toward the United States, 1986–1988," September 1986, CIAFOIA.
43. Carolyn Ekedahl and Melvin Goodman, *The Wars of Eduard Shevardnadze* (University Park, PA, 1997), 100–101; Jack Matlock, *Autopsy on an Empire: The American Ambassador's Account of the Collapse of the Soviet Union* (New York, 1996), 57–67.
44. Moscow to State, 11/11/1985, Box 47, Jack Matlock Papers, RRL.
45. Anatoly Chernyaev, "Gorbachev's Foreign Policy: The Concept," in Kiron Skinner, ed., *Turning Points in Ending the Cold War* (Stanford, 2007).
46. NSDD-270, 5/1/1987, NSDDs, ESF, RRL.
47. Reagan, "Gorbachev," 10/13/1985, Box 215, Donald Regan Papers, LC.
48. Carlucci to Reagan, undated, Box 92132, Robert Linhard Files, RRL.
49. Reagan, *American Life*, 637.
50. George Shultz, "How to Deal with Gorbachev," 11/18/1987, *FRUS 1981–1988*, VI: 94.
51. Joint Statement, 11/21/1985, APP.
52. "Debriefing of President," 11/19/1985, Box 215, Donald Regan Papers, LC.
53. Dobrynin, *In Confidence*, 592.
54. Brinkley, *Reagan Diaries*, 425–426; National Security Planning Group Meeting, 2/3/1986, NSPG 00127, RRL; Reagan to Gorbachev, 2/22/1986, Box 66, Jack Matlock Papers, RRL.
55. Gorbachev to Reagan, 6/1/1986, Box 214, Donald Regan Papers, LC.
56. National Security Planning Group Meeting, 6/12/1986, Box 2, NSDDs, ESF, RRL.
57. "First Meeting," 10/11/1986, EBB 203, NSA; MemCon, 10/11/1986, EBB 203, NSA; various MemCons, 10/12/1986, EBB 203, NSA; Shultz, *Turmoil and Triumph*, 757–779.
58. Politburo Session, 10/14/1986, EBB 203, NSA.
59. Shultz, *Turmoil and Triumph*, 372.
60. Dobrynin, *In Confidence*, 610.
61. Poindexter to Reagan, undated, box 91639, Alton Keel Files, RRL.

62. Skinner et al., *Reagan: A Life in Letters*, 384; William Odom, *The Collapse of the Soviet Military* (New Haven, 1998), 134.

63. Shultz-Gorbachev Meeting, 4/14/1987, Box 5, Oberdorfer Papers, SMML.

64. "Luncheon Toasts" and "TV Messages," 12/8–9/1987, *DOSB*, January 1988, 3, 6, 9; James Mann, *The Rebellion of Ronald Reagan: A History of the End of the Cold War* (New York, 2009), 238–240, 272–278.

65. Shultz, "How to Deal."

66. Chernyaev Diary, 8/28/1987, EBB 250, NSA.

67. Working Luncheon, 12/10/1987, EBB 238, NSA; Artemy Kalinovsky, *A Long Goodbye: The Soviet Withdrawal from Afghanistan* (Cambridge, 2011), chapter 4.

68. CIA, "The Costs of Soviet Involvement in Afghanistan," February 1987, DNSA.

69. JCS Cable, probably March 1987, DNSA.

70. Reagan Remarks, 8/26/1987, APP.

71. Reagan Address, 11/4/1987, APP.

72. Shultz-Shevardnadze MemCon, 3/23/1988, RAC Box 1, Nelson Ledsky Files, RRL; Svetlana Savranskaya, "Gorbachev in the Third World," in Artemy Kalinovsky and Sergei Radchenko, eds., *The End of the Cold War and the Third World: New Perspectives on Regional Conflict* (New York, 2011), 30–32.

73. Chernyaev Diary, 4/1/1988, EBB 250, NSA.

74. MemCon, 3/23/1988, Box 5, Dennis Ross Files, RRL.

75. Anatoly Adamishin and Richard Schifter, *Human Rights, Perestroika, and the End of the Cold War* (Washington, DC, 2009).

76. MemCon, 10/12/1986, EBB 203, NSA.

77. Shultz, *Turmoil and Triumph*, esp. 591.

78. Vienna to State, 6/20/1988, DDRS.

79. Matlock, *Reagan and Gorbachev*, 251.

80. Office of Soviet Analysis, "Where Is the USSR Headed?" undated, CIA-FOIA; Shultz, *Turmoil and Triumph*, 894; Sarah Snyder, "Principles Overwhelming Tanks: Human Rights and the End of the Cold War," in Akira Iriye, Petra Goedde, William Hitchcock, eds., *The Human Rights Revolution: An International History* (New York, 2012), 270–273.

81. Reagan Remarks, 6/12/1987, APP.

82. CIA Memo, 11/13/1987, *FRUS 1981–1988*, VI: 93.

83. Talking Points for Aspen Conference, 5/18/1988, RAC Box 2, Rudolph Perina Files, RRL; MemCon, 4/21/1988, EBB 481, NSA.

84. MemCon, 12/8/1987, EBB 238, NSA.

85. MemCon, 3/11/1988, RAC Box 1, Lisa Jameson Files, RRL; Mann, *Rebellion*, 282–285.

86. Reagan, *American Life*, 686; Robert Gates, *From the Shadows* (New York, 2006), 384.

87. Reagan Remarks, 5/30/1988, APP.

88. Reagan Remarks, 5/31/1988, APP.

89. Raymond Garthoff, *The Great Transition: American-Soviet Relations and the End of the Cold War* (Washington, DC, 1994), 352–353.

90. Private Meeting, 12/7/1988, EBB 261, NSA.

91. Daniel Moynihan, "The CIA's Credibility," *The National Interest* 42 (1995–1996), 111.

92. Excerpts from Gorbachev Speech, *New York Times*, 12/8/1988; Mikhail Gorbachev, *Memoirs* (New York, 1995), 459–460; Odom, *Collapse*, 136.

93. Gates, *Shadows*, 449.

94. Gorbachev-Grosz Meeting, 3/23–24/1989, CWIHP.

95. Chernyaev Diary, 10/5/1989, CWIHP; William Taubman, *Gorbachev: His Life and Times* (New York, 2017).

96. Bush Remarks, 5/31/1989, APP.

97. Scowcroft to Rice and Zelikow, 2/27/1995, Box 1, Zelikow-Rice Files, Hoover.

98. Philip Zelikow and Condoleezza Rice, *Germany Unified and Europe Transformed: A Study in Statecraft* (Cambridge, 1995), 20.

99. Bush Remarks, 5/12/1989, APP.

100. Bush Remarks, 5/12/1989, APP.

101. National Security Directive (NSD)-23, 9/22/1989, DNSA.

102. Bush Remarks, 5/31/1989, APP.

103. Hal Brands, *From Berlin to Baghdad: America's Search for Purpose in the Post–Cold War World* (Lexington, 2008), 23.

104. Bush-Momper MemCon, 4/19/1989, Presidential MemCons and TelCons, George H. W. Bush Presidential Library [hereafter GHWBL].

105. Bush Remarks, 7/11/1989, APP.

106. MemCon, 10/11/1989, Presidential MemCons and TelCons, GHWBL.

107. "Remarks and Question-and-Answer Session," 11/9/1989, APP; Mary Sarotte, *Collapse: The Accidental Opening of the Berlin Wall* (New York, 2014).

108. Bush Remarks, 12/3/1989, APP.

109. Thatcher-Gorbachev Conversation, 9/23/1989, EBB 293, NSA.

110. "Verbal Message from Gorbachev to Mitterrand, Thatcher, and Bush," 11/10/1989, CWIHP.

111. "GDR Crisis Contingencies," 11/6/1989, CF00182, Robert Blackwill Files, GHWBL.

112. Scowcroft to Bush, 11/29/1989, Box 10, OA/ID 91116, German Unification Files, Brent Scowcroft Collection, GHWBL.

113. Scowcroft Oral History, 11/12–13/1999, Presidential Oral Histories Project, Miller Center for Public Affairs, University of Virginia.

114. Excerpts from Soviet Transcript, 12/2–3/1989, EBB 296, NSA.

115. "First Restricted Bilateral Session," 12/2/1989, CF00769, Arnold Kanter Files, GHWBL; Bush-Kohl MemCon, 12/3/1989, Presidential MemCons and TelCons, GHWBL.

116. Mary Sarotte, *1989: The Struggle to Create Post–Cold War Europe* (Princeton, 2009), 85–100.

117. G. John Ikenberry, *After Victory: Institutions, Strategic Restraint, and the Rebuilding of Order After Major Wars* (Princeton, 2001), 226.

118. Acland to FCO, 1/30/1990, in *Documents on British Policy Overseas*, Volume 7, Series III, Document 109.

119. Scowcroft to Bush, undated, CF00182, Robert Blackwill Files, GHWBL.

120. Bush-Kohl MemCon, 2/24/1990, Presidential MemCons and TelCons, GHWBL.

121. Bush in Powell to Wall, 2/24/1990, Volume 7, Series III, Document 155, *Documents on British Policy Overseas.*

122. Bush-Mitterrand MemCon, 4/19/1990, and Bush-Havel MemCon, 2/20/1990, Presidential MemCons and TelCons, GHWBL; Robert Hutchings, *American Diplomacy and the End of the Cold War: An Insider's Account of U.S. Policy in Europe, 1989–1992* (Baltimore, 1997), 115–116, 123.

123. Scowcroft to Bush, February 1990, CF00182, Robert Blackwill Files, GHWBL.

124. Svetlana Savranskaya, Thomas Blanton, and Vladislav Zubok, eds., *Masterpieces of History: The Peaceful End of the Cold War in Europe, 1989* (Budapest, 2010), 679.

125. Bush-Kohl MemCon, 2/24/1990, Presidential MemCons and TelCons, GHWBL.

126. Mary Sarotte, "Not One Inch Eastward? Bush, Baker, Kohl, Genscher, Gorbachev, and the Origin of Russian Resentment toward NATO Enlargement in February 1990," *Diplomatic History* 33, 1 (2020), 119–140.

127. Bush-Kohl MemCon, 2/25/1990, Presidential MemCons and TelCons, GHWBL.

128. James Baker, *The Politics of Diplomacy: Revolution, War, and Peace, 1989–1992* (New York, 1995), 238–249; "Meeting with NSC Principals on Lithuania," 4/23/1990, CF00719, Rice Files, GHWBL.

129. Bush-Gorbachev TelCon, 7/17/1990, Presidential MemCons and TelCons, GHWBL; Bush News Conference, 7/6/1990, APP.

130. Sicherman to Ross and Baker, 3/12/1990, Box 176, James A. Baker Papers, SMML.

131. "The Future of Europe: Germany, NATO, CFE, and CSCE," undated, CF01308-001 through CF01308-013, Nicholas Burns Files, NSC, GHWBL.

132. Bush-Kohl MemCon, 2/25/1990.

133. Chernyaev Diary, 5/5/1990, EBB 317, NSA.

134. Bush Address, 10/2/1990, APP.

135. Engel, *When the World Seemed New*, 375.

136. U.S. Delegation (USDEL) with the Secretary in Namibia to State, 3/20/1990, Department of State FOIA.

137. See, for example, Matlock, *Autopsy on an Empire;* Mark Kramer, "The Collapse of East European Communism and the Repercussions within the Soviet Union (Part 3)," *Journal of Cold War Studies* 7, 1 (2005), 3–96.

138. Moscow to State, 5/11/1990, EBB 320, NSA.

139. Gorbachev-Jaruzelski Meeting, 4/13/1990, EBB 504, NSA.

140. Bush-Gorbachev TelCon, 12/25/1991, Presidential MemCons and Tel-Cons, GHWBL.

141. NIE 11-18-90, November 1990, CIAFOIA.

142. Cheney Oral History, 3/16–17/2000, Presidential Oral Histories Project; James Goldgeier and Michael McFaul, *Power and Purpose: U.S. Policy toward Russia after the Cold War* (Washington, DC, 2003), 33–34.

143. Bush-Mitterrand MemCon, 3/14/1991, Presidential MemCons and Tel-Cons, GHWBL.

144. Bush-Mulroney MemCon, 3/13/1991, Presidential MemCons and Tel-Cons, GHWBL.

145. TelCon, 6/21/1991, Presidential MemCons and TelCons, GHWBL; Chernyaev Diary, 6/21 and 7/23/1991, EBB 345, NSA.

146. Gorbachev, *Memoirs*, 609.

147. Bush to Gorbachev, 1/23/1991, Box 109, James A. Baker Papers, SMML.

148. "Meeting on U.S.-Soviet Economic Relations," 6/3/1991, Box 1, Burns-Hewlett Chron File, GHWBL.

149. Gates, *Shadows*, 501–502.

150. George Bush and Brent Scowcroft, *A World Transformed* (New York, 1999), 499.

151. Joshua Shifrinson, *Rising Titans, Falling Giants: How Great Powers Exploit Power Shifts* (Ithaca, NY, 2018).

152. Bush Remarks, 8/1/1991, APP.

153. MemCon, 6/20/1991, Box 2, OA/ID 91108, Brent Scowcroft Collection, GHWBL.

154. William Safire, "Ukraine Marches Out," *New York Times*, 11/18/1991.

155. Scowcroft Oral History.

156. Gates, *Shadows*, 531.

157. Baker Remarks, 8/21/1991, CF01526, Barry Lowenkron Files, GHWBL.

158. Bush and Scowcroft, *World Transformed*, 518–561, esp. 542–543.

159. TelCon, 12/25/1991, Presidential MemCons and TelCons, GHWBL.

160. Gates, *Shadows*, 506–507.

161. Richard Pipes, "Misinterpreting the Cold War: The Hard-Liners Had It Right," *Foreign Affairs* 74, 1 (1995).

162. Melvyn Leffler, "Ronald Reagan and the Cold War: What Mattered Most," *Texas National Security Review* 1, 3 (2018), 76–89.

Conclusion. Lessons of a Twilight Struggle

1. Richard Strassler, *The Landmark Thucydides: A Comprehensive Guide to "The Peloponnesian War"* (New York, 2008), 16.

2. Vladislav Zubok and Constantine Pleshakov, *Inside the Kremlin's Cold War: From Stalin to Khrushchev* (Cambridge, 1997); Michael McFaul, "Xi Jinping Is Not Stalin," *Foreign Affairs*, 8/10/2020.

3. Elbridge Colby and A. Wess Mitchell, "The Age of Great-Power Competition," *Foreign Affairs* 99, 1 (2019), 118–130.

4. John Lewis Gaddis, "After Containment," *New Republic*, 4/25/2005.

5. Ivo Daalder and James Lyndsay, *The Empty Throne: America's Abdication of Global Leadership* (New York, 2018).

6. Eric Sayers and Brad Glosserman, "Collective Resilience Is the Way to Address China Challenge," *Japan Times*, 8/14/2020; Hal Brands and Zack Cooper, "The Great Game with China Is 3D Chess," *Foreign Policy*, 12/30/2020.

7. A. W. Marshall, "Long-Term Competition with the Soviets: A Framework for Strategic Analysis," RAND Corporation, R-862-PR, April 1972.

8. Robert Work and Greg Grant, *Beating the Americans at Their Own Game: An Offset Strategy with Chinese Characteristics* (Washington, DC, 2019); Alina Polyakova, "The Kremlin's Plot against Democracy," *Foreign Affairs* 99, 5 (2020).

9. Christian Brose, *The Kill Chain: Defending America in the Future of High-Tech Warfare* (New York, 2020).

10. PPS Memo, 5/4/1948, *FRUS 1945–1950*, EIE: 269.

11. Elbridge Colby and Robert Kaplan, "The Ideology Delusion: America's Competition with China Is Not about Doctrine," *Foreign Affairs*, 9/4/2020.

12. Kissinger Staff Meeting, 10/6/1975, DNSA.

13. Aaron Friedberg, "Competing with China," *Survival* 60, 3 (2018), 7–64.

14. Joseph R. Biden Jr., *Interim National Security Strategic Guidance—The White House, March 2021*, https://www.whitehouse.gov/wp-content/uploads/2021/03/NSC-1v2.pdf; Richard Fontaine and Daniel Twining, "Standing Up for Democracy," *Foreign Affairs*, 7/18/2018.

15. Hal Brands and Toshi Yoshihara, "Waging Political Warfare," *The National Interest* 159 (2019), 16–26; Timothy Crawford and Khang Vu, "Arms Control and Great-Power Politics," *War on the Rocks*, 11/4/2020.

16. Alina Polyakova, "The Kremlin's Plot Against Democracy," *Foreign Affairs* 99, 5 (2020).

17. David Shambaugh, "As U.S. and China Wage a New Cold War, They Should Learn from the Last One," *Wall Street Journal*, 7/31/2020.

18. Graham Allison, *Destined for War: Can America and China Escape Thucydides' Trap?* (Boston, 2017).

19. Hal Brands, "Cooperate with China on Coronavirus but Don't Trust It," *Bloomberg*, 4/12/2020.

20. David Edelstein, "Cooperation, Uncertainty, and the Rise of China: It's about 'Time,'" *Washington Quarterly* 41, 1 (2018), 155–171.

21. Robert Kaplan, "Eurasia's Coming Anarchy: The Risks of Chinese and Russian Weakness," *Foreign Affairs* 95, 2 (March/April 2016).

22. For example, John Tirpak, "Roper Reveals NGAD Has Flown, but Doesn't Share Details," *Air Force Magazine*, 9/15/2020.

23. Jude Blanchette and Seth Jones, "The U.S. Is Losing the Information War with China," *Wall Street Journal*, 6/16/2020.

24. Anthony Vinci, "The Coming Revolution in Intelligence Affairs," *Foreign Affairs*, 8/31/2020.

25. Henry Farrell and Abraham Newman, "Chained to Globalization: Why It's Too Late to Decouple," *Foreign Affairs* 99, 1 (2020), 77–78; also Mark Pomar, "A U.S. Media Strategy for the 2020s: Lessons from the Cold War," *Texas National Security Review* 4, 1 (2020/2021). For early steps in this direction, see Bethany Allen-Ebrahimian, "Biden's Whole-of-National Security Council Strategy," *Axios*, 2/2/2021.

26. Elizabeth Redden, "Proposed Legislation Would Bar Chinese STEM Graduate Students," *Inside Higher Education*, 5/28/2020.

27. American Association for the Advancement of Science, "Historical Trends in Federal R&D," R&D Budget and Policy Program, AAAS, https://www.aaas.org/programs/r-d-budget-and-policy/historical-trends-federal-rd; Richard Wike et al., "U.S. Image Plummets Internationally as Most Say Country Has Handled Coronavirus Badly," Pew Research Center, 9/15/2020.

28. Paul Kennedy, *Rise and Fall of the Great Powers* (New York, 1988), 55.

29. Jeffrey Mervis, "U.S. Lawmakers Unveil Bold $100 Billion Plan to Remake NSF," *Science Magazine*, 5/26/2020; Kurt Campbell and Jake Sullivan, "Competition without Catastrophe: How America Can Both Challenge and Coexist with China," *Foreign Affairs* 98, 5 (2019).

30. Kennedy Interview, 12/17/1962, APP.

Index